CLASS & SOCIAL DEVELOPMENT

CLASS, STATE, & DEVELOPMENT

Series Editor:
DALE L. JOHNSON
Department of Sociology, Rutgers University

Class, State, & Development intends to provide class analysis perspectives on questions of the state and of development. Volumes will emphasize critical and Marxist approaches to the class structure and class relations of advanced capitalist societies, the social basis of contemporary states—both democratic and authoritarian—and the social and economic development of Latin America, Asia, Africa, and the Middle East. The series is published in cooperation with the Department of Sociology, Rutgers University.

Volumes in this series:
CLASS & SOCIAL DEVELOPMENT
(other titles in preparation)

CLASS &
SOCIAL
DEVELOPMENT

A NEW THEORY
OF THE MIDDLE CLASS

EDITED BY
DALE L. JOHNSON

SAGE PUBLICATIONS
Beverly Hills / London / New Delhi

For Salvador Allende,
who exemplified the best
that his class produced,
who sought to transcend
the limitations of his class,
and who died defiantly,
a victim of its contradictions.

For information address:

SAGE Publications, Inc.
275 South Beverly Drive
Beverly Hills, California 90212

SAGE Publications India Pvt. Ltd.
C-236 Defence Colony
New Delhi 110 024, India

SAGE Publications Ltd
28 Banner Street
London EC1Y 8QE, England

Printed in the United States of America

Library of Congress Cataloging in Publication Data

Main entry under title:

Class and social development.

  (Class, state, and development ; v. 1)
  Bibliography: p.
  1. Middle classes. 2. Middle classes—United
States. 3. Capitalism. I. Johnson, Dale L.
II. Series.
HT684.C55   1982   305.5'5   82-5897
ISBN 0-8039-0070-8   AACR2

FIRST PRINTING

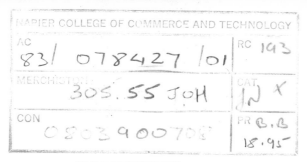
CONTENTS

Preface

This book introduces a series of volumes on the theme "Class, State, and Development." The series emphasizes critical and macroscopic appraisals of the class structure and class relations of advanced capitalist societies; the social basis of contemporary states, democratic and authoritarian; and the social and economic development of Latin America, Asia, Africa, and the Middle East. The main intent of the series is to provide class analysis perspectives on questions of the state and of development.

This first volume flaunts the overly ambitious aim of theoretical innovation. The effort is to draw on different currents of social theory, particularly within Marxism, to fashion a social scientific theory that is historical and dialectical. We are not rigorous in this effort, but we take very seriously the idea of social class relations as the dynamic source of social development. Within the networks of social relations designated social class, we analyze the shifting social functions, places, activities, and class situations of intermediate class formations.

The second volume in the series, a lively debate on theoretical disputes in the literature on Third World development, explores the dependency and mode of production perspectives of leading thinkers.

The third book of the series is less abstract. It extends the theoretical perspective developed in Volumes 1 and 2 to case studies of intermediate classes in the development and underdevelopment of several nations in the Caribbean, Latin America, Asia, and Africa.

Social Class and Social Development represents more a search for method and theoretical premise than a historical/empirical contribution on either social classes or social change and economic development—although there is much substantive analysis of the historical formation and present positioning within class relations of the American "middle class." This search for method and premise is conducted in the framework of an intellectual exchange with "structrualism," particularly the structuralist current within Marxist represented by Louis Althusser and Nicos Poulantzas.

A personal preface to my theoretical critique of structuralism is in order here. Years ago I picked up Althusser's *For Marx* and laid it aside after a few hours, impatient with the higher French intellectual culture. I had read Poulantzas's *Pourvoir politique et classes sociales* in Spanish translation (1968), before it appeared in English (1973). The prolix presentation and abstract formalism tried my patience; it did not seem to offer much as a guide for the main thrust of my research on local dominant classes, intermediate formations, and states in´ dependent (Latin American) societies. But I soon noticed that Latin American intellectuals for whom I had great respect were taking the structuralists seriously. Also, the pages of British and American journals began to reflect the growing influence of this tendency. At first I dismissed this as another intellectual fad. After reflection, I thought the growing interest might be attributable to the political failures of the Old and the New Left in the 1960s and the decline of activism and mobilization politics in the 1970s. What finally forced me to come to intellectual grips with Marxist structrualism, however, was the influence of graduate students with whom I worked closely over the years. Suffering through several brilliant dissertations which used an Althusserian/Poulantzian framework convinced me that structuralism had more to it than abstract philosophizing and a terrible penchant for unparsimonious sociological taxonomy. A generation of thoughtful, searching graduate students forced me to overcome my aversion to grand theorizing. This book is the outcome. It also is very much a collective product of ongoing work within the Ph.D. specialization in political sociology and development of the Rutgers University Sociology Department. I am especially grateful to the many graduate students with whom I have been associated over the difficult years of the past decade. With them I have enjoyed the contradictory relation of colleague and friend on the one side and Herr Doctor Professor on the other. It has not always been easy for me, or them, to break through the institutionally imposed inequalities of the professor/student relation. This book is partly about these kinds of relationships.

My first experience with broad questions of social and economic development came as a consequence of the formal requirement for a Ph.D. I lived in Santiago, Chile during 1964 and 1965, studying the industrial development of the country and the place of industrialists in the Chilean social structure. I did not find anything remotely resembling a "national bourgeoisie" determined to bring about economic and social development. It did seem to me, however, that the assertions of the nation's working class, and of the trade unions and Communist and Socialist parties that effectively represented workers' aspirations, together with the reformist role of the salaried middle groupings, offered real prospects for genuine social development. The Chilean middle strata (*capas medias* is the term used in Latin America) seemed to be the principal social support for the nation's long-established democratic civic culture and ferment for social reform. I was wrong about the *capas medias*. As the struggle polarized in Chile during 1972 and 1973, the *capas medias,* in overwhelming numbers and with great militance, were mobilized, in an almost classically fascist groundswell, on the side of the heeled boot of reaction.

The pattern of middle groupings playing socially/politically progressive roles in some historical periods and regressive roles in others can be observed in many nations. Indeed, internationally viewed, there is a bewildering display of seemingly contradictory places and activities among intermediate social formations in time and space. I resolved to try to make sense of it. This book represents the preliminary effort, and Volumes 2 and 3 of the series the next.

This book also reflects preoccupations with the North American middle class at the beginnings of a decade of incipient crisis in advanced capitalism; the 1980s will undoubtedly be difficult years. Since the following pages deal with the antecedents of the 1980s in an analytical manner, some additional personal reflections are appropriate here.

I am one of the beneficiaries of the Great American Celebration of the post-World-War-II period. Born of Scandinavian immigrants in the middle of the Depression on a bankrupt homestead on the South Dakota prairies, I, and many others, found it possible, during the 1950s and 1960s boom in demand for professional labor, to realize the American dream of "social mobility." So here I am among the Great Middle. And what do I make of it?

Like many college youth of middle-class origin or destination, I adhered to the "New Left" of the 1960s. (Already over 30 years old in the mid-1960s, I was a bit too "out of it" to relate closely to the counterculture of the period.) From New Left perspectives I developed an antipathy for the "Old Left" and even a certain disdain for the discipline of Marxist theory. I learned that declassed youth, the downtrodden peoples and oppressed minorities, the "marginals" of the Third World—and middle-class professionals, too, when they got their heads straight—were the source of revolutionary change. This seemed to correspond to events of the time. It took me a number of years in the 1970s to unlearn this.

Today I do not harbor expectations that middle-class professionals will play a central role in making a new and better world. I have worked and lived in the milieu of professionalism now for some 15 years. In the main, it is a culture of arrogant elitism, of personal careerism, of hypocrisy, and, most of all, of banality. The stirrings within the middle class of the 1960s, pressed by their kids and impressed with the assertions of oppressed minorities, have faded. In the 1970s the narcissism enshrined in the culture of professionalism became a sociopathology of fads and cults and a psychopathology of failed interpersonal relations. Perhaps one should worry less about the lack of progressive vigor in the middle class and more about a parallel with Nazi Germany or Pinochet's Chile—about the American middle class as a social base of right-wing reaction.

The book began with these preoccupations. The analysis of intermediate classes points decidedly away from mistaking the middle-class progressivism of one period, or the culture of narcissism of another, as indicating any kind of inherent propensity within the class. There is no fixed place for the middle class, no determined role, no necessary direction or certainty of outcome when the class asserts itself. The historical existence, the place in the social division of labor, the class situation of the middle are expressions of a larger set of class relations, as this book, I hope, will show.

Dale L. Johnson

Introduction

Great economic instability, social discontent, and political turmoil are as ubiquitous today as ever in the history of human society. The industrial countries suffer a relative stagnation, unemployment, inflation, and high interest rates. English cities are rocked by insurrections of West Indian immigrants and working-class youth, while Irish nationalists bomb symbolic targets of lingering colonial oppression. In American cities it is not safe to walk the streets or to breathe the air. The political response in England and America are law-and-order rhetoric and policies that bloat the military establishment, fatten the rich, cut social services to the poor, and further deteriorate the environment. In nonindustrial countries the problems are far more serious. Military dictatorships brutalize civilization while generals guide the transition from underdevelopment to a dependent development that benefits narrow local and foreign interests and pauperizes the great majority. In Central America a class war of ominous international implications is being waged. A modernized export agriculture expropriates peasants' means of subsistence; multinational corporations build manufacturing facilities that strengthen the old oligarchy and form a working class; a Common Market rationalizes production and regionalizes conflict. These conditions and events, multiplied a hundred times on a world scale, indicate more than merely a series of difficult problems. The 1980s perhaps mark a new era of social development of what many now call "the world system."

Prior transitions to a qualitatively new stage of historical development evoked cultural renaissance and serious intellectual reflection. While the technological innovations of the first industrial revolution remade the material world, social philosophy revolutionized ways of thinking about and guiding social development. Modern social science owes its existence to the confrontations of great nineteenth-century thinkers with the meaning of the new era.

Ideally, contemporary social science would attempt more than simply to address the roots of this instability, discontent, and turmoil; it would assess the meaning of the historical moment. Social science effectively does neither because there is little science in social analysis. The micro analysis of mainstream practitioners says very little about problems that are macro in scope. Quantitative research only superficially describes what can conveniently be computerized, and it utterly fails to analyze underlying structure. Marx was the supreme figure in assessing the antecedents and trends of nineteenth-century social development; yet today studies undertaken by Marxist social scientists tend to be ahistorical and guided by static premises adapted from the mainstream. A science adequate to the task of understanding the social world must proceed from premises that are macrostructural, historical, and dialectical.

This book does not attempt to address specific problems of instability, discontent, and turmoil, or to assess fully the meaning of the moment. It represents a search for premises that would allow study, evaluation, and prognosis of the emerging phase of development. An analysis of social class relations is at the center of this search for premises.

A dynamic quality to social science analysis can be achieved only when human individuals, and the phenomenal ways in which people are formed together in social groups and classes within institutionalized settings, are viewed in relation to the historically concrete structure of the total society, global in scope in the contemporary era. Structure shapes peoples' destinies as participants in institutions, as partakers of culture, as aggregates differentiated into races, sexes, and ages, as active members of groups, nations and, most of all, classes. Structure shapes, but people, participating and partaking, trying to live their lives as human beings, activate the structure; they act to maintain and transform it.

The fundamental placement of individuals in the global structure is into social classes. Class positioning presents people their "life chances." Classes within nations and on an international scale are the main forces of social development—and of underdevelopment. Dominant classes constantly face the problem of organizing and reorganizing their hegemony. Subordinate classes suffer exploitation and, as circumstances permit, act in response to the problems of oppression and everyday existence. What remains of the once substantial class of independent producers, small merchants, and farmers everywhere faces unstable dependency on big capital or annihilation. The salaried intermediate classes, once favored by historical developments now strive to retain their precarious privileges. Vast economic transformations, major crises, and, as Antonio Gramsci might have phrased it, the multifaceted struggles of subaltern classes and the varying hegemonic projects of the dominant classes come together in all their historical complexity in national arenas and on a world scale. This complexity must be unravelled so that the direction of movement can be deciphered and influenced. Mainstream professional social science offers information but little else; Marxism provides, when it returns to and builds on its classic premises, theoretical tools and a general historical, materialist, and dialectical perspective but no easy or exact formulae.

Social Class and Marxist Theory

[Social classes present the central conditions of human existence.] Philosophy and social theory from antiquity to the present have attempted to account for class and associated inequalities. The mid-nineteenth century philosophical and scientific achievements of Marx and Engels succeeded, directly or indirectly, in establishing the parameters of subsequent inquiry. The great thinkers at the turn of the century, men like Durkheim and Weber, engaged Marxism in intellectual confrontation to establish the division of labor, the economic basis of social organization, and class, status, and power as the central concerns of a new field of intellectual endeavor, sociology.]

[Modern sociology constructed two distinct yet interrelated tendencies on the foundations of nineteenth- and early twentieth-century social theory: functionalism and positivism. Functionalism turned Marx on his head by reforming his famous idea of "class struggle as the locomotive of history." For Marx, struggle against the injustices of the class system was the historical vehicle for the eventual elimination of class society. Among functionalists, "social stratification" (social inequalities in the distribution of scarce values and material rewards) is a "universal necessity" for the existence and maintenance of human society. Early versions, such as Davis and Moore's "Principles of Stratification" (1945), were simply scholasticized restatements of popular mythologies that formed part of the legitimating doctrines obfuscating class relations of exploitation and domination. The work of Talcott Parsons provided the foundation for a much more sophisticated, highly abstract systems theory that integrated the concerns of Weber and nineteenth-century social philosophy into a surbordinate place in a larger scheme of "equilibriated" social functioning.

But the great majority of Western sociologists, practicing within a newly professionalized academic "discipline," preferred earthy science to grand theorizing. Positivism generated an astounding mass of empirical studies of limited aspects of prevailing social realities, some of it lightly tinged with a permissible liberal concern for the injustice of social inequality. But these studies did not follow the logic of the scientific method of positivism—the facts never accumulated to become integrated into a systematic theory of class and inequality. A few bold practitioners of sociological enterprise did write marketable textbooks attempting to integrate empirical knowledge of social inequality with middle-range theoretical functionalism. But empirical research to this day largely remains at the level of the appearances that passing social realities assume, and research results are permanently buried in archives housing thousands of volumes of professional journals.

After Lenin and prior to the 1960s, Marxism remained barely alive in Communist parties and workers' movements in the West and, in more vital form, in Asian revolutionary movements. In metropolitan centers of intellectual production, democratic political culture, and anticommunist hysteria, Marxism was forced underground. Marx and Engels had provided the essential elements for the construction of a theory of social class that was at once historical, materialist, and dialectical, but Western Marxism could not rise to the challenge. Perry Anderson's interpretive survey of Marxist intellectual history (1976) places the weaknesses of post-Leninist Marxism in the context of the rupture of its organic links to the proletariat, its Sovietization as a ruling ideology, and the resilience of capitalism. Whatever the sources of Marxism's theoretical and politically strategic inadequacies, I think it fair to say that until recently a sterile, mechanical Marxism held sway, preoccupied with political economy, crisis, and fascism in the context of Stalinist hegemony over world communism. Several currents contrary to orthodoxy survived within the underground, notably the historical and empirical work of English Marxists and the critical theory of the Frankfurt School. Dialectics was preserved within the Marxist tradition by "Hegelian Marxists," but the contribution of the Frankfurt School in particular was limited precisely by its failure to base dialectical analysis in a theory of social class grounded in a materialist conception of history. Meanwhile, Lukács and Korsch remained without influence; Gramsci was not translated.

Though the belated Stalin revelations of the 1950s and the Soviet military thrust into Hungary opened the gates, it was not until the 1960s that a revitalized Marxism on a world scale reemerged. New, radicalized social forces made their presence felt in the West, and revolutionary nationalism confronted military dictatorship and a consolidated U.S. economic, political, and military presence in the Third World. In academic environments in Europe and for the first time in North America and the Third World, Marxism surged from the underground to challenge the hegemony of the mainstream doctrines that had come to form a "scientific" basis for ideologies of domination. Third World intellectuals, especially in Latin America, dulled the social science gloss given to imperial ideology by mainstream U.S. social science and reformulated the classic theory of imperialism as a theory of dependency. In the metropolis, critical theory circulated widely outside the confines of Frankfurt. Gramsci and Lukács were translated. Existing socialisms came to be recognized as new forms of class society. Studies of power structures, guided by instrumental notions of the ruling class-state nexus and inspired with "new Left" humanism and activism, intellectually (and to some extent politically) demolished the "pluralist" theories of power that obfuscated fundamental relations of power.

In Western Marxist sociology, Ralph Miliband's *The State in Capitalist Society* (1969) represented the culmination of an elementary Marxist theory of class, power, and the state. No sooner was the book published, however, than a new tendency, "Marxist structuralism," pioneered by

Louis Althusser (1970a, 1970b, 1971, 1976), rose to challenge the foundations of the "instrumentalist" views and down-to-earth Marxism of Miliband and others strongly influenced by Anglo-American positivism. The structuralist project did not confine its critical attention to empiricism: all the surviving historicist, humanist, and Hegelian Marxist currents were confronted. Altusser's concerns were anti-Stalinist, and his protégé, Nicos Poulantzas, composed a number of texts that challenged an economism viewed as the intellectual vestiges of Stalinism.

The sociological theory that finds its inspiration in the epistemological inquiries of Louis Althusser must be counted among the great contributions to social class theory, as we shall see in Chapters 1, 2, and 3, where I survey the main elements needed to construct a theory of social class and social development within a historical and dialectical framework. The work of Nicos Poulantzas stands out among that which has attempted to construct social theory on the basis of an Althusserian epistemology and use it in the analysis of major social phenomena. Poulantzas's *Classes in Contemporary Capitalism* (1975) is perhaps the most authoritative text on social class currently available. This is so not because it is adequate theory but because it is one of the few ambitious attempts to construct such a theory. The reviews of *Classes,* especially Eric Olin Wright's (1976) (and those of Geras [1972], Glucksmann [1972], Veltmeyer [1974-75], and Thompson [1978] on Althusser) and the offshoots, especially Carchedi (1978) and Wright (1978), have identified premises and perhaps advanced somewhat toward a more satisfactory historical materialist and dialectical theory of social classes, toward charting the path of social development.

Poulantzas's work is given extensive critical treatment, then, because it is one of a handful of available contemporary theoretical texts[1] specifically devoted to the analysis of classes. And the absence of works on social class bears out his critique of Marxism for its economistic bent. At the same time that economism continues to flourish, there is a rapidly growing body of literature on Marxist political theory. Yet research and writing on politics, the state, and other political questions is seriously hampered by the absence of solid work on social class. It is to Poulantzas's credit that he has recognized this lacuna and attempted to construct a theory of social classes on which an adequate political theory can rest.

But Poulantzas's books do not add up to a satisfactory theory of social classes (or of the state and the "political region," his main object). I argue in the theoretical chapters that follow, which are organized primarily as a critical encounter with "Marxist structuralism, that the Althusserian structuralism that permeates Poulantzas's work (and that of a still-growing number of others) tends toward a sterile, static, and dehumanized theoreticism. The critiques of these initial chapters are thorough and unrelenting. I try to recognize the limitations of the empiricist, historicist, and humanist currents so forcefully posited by Althusser, Poulantzas and others, while trying also to rescue from the structuralist onslaught those elements drawn from the different Marxist traditions that pertain to social classes—and to pose them in relation to problems of historical and dialectical method.

I want to differentiate this critique unequivocally from that of E. P. Thompson. The drafts of these chapters were prepared in 1977, before Thompson's *The Poverty of Theory* (1978) became available. I have not made substantial revisions of the manuscripts in light of Thompson's blast, although I invoke some choice Thompson quotes in places. (Also, in late 1979 the *Insurgent Sociologist* published a special issue on "Marxism and Structuralism" in which some of the critiques made here are also elaborated.)

Thompson's critique of Althusser and of structuralism within Marxism in general is devastating. I have been an admirer of Thompson, his sound historiography, his great theoretical and, most of all, empirical contributions to an understanding of class, his creative and independent Marxism, his principled stance as an articulate spokesman against Stalinism and all forms of dogmatic Marx*isms,* and his vital socialist humanism. On first reading, Thompson's critique appealed to me on another level. After a number of years of immersion in sanctified abstractions, a special characteristic of structuralism, I sometimes felt overwhelmed by pompous banality, some of which I undoubtedly have regurgitated here. I confess that one passage in particular from Thompson expressed my recurring feelings:

> All this "shit" (*Geschichtenscheissenschlopff*), in which both bourgeois sociology and Marxist structuralism stand up to their chins (Dahrendorf beside Poulantzas, modernization theory beside theoretical practice) has been shat upon us by conceptual paralysis, by the de-historicising of process, and by reducing class, ideology, social formations, and almost everything else, to categorical stasis. The sociological section: the elaborate differential rotations within the closure of the orrery; the self-extrapolating programmed developmental series; the mildly disequilibrated equilibrium models, in which dissensus strays unhappily down strange corridors, searching for a reconciliation with consensus; the systems-analyses and structuralisms, with their torques and their combinatories; the counter-factual fictions; the econometric and cleometric groovers—all of these theories hobble along programmed routes from one static category to the next. And all of them are *Geschichtenscheissenschlopff,* unhistorical shit.
>
> And yet, in these days, we are offered little else [1978:107-108].

One's feelings in moments of intellectual fatigue are one thing; one's rational appreciation are quite another. Thompson's blast is not a critique; it is a calumnious tirade of bitterness. Thompson has declared "unrelenting intellectual war against such Marxisms" (1978:189). What is at issue, he says, "is the defense of reason itself" (1978:4).

Thompson goes to considerable length to counter Althusser's antiempiricism and antihistoricism with a theoretical statement on the method of historical materialism. Thompson would purge structure and substitute soft molding clay for Althusser's orrery. Firm foundations are not built of clay. I have concluded, with Thompson, that any "mechanical apparatus for exhibiting relative motions and positions" (i.e., an orrery) will not do. Any form of structuralism provides too rigid a foundation, too "bourgeois" and elitist a base, to construct a socialist house. But who other than a fool would deny that structure is the foundation on which people construct their own shelters from structural imposition—as well as their own prisons. In impuning the motive of the structuralist interrogation of Marx*isms,* Thompson denies the very efficacy of structure. Moreover, politically, what could be more "Stalinist" than a declaration of war against a competing Marxism? What antidogmatism could be more dogmatic than to say that we "can have no business with theoretical practice except to expose it and drive it out?" What could be a greater attack on reason itself than this characterization of Althusser's explicitly anti-Stalinist project: "Althusserianism *is* Stalinism reduced to the paradigm of theory."

So much for the English master's insolent antipanegyrics. As for showing proper respect for the dead and institutionalized, I have opted not to make any changes in the critical stance adopted. Poulantzas was unquestionably the leading contributor to a revitalized Marxist social science, and I believe his intellectual presence will be preserved and enhanced by the close scrutiny merited by the work of great intellects. Poulantzas's suicide was followed a year later by the personal tragedy of Louis Althusser, who was alleged to have strangled his wife while in a deep mental depression. Again, I have elected not to make any changes in the criticisms to which Althusser is subjected.

Search for Method and Theoretical Premise

The bulk of this book is directed at a series of issues conventionally defined as "theoretical." The intent of what may seem endless, undoubtedly difficult, and probably confusing (even pedantic) discourse into theoretical premises is to attempt to distill a historical and dialectical method. The reader will note the frequent invocation of paired concepts: qualification/dequalification, professionalization/deprofessionalization, centralization/decentralization, and others. These are meant to capture dual and contradictory processes that exist in the same reality. Intervening in these processes is technology. And each duality is viewed as a specific manifestation of a larger historical process, a bipolarization of classes that forms some and undermines other specific intermediate class formations. For example, the increased salience of the capital/labor relation in the monpoly stage of development forms new sets of mediating class relations: technocrat/detail worker, administrator/office employee, professional/client. . . .

In the search for a dialectical method one of the themes that consistently recurs in the many texts drawn on to address theoretical/methodological issues is the evident disjuncture between historical tendency and actual empirical outcome. Another, related problem is structural determinism versus the indeterminism inherent in the dynamics of class relations.

The disjuncture is particularly glaring within that current within contemporary Marxism (disparagingly analyzed in Chapter 2 as the "return to original principles tendency") that would reduce method to the application of "laws of motion" of the development of the capitalist mode of production. The results of such investigations often have scant correspondence to the actual paths of development of capitalist societies. On the other hand, the bulk of intellectual production within both conventional academia and critical, radical, and Marxist social science is the limited empirical study of this or that phenomenon. These blindly reflect more often than elucidate an underlying tendency—a dual and contradictory process—in the development of capitalism. For example, the United States since World War II has experienced a rather one-sided class struggle, and the dominant class has enjoyed a solid hegemony. Critical theory inveighs against one-dimensional domination, and radical social science exposes power structure. The form of denouncing hegemony merely extends it. There is nothing omnipotent about any power structure. What is needed are studies carried out within the perspective of the immanence of change and development under capitalism; of the constantly shifting forms of struggle against systems of exploitation and domination; of the manner in which a dominant class struggles, as indeed it must, to achieve and maintain its domination in the face of resistance; of the structurally rooted "contradictions" of capitalist development.

The methodological problem of bridging the gap between historical tendency and empirical outcome extends to the best of the work that attempts to address class relations; it is these relations, not economic "laws," that we see as the driving force of social and economic development. Without doubt, Harry Braverman's *Labor and Monopoly Capital* is the major text of contemporary Marxism. We rely extensively on Braverman to develop an appreciation of the interrelations among the accumulation of capital, the labor process, and the formation of social classes. In addition, concluding chapters use his insights into the labor dequalification process as the framework for the empirical examination of the changes in the positioning within class relations of administrative, technical, and professional fractions of the intermediate (i.e., "middle") class in recent U.S. history.

The remarkable work of Braverman is useful because it—in contrast to the ahistorical framework of Poulantzas—explicitly provides historical grounding to the problem of social classes. But Braverman's book leaves something to be desired from the point of view of dialectics. Here we attempt to evolve a dialectical framework of class analysis that has some of the analytic rigor of Poulantzas and the historical perspective of

Braverman. Chapter 1 presents an analysis of social classes as historically structured social relations (as distinct from empirical groupings) and evaluates the contribution Braverman has made to understanding how the development of monopoly capitalism radically alters structured class relations. The problem of the other side of the dialectic remains, however, how class relations radically alter, shape, guide, and cushion the development of capitalist political economy.

Viewed from this side, there are serious deficiencies in Braverman's work: It embodies an excessive determinism; there is an implicit, backward-looking utoptianism; the class polarization thesis developed is oversimplified and the place of intermediate forces in class relations underestimated; his image of a vast, undifferentiated working class is seriously misleading; and workers are seen as subjected to the omnipotence of capital, rather than as struggling subjects shaping social development. These problems stem from Braverman's "original principle," by which all else is ordered: The law of accumulation impels capital's complete appropriation of the labor process, through which all other phenomena fall into determined places. Yet the labor process is not simply the private property of capital; it is the immediate and prime site of class struggle. The methodological problem here is the conflation of two necessary levels of analysis, the historical tendencies of the accumulation process and, within the context of that process, the varying course of class struggles that decidedly shape historical outcomes. "Braverman mistakes tendency for outcome."[2]

The book as a whole attempts to employ the concept of totality but without invoking assumption of either an "expressive" or "structured" totality. Burawoy has stated this theoretical problem succinctly:

> On the one hand, there is the idea of a Hegelian totality in which a single "essence" or dominant principle comes to pervade the entire society. Each part of the social structure becomes an expression of the whole, of the defining "sprit." For Lukacs (1971) "commodification" or "reification," for Marcuse (1964) "one dimensionality," for Braverman (1974) Taylorism . . .— these are the dominant principles which both order and are expressed through social relations, not merely within the economic realm, but in leisure, in the family, in politics, in the cultural realm—in short, throughout capitalist society. On the other hand, there is the idea of a structure totality, in which a single part (the economic) determines the *relations* among all parts. The economy, by virtue of its functional requirements (or, as Marxists say, conditions of reproduction), defines the contributions of different parts of society and thus the relations among those parts [Burawoy in McNall, 1972:17-18].

Chapter 3 contains a detailed critique of the expressive totality of Hegelian Marxists, and the bulk of the theoretical chapters is a critique of both economic determinism and the structuralist invention of ahistorical functionalist circumventions for economic determinism. We attempt to evolve a "genetic structuralism" (Goldman, 1976; Zimmerman, 1978-79) that moves away from static notions of structure toward conceptualizations of historical and structural tendency or the "logic of process" (Thompson, 1978).

In brief, I argue that the networks of social relations in which people are enmeshed are indeed produced by an underlying structure, one that is worldwide in scope. But this structured totality is constituted by distinguishable substructures that do not functionally mesh and which are moved by dual and contradictory tendencies. Moreover, structure at all levels is activated by people, and its transformation is a product of human activity, not inexorable laws of the system itself.

This seems to be in line with Aronowitz's comments on "capital-logic" and the necessity for conceptualizing the determining force of labor, culture, and consciousness on structure. "The rise of capital-logic theory is an important addition to Marxist theory if it is understood as an abstraction of one side of concrete historical processes which cannot be subsumed under its laws" (1978:141).

There is a related methodological problem in unraveling the determinism of structure from the indeterminism of human purpose and volition, of differentiating the determinants of the formation of class from the variant course of class struggle. The attempt is to develop an approach to the determination of class that focuses on structure without falling into structural*ism*. As a main current within Marxism, structuralism explicitly poses history "as a process without a subject." We refuse to see people as mere agents fulfilling system-defined functions. The view developed here is that thinking, struggling, active subjects shape, within the limits imposed by structures that themselves emerge in antagonistic social relations, the course of events. Dialectical method defines the structural forces that contextually define in the first instance the extent, forms, and circumstances of class struggle—and proceeds in the same methodological stroke to examine the structural transformations moved by class struggle.

This book is thus a theory of the historical dynamics of the structured social relations that we see as the source of social development. These structures are not revealed by the minds of great theorists. They have to be observed in the social world. In the academic disciplines of sociology and history there has long been, as Zaret notes, a "separation of ahistorical theory and atheoretical history." In sociology there is mindless number crunching; history is mainly ad hoc interpretation of chronicalized events. We concur that "a true synthesis of historical scholarship and sociological theory will emerge when concept formation is informed by research into the historically determinate nature of society" (Zaret, 1978:118).

We are not able, for the most part, to work within our own methodological injunctions. Individuals more or less fade into their abstracted space as subjects; there is very little in the book about class consciousness; the nature of ideology is examined in depth, but extant ideologies are not seriously analyzed; class struggle is treated in the abstract, yet concrete depictions of struggle are in the main absent. This is because, in the first instance, this is a book directed at salient questions of theory and method. A conscious choice was made to limit historical and empirical research to those areas that better serve methodological clarification than empirical enlightenment. And in this we have relied on secondary sources rather than extensive firsthand encounters. What the book does do that others do not is to leave conceptual space within historical/structural tendencies of the totality for empirical outcomes and within structure for its transformation by human agency. We have tried to fill some of this space with historical analysis of the formation of certain professions and with empirical investigation of trends affecting the positioning within class relations of professional, technical, and administrative labor—that is of transformations in the nature of the intermediate class.

It should be noted that there is no consensus even among the contributers to this volume on theoretical premises or method of analysis, nor do they agree on the principal thematic, substantive appreciation of intermediate classes. In the theoretical/methodological chapters I am highly critical of work that reverts to "laws of motion" of the capitalist mode of production. Among those singled out for criticisms are the "failing raters." Yet I have also included in this volume a provocative piece by Eisenhower that posits the falling rate of profit as the tendency underlying the "crisis" of the present "degenerative phase" of capitalist development. Similarly, I criticize the Althusserian notion of an "ideological region," yet the book contains a chapter by Heffren that departs from Althusser's concept of ideology as "an imaginary conception of the relation of subjects to their conditions of existence." Finally, Martin Oppenheimer and I have a disagreement as to whether the proliferation of intermediate groupings characteristic of advanced capitalist societies can legitimately be considered a class. Professor Oppenheimer, following E. O. Wright (1978), contends they constitute a disparate agglomeration of classless groupings meshed within "contradictory class locations." The approach I develop leads to a conceptualization of the intermediate *class* as a constellation of class fractions that have been historically formed as an expression of the process of class polarization.

Intermediate Classes

While mainstream sociology conceives of a multiplicity of "classes" based on "social stratification," Marxist social science has been captivated by two class models: lords and peasants under feudalism, bourgeoisie and proletariat under capitalism. Long preoccupied with the political roles of groups not clearly identifiable as working class, only recently have Marxists given serious analytic (as distant from political) attention to intermediate classes. I will not burden the reader with a discourse on the growing literature until subsequent chapters, but some summary observations on intermediate classes are in order.

One of the main generalizations is that capitalist development is characterized by a process of multiclass relations in a bipolarizing structure. We are concerned with late nineteenth- and twentieth-century development. The principal structural feature of the maturation of the monopoly stage of development is the bipolarization of classes. Capital becomes progressively more concentrated and centralized, and the great bulk of the population is reduced to the social position of wage earner. The elimination of preexisting intermediate classes is a historical condition of this process. The old petty bourgeoisie of independent producers, small farmers, and merchants, despite strong resistance, was dispossessed of property and forced directly into wage labor. But as the polarization process proceeded and the nineteenth-century petty bourgeoisie was eliminated, a new salaried intermediate class composed of technical, administrative, and professional employees was formed.

This class was formed in tempo with the movement of the capital accumulation process. Technological and organizational innovation gave scientists, organizational experts, and technicians an increasing importance. The internationalization of capital made the United States into the center of world capitalism, and administrative personnel manned the apparatus of empire. The growth of the interventionist/warfare/welfare state greatly augmented the ranks of professionals and functionaries. In this book we try to view capital accumulation as a good deal more than investment and sectoral development of the economy. It is a process of class formation/class dissolution and of structurally patterned social relations of antagonism. The proletarianization of the old petty bourgeoisie and the formation of a class of wage laborers was the principal historical source of the accumulation of capital, and this continues in new forms today. The intermediate class came into being mainly as an expression of that process. While we closely examine the functions of technical, administrative, and professional labor as agents in the social division of labor, our approach to class is a historical and relational one, not a static, functional one.

This intermediate class intervenes in or mediates the capital/labor social relation. It is located in the middle of polarizing social relations. For this reason we use the term "middle class." This is an unfortunate term, since the concept carries a lot of undesirable popular sociological baggage implying that class has to do with income distribution, occupational prestige hierarchies, lifestyles, and other social stratifications.

It is this class that constitutes the main substantive theme of the book. While we document a substantial numerical increase and growing social weight of intermediate groupings, the views expressed here have nothing to do with the notion that as the working class shrinks, the great middle expands. Originally formulated as a refutation of Marx's class polarization thesis, the expansive middle notion later became integral to the celebrated theory of "postindustrial society."

We refrain here from a sorely needed, extensive critique of the post-industrial society literature, its intellectual roots in the "end of ideology" ideology (Bell, 1960), its stumblings into "futurology" (Lipset, 1980), and its extension into recent writings on the "New Class" (Bruce-Briggs, 1979). (Oppenheimer reviews some of this literature and its intellectual origins in Chapter 4.) The thesis is plainly wrong. As Braverman has forcefully demonstrated for the United States, the working class, far from disappearing, encompasses an ample and growing proportion of the population; further, the labor force is not becoming more skilled but is instead being stripped of its skills. We argue that (a) in the latest phase of development, the bourgeoisie, far from having its class power usurped by a knowledgeable elite, has simply coopted from the middle class a servile technocratic staff, and (b) the bulk of the middle class, far from today constituting the main class undergirding a postcapitalist social order, is being pushed in the direction of the working class. The present phase of development is not postcapitalist, but one of incipient capitalist crisis—different in its specific manifestations than the booms and bursts of the nineteenth and early twentieth centuries and the period extending from World War I through the Great Depression to World War II, but an emerging crisis nonetheless. And the middle class in the United States and other industrial countries, we conclude in the final chapter, is at the heart of that crisis.

There are many aspects to the emerging phase and the place of the middle class within it. Our main concern is the "dequalification" of professional, technical, and administrative labor—that is, the deskilling and increased subordination in the division of labor of sizable sectors of the middle class. The general thesis of the dequalification of technical, administrative, and professional labor that we pursue is diametrically opposed to the main thrust of the literature in the sociology of occupations, which has molded its research in the postindustrial society framework.

The postindustrial society thesis has recently been extended and modified in the "New Class" literature. Among New Class analysts, Gouldner is undoubtedly the most provocative and interesting. He defines it as a "flawed universal class":

> The New Class is elitist and self-seeking and used its special knowledge to advance its own interests and power, and to control its own work situation. Yet the New Class may also be the best card that history has presently given us to play. The power of the New Class is growing. It is substantially more powerful and independent than Chomsky suggests, while still much less powerful than is suggested by Galbraith who seems to conflate present reality with future possibility. The power of this morally ambiguous New Class is on the ascendent and it holds a mortgage on at least *one* historical future [1979:7].

Gouldner's vision of the New Class as expressing a collective interest roughly parallels my argument (in Chapter 7) that the "service professional fraction" of the middle class is, in some sense, a bearer of universal functions of technologically and socially advanced society. Service professionals are engaged in the social production of use values, as distinct from the private production of exchange values. A system geared toward private profits lays bare human need and manufactures social problems that the state employs professionals to try to confront. While the "welfare state" is two steps backward toward social control of popular demand, it is a step or more forward toward a system that provides "to each according to his need." Capitalism does indeed produce the germ of a new society within its increasingly socialized institutionality. But nowhere are we so foolish as to posit professionals or any other category of knowledgeability or technical expertise as constituting a universal class which is assigned the historical realizing vision that historicists like Lukács attribute to the working class (Chapter 3). (Gouldner is not the first to assign historical mission to a middle class. See Oppenheimer's Chapter 4.) On the contrary, the middle class is not in a process of being constituted as the harbinger of a new order; it is gradually disintegrating as a class.

While the recent discourse on the New Class (whether the uncertain liberal preoccupations of Bruce-Briggs [1979] or the "Left neo-Hegelian" provocations of Gouldner [1979]) reflects its origins in the postindustrial society thesis, like all theoretical-ideological innovation, it also is rooted in actual social structural trends and their political concomitants. Today the great middle is less shrinking that bifurcating. Institutional centralization of power and the dequalification process of the "post-postindustrial" period (i.e., a developmental phase of incipient crisis) have tended to form not only a mass of specialized technical and administrative personnel moving toward (but not yet wholly into) the proletarian condition, but also a technocracy of sorts. The celebrated cases are those Chomsky (1969) denounces as the "New Mandarins," but the growing social weight of upper bureaucratic functionaries, staff experts, and purveyors of legitimating ideology does not serve to form a class as such, but a sector that is being elevated from a disintegrating middle class to the status of hangers-on of the managerial bourgeoisie. It may be that at times these elements act as "benign technocrats," but their place in evolving class relations is more likely to make them over into "servants of power," in Walzer's (1980) terms, a "neo-bourgeoisie." Still, as Straussman indicates in *The Limits of Technocratic Politics,* "It is necessary to separate the princes from their counselors" (1975:18).

Notes

1. A few other works are presented as theories of social class, but I did not find them useful in preparing this theoretical critique. Giddens's book, *The Class Structure of Advanced Societies* (1975), for example, applies a Marxized Weberian perspective to examine the

structuring of the working class and middle class in advanced capitalism and the "new class" in state socialist societies. A rather indiscriminate eclecticism in his theoretical position leads to some provocative critiques but does not lend itself to the construction of a coherent theory. Anderson's *The Political Economy of Social Class* (1974) is a well-organized general textbook that covers a wide range of questions relating to social classes. His main concern, however, is to apply a general Marxist perspective to social problems in the contemporary United States and not to systematically develop a theory of social classes. Ferrarotti's *An Alternative Sociology* (1974) is useful for a critical appreciation of a sociology of class. There is also a growing number of mainly descriptive studies of particular classes and the class structures of different nations. (On the United States see Hill, 1975, and Gilbert and Kahl, 1982; on England see Westergaard and Resler, 1975.)

2. See Vallas (1980). In the original drafts of this book, I did not recognize that Braverman "mistakes tendency for outcome." I am indebted to Vallas for this insight. At the time of this writing, Vallas is completing a dissertation on the labor process in the auto industry. This will undoubtedly represent a significant advance in more closely aligning outcome with tendency. In this respect, see also Gartman (1978) on the theoretical aspects and Walker's empirical study (1979) of the labor process in the British engineering industry.

Part One: Class Relations:

Theoretical Perspectives

Dale L. Johnson: Toward a Historical and Dialectical Social Science

The distinct preoccupation of Marxist social science has been the structure of capitalist society and its historical transformation. In this larger scheme of things the individual often disappears; the gap between structure and consciousness, being and thought, is unbridged. Yet the weathered pillars of the bridge between structure and consciousness, society and the individual, have stood for many years. There is no "human nature" as such, only a capacity for self-creation (Lichtman, 1977). A person is what he or she lives. A person's being is constituted by the social relations that comprise his or her natural and social existence. But people bring to the social relations that shape being a capacity for thought, imagination, creativity, purpose, and will. In social relations that are oppressive, the predominant mode of being may limit thought, stultify imagination, and inhibit creativity. Yet it is also the oppressed who quietly think the unthinkable and scheme their freedom. And it is in the nature of the mental capacities of humans to bring purpose and will not only to the mastery of nature, but to their relation to the social world—and to stubbornly seek to transform this relation.

The social relations to which I refer in the abstract are first and foremost class relations. In the social realities that theoretical constructs attempt to order and interpret, social classes are not abstract entities but groupings of concretely situated people engaging in the rigors of daily activities. The experiences of being born, living, and dying early or late; of making a living and eating well or going hungry; of being white or black, brown, yellow, or red, male or female, young or old; of acquiescing or rebelling; of being socially rewarded or arrested and tortured—all are set within fundamental patterned social relations of domination and exploitation, power and struggle. The subjective experience that is imposed by and constituent to these relations shapes and guides much of human activity. The day-to-day experience of living forces people to think their social being and to act in relation to their class situation, and this thought/activity shapes, guides and transforms the defining relations.

In this book we do not pursue a social psychology of the individual and society; our focus is the social relations of class. It is the purpose of this theoretical chapter to lay the groundwork for a study of the structural determination of social classes that does not forsake the individual, deny human agency, or freeze history. These difficult questions of theory and method are explored in a discussion of structural determination, subjects, and history. The chapter opens with a critique of the lifelessness of conventional sociology's notion of "social stratification" and of the excessive determinism of the contemporary Marxist texts on social class.

The term "social class" is too often understood as denoting empirical collectivities of occupational groupings positioned together through a common factor, such as wealth and poverty or relationship to the means of production. Upper, middle, and lower classes or bourgeoisie, petty bourgeoisie, and proletariat are seen as concrete groupings. Their wealth or poverty can be measured, their privileges or deprivations surveyed, their numbers counted. Of course, it is necessary to use terms that have an empirical referent and to investigate the situation of different classes. But immediately we encounter a problem: In capitalist society the empirical configurations of classes are in a constant state of flux. The division of labor shifts, technology revamps social structures, "life chances" vary, income distribution is altered, wealth is concentrated, over time new classes form, established classes are restructured, preexisting historical formations dissolve. Yet this is not the central problem; empirical designations direct attention away from the dynamic quality of class. The terms "upper class" and "lower class" are descriptive aggregations of individuals arrayed on one or more dimensions of social inequality; they have no relational component at all. The terms imply nothing of how the upper class got to be "haves" and the lower "have nots," or of the relationships between the two classes. The terms "bourgeoisie" and "proletariat" are also often used descriptively rather than analytically. This robs the concept class of its utility in the study of social development.

Social class is a dynamic, relational concept, and static, descriptive usages should be avoided. In the study of the workings of capitalist societies, the empirical configurations of bourgeoisie and working class are of less interest than the social relation of capital to labor. We know through empirical observation and theoretical generalization that this relation presents a central antagonism. It is a relation based on exploitation, the appropriation by capital of a proportion of the value produced by labor. It is in the interest of capital to increase the level of value appropriated; it is in the interest of labor to resist exploitation and to try to increase the proportion of value retained. It is in the interest of capital to see to the reproduction of the social relations that preserve its class privileges; it is in the interest of labor to modify or revolutionize prevailing social relations.

At any point in time we are interested in how the abstract relation capital/labor is empirically manifested. This requires a class concept at a lower level of abstraction. Capital is constituted as a social class designated as bourgeoisie and labor as working class. The internal structure and social character of the classes are viewed in terms of the forms of relations between the classes, forms that vary as the fundamental antagonism unfolds over time. The reproduction of relations of exploitation requires a panoply of forms of social domination on the side of the dominant class; on the side of the subordinate class it impels many and changing patterns of resistence. The forms of domination and resistance permeate the whole of society: supervisor/worker, technician/detail worker, social worker/welfare recipient, teacher/student, merchant/consumer, functionary/supplicant, doctor/patient, judge/defendant, landlord/tenant, IRS auditor/taxpayer, professional/client. . . . The permeation proceeds further: men/women, white/black, even parent/child are institutionalized as relations of inequality, of domination and subordination.

In this volume we are particularly concerned to understand how the relation capital/labor became concretized in the twentieth-century development of capitalism in industrialized countries like the United States. In America, capital is now highly concentrated and centralized as a dominant class whose power extends far beyond national frontiers and labor has been constituted as the proportionately largest working class in the world. The United States also has the world's most substantial middle class: the superordinates in the paired relations above, who are themselves subordinated to higher administrative authority. It is our thesis that this weighty intermediate class is a historical expression of the twentieth-century polarization of the working and capitalist classes.

The discussion above is the barest outline of views developed throughout the book. Unfortunately, this relational approach, rooted in the lived experience of human subjects, is not widely shared. In contemporary sociological studies of "social stratification," class as social relations is entirely absent. Also absent are people. Individuals are mere atomic units of a static society that functions without human agency, rather than living, thinking, acting human beings immersed within and molded by relational networks that people themselves activate and transform.

Social Class and Social Stratification

The term "class" is often suppressed in mainstream sociology, and attention is riveted on ascriptive and distributional social inequalities. Inequality in income distribution is seen as the main factor of social stratification, but invidious social distinctions based on occupational pursuit, educational level, lifestyle, and national origin or race are also viewed as important in stratifying the population of a nation. These social inequalities create a society in which individuals are placed on a series of hierarchies of social rank. To the extent that classes are visualized, they represent broad groupings of individuals aggregated into categories horizontally cross-cutting the different dimensions of social stratification. Individuals can achieve "social mobility" on any one of several such hierarchies and may suffer "status inconsistency" if their placement on different ranks is not in horizontal congruence.

In this conceptualization, classes exist outside the sphere of economic relations of exploitation and of the social relations of domination and oppression. To the degree that a class possesses a social unity, it is based on the congruence of rank in the various hierarchies and is achieved within the sphere of culture and lifestyle. This simple notion is continually produced and reaffirmed for popular consumption, although its simplicity is partially concealed when sociologists write to each other in highly complex descriptive, computerized quantitative studies of social stratification.

Income inequalities, the invidious distinctions of occupational prestige, differing educational attainments, ethnic and racial gradations, distinct lifestyles, and other factors of stratification are real social phenomena. But it is their social meaning that is important. Stratifications are *ideological* manifestations of prevailing social inequalities, and they are perceived and acted on by people in daily life. These are often mistaken by people (and by professional sociologists who specialize in ideological mystification) for social classes. Distributional and ascriptive inequalities and cultural and occupational attributes are integral to the social relations of exploitation and domination; they are facets of class relations in that the social meaning of stratifications systematically subordinates workers and serves to create divisions within the working class and to socially define boundaries between the working and middle classes.

When the term "class" is used in mainstream sociology, it is usually phrased in sanitized terms of upper, middle and lower, with gradations between. Social class divisions are typically drawn between blue-collar workers, who are lower class, and white-collar employees, who are middle class. Many conclude that skilled workers are now part of the middle class because their high incomes allow them access to middle-class lifestyles.

Stratification analysis and class analysis have remained in quite separate traditions. The former was historically produced (especially by Max Weber) as an "answer" to Marxism; and the empirical manifestations of social inequality continue to be extensively investigated by modern sociology. The Marxist tradition has evidenced very little serious concern with the multiple inequalities of any given social order in favor of a generalized emphasis on the class roots of broad, historical change in capitalist societies. This divergence has been excellently elaborated by Stolzman and Gamberg (1973-74). Since it is too much to expect that empirical sociology will begin to place social stratification within a class framework (since Marx still has to be "answered"), it is past time that class analysis is empirically applied to social stratification. This is being done with respect to race, and even more so in the area of sex and sexism. Research in social stratification guided by a class perspective could do much to indicate the specific forms of relations of domination between the main classes. The theoretical parameters for investigations of this type are provided in Chapter 2 discussions of ideology as the content of class relations.

At their scientific best, studies of social stratification remain ahistorical and descriptive. The Marxist theory of class pretends to be historical and analytic, though the different authors often fall short in both respects. Among recent works, two stand out. Harry Braverman's *Labor and Monopoly Capital* is an extraordinary study of the historical formation of the working class; Nicos Poulantzas's *Classes in Contemporary Capitalism* is a highly systematic analytic statement on the nature of the bourgeoisie and petty bourgeoisie.

The Historical Formation of Social Classes: Harry Braverman

Braverman's *Labor and Monopoly Capital* rivals Poulantzas's *Classes in Contemporary Capitalism* as a theoretical text on social class, though it was written to explore the labor process and not to expound a theory of class. *Labor and Monopoly Capital* achieves a synthesis of analytic sharpness and historical depth that is a rare scholarly achievement. The work is also an account of real life: Lucid presentation grips the reader and compels an exciting understanding of the forces that shape people's lives. Indeed, one is tempted to exclaim aloud: "That is why my life is the way it is!"

The analytic acumen, the sense of historical cause and effect, the excitement of knowing that "this is my life" all proceed from systematic analysis of the labor process as it is incessantly transformed by the driving force of capitalism, the accumulation of capital. The modes, avenues, and directions of the accumulation of capital and the interrelated transformations of the labor process together structure the social classes and shape the social conditions bearing down on the lives of people in the crisis-ridden cities and suburban housing tracts, in families in decomposition, and in the different occupations continually reshaped into degraded labor.

For Braverman, classes are not fixed, empirical entities but social relations in constant historical change. The accumulation of capital manifests itself in the labor process as an incessant transformation of the organization, character, and social relations of work in each of the sectors of production and as a continuous redistribution of the labor force among the sectors. This structures and restructures the social classes.

Since the end of the nineteenth century and at an accelerating rate with the development of the monopoly stage of capitalism, capital accumulation proceeded by the transformation of increasing sectors of the population into waged labor organized by capital for the purpose of producing surplus value and realizing it in the form of profits. The means of production were concentrated, control centralized; the small producers of farms and shops and the petty bourgeoisie in commerce and services were dispossessed of productive property, ruined with no alternative but to sell their labor power on the market. In recent decades, a large number of Third World peoples, dispossessed and geographically displaced by the internationalization of capital, have migrated to the metropolitan countries to be incorporated into the least desirable work or into the reserve army of labor.

Necessary community-organized services and family production for consumption were first disrupted, then replaced altogether by the "universalization of the market"—the extension of the commodity form of production, and the deterioration of social bonds that accompany commodification, into every intimate corner of life. In this manner, capital extended its markets while simultaneously incorporating the production of community and family services into the orbit of capital and incrementing the proportion of the labor force employed by capital to produce profit and accumulate capital. (In recent decades masses of women have been incorporated into the labor force, mainly as a growing sector of the working class.) Braverman states it cogently:

> In the period of monopoly capitalism, the first step in the creation of the universal market is the conquest of all goods production by the commodity form, the second step is the conquest of an increasing range of services and their conversion into commodities, and the third step is a "product cycle" which invents new products and services, some of which become indispensable as the conditions of modern life change to destroy alternatives. In this way the inhabitant of capitalist society is enmeshed in a web made up of commodity goods and commodity services from which there is little possibility of escape. . . . And while from the point of view of consumption this means total dependence on the market, from the point of view of labor it means that all work is carried on under the aegis of capital and is subject to its tribute of profit to expand capital still further [1974: 281].

The transformation of the bulk of the population into waged workers laboring in activities controlled by capital was historically accompanied by organizing an expanding labor force to maximize the production of surplus value (and its realization as profits, though Braverman does not deal well with this question). This was accomplished by management of the labor process according to "scientific" principles of the division of labor into broad functions and minute tasks and by the introduction of machine technologies that not only directly increased productivity but also permitted a more rigorous subordination of the labor force to an elaborately hierarchical and stultifying division of labor. The result was the eventual elimination of any residual control over work retained or gained by workers in previous periods and the destruction of their skills—that is, the degradation of labor. To this degradation were added the interrelated consequences of the universalization of the market: the atrophy of competence in urban and surburban conditions forcing people to turn to the marketplace for essential goods and services, and the erosion of satisfactory communal and family life—

> an all-powerful marketplace which, governed by capital and its profitable investment, is both chaotic and profoundly hostile to all feelings of community. Thus the very social services which should facilitate social life and social solidarity have the opposite effect. As the advances of modern household and service industries lighten the family labor, they increase the futility of family life; as they remove the burdens of personal relations, they strip away its affections; as they create an intricate social life, they rob it of every vestige of community and leave in its place the cash nexus [1974: 282].

The class structure was shaped and reshaped and continues to be molded by these powerful forces. There is no point in restating Braverman's substantive analysis of the historical formation of contemporary class structure here; I am more interested in his theory and method. Briefly, his main substantive conclusion is that the American working class has expanded during the monopoly stage to encompass roughly two-thirds of the population. As I will shortly indicate, this is totally at odds with Poulantzas's narrow conception of the contemporary working class. Braverman's analysis of the "middle layers of employment," while brief, is well-based in the history of the development of the labor process in the monopoly stage and fairly consistent with the in-depth analysis of intermediate groups in this volume. The historical grounding given to the formation of the middle class (and its growing tenuous position within the structure) is, again, in sharp contrast to Poulantzas's formal, analytic approach. Poulantzas reduces the analysis of the economic basis of the "new petty bourgeoisie" to a question of the place of unproductive labor in the capitalist mode of production, by and large conceived, as I will later argue, in abstract, ahistorical terms. Braverman's chapter entitled "The Structure of the Working Class and its Reserve Armies" is a major contribution toward an understanding of the place of the reserve army of labor under conditions of modern industrial capitalism, though it suffers from an excess of traditional Marxist orthodoxy in its conceptualization of the bottom layers of the class structure. Poulantzas, however, never raises the question of the reserve army of labor, despite the fact that the reserve army is sporadically incorporated largely into what he considers "unproductive" employment.

Braverman's main contribution, a perspective on social classes as historical and relational phenomena, provides a basis for a dialectical sociology. Nevertheless, Braverman's theory and method raise a number of problems. There is, first, an excessive economic determinism. As Walker (1981) and other critics point out, the labor process is the prime site of class struggle, and there is considerable variation across industries in the actual outcomes of these struggles. Moreover, technical innovations and market competition intersect with workplace struggle; again, there is considerable variation in the results. Braverman is trapped within a straightjacket of universal tendency. His excessive determinism results in an image of system omnipotence. And this image in turn makes his critique of the labor process take on the tone of a romantic outcry against the industrial division of labor. While Braverman is hardly the modern-day Luddite that Szmanski portrays (1978), the book is infused with a distinct element of utopianism—an explicit rejection of the division of labor characteristic of industrial civilization itself (capitalist or socialist) and an implicit longing for premonoply capitalism craft. There are also problems with Braverman's analysis of the capital accumulation process. He does not discuss those historic avenues of capital accumulation that have received attention by other analysts (but who have, unlike Braverman, largely ignored the impact of capital accumulation on the labor process): imperialism and epoch-making technological and product innovations (railroads, the automobile, electronics, computers, successive forms of cheap and efficient energy and their technical application, etc.). Nor does he adequately deal with the evolution of the state and its massive intervention in the accumulation and labor processes, its assumption of central functions in the system of class domination, and its place as a major employer of labor. These are perhaps legitimate omissions in a study that tries to limit its scope to the labor process. It is less clear, though, that analysis of the great social upheavals and class struggles that have been at the center of the accumulation and labor processes can be legitimately excluded from consideration. The heart of the labor process is the struggle between capital and labor. Social classes are indeed social relations structured by the historical movement of capital accumulation, but this structuring is not a mechanically determined consequence of capital's drive to accumulate through control of the division of labor and machine technology. The relations of classes, as they work themselves out historically, dialectically interrelate with the structural determinations that Braverman analyzes, but in isolation from their dynamic content.

Subsequent chapters attempt to build on Braverman's work by viewing the different sources of capital accumulation as historical processes of class formation, to add the struggle dimension to changing forms of class relations, and to view the state as a vehicle of class formation and as an expression of these relations.

Analytic Approaches to Class Determination: Nicos Poulantzas

The work of Nicos Poulantzas is situated within the post-Stalin context of wider efforts by European theorists to resurrect the scientific status of Marxism from empiricist, idealist, and historicist currents. Poulantzas's books became part of a second wave of critical intellectual enterprise that transcended the original, mainly epistemological inquiry of Althusser, Balibar, and other philosophers in attempting to construct systematic social theory and to use it in the analysis of significant problems. Poulantzas's works are explicitly attacks on the "economism" of official Marxism, including today's Eurocommunist parties.

Poulantzas's first books were mainly efforts to construct a theory of the "political region." His contribution to a theory of the state is unparalleled among contemporary Marxists. It incited one of the great debates on the nature of the capitalist state.[1] Toward the end of his short life, Poulantzas turned his attention to social classes. This followed logically from his work on the political region, as his theory of the state is based on the general view of the state as a "condensation" of the relations of classes. I have found particular ideas, such as his Gramscian concept of "power bloc," very useful.

Poulantzas's theory of social classes is structuralist in two senses. First, he is concerned with the structural determination of class. The thrust of his theory is the identification of the economic, political, and ideological factors that form social classes. Second, he draws heavily on the French structuralist school, developed in sophisticated non-Marxist versions by Claude Levi-Strauss and given a Marxized veneer by Althusser, Balibar, and others.

Structuralists, of course, do not hold a monopoly on a concern for structural determination; they share with diverse Marxist and non-Marxist social scientists the assumption that historical-empirical realities can be explained only in terms of the underlying structures that give rise to them. But how are these structures to be defined? How do they change? How is it that structures determine the realities that people confront in their everyday lives? And how do people, in experiencing structurally given, yet always changing, realities—in relating to each other cooperatively and antagonistically—accept and modify, confront and transform structures? What Poulantzas has to say about structures is taxonomically neat and intricately elaborate. Unfortunately, the distance he places between realities that people located in different classes experience and confront, his abstract mode of analysis, and the persistent use of the concrete only to construct a theoretical edifice does raise questions about the strength of the theoretical foundations.

Classes in Contemporary Capitalism is of a different order of achievement than his earlier *Political Power and Social Classes*, a book totally immersed in complex conceptualizations derived rather strictly from an Althusserian framework. This is toned down some in his book on classes and his final effort, *State, Power, Socialism*, in which a more dynamic, relational view of the state is expressed. *Classes in Contemporary Capitalism* has the virtue of situating the analysis historically and spatially: the present phase of monopoly capitalism/imperialism with a focus on the subordinate European nations of the imperial center. The vehicle for approaching these questions is even more concrete: the bourgeoisies, their internal structures and their relations to the state, and the petty bourgeoisies, old and new. Nevertheless, the themes are essentially posed from his earlier theoretical formulations in *Political Power*. While his analysis of the fractions of the European bourgeoisie is interesting (and his Gramscian concept of power blocs potentially useful), by and large he does not proceed to ever more concrete levels of analysis, bringing historical argumentation and empirical evidence to bear. Nor, to pose it less positivistically, does he explain historical events or current realities through methodological application of the framework. (This procedure seems implicitly dismissed by most structuralists as merely conjunctural analysis.) Instead, he poses central structuralist postulates alongside the concrete problems raised and then works inductively to reconstruct a global theory.

In a response to the critiques of Miliband and Laclau, Poulantzas (1976) admits to a certain formalism, "theoreticism" or abstractionism, and needless difficulty in language in his earlier work, but cites *Classes* as proof of the adequacy of his approach to the concrete. He denies the validity of any criticism of his work as "structuralist," but as I shall show below, Poulantzas's work continues to suffer from a number of problems, traceable to its Marxist structuralist origins, that limit its usefulness as a historical, materialist, and dialectical theory of social class.

The clearest statement of his approach to class determination, his main contribution, is contained in his essay on the "new petty bourgeoisie" (in *Classes)* Poulantzas elaborates three basic determinants of social class: the economic, political, and ideological. These determinants are derived from Althusserian regional theory in which political and ideological "regions" are "relatively autonomous" from the economic, which is determinant only in "the last instance." Perhaps his most important proposition is that classes are not themselves structures, but the "pertinent effects" of these regional structures.

With respect to differentiating the working class from the "new petty bourgeoisie," Poulantzas reduces the economic determination of class to a distinction between productive and unproductive labor. Workers who directly produce surplus value are the proletariat, because it is only this category of workers who are subject to the basic relation of exploitation of capitalist social relations, the appropriation of surplus value. All other waged or salaried workers are of the petty bourgeoisie, including, reardless of the conditions of work, all commercial employees, supervisory and nonsupervisory white-collar, service, or "mental" workers. This is because political and ideological factors, given their "relatively autonomous" character in capitalist social formations, act as codeterminants of class, especially in differentiating between the working class and the new petty bourgeoisie. Supervisory places, even those corresponding to direct production of goods and surplus value, since they function to control and subordinate labor in the economic process, are essentially determined by their political character. Production line foremen are thus members not of the working class but of the new petty bourgeoisie. The division between mental and manual labor, an ideological factor, acts as a determinant of class. This is because the social division of labor divides workers into experts and novices who are excluded from the "secret knowledge" of the production process. The development of industrial capitalism has resulted in a burgeoning army of petty bourgeois "experts," a process that also induces a dispossession of workers of any effective control over production and a disqualification of the skills of the bulk of the working class. (The latter tendency is developed by Braverman in a form superior to Poulantzas.) The division between mental and manual labor serves to mystify workers concerning the organization, planning, and relations or production.

This Weberian-sounding conception of the three-dimensional determination of social class[2] results in a reduced working class and an expansive

TABLE 1.1   Components of Social Classes in the United States
by Poulantzas's Criteria, 1969

All employers	7.5%	(bourgeoisie)	7.5%
Self-employed	4.5%	(traditional petty bourgeoisie)	4.5
Supervisors, mental labor	20.0		
Supervisors, manual labor	16.1	(new petty bourgeoisie	68.3
Nonsupervisory, wage earning mental workers	21.0	acccording to Poulantzas' criteria)	
Manual workers in unproductive sectors*	11.2		
Nonsupervisory, manual labor in productive sectors	19.7	(working class according to Poulantzas' definition)	19.7

SOURCES: Adapted from Wright (1976). Wright's data are based on a nationwide sample survey of occupations and working conditions (Institute of Social Research, University of Michigan, 1969).
*Unproductive sectors: commerce, finance, insurance, real estate, some services.

new petty bourgeoisie, a class most other analysts have defined in more limited ways and termed the "new middle class." The criteria of class determination are no small matter. Wright has compiled data on the United States which indicates the proportion of the economically active population that can be classified into the working and other classes by Poulantzas's criteria. (See Table 1.1).

Thus according to these criteria, the working class in the United States is a decided minority, one-fifth of the labor force, while the new petty bourgeoisie is over two-thirds of the labor force. Poulantzas does not give systematic data for European countries, but the working class there is a larger proportion of the population, according to Poulantzas's criteria and illustrative data.

In contrast, Braverman, using U.S. census data, designates the approximate size of the working class (operatives and laborers, craftsmen, clerical service and sales workers) as 69 percent of the U.S. labor force in 1970, having increased as a proportion of the labor force from 50 percent in 1900 (with the increase in recent decades disproportionately due to increased participation of women in rapidly expanding clerical, sales, and service activities).

To fully situate Poulantzas's theory of class determination and Braverman's approach to class formation as a historical process, I turn to an analysis of the problem of subjects in historical change and to a dialectic of class relations in the process of social development. There is need for an approach that combines structural analysis with historical analysis, while guarding against the different forms of reductionism and their corresponding ideologies that Veltmeyer has specified:

> historical empiricism (historicism), which collapses structural analysis (logic) into history, denying the specificity of theory as such; structuralist idealism-empiricism, which suppresses history in its structural analysis; and speculative idealism (theoreticism), which radically separates historical and structural analysis. Thus a structuralist analysis of history is possible or adequate to its object when it reconstructs a determinate social formation as historically specific, and analyzes both the impact of the whole on its parts, and the genesis and laws of development-transformation of the social totality. It approaches reality dialectically, as a historical process of human praxis rather than as an analytical system; it does not reduce historical change to structural identity [1974-75: 421].

Structural Determination, Historical Subjects, and Social Development

> All of the work of Marx is inserted within the most profound humanism, but a humanism of a new type not based in good intentions, but a humanism based in science, a scientific humanism rooted in real possibilities [Vuskovic Rojo, 1978].

In *The German Ideology* Marx observed that "living human individuals are the premise of all history." At the same time, Marx was emphatic in seeing individuals as totally enmeshed in a fabric of social relations. Further, people are active bearers (*trager*) of social relations and, above all, of relations of production. Luporini states:

> "Men" are always *internal* to "social relations," though they create them (with their labor: man makes his own history, etc.). That is, the individual is in the first place conditioned and determined by these relations before he is able (eventually, and under determinate conditions) to modify them [1975: 292].

Althusser, in his efforts to purge Marxism of "philosophical twaddle about man" (1976:173), dispenses with the living, human, individual side of the dialectic:

> The structure of the relations of production determines the *places* and *functions* occupied and adopted by the agents of production, who are never anything more than the occupants of these places, insofar as they are the "supports" (*Trager*) of these functions. The true "subjects" (in the sense of constitutive subjects of the process) are therefore not these occupants or functionaries, are not, despite all appearances, the "obviousness" of the "given" of naive anthropology, "concrete individuals," "real men"—but the *definition and distribution of these places and functions. The true "subjects" are these definers and distributors: the relations of production* (and political and ideological relations). But since these are "relations," they cannot be thought within the category subject [1970b: 180; italics in original].

This purging of subjects and reification of structure must be critically interrogated: How can the "structure of the relations of production" be conceptualized without its corresponding component rooted in consciousness, in the experience and thought of the women and men that give life and movement to structure? What else are "ideological relations" than the thought component that meshes subjects with structures? And is not thought (for example, the internalized social definition of *being* a worker, a woman, or a French philosopher) an acted on and lived experience of subjects within structures? Thompson is correct to say that structuralism "has no way of handling 'experience' (or social being's impingement upon social consciousness)" (1978:4) or of how consciousness "thrusts back into being" (p. 9).

This can be phrased in class terms, for I am not speaking of men and women as individual, autonomous subjects, and certainly not as individuals exercising utilitarian free choice. Persons are indeed "assigned their places" by the workings of the class order; persons—men and women, bosses and workers, blacks and whites, youth and adults, professionals and clients—are enmeshed in definite social relations and thereby have to make sense of this experience in their consciousness; and this consciousness shapes how people act within social relations. People *live* the material conditions of their existence; they are thrust within and directly encounter a panoply of social relations that are exploitive and oppressive; they experience a class situation, act within class relations; they develop a self-consciousness of this experience and activity; and this consciousness finds expression (material, ideological, political) within structure. The "structure of class relations" cannot be *dialectically* "thought" without the category subject. Classes are formed in given, yet changing, relations of production; people of similar positioning suffer or enjoy similar social conditions, develop common social bonds and interests, think and value in class ways, and, as thinking and valuing subjects, live out the relations as best they can and, sometimes, as subjects with collective interest and will, effectively struggle together to transform the social relations that form their consciousness and make up their lives. The structural determination of class, class consciousness, and class struggle can be analytically segregated and discussed, but in "real life" they are not separable phenomena.

Althusser's statement is from his earlier work. Later he and other structuralists attempted to reinsert the categories of process and subject in an otherwise lifeless structuralism and to get around some of the problems posed by what can only be described as a complete reification of structure. The concepts of "practice" and ideological "interpellation" later achieved a certain conceptual integration in the structuralist "theoretical orrery" (Thompson, 1978) but without substantial modification of the approach.

Althusser was concerned with the meaning of theoretical practice (i.e., Science). His notions were much criticized.[3] In *Essays in Self-Criticism* (1976) Althusser retracted much of what he had to say about theoretical practice. Poulantzas uses the concept of practice more pervasively than

Althusser; he talks about "class practices." The intent seems to be to introduce a dynamic notion of practice as activity of transformation. Given that Poulantzas incorporates the structuralist assumptions of Althusser (quoted above in its fundamental statement) without any appreciable modification, I cannot understand how practice can be conceptualized as anything other than the acts of carrying out defined functions by agents. The most dialectical statement of practice that I found in Poulantzas is this: "The determination of the practices by the structure and the intervention of the practices in the structure, consist in the production by the structure of limits of variations of the class struggle; it is these limits which are the effects of the structure" (1973:95). Wright (1978) has formalized the idea of limits in even more "rigorous" terms. This problem I will again discuss in a later analysis of the concept of class struggle, which the structuralists seem to have managed to exorcise of all meaning.

In an essay on ideology (1971), Althusser again took up the subject of subjects, which Poulantzas and other structuralists uncritically accept. Ideology, "an imaginary relation," links subjects to their "conditions of existence." The "ideological state apparatuses" "hail" subjects and "interpellate" their assigned places in the structure. In this way, once again, subjects are not subjects at all, but "agents" of the structure. Therborn (1980) has criticized Althusser's undialectical notion of ideology, and I shall have more to say about this form of purging of subjects and the fallacy of ideological and political "regions" in a subsequent discussion of ideology and politics as "the content of class relations and expression of class struggle" (Chapter 2).

To return to the main contemporary texts on social class: The approaches of both Poulantzas and Braverman emphasize objective structures rather than subjects and their activities within and struggles against these structures. This could be proper as long as "living humans" as "the premise of all history" are not left aside. Yet for Braverman, subjects appear more as victims of capital's control of the capital accumulation and labor processes than as makers of history, an approach only partially corrected by "post-Braverman" studies of the labor process, such as Edwards (1979; critical reviews by Vallas, 1980, and Johnson, 1982). In Poulantzas's ahistorical, analytic framework subjects are replaced by the concept of "agents" as "bearers" of the "ensemble" of structured social relations. (Agent is the structurist equivalent to the Parsonian concept of "actor"; the German for bearer, *trager*, is usually put in parentheses to call on the authority of Marx; and ensemble is meant to invoke complexity). The point is that an analysis of class formation and determination, the structure of class relations, and societal transformation that is historical and dialectical must be extended into class situations, into the subjective experiences of class, and into the experience, forms, effects, and outcomes of class struggles. The accumulation process historically transforming the structure of social classes exists in dialectical relationship with the activities of people situated in different classes and in struggle—and accumulation, I later argue—is in the main a social process of class formation.

For Poulantzas, classes are no more than the "pertinent effects" of "regional structures" (i.e., the economic, political, and ideological). In this conception there is nothing that gives a class structure any social reality in its own right, any determining effect on social and economic development. Classes are not simply "pertinent effects," they are antagonistically structured social relations made up of living, thinking, acting human beings who activate the relational structures. These classes, not some reified set of given "places" defined by function, are the main historically formed, structural elements of society. As the major structural feature of society, classes are dynamic forces. The social struggles of living, thinking, and acting subjects, when viewed dialectically, shape the direction of movement of the very processes that determine classes and constantly transform society through different developmental stages and historical phases within stages.

Though Braverman's economic determinism implies a restricted dialectic, in that people are victims rather than active subjects, the book does provide a solid basis for one central element of social class theory—a historically grounded theory of class formation. Braverman's approach to class formation, in contrast to most interpretive or descriptive history, is analytically precise. The objective determination of social class seen first and foremost as a historical process of formation of polarizing classes, capital and labor, proceeds from an analytically derived and historically grounded perspective on the transformations associated with the capital accumulation process. At this first and necessary step Braverman ends his work.

Dialectical methodology builds on this approach by examining the impact of productive forces on class relations and class relations in interrelation with the productive forces. The absence of a dialectic of class results, as in the case of Braverman, in an analysis of the labor process in which it appears that capital commands and it is done.

Nevertheless, implicit in Braverman is an ultimate concern for establishing the objective basis for the subjective experience of class under the social conditions of contemporary monopoly capitalism. His analysis develops the Marxist concept of alienation in the most profound sense, concretizing a concept in history and sociology that has largely remained in the realm of humanist philosophy since the early Marx and the young Lukács. Braverman's work, because it deals with historical class formation in relation to the human consequences of capitalist development, at least provides an objective basis for an analysis of class structure, the subjective experience of relations of class, and class struggle.

This is in sharp contrast to Poulantzas, whose theory has no clear relation to the human experience of social class and class struggle. Poulantzas dismisses the "problematic of the subject," in effect, as so much "bourgeois subjectivist idealism":

In this view, I am a Marxist structuralist because I do not grant sufficient importance to the role of concrete individuals and creative persons; to human freedom and action; to free will and to Man's capacity for choice; to the "project" as against "necessity.". . . I would like to state quite clearly that I have no intention of replying to this. We are not here concerned with any genuine alternative of humanist Marxism against structuralist Marxism, but simply with an alternative of idealism against materialism [1976:70].

Paradoxically, Thompson (1978) has dismissed Althusserian structuralism as the ultimate "idealism." These charges and countercharges of "idealism" are no more than banal polemic.

Poulantzas also defends himself against charges of "structuralism" as "a theoretical conception that neglects the importance and the weight of the class struggle in history" (1976:71). Yet it is emphatically the case that Marxist structuralists in general disdain concern with subjective experience and concrete historical social struggles as preoccupations of "humanist" and "historicist" or "empiricist" perspectives. It seems that a legitimate philosophical inquiry into the "problematic of the subject" by Althusser has resulted in a theoretical stance that purges subjects. A focus on historical development, on the ways in which people can and do shape their own lives and destinies, is not possible—at least without substantial modification of the structuralist perspective.

Poulantzas's notion of class struggle will be dealt with shortly. For now, suffice to note that the image of the social formation provided by Poulantzas (in an even farther-reaching way than Braverman) is that of an omnipotent system. Social formations do not contain people, only "agents" who carry out the structurally given obligations of functionally defined social positions. This moves Poulantzas's work in the direction of dehumanized and static theory or, as I analyze in Chapter 2, toward a "radical functionalism," or "left-wing Parsonianism." Poulantzas's conceptualization of the relations of production yields an historical focus on the continuation of these relations through the reproduction of social classes.

It is not the intent of this work to engage the Marxist structuralists in philosophical debate on the shortcomings of the historicist and humanist currents in Marxism—there is much to be learned from their critiques. My general point is that the contributions these currents have made over many decades (see Chapter 3; see also Best and Connolly, 1979) cannot be dismissed without running the risk of dehistoricizing and dehumanizing Marxism. Nor is there an intent here to reduce the question of classes to class consciousness or to develop subjectivist or historicist perspectives as the foundation of a theory of social classes.[4]

It is not the lack of concern of Poulantzas and other structuralists with consciousness or the human experience of class that is the problem, for a focus on the basic structure of society at any point in time is a legitimate endeavor, just as Braverman's account of the forces behind the historical formation of class structure is legitimate. A reasonable case can also be made for the analytic premise that structure precedes genesis (see Chapter 3). The problem is the structuralist purging of subjects, such that a focus from within a structuralist perspective on historical development and the ways in which people make history is impossible.

I will state it bluntly: Any theory that assumes people to be mere "agents" of overwhelming structures, that negates human agency in history, that poses history "as a process without a subject," even denies history itself, runs the risk of degenerating into a dehumanized theory, both in its content and in its ideological implications. Such an approach results in a static theory as well. Recall Marx's enduring insight into the relationship between structure and history: People make their own history, but only under circumstances that are objectively given. Like other great insights of Marx (discussed in Chapter 2), this generalization is subject to myriad interpretations, but it does provide a definite clue to a dialectic of change and development. This aphorism is Marx's clue to the basis for a contemporary dialectical social science. Circumstances are continuously presented to people by the intersection of historical-structural conditions and the accumulated effects of the outcomes of social struggles that have shaped people's economic conditions and their social, political, and cultural heritages. The Althusserian concept of structure denies that people play a role in making their own history. Veltmeyer states it succinctly:

> The objective structure of social formations is imposed on men by a "hidden mechanism" which determines that structure as the objective mode of the appearance of reality. Thus history is a process without a subject, and men are not the "active subjects" of this process; they are simply its "supports" (Trager) [1974-75:397].

Abercrombie, Turner, and Urry suggest that Poulantzas's "argument can be seen as a form of omnipotent structuralism" (1976:537). Geras has a similar critique: "The Althusserian universe is governed by structures and the only subjects that populate it are those subject *to* this government, their places and functions marked out for them by its ubiquitous hegemony" (1972:76). Geras, with Thompson, goes so far (I would not) as to characterize Althusserian Marxism as a new form of idealism.

Structural analysis is necessary for an understanding of the circumstances and objective conditions, the raw material of history, which is presented to people. It is the study of social classes as structured social relations in historically concrete formations and of all forms of social struggles that yield life and movement to structures that indicate in what direction people move—or potentially can move—their history in given circumstances.

A Note on Class Struggle

At the level of observed everyday experience, what is ordinarily understood as class struggle is readily identifiable: political clashes and ideological proclamations, demonstrations and police actions, strikes and lockouts, a multitude of forms of employers' impositions and workers' resistance, insurrections and violent repressions, and so on. At the theoretical level, however, the concept of class struggle is elusive.

The traditional Marxist notions of "class in itself" and "class for itself" are meant to differentiate problems of the structural determination of class from classes as agents of historical transformation. Numerous analysts have attempted to study (even to enumerate empirically) the conditions under which a class in itself develops class consciousness and through its actions moves history. Still, there does seem to be a growing recognition that there is a problem. While the distinction has a certain simple, heuristic value, it lacks a firm theoretical foundation linking class determination to class consciousness and class struggle. To bridge this gap dubious notions like "false consciousness" have been invented.

Poulantzas studiously avoids the class in itself, class for itself distinction. In his later work he makes frequent statements to the effect that classes have no existence except in class struggle. This assertion is hard to square with the thrust of his work, which is predominantly concerned with structural determination (e.g., of class in itself). The social division of labor determines "places" for "agents" to engage in "class practices." Are these "class practices" equivalent to "class struggle"? He says so: "Social classes coincide with class practices, i.e. class struggle" (1975:14). But the answer seems to be no, because the practices—combinations of economic, political, and ideological activity—correspond to the places that are defined in the first instance by the structure.

Despite his "class practice, i.e., class struggle," Poulantzas implicitly seems to recognize that class practices are not the same thing as class struggle, since he superimposes another concept on his social division of labor, class place, agent, class practice theoretical apparatus: the concept of "class position." This concept (perhaps taken from Gramsci's "war of position") refers to the orientation of classes in the concrete class struggles within specific social formations at particular moments in time ("conjunctures"). This seems to be a restatement of the class in itself/for itself idea (which was not Gramsci's usage). On the one hand, there are the determinations; on the other, conjunctural class positions.

In a sympathetic critique of Poulantzas, Andor Skotnes proposes a distinction between determined class practice and class struggle. The former is "a fundamental function generated by the structure relative to its needs of reproduction." Class struggle "is a practice which engages, opposes, or resists another class to improve or defend a class place" (Skotnes, 1979:51). Skotnes argues that submission is the structurally determined class practice of exploited and subordinated classes. "(This submission) is in no way a class struggle for it opposes and resists nothing" (p. 51). He goes on to argue that for the dominant class the "determined class practice of exploitation and domination is certainly a class struggle" (p. 51). It is probably an advance to think of structural determination, not as principles of political economy, of "laws of motion," but as the ways in which a dominant class struggles to maintain its domination (explored in discussion of hegemonic projects Chapters 2 and 6). But this does not provide a perspective on class struggles of the dominated classes.[5]

Poulantzas's assertion, widely reiterated in the literature on class, that "classes exist only in struggle" is rather dubious. (But, as noted, even if the assertion is accepted, this evidently has no meaning in this larger schema.) Classes existing only in struggle seem to represent a reaffirmation of the "class struggle as motor of history" idea. The problem with this is that it poses history as inert substance waiting its propulsion. Class struggle does not exist independent of history to then act on it; it *is* history.[6] A generalization of this order is hardly a definition. The method employed in subsequent chapters is to let the concept of class struggle emerge within a historical and dialectical appreciation of social class. Class struggle is not something that only dominant classes engage in (or at least are successful at), nor is it something that the working class, after seizing consciousness, promotes as it becomes a class for itself and a historical agent. Class struggle *is* history because it is endemic to the "ensemble" of social relations of class societies. A social relation of exploitation is inherently antagonistic; it is an institutionalized, permanent struggle. This being so, a coterie of secondary relations, also antagonistic, necessarily emerge to surround the fundamental relation. Struggle is not something that erupts; it is, in a plethora of forms, omnipresent. Some analysts refer to the network of relations of exploitation as the "base" and the set of relations that surround this "base" as "superstructure." As I put it in Chapter 2, class struggle is the dialectic between "base" and "superstructure."

Notes

1. Main contributions to the debate on the state are Poulantzas (1969, 1976), Miliband (1970, 1973), and Laclau (1977). This debate has theoretical significance beyond the question of the state. It is incumbent upon those of us in the Anglo-American tradition of excessive empiricism, "instrumentalism," and liberal humanism to try to confront the legitimate criticism unleashed by the Althusserians. Questions of humanism and historicism are addressed here and again in Chapter 3 with specific respect to conceptualizing the middle classes. A dialectical method that permits investigatory immersion in history and social facts is developed in Chapter 2. Personally, I have come to agree mainly with Poulantzas's (1976) well-stated comment on empiricism (though not with his characterization of Miliband as a "fervent advocate of the palpitating real"): ". . . for in fact nothing could be more academic than the demagogy of the 'empirical real.' Real history can only have an impact upon theoretical positions (and not only upon mine). It can never do so upon positivist empirical positions because, for the latter facts 'signify' nothing very much: they prove nothing for the simple reason that they can be reinterpreted *ad infinitum* in any way one chooses. It is this noisy illusion of the evident that gives rise to immutable dogmas." Unfortunately, in Poulantzas's work this antiempiricism is reflected in a "theoreticism" that inhibits understanding of the real-concrete.

2. The Weberian multidimensionality of social class encompassing economic class, social status, and "party" roughly approximates Poulantzas's economic, ideological, and political criteria, but the correspondence should not be taken too far. In Chapter 2 I also point to a certain affinity between Althusserian regional theory and functional system theory, the Parsonian version of which posits three regions: the social, cultural, and personality systems.

3. See especially Geras (1972:84). Geras's critique was written prior to Althusser's self-criticism for his "theoreticist deviation" (Althusser, 1976). Jane Canning and James Cockcroft (1978) have commented nicely on these questions.

4. While there are few theoretically informed studies of the structure/consciousness interrelation, persons like Lefebvre (1971) have at least provocatively analyzed the permeations of the production-distribution-exchange-consumption cycle into everyday life. Goran Therborn has studied ideology in "the constitution and patterning of how human beings live their lives as conscious, reflecting initiators of acts in a structured, meaningful world" (1980:15). Lucien Goldman (1976) has developed a dialectic of "genetic structuralism" (as opposed to static structuralism) that links structural process to cultural creation (see Zimmerman, 1978-79; Mayrl, 1978-79). Raymond Williams (1977) has contributed greatly to an understanding of structure, consciousness, and cultural production.

5. Erik Wright (1978) provides a rather elaborate conceptualization related to the problem of class struggle. This is analyzed later. Wright has a great affinity for formalism. A formal, definitional sociology of class may enhance the reputation of Marxist sociology within rigor-respecting, structural functional institutional communities of academicians, but it does not, shall we say, advance the class struggle itself.

6. Adam Przeworski has extensively analyzed the problem of class struggle in the formation of classes. He argues that "classes are not solely determined by means of objective positions, since they are effects of struggles, and these struggles are not solely determined by the relations of production" (1978:117).

Dale L. Johnson: Dialectics and Determination in the Theory of Social Classes

In Chapter 1 I stated that Marxism offers a number of theoretical and methodological guidelines for a dialectical sociology, but it provides little rigor and no exact formulae. The Marxist structuralist attempt to impose conceptual rigor has resulted in a sterile, static, and dehumanized theory. This chapter draws on the preceding theoretical stance (especially the need to focus on the interrelationships among the forces of structural determination, subjective experience, and class struggles) to offer a theoretical critique of the concepts of productive and unproductive labor, the Althusserian version of the base-superstructure distinction in "regional theory," and the idea that the fundamental contradiction of human society is that between the forces of production and the relations of production. The purpose of the critique is to derive what is useful from these loose, sometimes mechanized, or frequently misapplied conceptualizations to work toward the development of a theory of social classes that adequately guides the specific studies in this volume of intermediate classes and class relations in the advanced capitalist societies and (in Volume 3 of this series of books) of the Third World. The chapter concludes with a pointed critique of several contemporary currents in Marxist theory.

Productive and Unproductive Labor

Much has been made in recent literature of the question of productive and unproductive labor. Braverman develops an analysis of the significance of the generation under monopoly capitalism of a labor process that depends on a constantly increasing number of workers who do not produce surplus value. Poulantzas builds his theory of social classes on the distinction between productive and unproductive labor. And it should be noted that Poulantzas's grounding of his theory of the economic basis of class determination in productive/unproductive labor is consistent with Marx's original theory.

It is my position that the characterization of work as either productive or unproductive has no direct bearing on a theory of the determination of social classes. At best, the productive or unproductive nature of work activities may have some limited relevance to the fractionalization and internal stratification of the working class, but this remains to be historically/empirically demonstrated. On the other hand, the growing proportion of the labor force performing unproductive activities has serious implications for the emerging economic crisis in the most recent phase of development within the advanced industrial countries—and thus implications for the class situation of the working class and the class relations of a difficult period. The elaboration of this position requires considerable exposition, and I begin with a restatement of the elements of the theory.

The Theory

A thorough study by Gough (1972) of Marx's theory of productive and unproductive labor reveals that Marx's writings on the subject, while always based on the labor theory of value, were not always consistent with each other. Gough is nevertheless able to derive a reasonably clear conception of unproductive labor on the basis of his reading of Marx. Marx was clear on excluding some categories of workers from productive labor. These include workers who produce neither use values nor surplus value. ("Use values" are produced by the transformation of human labor into something to satisfy a human need or want.) There are two categories: "pure" circulation workers, such as salespersons, advertising workers, and the like; and "unnecessary" supervisors. Workers in the sphere of circulation do not add to or alter the use value of goods; their activities are not necessary to production in general but are peculiar to the commodity form of production under capitalism. While some supervisory activity is technically necessary to the production process, most supervision "merely arises from the antagonistic contradiction between capital and labour."[1] Also, some labor produces use value but not surplus value and is defined as unproductive labor. This includes all labor that is supported out of revenue, such as state employees, and those who provide services in the sphere of personal consumption.

Gough interprets Marx as including many types of distributive and service workers in the productive labor category. In contemporary capitalism many services are organized and produced as commodities for a market. With respect to distributive workers, "those who are really part of the production process working in the sphere of supply (such as workers who unload goods, move them to the counters, etc.) are productive labourers; those who operate cash registers and are otherwise employed solely because the products assume a commodity form are, on Marx's criterion, unproductive labourers" (1972:12).

O'Connor also elaborates on Marx's theory of productive/unproductive labor. He conceptualizes the predominant form of unproductive labor as "guard labor":

> Workers behind cash registers, bank tellers, store guards, watchmen, etc. are in whole or part engaged as special police enforcing the property rights of

commodity owners. Money counting is also a kind of guard labor. Book-keeping and accounting and related activities are required to guard products and services as commodities, i.e., to insure that objects and services function as commodities in the sense of making sure that only those who pay the full price of the commodity actually get it, figuring out whether prices are sufficiently high to cover costs, etc. Guard labor reproduces the formal structures of capitalism and maintains and reproduces capitalist production relations. Guard labor does not produce commodities (or in capitalism, surplus wealth) yet without guard labor commodity production (and surplus wealth production) would be impossible. [1975:303-304].

The other form of unproductive labor identified by O'Connor is "realization labor:"

This is the activity of advertising, publicizing, marketing etc., which is required for the reproduction of the system as a whole but which is not productive of values. The function of realization labor is not to guard property, count money, etc., but to communicate symbols about the commodity to make it appear that it is a definite use value [1975:305].

According to O'Connor, labor organized by the state is "guard labor." This is clear in the case of the police and armed forces, as well as the judicial and penal systems. O'Connor suggests that all labor organized by the state has this guardian quality, though I find it difficult to understand how postal, utility, and other state workers who produce marketed goods or services are "guard labor." Carchedi views the economic identification of state employees as dependent on the nature of the activity in which they are employed. State activities may consist of "capitalist" and "noncapitalist" production. Unproductive activity by the state, Carchedi suggests (1978:-107-109), is production *for* but not *of* surplus value.

In my estimation, those who textually and uncritically adopt Marx's theory of productive and unproductive labor fail to appreciate the need to evaluate the theory in the context of the great changes wrought by the development of capitalism since the early nineteenth century. For example, the characterization of all state employees as unproductive workers ignores the enormous transformation of the state with the development of the monopoly stage of capitalism. The modern state is interventionist and entrepreneurial, engaging in a wide range of production and other activities that facilitate capital accumulation (see Chapter 7).

It is also necessary to invoke a historical "sociology of knowledge" appreciation of the theory. Marx's categorization of state workers as unproductive because their salaries are paid out of revenue needs to be interpreted in the historical context in which Marx was writing. The classical political economy on which Marx based his work originated as a principle element within the ideological arsenal of an ascendent bourgeoisie which engaged in a struggle for the demolition of the mercantilist state. Classical political economy elaborated the labor theory of value and laissez-faire ideology, developing a highly critical perspective on the precapitalist state. Employees of merchantilist states were condemned as parasites whose functions were to thwart progress. Marx, of course, adapted and transformed the labor theory of value into a powerful theoretical advance. But he also adopted uncritically the idea of the state as primarily a repressive apparatus, paid for out of tax revenues. During his lifetime bourgeois states became consolidated, yet played a minimal direct role in the process of production, circumstances which no longer hold.

In any case, returning to the principle modern proponent of the theory of productive and unproductive labor, Poulantzas, following strictly in Marx's footsteps, posits a narrow definition of productive labor: Labor is only productive when it produces surplus value. Only labor involved in the direct production of marketed commodities produces surplus value. Consequently, in twentieth-century capitalism, the working class shrinks and the "new petty bourgeoisie" of unproductive employees expands.

Poulantzas's critics mainly accept the thesis that the productive/unproductive labor distinction has a bearing on class determination, but they differ with him in important respects.[2] Wright (1978) suggests that Poulantzas's definition of productive labor is far too narrow: Workers producing marketed services, he argues, produce surplus value. This is consistent with Gough's reading of Marx. Wright also contends that the distinction obscures the complex nature of workers' actual positions in the social division of labor: Jobs of most workers actually contain a mix of productive and unproductive labor. Wright's most significant critique of the distinction is that its application by Poulantzas does not demonstrate a divergence of fundamental class interests between the two categories of workers, though there may be immediate interests that differentiate productive from unproductive workers. He seems, therefore, to qualify the bearing of the distinction on class determination. Wright suggests that Poulantzas has shown that the "formal mechanisms of exploitation are different for the two types of workers; but he has not shown why this formal difference generates a difference in basic interests and thus can be considered a determinant of a class boundary" (1976:17).

In many ways, Carchedi's analysis, which takes off from Poulantzas and Althusser, presents the most developed, interesting, and useful of the formal, analytic approaches to social class. The bulk of two lengthy articles (1975a, 1975b), later expanded into a book (1978), deals with an intricate exposition of production relations, which he then applies to the question of the economic identification of the new middle class and state employees, questions I will examine in a later chapter. To oversimplify Carchedi, there are those who do not own the means of production but who sell their labor power, and produce (the working class), and there are those who own the means of production, are nonlaborers, and do not produce (the capitalist class). The "new middle class" is composed of those "agents" who do not own the means of production but do perform the "global function of capital," while also in part carrying out functions of the "collective worker." The implication of Carchedi's analysis is that productiveness or unproductiveness of labor is a less central aspect of production relations (though he brings this to bear) than functions performed in the capitalist social division of labor.

Unproductive Labor and
the Experience of Social Class

There are, of course, great practical difficulties in determining who is a productive or unproductive worker, given the complexities of the labor process and occupational structures. Moreover, under conditions of advanced industrialism, the work day for a substantial proportion of the work force is divided between productive and unproductive activities. These practical difficulties are not, however, sufficient to discard the productive/unproductive distinction in relation to a theory of class determination. How, then, is the theoretical adequacy of the distinction to be evaluated? The previous chapter's analysis of the objective determination of class in relation to the subjective experience of class can be used to address this question.

One important test of the validity of any analysis of class determination is whether or not it can be historically and empirically demonstrated that the presumed determining factor actually conditions class situations such that people within that class experience life in fundamentally different ways from other classes. In this framework, the significance of the productive/unproductive labor distinction could be viewed in relation to class experience and class interests that arise from the actual changing historical and day-to-day experience of people who labor (mainly) productively or (mainly) unproductively. What, then, is different between the life experience of workers who produce value that is directly appropriated by capital in the process of production and the life experience of employees who do not directly produce value but perform the service of its realization or of "guard labor"? At the analytic level, the productive/unproductive distinction implies that the principal differences is that productive workers experience direct exploitation. They receive in wages considerably less than they produce in value, a basic relation of capitalist production that is buttressed through a panoply of oppressive institutional means. In contrast, circulation workers and those performing "guard labor" by carrying out state functions or by subjugating and supervising the labor force (O'Connor, 1975) draw their wage and salary not from what they produce, but from the value that capital appropriates from production and redistributes to them. In terms of the political sociology of class, it would follow—if the determination has any validity—that the life experience of the people who make up these "classes" are differentially conditioned. *If life experience differs, the primary reason would have to be that the social relation employer/productive worker is qualitatively different than the social relation employer/unproductive worker.* Though not made explicit in the literature on unproductive labor, the assumption seems to be that it is very different to experience a social relation of direct exploitation than to live off the fruits of the exploitation of others.

In my opinion, it is nonsense to suggest that sales clerks, office workers, service workers, security guards and bank tellers consume the fruits of the exploitation of industrial workers.[3] All categories of workers are hired so that their employers can gain a profit. This is the primary determinant of their class location, as I will argue in more depth below. Even so, a bank guard and an assembly line worker perform different functions, and one can still ask if there is any reason to suppose that the great majority of commercial, service, or office waged workers who sell their labor so that they can live and capital can profit have a fundamentally different class experience of exploitation and oppression than industrial workers. The total experience of class does, of course, differ markedly among different fractions and strata of the working class. The working class is composed of a shifting array of occupational groupings that perform different functions in the economic process. Working-class occupations are subject to differing forms and degrees of exploitation and class domination. The structure of occupations and the forms of exploitation and domination change with historical development. Moreover, the working class is divided by type of work, differing wage levels, relative security or insecurity of employment, and other factors and is stratified by race, national origin, and sex (Edwards, 1979: chap. 10). But it seems that there is no reason to suppose that engaging in work that is analytically considered productive or unproductive has any greater bearing than a number of other factors that divide, fractionalize, and stratify workers and shape the experience of class within the working class. In the earlier phases of development, for example, unproductive "white-collar" workers were accorded special privileges of income, status, and working conditions. Today, some strata of unproductive white-collar workers retain relative privileges, while the great bulk of service, sales, and clerical workers are among the most economically and socially oppressed sectors of the working class.

Each of the factors that divide and stratify the working class has distinct historical origins in different national contexts that demand historical/empirical investigation, rather than theoretical assertion as fixed criteria of class determination. The different forms of class oppression and degrees of exploitation and the divisions and stratifications among workers directly affect class situation and, therefore, the forms of class consciousness and the ways in which structurally antagonistic class relations are acted out. But these factors do not make the working class anything other than a working class. All waged workers place their labor power on the market and exchange it against capital. Capital utilizes this labor to produce a profit and expand itself. The form in which capital's profit is appropriated in the case of workers producing material goods is surplus labor that produces surplus value. The form of capital's profit in the commercial sector is primarily in the realization process through exchange of values, *which is enabled by the use values appropriated through the surplus labor provided by commercial workers.* In either case—and from the class-determined point of view of both capital and labor—the primary social relation, the relation that conditions class interests and antagonistic class relations, is the exploitation of labor to produce a profit and expand capital—that is, the appropriation of the use values in money form embodied in the diverse forms of surplus labor. The same is the case of workers in the financial sector and, in a more indirect form, among most categories of state employees. The form of appropriation of profit differs by economic sector; the content is invariant in that all capital requires labor to produce a profit. For capital, the form in which profit is gained is not particularly relevant. In the present phase of industrial capitalist development, the most unproductive, wasteful, and socially destructive activities have become principal sources of capital accumulation. Moreover, one of the primary characteristics of corporations in the modern era is their vertical and horizontal integration (and recently their conglomeratization) with the end being appropriation of profit from every phase of economic activity. On a larger scale of concentration, centralization, and organization of capital, the ascendance of finance capital to its supreme position is an expression of the tendency to accumulate capital and appropriate profit in diverse sectors. Similarly, the fundamentals of the class situation of workers flow from the fact that their surplus labor produces profits for a capitalist class that is organized for the purpose of appropriating value wherever it can be produced or realized. A young worker today may drift from employment as a supermarket cashier to routine clerical work, or to minimum wage work in a factory or as a security guard or fast food attendant—work functions and specific work conditions may differ, but it's all the same misery to him or her.

The theory of productive/unproductive labor may also confuse function in a highly articulated social division of labor with source of income. As previously noted, the theory implies that unproductive workers live off the sweat of productive workers. Workers employed by the state are said to be unproductive because their income is derived from revenue provided by taxes on the population. Thus, the distinction ultimately depends on the source of income as the criterion of class determination. This results in the peculiar stance by those using the theory that production determines all, while, at the same time, class placement depends on whether a worker's income derives from producing or from living parasitically off those who produce.

In my view, production and consumption are two sides of a coin linked by distribution and circulation of money. The minting of the coin is jealously guarded by the state. In a unique contribution on the dialectics of the mode of production, Lebowitz (1978) has argued that the entire economic cycle is a unity of opposites. I would add to Lebowitz's rather Hegelian formulation of the whole the sociologically concrete idea that social relations of exploitation and domination permeate every aspect of this unified, contradictory process. It is these relations which structure the social classes. It is not, therefore, whether income is derived from one moment of the process or another, from production or distribution or state revenue, that is important but, rather, the varying forms and human experience of exploitation and domination.

Even Carchedi, who depends heavily on the concept of productive/unproductive labor, does not hold that unproductive workers do not form part of the working class:

> The commercial worker (as with all workers in the circulation sphere), being unproductive, does not produce value and thus, strictly speaking, cannot be exploited. However, he is expropriated of surplus labor and is therefore economically oppressed [1975b:363].

In an implied criticism of Poulantzas, Carchedi suggests it is wrong to use the concept of productive worker to divide the working class from the middle class: "Within the working class we find both productive and unproductive workers, both workers who are exploited and workers who are economically oppressed" (1975b:363). I suggest that the distinction between exploitation and economic oppression is unlikely to occur to any worker because it is not in his or her class experience. Nor does it require great perspicacity or in-depth social research to observe the abysmal class situation of the growing masses of unproductive commercial, office, and service workers, or to note that unproductive activity is the main sporadic occupation of the floating sector of the reserve army of labor.

Unproductive Activity, the Middle Class, and Crisis

The transformation of unproductive sectors of the labor force into new segments of the working class, a process analyzed extraordinarily well by Braverman, is a product of development in recent phases of the monopoly stage of capitalism. The ahistorical, analytic conception of unproductive labor cannot grasp this transformation as a historical process or relate it to the human experience of class.

I have suggested that historical/empirical investigation rather than theoretical assertion is necessary to fully understand the formation of class structure, the divisions and stratification within classes, and the boundaries between classes. Of course, this investigation must be theoretically informed. The theory of productive/unproductive labor, I suppose it could be argued, at least has the advantage of being a coherent framework rooted in the labor theory of value. Given the problems raised so far, this does not seem to me a very strong argument, but before discarding the theory altogether, one further avenue of examining its validity can be explored. If it is erroneous to exclude a substantial segment of the labor force from the working class by the criteria of unproductive activity, the question remains whether the productive/unproductive distinction might nonetheless be important in differentiating at least certain occupational categories from the working class. Poulantzas's main effort is to analyze the differentiation of the working class from the "new petty bourgeosie," and this is an exceedingly important problem. What, for example, are the criteria of class determination of supervisors and middle-level managers, or of highly trained and well-paid technicians, or of professionals and state bureaucrats? A later chapter is devoted to these questions, so only a few points need to be made here.

Clearly, most employees generally considered "middle class" do not engage in productive activity. But it is not the unproductive quality of the work of managers, professionals, and other middle-class employees that determines their location outside the working class—it is, to frame it in Carchedi's terms, their function in the social division of labor. Perhaps a better way to put this (because it implies a structural-functional perspective) is that class positioning has to do with place and role in the relations of production, or, more operationally posed, with the relationship of different occupational groupings to the system of exploitation and the class domination that sustains and reproduces the system of exploitation. Thus any occupational grouping that has surplus labor appropriated and converted into profit and is subordinated with the system of class domination is working class. Yet one of the distinguishing characteristics of twentieth-century capitalist development has been the proliferation of employees retained to carry out the control functions of capital—control over the means of production and the accumulation process (that is, over the system of exploitation) and control over the labor process (that is, the means of domination over the working class). Insofar as certain categories of employees are delegated the control functions of capital, by virtue of their employment, they occupy superior positions in hierarchically ordered systems of class domination and in these positions act to facilitate exploitation and oppression. Their livelihoods and class interests depend on the maintenance and reproduction of relations of exploitation and domination. While these employees do not produce anything, it is not the unproductiveness of their labor in itself that is important but the *acts* of exploiting and dominating that correspond to the social positions of those performing control functions. While I have overstated this argument, in that middle-class employees are portrayed as agents, their defined function in the division of labor is one of the factors that differentiate them from the working class and that creates antagonistic social relations between the two classes. I will later add some correctives to this overly functional view.

No matter how viewed, then, the productive/unproductive distinction raises more problems than it resolves, at least with respect to class determination. Yet, if the criticisms posed here are valid, how is it that Braverman's work is so solid, while also invoking a version of the theory of productive/unproductive labor? Braverman's book contains a chapter in which he generally subscribes to this new orthodoxy based on mid-nineteenth-century political economy, though he uses it in a much more creative fashion than Poulantzas, Carchedi, O'Connor, and others. Given his excessive determinism rooted in a predominant concern with the effects of the production side on the labor process, Braverman's turn to orthodoxy is logical. But there are two curious aspects. One is that his restatement of the concept of unproductive labor is hedged by qualifications when he attempts to show the relevance of the concept to his work. In earlier days, he suggests, unproductive labor was not extensively employed by capital and was "a favored stratum, closely associated with employer and the recipient of special privileges". (1974:417). With the development of monopoly capitalism, however,

> The unproductive labor of the corporation, having been so tremendously expanded, has been given the same twofold structure as productive work by the capitalist division of labor. The individual functionary, closely associated with the capitalist, has, as we have described, given way to the department or division of the corporation, in which only the heads remain associated with capitalist management while the rest occupy positions akin to those of workers in production. Thus, while, on the side of productive labor, the individual worker loses those characteristics as producer of a finished commodity which made him or her a productive worker, and retains those characteristics only in the mass, on the side of unproductive labor a mass has been created which shares in the subjugation and oppression that characterizes the lives of the productive workers [p. 418].

Braverman's analysis of "shadow production" in the offices which presumably partition white-collar, salaried employees from blue-collar shop workers is illustrative of the need for a historical perspective. In the monopoly stage of capitalism, the scale of production and control of the process require that production "is replicated in paper form before, as, and after it takes place in physical form" (1974:125). Hand and brain are separated, each subject to an elaborate division of labor fashioned by a combination of Taylorism and machine technology. In the end, the mental work of offices is transformed into the manual work of typing, keypunching, filing, and so on in a continuous flow operation of paper.

Unproductive workers "have become mere cogs in the total machinery designed to multiply capital" (1974:419). If this is so, if the concept of unproductive labor had "lost its social force as a line of division between the middle class and the working class," if it does not even clearly differentiate between fractions of the working class, what utility does it have in the analysis of social class? This is the other curious aspect to Braverman's treatment of this theme: its lack of any real relevance to his excellent analysis of the forces underlying class determination. Braverman's chapter on unproductive labor pays tribute to orthodoxy, but it does not noticeably contribute to his analysis.

Insofar as a theory of class determination is concerned, the productive/unproductive labor distinction is seriously deficient. Are we then to throw the theory out altogether—and, by implication, discard the labor theory of value from which it proceeds as well? I think not. Some French analysts, especially Berthoud (1974), have argued that the theory is not pertinent to a theory of social classes, but that it is useful in relation to questions of capital accumulation and labor productivity. Skotnes (1979) makes similar assertions. O'Connor (1975) has pursued the relation between unproductive labor and "capital disaccumulation."

The idea of unproductive activities as principal avenues of capital accumulation was first systematically developed by Baran (1957) and

Baran and Sweezy (1966). This approach steps outside traditional formulations of the labor theory of value to develop a concept of unproductive activity. Investments and the utilization of labor are examined in terms of social usefulness. Large segments of the labor force work to produce wasteful, destructive, or superfluous goods and services that would be absent in a "rationally ordered society" but are essential as a form of "surplus absorption" under monopoly capitalism. The concept has the virtue of being tied to a Marxist interpretation of a particular stage of the development of capitalism, the monopoly stage. Labor employed in the military sector, in the sales effort, and in other wasteful and irrational activity is necessary to the growth and stability of the economy under monopoly.

Skotnes suggests:

> Productive/unproductive labor conceptualizes the allocation of surplus value and labor power between the sector that produces more capital (and thus accumulates capital), and the sectors that drain capital away from accumulation but are necessary to the reproduction of the social formation. Such a concept can be utilized in a wide range of concrete studies—from those that analyze the secular trends of capitalist development to those that analyze symptoms of cyclical crisis [1979:39].

I believe the most promising avenue for viewing the significance of unproductive activity has been opened by Becker (1973-74, 1977) and Eisenhower (1977 and Chapter 5, this volume). Both authors examine the relation between increasing investment in activities that do not directly produce surplus value, the growing proportion of the labor force employed in these unproductive activities, and the problem of crisis. This is also important to O'Connor's "fiscal crisis of the state" (1973) and Wright's theory of crisis (1978). The chapter by Eisenhower explores the sources of the contemporary crisis of American capitalism in some depth. Whereas Baran and Sweezy see unproductive activities as the primary sources of capital accumulation, growth, and stability of monopoly capitalism, Eisenhower views the costs of the necessarily unproductive and increasingly wasteful expenditures of both private capital and the state and the growing army of unproductive workers and middle-class employees that must be sustained and reproduced as clear signals of the "degenerative phase" of capitalist development. Eisenhower implies that the net social costs are approaching the point of being greater than the benefits accruing to capital in the form of the contributions that unproductive labor and state activity make to increasing the productivity of productive workers, to extending markets, or otherwise facilitating capital accumulation and counteracting the tendency of the rate of profit to fall. This threatens profitability and undermines the potential of continued accumulation. The historical countertendencies to falling profit rates are becoming exhausted; the system sinks into an ever deeper morass. This has forced the trimming of state expenditures for social purposes, incited attack on the working conditions and living standards of the working class and the great middle class of unproductive employees, and exacerbated existing social tensions; it has forced American business to engage in fiercer competition with foreign capital and to attempt to tighten the reigns of imperialist relations.[4] To the degree that Eisenhower's crisis thesis is valid (I have some doubts as to the sources of crisis in unproductive activity and declining profits), the effect on class relations can be substantial, for in periods of transition to a new phase of capitalist development and of sharpening crisis, class relations assume new forms, class struggles intensify, and the possibility of projects to establish a new basis of hegemony loom on the horizon. (Hegemonic projects are discussed below and in Chapter 6.)

If Poulantzas's theory of productive/unproductive labor has no real bearing on class determination, his book *Classes in Contemporary Capitalism* does succeed in posing a significant problem that had hardly been addressed in social theory previously—the problem of the place of politics and ideology. His formulation is nonetheless deficient from the point of view of dialectics. Below I develop at some length the view that politics and ideology are the content of class relations and the expressions of class struggles (not "relatively autonomous regions" that exercise determination over classes).

Class Determination and Class Relations

Some of the most difficult questions concerning social class are those that have to do with the structuring of class relations in interrelation with the content, effects, and expressions of these relations. What historical forces can be identified that propel the development of the mode of production through historical stages, and how are these developments reflected in or a response to the social, political, and cultural forces of history? How do the economic relations basic to the mode of production manifest themselves as structured social relations with varying political, ideological, and cultural contents? In what manner do the social, political, ideological, and cultural relations transpiring within social structures in transformation interrelate with, or themselves become, forces propelling the development of the mode of production?

The Political and Ideological

Marxism has produced a number of premises that enable one to address questions of structural determination and dialectical relations on many fronts. These premises are "discovered historical truths" (as orthodox Marxists sometimes put it); better stated, they are basic methodological starting points in historical materialist and dialectical analysis. They include the proposition that social being determines social consciousness; the base/superstructure distinction; the class struggle as "motor of history" concept; the view of the capitalist state as "a committee for managing the common affairs of the whole bourgeoisie"; and the "primary contradiction" as rooted in the conflict between the forces of production and the relations of production. But these premises are starting points; they do not present a rigorous theoretical basis for a historical materialist and dialectical methodology. On the contrary, most of the premises do not even rise to the status of scientific concept; they are, no matter how enduringly profound, mere metaphors.

Take, for example, Marx's statement in *The German Ideology*: "Life is not determined by consciousness, but consciousness by life." In the context of Marx's materialist polemic with German philosophical idealism "which descends from heaven to earth," this is a perfectly cogent statement. In isolation from the whole of Marx's thought it is not a dialectical statement. Thompson speaks of a "dialogue" between social being and social consciousness:

> If social being is not an inert table which cannot refute a philosopher with its legs, then neither is social consciousness a passive recipient of "reflections" of that table. Obviously, consciousness, whether as unselfconscious culture, or as myth, or as science, or law, or articulated ideology, thrusts back into being in its turn: as being is thought so thought also is lived [1978:9].

Another example is the term "class": It is a central concept, but not an entirely adequate one, for in its general usage it denotes too little and connotes a multitude of contradictory ideas. The class struggle as the "motor of history" is simply a metaphor connoting a central dynamic. Class is also one of those terms Thompson calls "junction concepts." The power of the struggle metaphor is that it joins the concept of "relations of production" from political economy to the sociological denotation of "class" and both to the concept of "history."

Perhaps the major contribution of the Althusserian School has been the forced rethinking of these premises. Althusser (1970a, 1970b, 1971, 1976) and his followers subjected each to diligent study and reformulation in an attempt to construct a sounder theoretical foundation for historical materialist methodology. The wide-ranging critical response to their efforts has at least opened up the possibility for a more precise conceptualization of historical materialist theory and methods.

It is not my purpose to hold up for scrutiny the elaborate conceptual apparatus invented by the Althusserians to force greater rigor on each of the premises (as Wright [1978] has attempted in his peculiarly American version of a systematic structuralist sociology). But the rather tired metaphor "base/superstructure" is at the heart of the problem.

The Althusserian framework of determination, "overdetermination," and "relative autonomy" of the superstructures (i.e., political and ideological "regions") is extraordinarily complex. Excellent critiques are available in the literature (Geras, 1972; Glucksmann, 1972; Veltmeyer, 1974-75; Laclau, 1977; Thompson, 1978; Mayrl, 1978-79; *Insurgent Sociologist*, 1979; Canning and Cockcroft, 1978), and there is no need here to fully explore the subject. It is sufficient for present purposes simply to restate the main points of what I understand to be the traditional Marxist idea of economic determinism and dialectical relations between "base and superstructure" and to compare this to Althusserian regional theory.[5] In the classical view, the forces and relations of production, in their contradictory unity and historical movement, broadly shape a wide range of superstructural phenomena: culture, ideology, law, the state. Relations of production between controllers of the productive process and those who sell their labor power in order to survive and to produce surplus value for the controllers are tied to the political, ideological, and legal relations that sanction and legitimate them. This is what gives these phenomena their superstructural quality. Downgraded in this stance of economic determinism is the premise that, in a dialectical relation, superstructures act back on and modify the forces and relations of production and that, as I will explore later, the main expression of this dialectical relation between base and superstructure is the class struggle.

In the Althusserian formulation, the determinant instance (the economic) determines the determined instance (the political and ideological), in that the economic "calls into existence" the political and ideological as a "condition of its own existence." According to structuralist logic, the economic is determinant only in "the last instance." Inasmuch as the determined instances, according to Althusser, feed back[6] into the determinant instance, the economic is "overdetermined" and the superstructures "relatively autonomous."

This intriguing, if tortured, reformulation of base and superstructure is employed by Poulantzas (1975) in his analysis of classes. Poulantzas's thesis is that the ideological and political are "relatively autonomous" regions of capitalist social formations and as such exercise structural determination over social classes. This is the most controversial aspect of his theory. Wright takes issue with Poulantzas on this score. His main contention is that Poulantzas, in spite of assertions to the contrary, does not maintain the primacy of economic relations in the definition of classes.

> Thus, an agent who was like a worker on the economic and political criteria, but deviated on the ideological criteria, would on this basis alone be excluded from the proletariat (this is the case for subaltern technicians). In practice, therefore, the ideological and political criteria become co-equal with the economic criteria, since they can *always* pre-empt the structural determination of class at the economic level [Wright, 1976:18].

Poulantzas conceives of the supervisory/nonsupervisory division as a political determinant of the class boundary between proletariat and petty bourgeoisie. This is because supervision entails the "direct reproduction within the process of production itself, of the political relations between the capitalist class and the working class" (1975:228). Extensive supervisory positions, according to Wright, are basically a reflection of economic differentiation; there is no particular reason why supervision should be a *political* criterion of class determination. Stated in terms I will develop further in Chapter 7, supervision is an extension—an extensive and highly differentiated one in advanced industrial capitalism—into the social division of labor of the control functions of capital—control over the means of production, over the accumulation process, and over labor. From this standpoint, supervision is not a political criterion, in the customary sense of politics in any case, but flows directly from the relations of production inherent in the capitalist social division of labor. As such it can be operationalized as an economic criterion of class determination.

Also open to question is the use by Poulantzas of the mental/manual division as an ideological criterion of class determination. Wright cites racism, nationalism, and other ideologies of domination as factors in *creating divisions* within the working class. Wright's implied question is why the mental/manual distinction should have any special weight as an ideological criterion. It might be added that a whole range of these factors (what I previously termed "social stratifications") have the effect of dividing classes. Stratifications are highly variable (historically and crossnationally) and mutable ideological reflections of a range of social inequalities within class societies. Stratifications reflect the dynamics of class relations, especially as ideologies of domination, but do not form classes. (See Heffren, Chapter 6, on dominant ideologies.) As Poulantzas himself notes in a criticism of non-Marxist theories of social stratification: "The division into class forms the frame of reference for every social stratification" (1975:199).

Ideological factors create social divisions within classes and may, in particular historical or national instances, rigidify boundaries between classes, but they should not be employed as factors of class *determination*. Braverman (1974) and even C. Wright Mills (1951) suggest that the mental/manual distinction becomes less and less important with each new phase in the development of monopoly capitalism.[7]

Skotnes notes:

> The division between manual and mental labor is a basic notion within the systems of notions that comprise bourgeois ideology—and a notion is not at all the same thing as ideological class practices. . . . It depicts the relation between capital and labor as the relationship between those whose naturally superior intelligence elevates them to "brain work," and those who are relegated to the labor of hand and brawn because of inferior intellect [1979: 43-44].

Wright's approach is to suggest that only after analysis of class determination in terms of contradictory locations can political and ideological criteria be employed in the analysis of social class:

> *The extent to which political and ideological relations enter into the determination of class position is itself determined by the degree to which those positions occupy a contradictory location at the level of social relations of production.* The more contradictory is a position within social relations of production, the more political and ideological relations can influence its objective position within class relations. The more a position coincides with the basic antagonistic class relations at the level of social relations of produc-

tion, the less weight political and ideological forces can have in determining its class position [1976:36-37; italics in original].

Phrased in terms of class determination, this formulation seems dubious, but Wright uses the idea of contradictory locations to good effect. Political and ideological class struggle can push intermediate strata in the direction of the working class or can deepen their contradictory location between the bourgeoisie and the working class. One example cited by Wright is white-collar workers' sense of social superiority induced by the status division between mental and manual labor, which might be counteracted by a strong union movement. These considerations point to the need for a more thorough analysis (drawn out here in various parts of the book) of the extent to which classes are structurally or "objectively" determined and the degree to which classes, through self-consciousness and struggle, are self-forming. (Przeworski [1978] is particularly clear on this).

I think that Althusserian regional theory obfuscates the question of base and superstructure, which, while a discomforting metaphor, is yet to be surpassed as a means of cutting through to the quick. In utilizing this approach, Poulantzas, by heavily weighting the relations of production and downplaying the dynamic movement of the forces of production and by yielding a determinative quality in the formation of classes to ideological and political factors, denies the historical truth and methodological premises of the base/superstructure distinction. A methodology for determining cause and effect is thereby renounced. Statements about dialectical relations between base and superstructure cannot ignore the direction of cause and effect. To state that ideological and political factors *determine* classes gives causal weight to what are more properly seen as effects (effects which in turn have their effects on the base). Wright's concept of contradictory locations is interesting yet limited by his stepping within Poulantzas's problematic to quarrel with the application of structuralist noneconomic criteria of class determination.

Here I contend that political and ideological forms of struggle are expressive of the dialectics of base and superstructure, and as such are constituent elements in the concrete, historical process of class formation. But attempts to integrate ideological and political factors into social class theory are made all the more difficult by virtue of theoretical differences within Marxism. (Wood [1981] has acutely analyzed how these theoretical differences come about through distinct interpretations of the base/superstructure metaphor and through economistic as versus social and historical determinate views of the mode of production.) Many of these differences result from the relative weight given to the productive forces and productive relations. Among the historical truths and methodological premises of traditional Marxism there is perhaps no looser and more confused a formulation than the idea that the fundamental contradiction of human society is that between the forces of production and the relations of production. Baran and Hobsbawm broadly define the terms:

To be sure, neither "forces of production" nor "relations of production" are simple notions. The former encompasses the existing state of rationality, science, and technology, the mode of organization of production and the degree of development of man himself, that "most important productive force of all" (Marx). The latter refers to the mode of appropriation of the products of human labor, the social condition under which production takes place, the principles of distribution, the modes of thought, the ideology, the *Weltanschauung* which constitute the "general ethos" (Marx) within which, society functions at any given time. The conflict between the two—sometimes dormant and sometimes active—is due to a fundamental difference in the "laws of motion" of forces and relations of production respectively. The forces of production tend to be highly dynamic. . . The relations of production on the other hand tend to be sticky, conservative [1961:238-239].

There is general agreement on the constitution of productive forces. Baran and Hobsbawm's definition of the relations of production as including ideology, however, may very well violate another basic methodological departure, the base/superstructure distinction. Relations of production have first to do with property relations (most analysts include distribution and exchange relations): "One class owns or controls the means and objects of production and organizes the labor of the producing class with the purpose of producing and appropriating a surplus product" (O'Connor, 1975:298). While these relations are normally "sticky, conservative," we also know through observing historical events that they can be dynamic, explosive. Moreover, the particular *forms* assumed by the relations of production in different times and places are complex and variable.

Historical observation led Marx and many Marxists to posit the primacy of the forces of production over the relations of production and to emphasize that the development of the forces of production fundamentally determine all economic, social, political and cultural developments. Still, there are lengthy historical periods—Western capitalism since World War II, for example—of rapid economic development, vast technological change, and sweeping, new avenues of capital accumulation guided by and subordinated to the relations of production, which have modestly changed in form but remained relatively unaltered in their fundamental expressions. During the same period the development of the productive forces in much of the Third World has been grossly distorted or effectively blocked by the articulation of dominant international and national class forces. The persistent underdevelopment of many peripheral nations stands as monumental evidence of the fettering of the productive forces by the prevailing productive relations. I do not think, though, that the problem of the primacy of the forces or relations of production can be solved by historical/empirical observation.

Nor can it be solved by reading Marx. His 1859 preface to the *Critique of Political Economy* is an unequivocal statement on economic determinism as the method of political economy. Cohen's *Karl Marx's Theory of History: A Defense* (1978) builds a reasonable, though I think overstated, case that Marx was a technological determinist. (Cohen has been excellently evaluated by Levine and Wright [1980] and by Wood [1981].)

If any historical generalization based on observation and a synthesis of the views of analysts can be simply stated, it is that, while the relations of production restrain the forces of production and guide their movement, the forces of production, driven by the imperative of capital accumulation and however restrained and channeled, continually move the mode of production through different stages and phases, thereby giving form to the evolution of social classes, bringing on new dimensions of class struggle, presenting periodic crises, and eventually forcing the relations of production into new forms of existence. And these new forms may involve, or hold out the potential for becoming, radically altered relations of production in their most essential expression—the social relation between exploiters and exploited, oppressors and oppressed. Yet, as Levine and Wright (1980) argue, the relations of production may or may not be forced into new molds consistent with the full development of the productive forces. This depends on the *capacity* of classes to translate their interests into "practices" of transformation—that is, to effectively mobilize their material, organizational, and ideological resources in class struggle.

The uneven unravelling of the forces and relations of production may indeed present human society with a fundamental contradiction, but the statement of contradiction in such general terms does not point to the manner of its resolution. Moreover, attempts to unravel the manifestations of the contradiction at all levels of the totality is a methodological quagmire. That this contradiction propels the totality toward its inevitable end is teleology, not science.

In contemporary Marxism these theoretical/methodological differences with respect to the forces and relations contradiction are at least implicitly recognized. Yet distinct tendencies have grown out of the problem of primacy. A predominant emphasis on the forces of production results in an excessive technological or economic determinism—or, in some currents, a preoccupation with the "laws" of the mode of production at an abstract level. An overemphasis on the sticky and conservative quality of the relations of production tends toward a static, functional analysis and does violence to some of the other historical truths and methodological premises of historical materialism. In contemporary Marxism this is the predominant mode of analysis.

Consider a proposition by Poulantzas: "This dominant role of the relations of production over the productive forces and the labour process is what gives rise to the constitutive role of the political and ideological in the determination of social classes" (1975:21). In this view, the political and ideological are not superstructural reflections of the economic base but exist on a par with the economic as distinct "regions." The three regions are articulated, with an "overdetermined" economic region determinant in "the last instance."

The structuralist insistence on the articulation or interrelatedness of all elements of a social formation must be recognized as legitimate. But one does not have to postulate "regions" to capture this interrelatedness. Moreover, it is one thing to say how political, ideological, and economic elements of a social formation articulate, and quite another to analyze how these elements came together in the first instance. (The problem of structure versus genesis is discussed in Chapter 3; see also Zimmerman, 1978-79, on Goldman's "genetic structuralism.")

It seems to me reasonable to suggest that, within particular historical stages of development, the elements of a social economy constitute a unified whole into which political and ideological phenomena are *subsumed within* the relations of production. Competitive capitalism was an integrated system with a distinctively ideological underpinning-reflection (economic liberalism, utilitarianism, individual freedom, Social Darwinism, etc.) and a highly competitive political struggle. Monopoly capitalism is a system of articulated parts in which ideology, politics, and the state are integral to it. They are not mere epochal "reflections" of the economic base, but neither are they semi-autonomous regions.

A dialectical rather than functional appreciation of a system might be stated in this way: The social economy (analyzed as a process) must be taken as a whole and conceptualized as a contradictory unity, with each element of the unity (or moment of the unitary process) exercising determination on the other elements (or moments). We might further postulate that the structural determination of class proceeds out of this contradictory unity, and that it is out of the relations of class that politics and ideology in turn emanate. Only in this proceeding are politics and ideology "superstructural"; they "express" underlying class relations. That both may exhibit a certain "relative autonomy" (if indeed the term can be dialectically posed) is not in dispute. That they hold an autonomous "regional" status is highly disputable, unless one is willing to deny Marx's premises and substitute functionalist notions of regional articulation for dialectical interrelation.

Class relations become the concrete locus of structural contradictions and antagonisms, and ideological proclamations and political clashes articulate and express them. These and other forms of struggle then relate back directly into the economic process, exercising direction and constraint over the development of the productive forces, over the process of capital accumulation, and over the unfolding of the labor process and all other aspects of production. In this way, classes in action actualize their structurally determined existence and become the bearers of dialectical movement.

Thus conceptualized, ideological and political factors do not have a "constitutive role . . . in the determination of social classes." *Ideology and politics are elements of class relations and expressions of class struggle.* As "superstructural" phenomena (i.e., as expressions) politics and ideology are given their basic content by the development of the economic process as a whole and are set in motion by class situations, by the life experiences of people within classes, their forms of consciousness, and their practical activities. As the content of class relations and the expressions of class struggle, ideology and politics then relate back to and impact on the economic process and, in mediated and reciprocal form (to add a third dimension to the dialectical interrelation), on the constitution of classes as historical actors.

Below ideology is considered in greater depth. What does it mean to say that ideology is the content of class relations? It is again imperative to invoke the active subject: A class relation is a lived, real-life experience of exploitation and the domination that is necessary to sustain exploitation. This relation necessarily involves systematic thought which interprets and organizes its continuing transpiration. A social relation cannot exist without it being lived in thought, experienced in consciousness, as it occurs and reoccurs in action. This thought, organized by and constituent to the relation, is thereby a content of that relation. Yet an exploitive, oppressive relation is experienced differentially and antagonistically by the parties to it. The relation therefore presents a clash of conflicting ideational representations—that is, it founds the ideological-political expressions of class struggle.

Class, Ideology, and Hegemony

> Generalizing, one may put forward the idea that every social relationship *is born and exists at once within thought and outside it*—that every social relation contains an ideal part, from the outset, which is not an *a posteriori* reflection of it, but a condition of its appearance, which becomes a necessary component to it. This ideal part exists not only in the form of the content of consciousness, but in all aspects of social relations which make the latter into signifying relations and reveal their *meaning*, or meanings [Godelier, 1978:92].

Ideology is a most perplexing subject of inquiry. In this volume Heffren's chapter deals extensively with the subject in what is a considerable and unique achievement. Heffren, beginning with an Althusserian notion of the "ideological region," sees ideology as a "socially determined, imaginary conception of the relation of subjects to their conditions of existence." But Heffren does not confine himself to the abstract world of structuralist generalizations. He examines the constitutent elements of ideology and the *process* of establishing hegemony. His work needs to be commented on here insofar as it relates to the question raised above: ideology as the content of class relations and expressions of class struggle.

A "modal ideology," according to Heffren, represents the point of connection between the mode of production and the deepest layer of the ideological region and is distinct from "particular ideology," which, as the most common form of ideological expression, is specific in both object and social base or origin. The modal ideology originates as an intrinsic aspect of the relations of exploitation and domination under capitalism and becomes generalized to all social relations and institutions. The modal ideology is composed of a cognitive style (a socially acquired mode of thought such as the instrumental rationality of monopoly capitalism) and a conceptual field (unexpressed elements tied up in the relations of production, such as ideas of the virtues of individualism, formal freedom, acquisitiveness, competition, and so on). Modal ideology has two functions: to limit ideological discourse to ideas compatible with the prevailing order and to select out from the wide range of ideas always present those that have a good fit with the underlying relations.

Ideology viewed as "an imaginary conception" implies that social relations are seen by subjects as objective realities that exist independent of one's will. People internalize a mental relation to the objectivity of social relations, which includes a construction of their own subjectivity. Unlike many of the critical theorists (whose work is too often one-dimensional) and perhaps Althusser himself, Heffren's theory of ideology embodies a dialectic. Changing realities contradict peoples' internalized imaginary relation to them and allow subjects to think (and to act) a critical relation to their conditions of existence. Moreover, since the social relations of exploitation and domination are structurally antagonistic, it follows that the modal ideology rooted in these relations is likewise contradictory, the more so as the social forms of the relations change with economic and social development.

Heffren also analyzes the "ideological apparatuses" (schools, the family, the church, media, the military, political parties, trade unions) which are mediating institutions, the means by which modal ideology is brought into everyday life. These institutions are not instruments of a dominant class (since they have a history and dynamic of their own and since antagonistic class relations are sharply experienced within them), but the dominant class always struggles to make them theirs, to use them to maintain domination—or to establish a new hegemony.

Hegemonic projects are particular forms of class ideological struggle. While Heffren's analysis is of bourgeois projects, Gramsci has instructed us that the working class and its allies can also struggle to achieve hegemony in a revolutionary process. In this volume, a hegemonic project is posed as a response to crisis, which can originate from different sources, such as a transition from one stage of development to another. In this crisis, a particular class (or fraction of a class, usually one in ascendance as an economically dominant fraction, but one that does not enjoy a wider hegemony) attempts to carry through the logic of the transition and realize it—and thereby its class interests—throughout the social order. The objective of the project is state power; it aims at transformation of the state and the ideological apparatuses, at the subordination of rival projects and the class interests behind them, at changing the balance of power in society as a whole. To accomplish this it is necessary to secure a new alliance of classes and social forces—to form a new "power bloc"—and to engage in concerted ideological and political struggle. Hegemonic projects are always risky ventures for the bourgeoisie, since they imply an alteration of basic social relations and the modal ideology, with the associated instability. Put in motion, the project can provide—since the established powers themselves question the crisis-ridden established order and its ideological props—an opening to a counter hegemony, or to the exercise of revolutionary or counterrevolutionary force.

Therborn (1980) has tried to define the dialectical character of ideology: "a dialectic indicated by the two opposite senses of the word 'subject' ('the subjects of history'/'the subjects of the prince'). Ideologies not only subject people to a given order. They also qualify them for conscious social action, including actions of gradual or revolutionary change. Ideologies do not function merely as 'social cement'" (1980:vii). Therborn views ideologies not as doctrines, bodies of ideas, or texts, but as ongoing social processes. His book is concerned with the dialectical operation, material determination, and class structuring of ideology.

> Ideologies subject and qualify subjects by telling them, relating them to, and making them recognize: 1. *what exists*, and its corollary, what does not exist . . . 2. *what is good*, right, just, beautiful . . . and its opposites . . . 3. *what is possible* and impossible; our sense of the mutability of our being-in-the-world [1980:18].

Ideologies are highly articulated with class modes of existence and class-rooted discourse. (See also Kellner's [1978] excellent analysis of ideology and hegemony).

The formulations posed thus far on class and ideology are necessarily abstract. The only way in which the dialectical interrelations of productive forces and productive relations (expressed in diverse forms as relations of class and class struggle, including ideological and political forms) can be concretely stated is through historical and empirical analysis. This volume provides two studies which specifically link ideological struggle to a dialectic of class.

In applying his theory of ideological struggle, Heffren studied the early twentieth-century alliance between a newly formed fraction of the American bourgeoisie, corporate finance capital, and the new middle class. The object of the "corporate liberal" project, which found fundamental expression in the middle-class "progressive movement" and reform and technocratic ideas of the period, was a restructuring of the state, the ideological apparatuses, and of the ideological basis of social relations, all of which were already undergoing substantial modification in form and content through the transition from nineteenth-century competitive capitalism to twentieth-century monopoly capitalism.

The second study is Gorelick's chapter on class relations and public education. This is a case study of the historical formation of teaching as a profession in the context of the struggle of immigrant labor and the marriage of turn-of-the-century American progressivism and the interests, thinking, and activities of corporate capital. Ideas about education, the practice of the teaching profession, and teachers as constituent elements of a newly formed intermediate class were molded in the complexity of turn-of-the-century social struggle.

I have elsewhere developed the concept of hegemonic project in the analysis of Latin American authoritarian states. An article, "Chile: Before,

During, After," links an appreciation of changing Chilean political economy and the heightened class struggles of 1970-1973 to the project of the post-1973 military dictatorship. Chile's military rulers "have embarked on a brave attempt to achieve a long-term and stable hegemony that cloaks itself in nineteenth-century economic liberalism, twentieth-century technocratic authoritarianism, and Pentagonese doctrines of 'national security'" (forthcoming: 29). Volume 3 of this series contains an analysis of military dictatorship in the Southern Cone of South America as outcomes of particular projects of hegemony. These projects (which were only conjuncturally successful and are now disintegrating) were based on crises of transition from one stage of "dependent development" to another (combined in Chile, Argentina, and Uruguay with heightened levels of class struggle resulting in "organic crisis") and particular alliances of internal and international class forces.

In contrast to the ways in which ideological phenomena are conceptualized in studies by Heffren, Gorelick, and me—as the content of class relations and the expressions of class struggle—the traditional way in which Marxists have dealt with ideology has not provided a particularly satisfactory guide to the analysis of concrete historical processes. In commenting on the great confusion that Marx's metaphor of base and superstructure has caused,[8] beginning with Engels's backtracking from it, Karl Korsch noted as long ago as 1935:

> The entire problem disappears just as soon as we substitute for the general question of the effect of "economics as such", upon "politics as such", or "law, art and culture as such", and vice versa, a *detailed description* of the definite relations which exist between definite economic phenomena on a definite historical level of development and definite phenomena which appear simultaneously or subsequently in every other field of political, juristic and intellectual development [1972:64-65].

I shall have much more to say about the imperative of linking historical/empirical research of the concrete with the theoretical moment of the scientific endeavor in the discussion of "historicism" and the question of intermediate classes in Chapter 3. Meanwhile, it can be concluded that the concrete study of ideology and political-ideological struggle in particular conjunctures (which may or may not involve hegemonic projects) is a principal ingredient in dialectical analysis of class structure, class struggle, and all the specific forms assumed by the relations of production in developmental stages.

Neither Poulantzas nor Braverman approaches questions associated with the relations of production from this perspective. Poulantzas rejects any validity in the base-superstructure metaphor and avoids the concrete. Braverman takes the metaphor literally. He does not discuss political struggle and confines his analysis of ideology to the phenomenon of Taylorism. His emphasis on the forces of production over the sweep of history makes the relations of production appear as derivative from the movement of the productive forces. This, while giving his work a decided quality of economic determinism, does provide insight into how classes are historically structured and restructured. Braverman also tries not to lose sight of the relations of production. He demonstrates how new forms of organizing the labor process and new technologies give rise to new relations of class domination. But for Braverman, cause and effect is more a one-way street than a two-way process. In contrast, Poulantzas's emphasis on the relations of production yields an ahistorical focus on the reproduction of these relations. Broad questions of class formation, struggle, change, and development cannot therefore be adequately addressed.

More needs to be said about the conceptualization of the concrete forms assumed by the relations of production in different historical stages and phases. The foundations of an adequate theory of social classes reside in a historical materialist framework that is analytically rooted in the principles of political economy and in a dialectical method. An analytically sound theory proceeds from abstractions concerning the mode of production. The capitalist mode of production is characterized by relations of production of a given character that are distinct from those of precapitalist modes of production. The essential character of these relations of production (exploiters/exploited, oppressors/oppressed) are invariant throughout all stages of capitalist development, though the social forms, including ideological and political forms, through which these relations are expressed change radically. The forms assumed by the relations of production in different developmental stages or in different concrete national societies may serve to conceal the essential relations determined by the mode of production (this is the main function of ideologies of domination). Most historiography is analytically weak because it mistakes historical forms for essential relations. (This is not the case for Braverman's historical method, despite the shortcomings already mentioned, because he proceeds from the main features of the capital accumulation and labor processes characteristic of the capitalist mode of production to the study of the concrete forms assumed by these processes during the monopoly stage of capitalist development.) Purely analytic theories are historically ungrounded because they do not proceed to study the transformation of historical forms to then determine the consequences of these transformations. This is the main weakness of Poulantzas's work, shared to some degree by Carchedi (1978) and Wright (1976). This problem is even more evident among those who would explain whatever phenomena by an analysis of one or another abstract, tendential law of political economy (see the section below on theoretical tendencies). As an analysis of the manner in which the capitalist mode of production yields a basic structure to social classes and determines primary relations of class, the works of Poulantzas and Carchedi are real contributions. Unfortunately, Poulantzas in particular does not historically ground his analytic theory, and therefore one learns little of changing forms and their consequences. Worse still, when Poulantzas does get down to the real, he mistakes concrete forms (e.g., the mental/manual distinction) for essential relations.

The development of a dialectical method raises even greater problems than the framing of an adequate analytic framework. In this chapter (dialectics is further developed in the next offering), I have tried to develop a non-Hegelian conception, rooting dialectical movement in the structural determination of class relations and the reciprocal impact of these relations (in the concrete forms of ideological, political, and other class struggles that demand historical/empirical specification) on the determining structures.

Perhaps an appropriate footnote to add here is that the great differences within Marxist approaches to social class proceed not simply from different theoretical stances but from historical realities in the development of Western capitalism. Marxist theory is itself an ideological expression of class relations. (See Mayrl [1978-79] on the roots of structural and phenomenological Marxism; Anderson on Western Marxism [1976], and Wolff's critique of Anderson [1978]). The advance of the forces of production in the monopoly stage, especially in the most recent phase, has reinforced the stultifying effects of the prevailing relations of production by multiplying the means by which capital dominates all forms of labor and sees to its reproduction. Marxist theory both reflects this and attempts to grasp it and confront it. Braverman documents this well: Scientific management, technology, and the corporate form of organization place increasing control in the hands of capital while multiplying the sectors of the population brought into the labor process under conditions determined by capital's control of the entire process. The contours of the class structure are constantly reshaped without bringing about an explosive quality to class struggle. The relations of production and the institutional means of social reproduction increasingly appear as systems of total domination. This may be an important factor that gives Marxist structuralism, with its emphasis on relations of production and their reproduction, its growing influence.[9] Perhaps this also accounts in part for the continuing presence of critical theory, with its emphasis on ideological aspects of domination, as well as German "state derivation theory" (Holloway and Picciotto, 1978).

But the grand task of theory is to elucidate and liberate people from prevailing realities, not simply to reflect them. Althusserian structuralism reflects more than it penetrates. With this in mind, I turn to remarks on current theoretical tendencies in Marxism.

Theoretical Tendencies

So we have to say that when we talk of 'the base', we are talking of a process and not a state. And we cannot ascribe to that process certain fixed properties for subsequent deduction to the variable processes of the superstructure. Most people who have wanted to make the ordinary proposition more reasonable have concentrated on refining the notion of superstructure. But I would say that each term of the proposition has to be revalued in a particular direction. We have to revalue 'determination' towards the setting of limits and the exertion of pressure, and away from a predicted, prefigured and controlled content. We have to revalue 'superstructure' towards a related range of cultural practices, and away from a reflected, reproduced or specifically dependent content. And, crucially, we have to revalue 'the base' away from the notion of a fixed economic or technological abstraction, and towards the specific activities of men in real social and economic relationships, containing fundamental contradictions and variations and therefore always in a state of dynamic process [Williams, 1973:5-6].

The weak presence of historical and dialectical perspectives in contemporary social class theory is manifested in the intellectual and political weight of two contemporary theoretical tendencies within Marxism, what might be termed "radical functionalism" and the "return to original principles." The first tendency moves in the direction of mainstream, functionalist systems theory; the second, toward a methodological rigidity, mechanical determinism, or, in extreme cases, a theoretical and political dogmatism. In a curious way Marxist structuralism may be stimulating both tendencies, though it represents neither and the effect is completely remote from the intention of Althusser, Poulantzas, and others influenced by their theoretical renovations. Here I ignore the strategic political implications of theory, but elsewhere I have made a similar point about intentionality: the anti-Stalinist, anti-reformist, and anti-"ultra-left" political intent of Marxist structuralism seems to have gone awry in the context of Eurocommunism and Red Brigades.[10]

Althusser's work is inspired by a desire to confront intellectually and politically both the influence of what he defines as bourgeois philosophy and social theory within Marxism and the deformations that Marxism has suffered at the hands of a variety of dogmatists. Unfortunately, the Althusserian School's assault on economism, the emphasis on reproduction, and the notion of economic determination only "in the last instance" may be encouraging a kind of Parsonianized Marxism, or "radical functionalism," especially in Germany and the United States. At the same time, structuralism's emphasis on Marx's mature science of political economy and the rejection of Marx's historicism and early humanism feeds the rigidity of those who would explain whatever phenomenon in terms of a theoretical generalization lifted from one of the volumes of *Capital*. I have already demonstrated the difficulties this has created in one such case, the theory of productive and unproductive labor, and I now turn to the broader implications of these class theoretical tendencies as they relate to social class theory.

Radical Functionalism

As is well-known, functional systems theory has no means of differentiating cause from effect, or of analyzing processes of fundamental change.

Parsonianism, exchange theory, cybernetics, feedback models, equilibrium analysis, or any systems approach is entirely remote from dialectics. The study of the articulation of the different phases of the social economy—and the structural determinations that emanate from, have their effects on, and interrelate back into the economic process—must therefore proceed from assumptions other than those involved in systems theory. (Frank's analysis [1969], "Functionalism and Dialectics," is very useful.) From a historical perspective, systems are never stably articulated or in equilibrium. This is because the unity of a social system is a contradictory unity. The parts of a whole do not fit smoothly together; the different phases of what may be at a certain level a unified process are out of joint. The central contradiction of the system called capitalism is the structurally antagonistic relations of social class; these are lived experiences acted out in political, ideological, and other forms of class struggle. Dialectics is the only method that does not result either in a static, functional analysis or in a crude determinism.

Analyses that are quite divergent in most respects from Marxist structuralism often also depart from a radical functional perspective. Ehrenreich and Ehrenreich have invented a theory of the "professional managerial class." The major function of this class in the social division of labor is "the reproduction of capitalist culture and capitalist class relations" (in Walker, 1979:12). Wright's work on social class invokes an academic formalism that, against his best intentions, often slides into a radical functionalism. (The Ehrenreichs, Wright, and others are discussed in Chapter 3.) The 1960s tradition of North American "radical" social science remains largely concerned with exposing how the system maintains itself. This remains reflected in many contributions to such journals as the *Review of Radical Political Economics*, *Politics and Society*, and the inappropriately named journal of radical sociology, the "*Insurgent" Sociologist*. The theoretically sophisticated work of German state derivation theory (Holloway and Picciotto, 1978), as well as the inheritors of the tradition of the Frankfurt School, remain bound up in the study of forms of ideological domination and could also be considered forms of radical functionalism. While radical functionalism originates in social systems of Europe and America that have been maintained very well, the approach has inevitably diffused to the dependent periphery, though it is interpreted more dynamically there (see, for example, Guitierrez Garza [1978] and Cueva [1979].) I will confine analysis to one example or work directly related to social class theory, Bowles and Gintis's contribution on education.

Schooling in Capitalist America (1976) is an in-depth and excellent analysis of education's functions in meeting the historical and contemporary demands of capital accumulation and of the reproduction of prevailing "social hierarchies" (a term the authors substitute for social class and that reveals the absence of a dialectics of class). The central concept in their analysis is the "correspondence principle." Education corresponds to the changing needs and structure of the economy and prevailing economic interests. Bowles and Gintis confirm the radical critiques of education of the 1960's: School curricula mirror the needs of employers for a differentiated and stratified labor force with requisite skills, while the authoritarian structure and imposed competitive culture of schools prepare young workers to accept subordinate roles in the bureaucratic corporate hierarchy and socialize them into properly conservative, compliant attitudes. The schools function to intergenerationally reproduce the social hierarchy, together with its legitimating mythology and its racial and sexual stratification, not, as mythology holds, to equalize opportunity and reduce social inequality in a democratic society. The final chapters of the book add a dynamic quality to the analysis, in that historical changes in American education are held to reflect contradictions within the political economy as a whole. Nevertheless, the central focus is a functional analysis according to the "correspondence principle."

Bowles and Gintis avoid explicit Althusserian concepts. But their analysis is consistent with Althusser's concept of "ideological state apparatus." According to Althusser (1971), education has supplanted the church as the dominant apparatus with a broad yet specific function, to reproduce the conditions of production.

Institutions like education are, of course, social instrumentalities. Examination of institutional functions therefore forms a legitimate and necessary part of analysis. In application to the class determination of people working within particular institutions, however, an exclusively functional analysis inevitably reduces people to mere agents of institutionally given instrumentalities. Institutions and the people whose lives are enmeshed in them are rife with noncorrespondence, with contradiction, conflict, struggle. I have taken Bowles and Gintis somewhat to task here because their book is undoubtedly the best analysis of education available today. (For a more critical view than I would like to make see Gorelick [1977]; see also her contribution on education in this volume.) Unfortunately, their work does not readily recognize the contradictory nature of education, the forces at work shaping it in noncorrespondence, and the degree to which education is central not only to reproduction of a trained, docile, and stratified labor force, but to the formation of classes and to the intense social struggles of contemporary society.

Within Marxist theory proper structuralist perspectives have become pervasive. At the most general theoretical level, Marxist structuralism's main problem is its affinity with functionalism. The Marxist concept of "reproduction"[11] becomes transformed into an almost Parsonian preoccupation with "system maintenance." Of course, questions of reproduction are central to social theory. Preoccupation with these questions in theoretical endeavor or historical/empirical research is scientifically legitimate to the extent that these endeavors and research are guided by a perspective that is materialist, historical, and dialectical.

To be sure, the Marxian variant of structuralism can be considered a real advance over Levi-Strauss or Parsons. Structuralism posits underlying or "hidden" structures that render observable phenomena intelligible. And an attempt is made to identify structural contradiction. Appelbaum has written a critique that differentiates Althusserian structuralism from systems theory. Althusser is right, he suggests, to recognize "that the underlying logic of a system must be theoretically reconstituted if surface events are to be rendered intelligible" (1979:26). Appelbaum argues that Althusser has also made a contribution in opening a sophisticated contemporary avenue of distinguishing

> Marx's dialectic from Hegel's by pointing to its sociological nature—that is, the fact that the Marxian contradiction entails an 'accumulation of circumstance' and 'currents' and is therefore complex and overdetermined in a way that the Hegelian contradiction is not. The Marxian contradiction is specified by historically concrete conditions, including those characterizing the superstructure, . . . the internal historical situation (state of the bourgeois revolution, remnants of the feudal past, customs, national traditions, political 'etiquette'), and the external historical situation (most notably the extensiveness of capitalism as a world imperial system) [1979:27].

Even while applauding Althusser, Appelbaum goes on to note that the concept of "unity in dominance" that embodies this dialectic "appears to be little more than a pluralist functionalism recast in Marxian categories."

Structuralism borders on[12] substituting a radical form of ahistorical, abstract systems theory for materialism and dialectics. For the traditional Marxist concept of base-superstructure, and the much-abused economic determinism associated with this distinction, the Althusserians substitute the idea of "relatively autonomous regions." Thus, instead of a dialectical process of interrelation between base and superstructure, the Althusserians abstractly posit formal relations between regions, with economic determination in the "last instance." Yet, like all systems theory, structuralism never seems to arrive at any "last instance."

Althusserian/Poulantzian regional theory, it seems to me, falls into the indeterminism characteristic of all systems theory. Laclau refers to Poulantzas's application of the Althusserian regional conception of the economic, political, and ideological in terms parallel to those used by critics of Parsons. The "Holy Trinity of Levels" and the "metaphysic of instances" are applied with "taxonomic fury" when faced with complex reality:

> This distinction between determinant in the last instance and the dominant role seems to be no more than a series of metaphors which attempt to resolve, through symbols of little theoretical content, an artificial problem created by

a metaphysic of instances. . . . We have here a new example of the fusion between taxonomy and formalism [1977:77].

In the previous chapter I concluded that structuralism represented a theory with objects but a history with no subjects; a dehumanized, undialectical theory in which people are merely "agents" of overwhelming structures. The critique can now be extended. The "relative autonomy" yielded by Marxist structuralism to the ideological and political instances (including the state, whose "relative autonomy" I have not discussed), combined with a preeminent concern with reproduction and broad social functions, leaves one with a sense of a theory that verges on a left-wing Parsonianism; a static systems theory of functional articulations between regions with no method for differentiating cause from effect; an indeterminism of the historically concrete that perhaps becomes, in the end, a "structural superdeterminism" and "structuralist abstractionism," as Miliband (1973) put it, where "structures" actually amount to abstract functional requisites of the mode of production.

The "Return to Original Principles" Tendency

The growing stature of Marxist structuralism has coincided with a wave of recent analytical work that might be termed the "return to original principles" tendency. Work within this tendency selectively borrows method rather than content from the Althusserians. Contradictions are located at the level of the mode of production, and whatever is to be explained is treated as a consequence of the falling rate of profit or one or another iron "law." Few who work within this framework bother to situate these contradictions historically—according to the various stages and phases of the development of the mode of production—or concretely—in the class struggles that emerge out of development in widely different historical and geographical contexts. Subjects are purged and history is formal method.

The falling rate of profit tendency is the cardinal axiom of the original principles fundamentalists. The theory states that the imperatives of capital accumulation and competition lead to an increase in the "organic composition of capital" (e.g., "dead labor" as embodied in the means of production). Since the variable capital of "living labor" is the only source of surplus value, the increased ratio of constant to variable capital necessarily means a decline in profit rates. The theory has a certain respectability because Marx derived it (or perhaps because it can be stated in an algebraic formula). Falling profits mean "overaccumulation" and "overproduction" in relation to declining demand—in other words, "crisis." Crisis can be averted or overcome only by "countertendencies" to the falling rate of profit, such as increasing intensity of exploitation and cheapening of constant capital.

There is a great dispute in the literature whether or not the tendency empirically conforms to historical patterns. Fine and Harris (1977), for example, argue that, while not an observable empirical law, the falling rate of profit is nevertheless an "abstract tendency" that operates in the dialectical interrelations of declining profits and counteracting tendencies. Hodgson comments on Fine and Harris: "The astounding feature of this 'dialectical' interpretation is that it does not matter what happens in the real world as far as the vindication of the 'law' is concerned; it is valid if the rate of profit has a tendency to fall, and it's valid if the rate of profit has a long-run tendency to rise!" (1977:98). Superior presentations of the dialectics of this presumed law have been contributed by Lebowitz (1978), Appelbaum (1978), and Castells (1980); but in its most compelling formulations, this approach would reduce political economy to a method for examining tendencies and countertendencies in profit rates and their effects.

"Class struggle" is dealt with in this literature mainly as a source of pressure causing profits to fall. Thus, we have the paradox of Marxists agreeing with capitalists that the way to avert crisis is to keep wages down and profits up.

Another absurdity is the invocation of "law" to discard Marx's sociology. In this vein, one of the first formalistic analyses (of the contemporary period) that related the labor theory of value to classes was Martin Nicolaus's 1967 article, "Proletariat and Middle Class in Marx." In keeping with "New Left" orthodoxy of the time, Nicolaus pronounced the Marxist idea of the historic mission of the proletariat fallacious: "If one denies, as it seems to one must, the validity of Marx's class polarization and proletarian revolution predictions from the Manifesto, . . . one cuts out of Marxism only its youthful optimism, the product of excessive captivation with the elegance of Hegelian idealism" (1967:46). On the other hand, Nicolaus suggests that Marx's mature work "laid down the fundamental economic and sociological principles which explain its [the middle class's] rise and its role in the larger class structure" (p. 46). The middle class of unproductive workers, "or servants for short," is required "to fulfill the functions of distributing, marketing, researching, financing, managing, keeping track of and glorifying the swelling surplus product" (1967:46). Paradoxically, Nicolaus's "new left" break between the youthful optimism and the mature Marx coincided with Althusser's "old left" discovery of Marx's "epistemological break."

Sociology, like economics before it, becomes a dismal science when analysis of all phenomena is reduced to formal laws "discovered by Marx," when the working class is seen as permanently incorporated and pacified, and when the middle class is dismissed, following Nicolaus, as unproductive workers "or servants for short."

A desperate search for scientific rigor ensued in the collapse of the New Left in the early 1970s.[13] At the epistemological level, Althusser gave this tendency a new breath of life in his systematic "reading" of Marx (1970a, 1970b). By the early 1970s the standard works in political economy of the 1960s were subject to devastating critique by those espousing a "return to original principles." Baran and Sweezy's *Monopoly Capital* (1966) and Frank's pioneering work on dependency theory (1969) were subjected to virulent attack for alleged departure from the fundamental laws of the capitalist mode of production. Some such criticisms were motivated by sectarian ideological considerations;[14] others were offered as exercises in socialist scholarship by intellectuals unaffiliated with a vanguard sect.[15]

Most work in this vein has been accomplished at the level of theoretical critique. Among those who have transcended this level to make theoretical contributions (Althusser and Poulantzas, of course, prominent among them) there is abstractionism that severely detracts from the tendency's usefulness in historically concrete research. Of course, from the point of view of some of the structuralists, historical or empirical research is worthless. Hindess and Hirst go so far as to state that "the study of history is not only scientifically but also politically valueless" (1975: 312), a proposition that is a direct *reductio ad absurdam* from Althusser.

The problem with this tendency is not the rediscovery of the "laws of motion" originally revealed by Marx in *Capital.* These works contain theoretical elaborations of the capitalist mode of production in the abstract that are remarkable for their coherence and profundity. Yet, they are also historical documents grounded in the economic realities of nineteenth-century Europe, in theories of political economy evolved by the classic ideologues of the bourgeoisie from Smith to Ricardo, and in Marx as the ideologue of the emerging proletariat. Fundamental or tendential laws of nineteenth-century political economy perhaps remain valid under modern conditions, but only to the degree that they can be concretely historicized to the latest phase of capitalist development and formulated so as to bear on contemporary peoples' struggles to transform society.

Eisenhower's work in this volume (Chapter 5) is one such concretely historicized study that departs from "original principles" while making an original contribution. Eisenhower succeeds in examining the basis of the contemporary incipient crisis in the United States by relating the growing weight of unproductive activity (which is a characteristic of middle-class labor) to the falling rate of profit in the current "degenerative phase" of capitalist development. Castells also invokes the falling rate of profit in his impressive work, *The Economic Crisis and American Society* (1980). He concretely relates tendencies and countertendencies to the crisis of the present period in the United States.

But Eisenhower's and Castells's excellent treatises are exceptions. In general, there is analytic rigor and determination among the original principalists, both to considerable excess, but no history. Dialectical movement is expressed not in class struggles endlessly waged through different historical stages and phases of capitalist development, but in the inexorable laws of motion of the capitalist mode of production. Paul Sweezy's response to this tendency is worth quoting:

> The question I would like to put to Cogoy and the others who think like him is this: Do you maintain that these laws were established once and for all by Marx, that they are invariant to changes in the forces which underlie them, and that there is therefore no reason for us to follow Marx's example in studying capitalist reality and drawing our own conclusions from our studies?
>
> If the answer is yes, if these theorists really believe that Marx said the last word on capitalism's laws of motion, then I for one can only say that I cannot take them seriously. Their Marxism has degenerated into a sterile orthodoxy which cannot help us to understand and deal with the problems of capitalism in the last third of the twentieth century.
>
> On the other hand if one rejects the notion that all of Marx's laws are as valid now as they were in his time, and if one concludes on the basis of the data available to us today that the law of the falling tendency of the rate of profit is no longer operative, then one must conclude that an analysis of accumulation which, in Cogoy's expression, "rests on the tendential fall of the rate of profit" is doomed from the outset to futility. And it follows of course that one must pursue a different course in seeking to unravel the contradictions of the accumulation process [1974:52].

Thompson suggests that the iron concept "law" should be dropped in favor of "the logic of process" (1978:86, 110, 159-163). This would represent an advance. In any case, analysis cannot be limited to formal application of the laws governing the functioning and movement of the mode of production. The labor theory of value, the theory of productive/ unproductive labor, the laws of capital accumulation, the falling rate of profit—all laws derived from analysis of the mode of production in the abstract—*must* be interpreted in the concrete forms assumed by capitalism in different stages (in the imperial center phases within the monopoly stage, and in the dependent periphery of world capitalism according to the stages of the development of underdevelopment). Further, there can be no social science dialectic without an appreciation of people as subjects within a framework of structural and dynamic class analysis.

I don't think it is necessary to postulate any epistemological break to recognize that Marx himself dealt with the problem of alienation, the principles of political economy, and class struggle almost independently, without reconciling the differences in approach.[16] The development of an analytically sound, historically grounded, and dialectical theory of social classes provides contemporary Marxists an opportunity to bring these approaches together. This volume tries to move in that direction by examining the question of the intermediate classes in the advanced capitalist countries (mainly the United States).

Notes

1. Marx, *Capital*, Vol. III, cited by Gough (1972:12).

2. Skotnes (1979) is an exception. Poulantzas serves as a point of departure for Juan Manuel Carrion's work, which contains by far the most sophisticated theoretical treatment of productive/unproductive labor (1978). Particularly important is Carrion's careful treatment of the levels of abstraction involved in the theory, since its application to the capitalist mode of production in general (i.e., apart from stages of development) has given the distinction a formal, abstract, and ahistorical quality. Nevertheless, I think Carrion's study of the Puerto Rican petty bourgeoisie was advanced not so much by the theory of productive/unproductive labor as by his insightful historical analysis and careful empirical study of the contemporary Puerto Rican class structure.

3. This argument has somewhat of a parrallel, equally wrong, in the thesis of American workers living off the "spoils of imperialism" appropriated by American corporations operating in the Third World (Evanson, 1977).

4. Immanuel Wallerstein has formulated an argument somewhat parallel to Eisenhower's. He suggests that as the "world-system" further integrates and develops, repression increases. "The reason is simple. The 'cost' of repression is the partial redistribution of the surplus to the repressors, who are in fact the intermediate strata. The process is called 'co-optation.' But each cooptation is less 'worthwhile' than the previous one, since it involves further deductions from a *declining percentage* of the surplus controlled by the top strata, in order to buy off once again the intermediate strata" (Wallerstein in McNall, 1979:48).

5. This is, of course, a simplified notion of the base/superstructure, which I consider an apt metaphor. I try to delve into the complexities of dialectics and determination throughout the book. William's excellent article, "Base and Super-structure in Marxist Cultural Theory" (1973), serves as a guideline for my own thinking, and Godelier (1978) is helpful.

6. This systems theory language is not that of Althusser, but it is appropriate given a certain affinity between structuralism of all tendencies and functional systems theory. Richard Wolff, an American economist sympathetic to the Althusserian perspective, has stated the idea of articulation of parts of a system in less functional terms: "Marxism's theoretical focus upon class as the basis for constructing an understanding of any social formation is all that is meant by 'determination in the last instance by the economy.' Class is first and foremost an economic concept. Marxism's focus on the primacy of class, and in that sense the primacy of economics, amounts to an insistence on how to think about the complex mutual determinations that constitute a society" (1978:64).

7. Important commentaries by Latin American social scientists on these issues are contained in the proceedings of a 1972 conference on Social Classes in Latin America sponsored by the National University of Mexico (UNAM, 1973).

8. Godlier (1978) has developed a valuable theoretical innovation on the structuralist muddling of the infrastructure-superstructure conception by demonstrating that superstructural elements (e.g., kinship, religion) can, when embodied as the principle "ideal reality" of the relations of production, become dominant, organizing instance of the social order. Also, Aronowitz (1978) develops an approach to base and superstructure more or less to consistent with that elaborated here.

9. Another caveat should be entered in my criticism of Marxist structuralism. No theory remains stagnant, unless it has no interconnection at all with reality. Althusser's structuralism is a considerable advance over Levi-Strauss's; Poulantzas's concept of structure is an advance on the original metaphysical notion of Balibar; of particular note in terms of innovation within this perspective is a recent theoretical work applied to the transition from feudalism to capitalism by Resnick and Wolff (1979). They proceed from Althusserian regional theory while also positing class relations as the central "organizing concept" of Marxism. This gives their work a dialectical quality that is generally absent within Marxist structuralism. The same may be said of Agustin Cueva's work on classes (1979).

10. "A political strategy consistent with a theory that posits a reduced working class and an expansive petty bourgeoisie together with an image of system omnipotence, can only be defensive in character. A defensive posture results either in a reformist strategy of broad class

alliance (e.g., Eurocommunism) or an adventurist politics of desperation (e.g., the Italian Red Brigades), or both" (Johnson, 1978:43).

Another way to look at the political implications of the structuralist penetration of Marxism has been stated by Gonzales Casanova:

> A great number of studies since 1960 deal with the crisis of society and with the state in such a way that these concerns appear to displace the problematic of progressive and revolutionary movements; these tend to be viewed only in function of an analysis of the "System" in which movements of liberation, of the masses, of the workers, disappear with their flesh-and-blood actors. Their history is often reduced to variations and mutations with the "System." The System has been converted into an omnipresent and exclusive protagonist, a Leviathan or a Behemoth.... What is omitted is anything that bears on the alteration or suppression of the System by the social, political and revolutionary forces that are trying to modify or replace it [forthcoming: 1-2].

11. The Marxist concept of "reproduction" demands a thorough reexamination in terms of its epistemological roots and theoretical consequences that is well beyond the scope of this book, though I comment on the problem in Chapter 3. If the concept is to be retained, it needs to be purged of its static and functionalist implications and integrated into a historical and dialectical methodology. David Noble (in Walker, 1979) has contributed a stunning critique of the concept's current one-dimensional, functional use.

12. In a critical comment on the draft of this chapter, Wright contends that I have overstated the case for a left-wing functionalism. I do not think so, but Wright's observations are worth noting:

> The notion of "last instance" does have a fairly precise meaning, namely that the forms and general limits of development of the superstructural regions are constituted as "conditions of existence" of the system of exploitation/production. Johnson is correct that this is a functional argument: those conditions are explained by virtue of the functional requirements they fulfill for the existence of the system of production (that is what is meant by a condition of existence). But it is not obvious that this deviates very much from Marx's discussion of forms of "correspondence" of superstructures to bases. And, in any event, it is not functional*ism* even if it is a functional argument, because: a) there is no symmetry between regions: the base is not constituted as a condition of existence of the political, for example—the functionality of determinations is determined itself by economic (production) relations; b) the notion of differential historical time allows for systematic disjunctures between regions, so that even if the ideological and political regions are called forth as conditions of existence of the economic, it does not follow that they necessarily adequately fulfill those conditions of existence; c) the notion of the state (and one could add, ideology) as crystallization implies that the form of the state is the result of class struggles; "conditions of existence" implies that the stakes in the struggle is the reproduction of the relations of production. Thus, one way of restating these interconnected arguments is that the theory of regional structures involves two axes: one which specifies that what is at stake on a terrain of struggle (the conditions of existence of the system of production relations—this is the functional moment in the analysis) and one of which specifies the structural outcomes of that struggle (the condensation of class struggle). Now it is the case that Poulantzas often lapses into a functional*ist* mode of thought, particularly in *Political Power* . . . when he seems to suggest that the structural resolutions of struggle always fulfill the functional requirements, but later he partially rectifies this tendency by stressing the contradictory character of the solutions. And certainly other Marxists informed by the Althusserian starting point have categorically rejected the necessity of functional outcomes even if they retain a notion of regions as the sites of struggles over conditions of existence, see especially Therborn, Castells (particularly his new book on Crisis), and Wright (the analysis of the

contradictions between limits of functional compatibility and limits of structural possibility, which is another way of talking about these issues).

13. How could the New Left not fail with a theory that writes off the working class as hopelessly coopted and the middle class as "servants"? In many ways Nicolaus's articles reflected the sentiments of radicalized middle-class youth of the time who placed their hopes for change in themselves in coalition with the totally dispossessed minorities and the Third World. He does not, though, figure prominently among the "Falling Raters."

14. See, for example, the virulent critiques of dependence theory in *Latin American Perspectives*, 1 (No. 1) 1974 and subsequent issues in 1975 and 1976.

15. These are too numerous to cite in theoretical journals in Europe and in such U.S. journals as *Review of Radical Political Economics* and *Kapitalistate*. See Sweezy's critique (1974) of Cogoy, Yaffe, Mattick, and "others who think like them."

16. This is not to deny that Marx's early dialectical method based on inverting Hegel's idealism, subjectivity, and expressive causality—for example, his philosophical conception of history—are not qualitatively distinct from his later, "mature" method based on materialism, structural causality, and objectivity in a framework of class analysis, such as his science of history. Veltmeyer (1978), a critic of Althusser, also postulates this transformation of Marx's method as "an epistemological break." A recent effort to deal with alienation, political economy, and class struggle in the context of advanced capitalism is Horton and Moreno (1978).

Part Two: Theoretical Perspectives

on Intermediate Classes

Dale L. Johnson: Class Relations and the Middle Classes

The very substantial middle classes of advanced industrial societies have been formed by the mature development of the stage of monopoly capitalism. These are *classes,* not indeterminate strata, unmistakably distinct from the working classes and bourgeoisies. In the dependent, underdeveloped countries the intermediate groups take on quite different configurations; but within the metropolitan countries, the middle classes are composed of analytically identifiable groupings (the technical term used is "fractions") that coalesce to form a social whole. They have experienced a particular (and until recently a very privileged) formation in the process of capital accumulation; they perform particular functions in the social division of labor as it evolves through different phases of development; they have particular positionings in the changing social relations of capitalist development; they share common class interests and achieve a coherent unity in the sphere of class culture and lifestyle; and they have played and will continue to play key roles in the social struggles that shape the development of monopoly capitalist society.

Examination of recent literature on the middle classes reveals quite diverse approaches to the problem of historical formation, structural determination, and social existence of a middle class as a class in itself. There is no agreement on terminology, much less on the ideas underlying such different concepts as "new middle class," "new petty bourgeoisie," "new working class," "intermediate class," "professional managerial class," "new class," or "middle strata." Most of the literature is more analytic than historical and rather static in conception. While there is a considerable advance in this literature that enables a better understanding of the social and technical divisions of labor and the places of professional, technical, and administrative labor within it, it suffers considerably from its "radical functionalist" theoretical underpinnings. None of the authors seriously tries to root class formation in the process of capital accumulation, following the example of Braverman's study of the labor process and the formation of the American working class. While attention is given to the social movements and cultural expressions of the middle class, there is little effort to see the different segments of the middle class in terms of their places in the changing social relations of capitalist development.

I am fortunately relieved of the obligation here to insert a review of the diverse literature on the theme by the presence of the excellent summary and critique of Martin Oppenheimer in the following chapter. The present essay draws on the theoretical premises of the preceding chapters to first examine in broad outline the manner in which the capital accumulation process has formed the middle classes of the industrial countries, then turns to analytic and "radical functionalist" approaches to class determination, contrasting them to a more historicist perspective, and finally discusses the questions of the "fractionalization" and social unity of the middle class.

In keeping with the argument of Chapters 1 and 2, capital accumulation is not viewed here as a purely economic process. The macroeconomic variables of Keynesian economics (savings, investment decisions, interest rates and money supplies, technical innovations, etc.) are devoid of social content and history as process. In Marxist political economy, a focus on the development of the forces of production or the tendential laws of the mode of production often slide over into an economic determinism. This economism always presents a very sterile sociology. While the accumulation of capital is indeed rooted in macroeconomic forces, it is simultaneously not only a process of class formation (as Braverman brilliantly shows) but also constituently involves changing forms of conflict relations between classes (this Braverman does not bring to bear, but see Edwards [1979] and Zimbalist [1979]). The great middle classes of the Western capitalist societies have been formed in tempo with, and as an inherent part of, the process of the accumulation of capital through the distinct phases in the development of the monopoly stage of capitalism.

This middle class is made up of the administrators of the large bureaucracies and technical, scientific and professional sectors of the labor force that have grown by leaps and bounds in the twentieth century. Yet statistics on the changing composition of the labor force with successive phases of development are but descriptive indicators of a fundamental social process. To avoid viewing the historical formation of new sectors of the labor force as something other than the simple expansion of employment in new activities opened by economic development, it is necessary to understand labor force shifts as new developments in the social and technical division of labor—and how developments in the division of labor are embedded in changing social relations. This is another way of saying that the formation of classes is constituent to the accumulation process and should not be seen as an empirical process (though the numbers involved can be ordered). The accumulation process precipitates and subsumes changing forms of antagonistic social relations.

Despite all the problems, analyzed in the preceding chapters, associated with Poulantzas and others concerned with developing "analytic approaches to the structural determination of social classes," it remains true that they at least attempt to view the social division of labor as a relational process. The work of Poulantzas, Wright, Carchedi, the Ehrenreichs, and Burris analyzed in this essay (Oppenheimer reviews many others in Chapter 4) places the middle class in the always changing social relations of capitalism. They begin by arguing, quite correctly, that the middle class has to be understood in the context of a structurally polarized social order. Capitalist societies are divided into two fundamental classes, capitalists and workers, each with a determined place and function in the social relations that undergird the economic process. The "global function" (Carchedi, 1978) historically usurped by capital is that of overall control of the accumulation and labor processes. Workers, on the other hand, sell their labor power and produce value that is appropriated by the controlling, employer class. The basic social relation of capitalism is the appropriation by one class of a proportion of the value produced by the exercise of the labor power of the other class. And, as the Althusserians might put it, this relation has "as a condition of its existence" a panoply of other relations of domination that assure its reproduction. Class polarization and the relations of exploitation and domination are a commonplace assertion to Marxism. But what these authors bring is an extraordinary sophistication to the analysis of polarized class relations and an attempt to pose the place of nonworker and nonemployer groupings (i.e., intermediate classes) in these structurally polarized relations. The main problem with the analytic approaches examined here (with the possible exception of Burris and Wright) is that, as a consequence of their abstract and static or "radical functionalist" premises, the middle class is seen, by and large, as composed of the bosses' agents. This results in an undialectical view which the concluding sections of this chapter try to correct.

Capital Accumulation and the Formation of the Middle Class

The intermediate social elements which intervene in the capital to labor relation are formed in tempo with the movement of the accumulation process. Here accumulation is understood to involve a much broader range of historical developments than simply movements of the forces of production into innovating technological pursuits and new sectors of growth. Accumulation is a process of transformation of the relations of production. Of particular interest is how accumulation undermines existing patterns of class relations and forms new sets of these relations. Historically, the opening of the diverse avenues of accumulation has had a profound effect on the entire range of social structural phenomena. Old classes wither; new classes ascend; the social conditions of the population are radically changed; and social struggle changes in form, character, and effect. One of the principal outcomes of the accumulation process in advanced capitalist societies has been the augmenting of space accorded new social elements intermediate between capital and labor in a growing, complex social division of labor.

The historical avenues of accumulation have precipitated basic structural changes in economic organization, in technology, in the labor process, and in markets. The changes proletarianized widening sectors of the population (farmers, artisans, small businessmen, immigrants, women) while creating ever-increasing demand for educated and skilled labor that also formed growing markets to provide a continuing base for the realization side of the accumulation process. New occupations proliferated to minister to a needy, dependent population and to administer an interventionist, "welfare-warfare" state. This brief exposition sums up the most important avenues of accumulation as they bear directly on the question of the historical formation of the middle class with particular reference to the United States. Later (Chapters 10 and 11), we analyze how an incipient crisis of capital accumulation in the United States affects the situation of the American middle class in the present period and what this may mean for the decade of the 1980s.

Historical studies of accumulation often view technological innovation as the main source of development. The application of power to mechanical devices in the Industrial Revolution, the steam engine and railroads of the nineteenth century, and the automobile, electronics, and computers of the twentieth century indeed were "epoch-making" innovations. But there is one source of accumulation that is even more important than technology: the incorporation of increasing proportions of the population into the waged labor to capital social relation. And there are other sources of accumulation that rival technology in significance: the internalization of capital and the growth of the modern state.

First, it should be clearly understood that without the production and appropriation of economic surplus that is reinvested in expanded production there is no accumulation and economic development. Under the capitalist mode of production this means that capital must be in a position to exploit labor directly or to appropriate surplus that is generated outside the capital to labor relation. In its earlier stages of development, capitalism depended considerably on the appropriation of economic surplus through relations of unequal exchange with noncapitalist sectors. For example, the slave plantation system of the Caribbean, parts of Asia, and the southern United States produced a considerable surplus that merchant capital appropriated through a variety of mechanisms. Some of this surplus found its way into the accumulation process, furthering capitalist development in Europe and the northern region of the United States. Similarly, in nineteenth-century America the surplus produced by a vast class of independent commodity producers (farmers and ranchers of the expanding frontier, artisans and other small producers) was, through unequal exchange mechanisms, diverted into the hands of investors.

With the monopoly stage of capitalist development, however, the principal means of accumulation shifted from unequal exchange to the dispossession of independent producers and their incorporation by carrot or by stick into the waged labor to capital nexus. This permitted the subsumption under the aegis of capital of production previously outside the sphere of capital and the direct appropriation of value from a labor force subjected to relations of exploitation. In plantation areas, slave labor became waged labor on modern capitalist plantations. In America the supply of exploitable labor was greatly increased by immigration. Through the course of the twentieth century, accumulation proceeded rapidly on a basis of dispossession and proletarianization, so that today the great majority of the population (including, in recent years, the majority of women) has been transformed into a dependent mass of waged workers. They are, without alternative, fixed in the employment of capital, yet they are entirely dependent on the consumption of marketed commodities.

The first and primary source of capital accumulation is incorporation of increasing sectors of the population into the capital to labor social relation. Different segments of a qualitatively new intermediate class were formed in the context of the polarization between increasingly concentrated and centralized capital and a growing mass of proletarianized peoples. Large-scale production employing new industrial techniques greatly increased the productivity of the growing labor force and created a sharply rising demand for engineers, scientists, and experts in organizational work. Scientists and engineers designed new means of augmenting worker productivity; organizational experts reorganized the labor process to more effectively subordinate labor; workers were subjected to routinized, dequalified work and the skills they were stripped of were transferred to the new experts. Control of the production process and labor became a central concern; supervisors proliferated. Reproduction of a labor force now entirely dependent on wages and stripped of the folk arts and communal survival services of the previous era became a problem; a growing army of professionals was formed to deliver babies and cure illness, provide schooling, produce culture, and apply a presumed expertise to all manner of acute social problems.

Of course, this vast, exploitable, and market-dependent working class and expanding middle class could not have been formed if concrete, new investment opportunities had not been explored. In the nineteenth century railroads and splendid new technological innovations opened up great new opportunities for profits and expanding corporate enterprise. The second source of accumulation is the great "epoch-making innovation." The automobile, cheap energy, and electronics created boom conditions. The assembly line and computers represent new ways of more profitably organizing production. As I have noted elsewhere:

> New occupational groupings within the working class and middle class followed quickly in the wake of large-scale capital extension into new economic activity and new technological accomplishments. The organizational and technical aspects of these developments required large numbers of qualified employees who swelled the ranks of new occupations that consolidated into sizable segments of a newly constituted middle class, a class set squarely between and within the polarizing relations of increasingly concentrated and centralized capital and the growing mass of proletarianized workers [1981: 6].

Third, the internalization of capital has constituted a principal source of accumulation. The development of England and Spain as the first imperial powers depended on pillage of the tangible wealth of the world. Later, relations of unequal exchange between primary production on the world periphery and industrial activity in the industrializing center were established and the European continent and America began to rival England. Still later, the export of modern capital from the center into the areas previously underdeveloped by colonialism and imperialism became a main source of international accumulation.

The internationalization of the accumulation process has tended, particularly in the latest "transnational phase of development," to internationalize class relations. Local bourgeoisies, a growing working class, and intermediate classes are formed in the periphery under conditions of dependency that are structured by accumulation on a world scale. These classes are involved in rapidly changing relations within national contexts, and these relations are necessarily seen as fixed within an international dimension. Similarly, the formation of the North American middle class is necessarily analyzed in part as an outcome of the rise of U.S. corporations as the dominant productive force on a world scale. During the post-World War II period the United States became the technical and administrative center of transnational capital and "free world" empire; middle-class employees man the administrative and technical apparatuses of the global reach of the transnational corporation. (Class formation and class relations on the periphery in relation to the internationalization of capital are discussed extensively in Volume 3 of this series.)

The internationalization of capital is related to the final principal source of accumulation: the growth of the modern state. The "imperial" or "warfare" dimension of the "welfare/warfare" state is a source of employment of administrative, technical, and professional labor. That the United States has a larger and more prosperous middle class than Europe is related to the hegemony (even though now declining) of American capital in the international sphere.

The "welfare" dimension of the modern state has evolved in the context of the difficult social conditions produced by development and in relation to the level and complexity of social struggle accompanying development. The decline of necessary social services previously part of community life, the misery among urbanized workers and immiserated populations, and the social demands of peoples' movements have required the state to provide a wide range of services.

The "interventionist" or "positive" dimension of the modern state has come about in response to periodic crises and the need for regulatory, monetary, and fiscal policies that facilitate accumulation. The middle class, then, was formed in considerable part to fill the multiplying interstices of the warfare/welfare/interventionist state.

While the middle class has been in rapid formation throughout the twentieth century in all the industrializing countries, its social weight, especially during the post-World War II period, became greater in the United States than elsewhere. By 1970, 17 million technical, administrative, and professional employees, or one-fifth of the labor force, formed the great American middle class. As the United States became the administrative and technical center of empire and made technological leaps in electronics and computers, both the concentration and centralization of capital and the proletarianization of the population proceeded to an extreme degree, making intermediate formations more important in the United States than elsewhere.

By way of anticipation, I add that the future of this class may not be as bright as its history was favored. Chapter 11 argues that most of the historical avenues of accumulation that once swelled the American middle class have very nearly reached the limits of their expansion—and vast new avenues of accumulation are not readily in sight—greatly affecting its class situation and its positioning within the polarizing relations of capital to labor.

Analytic and Functional Approaches to the Structural Determination of the Middle Class

The concept "middle class" is extremely loose and ambiguous. The greatest problem is that it carries the popularized sociology of "social stratification," in which groupings of individuals or occupations are ranked on various dimensions, such as income and social prestige, on an upper-to-lower continuum. The formations that modify middle class, petty bourgeoisie, or working class by the term "new" carry with them a much too specific, narrow, or, in my view, misleading theoretical implication. The popular sociology baggage carried with the concept middle class obviously is to be discarded. But I resist inventing some new term (such as the Ehrenreichs' "professional-managerial class" or "PMC"). So for want of a better term, I try to specifically redefine, through the course of this and succeeding chapters, the concept to give it a meaning that pertains to certain prescribed historical formations and patterns of class relations specific to capitalist societies, especially those of the advanced industrial countries, during the monopoly stage of development. (Class formations and relations in the Soviet Union are treated in Volume 3 of this series.)

The recent literature on social classes has been very helpful in defining the nature of these social formations and relations. This literature raises a series of implicit questions about the middle class. To what extent can it be said that the middle class has been historically "called into existence"

(a) to perform, together with the top managerial fraction of the bourgeoisie, the control functions of capital?

(b) to perform the technical aspects of coordination of production and the development of the productive forces?

(c) to perform the social coordination corresponding to the productive, repressive, ideological, regulatory, reproductive, service, and other activities of the state?

These are the questions posed directly or indirectly by those recent authors (Poulantzas, Wright, Carchedi, Burris, and the Ehrenreichs) who pursue what might be termed an "analytic" or "functional" approach to class determination. The answer to these questions is yes, the middle class has been "called into existence" to do these things. The problem is that this is not a dialectical way to pose questions.

Among the authors formulating an analytic approach, Poulantzas builds a determined case for a large and expanding middle class; in his terms there is a "new petty bourgeoisie" (constituting as much as two-thirds of the population in the United States, somewhat less in Europe) that is structurally determined to be a distinct social class. But this determination, as I made clear in Chapter 2 (where Poulantzas's theory of the new petty bourgeoisie is outlined), is posed in terms of Althusserian regional theory and a misapplication of the theory of productive and unproductive labor.

Poulantzas's critic, Wright, avoids the issue of whether or not there is a new petty bourgeoisie or any *class* in the middle between bourgeoisie and workers. He argues that "not all positions in the social structure can be seen as firmly rooted in a single class" (1976:4). Wright posits social categories that are characterized by "contradictory class locations": between the bourgeoisie and the proletariat, between the proletariat and the petty bourgeoisie (defined in the traditional sense of self-employment), and between the petty bourgeoisie and the bourgeoisie. This includes most of the locations that Poulantzas designates as the new petty bourgeoisie. (Wright's original 1976 critique of Poulantzas [1978] is a real substantive contribution and was subsequently extended and placed with other essays in a book.) Oppenheimer (Chapter 4, this volume) shares this concept of intermediate strata.

Wright, in effect, postulates classless strata.[1] These include (a) technocrats and top- and middle-level managers (presumably those with no ownership stake)—he estimates that this stratum in the United States constituted 12 percent of the economically active population in 1969; (b) bottom-level managers, foremen, and line supervisors—18-23 percent of the 1969 U.S. labor force; (c) employers hiring less than 50 workers—6-7 percent of the labor force; (d) semi-autonomous employees, including all professionals, technicians, teachers, and craftsmen—5-11 percent of the labor force. Thus, between 41 and 53 percent of the U.S. labor force (1969) can be classified in terms of "contradictory class locations" (Wright, 1978:86). The main differences with Poulantzas, apart from terminology, are that Wright does not recognize intermediate groupings as forming a class, that he includes "unproductive" blue-collar and lower-level white-collar workers in the working class (making it about 40-50 percent of the labor force in the United States, as compared to 20 percent for Poulantzas), and that he employs a somewhat different method of applying criteria of class determination.

The economic determinations of these strata are contradictory. These are analyzed by Wright in terms of three processes underlying production relations: "The progressive loss of control over the labour process on the part of the direct producers; the elaboration of complex authority hierarchies within capitalist enterprises and bureaucracies; and the differentiation of various functions originally embodied in the entrepreneurial capitalist" (1976:28). These processes in turn are reduced, following Poulantzas's analysis, to changing relations of economic ownership (control over the accumulation process) and possession (control of the means of production and command over labor power), changes which are occasioned by the concentration and centralization of capital. Though, like Poulantzas, Wright suffers from a certain inclination to substitute taxonomy for analysis, his is a considerably more dynamic approach than his European counterpart and will be utilized in part in later chapters.

An interesting variant on the analytic approaches to the determination of the middle class is the work of Carchedi (1975a, 1975b, 1978). Unlike Wright, Carchedi has a specific conception of the "new middle class," which is defined as that class which shares the *functions* of capital and of "collective workers" in the social division of labor:

> With the separation of the legal from economic ownership of the means of production . . . capital takes on a global function and is no longer concentrated in the capitalist class but is diffused among those who are neither the legal nor the real owners of the means of production. That is, the function of capital (now a global function) is performed not only by the capitalist class (at this level of abstraction, the managers) but also by another class the characteristics of which are: 1) it does not own either legally or economically the means of production 2) it performs both the global function of capital and the function of the collective worker 3) is therefore both the labourer (productive or unproductive) and the non-labourer and 4) is both exploiter (or oppressor) and exploited (or oppressed). It is this class which I call the *new middle class* [1975a:51].

It seems reasonable to suggest that the middle class is composed largely of people who are the bosses' agents but who also work for a living by producing something of value. But this is not a new or terribly profound insight. The more interesting part of Carchedi's work is that his approach lends itself to an analysis of the consequences of capitalist rationalization of the functions performed in the labor process. In Chapter 10 we analyze the "dequalification of technical, administrative and professional labor" and, in part, this analysis is based on Carchedi's formulation concerning the new middle class:

> Proletarianization of these agents is explained in terms both of devaluation of their labour power . . . and in terms of the progressive disappearance, for the majority of the agents making up the new middle class, of the global function of capital *vis-à-vis* the function of the collective worker [1975:1].

Carchedi is not very precise in defining the functions of capital, beyond the "global function"—control. From his point of view, the middle classes are formed historically of those elements whose labor is purchased in whole or in part for its value in the controlled and delegated exercise of the functions of capital. The relational side to this formulation of the class, which is mainly implicit in Carchedi's formalism, is that as controlled agents they carry out their controlling activities in antagonistic relations with workers and client populations. Yet, at the same time, inasmuch as the labor power of middle class employees is purchased and its use value appropriated by capital, and insofar as part of their labor time is devoted to workers' work and they are subordinated to the despotism of capital in the labor process, they exist in simultaneous antagonism with their masters.

These authors, I think, do have something to offer. In general, an analytic perspective on class determination begins with a characterization of capitalist development as one continuously moving toward an ever more extreme concentration of production and institutional centralization. It is reasonable to suggest that this is the first step in achieving an analytic basis on which to rest a historical account of the formation of the middle class and an analysis of its growing place in the social and technical division of labor and in the social relations of exploitation and class domination.

The determination of the middle class (and its fractions) is directly related to the way in which capital is organized to carry out the production process and what capitalists and their top managers do. The activities of capital rest on a global function—control. This "global function," which Carchedi does not disaggregate, has several aspects: control of the means of production, of the process of capital accumulation, of the labor process, and of the panoply of institutional means by which exploitation and class domination are facilitated. The maintenance of control assumes overall management, the planning and coordination that are technically necessary to the economic process. The striking feature of monopoly capitalism is the degree to which the functions of planning and coordination by capital (and sundry managerial agents) are both concentrated at a high level of bureaucratic organization and widely dispersed within a technical division of labor. Corporations delegate and rationalize planning and coordination through extension of the division of labor; that is, capital converts planning and coordination into functional divisions (research and development, engineering, production, sales, etc.) and within these, into a series of specialized tasks performed by workers who produce value and profit only in their collectivity. This permits the concentration of the control functions that assure appropriation of profit at the highest administrative level permitted by the technical division of labor; it also permits a certain degree of organizational rationality in decentralized coordination that promotes productivity. The technical and social coordination of economic activity is converted into a management science of control. For all those located below the pinnacles of administrative hierarchies there is great responsibility but little authority. Historical trends have been such that within economic enterprise today the technical and social cooperation necessary to production has been largely organized by capital into despotic control of a highly differentiated, bureaucratized division of labor. The social form that coordination of economic activity has taken is complex differentiation of coordinative activity accompanied by tight control of the labor process, while diverse control functions necessary to maintain the relations of production (i.e., those activities required to reinforce and reproduce the system of exploitation and class domination) are delegated to the state.

Capital organizes itself to exercise its global function in diverse ways. Among these is the employment of agents to exercise specialized coordinative, planning, and control functions. The historical process of concentration and centralization of capital has resulted in operations of such magnitude that legal owners cannot exercise direct dominion over property and retain managerial agents to act in their stead. Managers in turn employ assistants, and assistants dispose of various levels of subassistants. Capital also organizes itself through the medium of the state. Massive state agencies have evolved that seek to impose order on the anarchy of the economic and social order. Activities of the state expand increasingly to centralize key functions: to facilitate private capital accumulation, to enforce and reproduce the system of exploitation and class domination, and to provide for social needs that cannot otherwise be met.

Burris has provided a succinct statement of the functions of middle class positions with respect to the capital accumulation process:

1. *The supervision and control of the labor process:* managers, foremen, supervisors, etc.

2. *The reproduction of capitalist social relations:* teachers, social workers, health professionals, state administrators, lawyers, cultural workers, etc.

3. *The accounting and realization of value:* professionals in advertising, sales, accounting, banking, finance, insurance, etc.

4. *The transformation of the technical means of production:* scientists, engineers, research technicians, etc. [1980:29].

On the basis of this functional breakdown, Burris then interpreted census data on occupational changes from 1900 to 1978. These data (which complement empirical data on "fractions" of the middle class provided in Chapter 7) are shown in Table 3.1. Burris, unlike others of a functionalist bent, is careful to place the functions of the middle-class positions in the context of the accumulation process and the historical struggles of capital and labor.

This functional perspective is valid—as far as it goes. But it has also to be understood, at the very least, that the evolution of functions in the social division of labor, like the movement in the accumulation of capital in which the division of labor unfolds, is itself a dynamic and uneven relational process and in no way a mechanical, evolutionary process. The positions of the middle class are determined within a dynamic process of the unfolding social relations of the accumulation process, of capitalist development as a

TABLE 3.1   New Middle Class Positions Within the U.S. Labor Force, 1900-1978

	1900	1910	1920	1930	1940	1950	1960	1970	1978
Total	1,605	2,536	3,785	5,314	6,026	8,844	12,240	18,131	23,885
Percent of Labor Force	6.0	7.3	9.5	11.3	13.3	15.9	18.9	23.6	25.3
Sector (% of labor force)									
Private	3.7	5.0	6.8	8.0	9.6	11.6	14.1	16.7	18.3
State	2.3	2.3	2.7	3.0	3.7	4.3	4.9	6.9	7.1
Function (% of labor force)									
Supervision	1.6	2.3	3.1	3.3	4.1	5.6	6.3	6.8	7.9
Reproduction	3.2	3.5	3.9	4.7	5.2	6.0	6.2	8.4	9.6
Realization	0.9	1.2	2.0	2.5	3.3	3.8	4.1	5.0	5.2
Technological innovation	0.3	0.4	0.5	0.8	0.7	0.8	2.2	3.4	2.6

SOURCES: Burris (1980: 30) based on U.S. Department of Commerce, Bureau of the Census, *12th Census* (1900), vol. 2; *13th Census* (1910), vol. 4; *14th Census* (1920), vol. 4; *15th Census* (1930), vol. 5; *16th Census* (1940), vol. 4; *Comparative Occupational Statistics for the United States, 1870-1940; 17th Census* (1950), vol. PE-1B; *Occupational Trends in the United States, 1900-1950; 18th Census* (1960), vol. PC(2)-7A; *19th Census* (1970), vol. PC(2)-7A; U.S. Department of Labor, *Employment and Training Report of the President* (1979); Spurgeon Bell, *Productivity, Wages and National Income* (Washington, D.C., 1940).

never-ending propellent of economic and social transformation. As industry grew to gigantic size, administrative control and coordinative functions proliferated. As technological and organizational innovations opened new avenues of accumulation, skilled craftsmen were brought screaming and kicking into the proletarian condition, while elite engineers and an army of technicians were trained and credentialed. As the state assumed new responsibilities for the overall management of a near unmanageable process, a battery of intervening functionaries came into being.

To recapitulate before turning to other distinctly functionalist formulations and an attempt to distill a more dialectical view of class determinations, the middle class is made up of technical, administrative, and professional employees who are not, in the main, hired to produce surplus value as such. Their places in the social division of labor are to perform functions appropriated from deskilled workers, to exercise coordinative and developmental activities as delegated by managers, or to supervise the labor of workers who do directly produce surplus value. Yet technical personnel, administrative functionaries, and professionals are not simply agents of capital. As Carchedi emphasizes, they also perform, in some measure, the productive functions of workers. They sell their labor on a market, and its value within the process of production, whatever the mix of controller or productive activities, is appropriated by capital. They are subordinated within technical and administrative labor processes that today are infinitely hierarchized. For these reasons they necessarily relate antagonistically to their employers, as well as to the producers who are their subordinates and, in some cases, their victims. But the real issue is not that they are crossbred between bosses' agents and productive workers, but that they are intermediate class formations intervening within and mediating the defining relations of capitalist society, the capital to labor relation.

The main problem with Carchedi is that his abstract notion of function does not contain a focus on the social relations of class, which I have tried to pose above in a general way.[2] The same is true of Poulantzas, who uses functions performed in the social division of labor to define large groups out of the working class and into the new petty bourgeoisie. Function performed is not, by itself, a structural determinant of class; it does not define social groupings into or out of a class (Szmanski in Walker, 1979). Function is simply one indicator of relational placement. Ehrenreich and Ehrenreich (Walker, 1979), while departing in some ways from an even more functionalist conception of the middle class, attempt, at the same time, to carry out a dynamic study by placing a larger emphasis on class relations. This is particularly interesting work because it starts from many of the assumptions of the "radical functionalism" criticized in Chapter 2. Theirs is an approach straining to escape its functionalist straightjacket.

This straining is also true of Glucksmann, who searches the terrain of intellectual labor for the means of escaping its system-reproducing functions. But, much like the Ehrenreichs, his answer resides in ideological exhortation: "The new middle class can directly discover that the 'intellectual labor' that qualifies it is an abuse of power and a power of abuse" (1976:83).

The Ehrenreichs define the professional-managerial class (PMC) "as consisting of salaried mental workers who do not own the means of production and whose major function in the social division of labor may be described broadly as the reproduction of capitalist culture and capitalist class relations" (in Walker, 1979:12). While cultural workers, managers, engineers, and scientists perform different specialized roles, they "share a common function in the broad social division of labor and a common relation to the economic foundations of society" (1979:12).

The Ehrenreichs' work is not the usual static, functional conception of class. This common function, since it is to manage, maintain, service, and reproduce the working class, places the PMC directly in conflict with workers. Moreover, the antagonisms are a historical product of the appropriation, carried out by the PMC—in part at the behest of capital but also in its own self-interest—of the skills, knowledge, and culture of the working class. The PMC is also in conflict with the bourgeoisie. Not only is it in a position of having to sell its labor power, but the PMC's propensity for planning and rationalism frequently encounters capitalist irrationality and strives for profits:

> Although objectively in the service of capital against the working class, the PMC identifies its interest with that of society as a whole (and progress), an ideology grounded in notions of professional autonomy, scientific rationality, and the disinterested political objectivity of expertise [Noble, in Walker, 1979:124].

They also see the PMC in terms of its social cohesiveness (discussed in the next section): higher educational attainments (which is how the PMC reproduces itself), shared lifestyles and consumption habits, inter-marriages, and similar world views.

This approach embodies to some degree the relational component of social classes that is too often missing in the literature. Yet in the end, when all is reduced to the social function of reproduction, their idea of class relations loses its dynamic and contradictory power, its dialectic. A tentative critique of the notion of "reproduction" was made in Chapter 2. Noble's observations reinforce this critique:

> What is reproduction? Is it something people can specialize in?

> The Ehrenreichs have here too substituted a static, one dimensional notion for a dynamic, contradictory one. . . . They have lost a sense of potential, motion, history; their concept kills. When they use the term "reproduction," they mean reinforcement; to reproduce capitalist social relations is to strengthen, repair, revitalize, renew, sustain those relations and nothing more. Reproduction stops history, for the Ehrenreichs . . . (yet) reproduction and production are but two aspects of the same, single, process of social production. . . . Reproduction thus has a twin identity: it is at once the strengthening of capitalist relations and movement beyond them [Noble, in Walker, 1979:130-131].

The Ehrenreichs are hardly the first to conceive of the middle class mainly as purveyors of capitalist culture. A "New Left" theorist of the 1960s, Martin Nicolaus (his 1967 work is analyzed in Chapter 2) referred to the middle class (the social basis of the New Left of the era) as "servants for short."[3] This kind of disdainful view of the class goes back to the heyday of its formation and celebrated progressivism; Veblen had noted as early as 1919:

> The class of gentlefolk, the legally constituted wasters . . . can not be expected personally to take care of so large a consumption of superfluities as this posture of affairs requires at their hands. They would, as the Victorian peace teaches, necessarily have the assistance of a trained corps of experts in unproductive consumption, the first and most immediate of whom would be those whom the genial phrasing of Adam Smith designated "menial servants." Beyond these would come the purveyors of superfluities, properly speaking, and the large, indeed redundant, class of tradespeople of high and low degree—dependent in fact but with an illusion of semi-dependence; and farther out again the legal and other professional classes of the order of stewards, whose duty it will be to administer the sources of income and receive, apportion and disburse the revenues so devoted to a traceless extinguishment [1964:346].

This "substantial middle class" Veblen saw would be dependent on the "kept class" and contribute to the "income streams" of the owners of invested wealth (Veblen, 1964:347).

Nor are the Ehrenreichs the last to proceed in the radical functionalist vein. The approach is rapidly spreading in Marxist circles outside Europe and the United States. Gutierrez Garza, writing in *Cuadernos Politicos,* an influential Mexican journal, considers the "salaried petty bourgeoisie" as those who do not produce surplus value and "live from the surplus value that is transferred to them from the rest of society" (1978:115). She evidently looks at the salaried petty bourgeoisie in terms of their function, which is that of exercising the domination of capital. The petty bourgeoisie is viewed as the "organic intellectual" of the bourgeoisie; the class performs the functions of direction and vigilance over the labor process and of exercising political domination through the state. (A similar, though less explicitly functional, approach is applied by the Latin American sociologist Agustin Cueva [1979].) Gutierrez's notion explicitly makes the petty bourgeoisie parasites who live off production workers. Moreover, to view an entire class as "organic intellectuals" of the bourgeoisie (a notion also implicit in the Ehrenreichs' work) considerably distorts Gramsci's concept.

The main problem, however, is that the entire approach, whether Gutierrez, the Ehrenreichs, or others, takes as a given the functions which the bourgeoisie *struggles to impose on institutions* as characteristic of the people themselves, of the "functionaries" or "agents" who work within these institutions. Few would think of Lockheed Corporation assembly line workers producing strategic bombers for the United States Air Force as "agents of the Pentagon" or "war-mongers"; why, then, should an engineer, technician, production foreman, teacher, or social worker be considered an "agent" of another class? Institutionally defined roles are one thing; how people actually perform these roles and the kind of people they are may be quite another. Thinking back to the previous chapter's discussion of subjects and history we can reaffirm here that people are formed in the social relations in which they are enmeshed, and, in living and thinking the relations that shape their lives and their self-conceptions, they engage in a process of self-formation. Middle-class people are nobody's agents (though they may often act so); they are human beings (though some have been robbed of their humanity) caught between their defined roles and their actual circumstances.

I will try to state briefly what seems can be usefully extracted from the more dynamic "radical functionalist" approach to class determination. The structural determinations of the middle class (and its "fractions") derive from the particular place and form of insertions of different occupational groupings into the relations of production, as these relations are transformed with the continuous development, driven by the forces of capital accumulation, of monopoly capitalism through different phases. The "relations of production" is an exceedingly generalized concept. For purposes of analytically deriving the determinations of the middle class, the relations of production can be viewed from the angle of the underlying social relations of a capitalist economic order, those of exploitation and class domination. This permits a more specific examination of the many forms these relations assume and the place of distinct fractions of the middle class within them.

The basic social relation of the capitalist mode of production at all stages of development is the appropriation by one class of a proportion of the value produced by the exercise of the labor power of the work force. These exploitive social relations necessarily require social means of enforcement, reinforcement, and reproduction. A panoply of relational forms of oppression, suppression, and repression evolve as means that facilitate exploitation. These forms change with historical development and are variable between nations. In their totality, relational forms can be conceptualized as a *system of exploitation and class domination*. The many varied and changing social forms assumed within the system become the primary relational bases of institutions and social structures; in fact, these forms leave their stamp on the entire range of social, political, and cultural phenomena within a given society.

At the analytic level, the determination of the middle class proceeds by examination of the places and activities of different segments of the technical, administrative, and professional labor force in the system of exploitation and domination. To avoid falling completely within a version of radical functionalism, it should be emphasized that a "place" within a "system" is never fixed for any appreciable period of time. A place is not simply a precise location in a given structure, but a patterned, purposive, repeated, yet fluid set of activities that brings people together in relationships. What it is that people do defines the place. People do different things, relate differently to other people, and change themselves as circumstances change and as people interrelating change circumstances. A system, then, is not a static set of categories arbitrarily conceived by a social scientist, whether it be a functionalist like Talcott Parsons or a Marxist structuralist like Louis Althusser. A system is a highly dynamic pattern of social relations that permeates the everyday realities of people living out their lives. The patterns of social relations within a system of exploitation and domination are in constant flux because they are inherently antagonistic, because the acting out of relations of antagonism between the parties involved changes the form, expression, and intensity of relations over time, and because the structural forces and conditions that contextually define the system are in constant change.

Drawing again on some of the premises of Chapter 2, we can say that the study of the determination of social classes (and the "fractionalization" of classes to be discussed below) involves analyses of highly dynamic social relations. The structure of these relations are transformed with the movement of the forces of production, by the different avenues and modes of capital accumulation. Relations of exploitation and domination are by their nature antagonistic. Therefore, the actual, concrete ways in which individuals, groups, and classes interrelate become dialectical forces that, over time, change the prevailing relations and provide a structured context for the movement of the forces of production and the accumulation process.

Class struggle, which is itself structurally limited and selected by various social structures, simultaneously reshapes those structures. The word "simultaneously" is important in this formulation: social structures do not first structurally limit and select class struggle, after which class struggle transforms those structures. Class struggle is intrinsically a process of transformation of structures, and thus the very process which sets limits on class struggle is at the same time transformed by the struggles so limited [1978:21].

With this dialectic of class struggle interjected, the "analytic" conception of class determination focusing on "function," "system," and "places" is more or less proper but, again, only as far as it goes. I think it can be taken further by interjecting a certain degree of "historicist" Marxism.

Historicism and Problems of Empirical Specificity

Coming to grips with the question of the middle class requires a historical understanding of multiclass relations in a bipolarizing structure.[4] And this implies a theoretical position that assumes history is a process with subjects and that points to and makes sense of the great historical and empirical variations in class formation and class relations. A problem, in addition to those identified above, with the analytic conceptions of class by Poulantzas, Wright, the Ehrenreichs et al. is that they invoke structure with either formalism or, like the historicists the Althusserian structuralists criticize, they assume an implicit teleological notion of genesis and process. Questions of historical formation of classes are ignored and the relational component of the class concept is hypostatized as stasis. Moreover, analytic theory does not readily point toward important issues that require empirical clarification. It is therefore vital to rescue what is essential within historicism and within Marxism as an empirical science from the structuralist onslaught.

Historicism (best exemplified by the Hegelian Marxists) is an approach that is preoccupied with a kind of philosophical genesis, or at best ontological process, to the neglect of structure and is contemptuous of empirical investigation. Alienation and reification mark the origin of social being and determine its course of evolution. In Lukács's view, only the essential contradiction of a true proletarian social consciousness moves history. I have already made clear my position (Chapters 1 and 2) that a dialectical science proceeds from structural analysis to an examination of historical process. But it is also the case that our conceptualization of structure and derivation of any genetic principle has, in the first instance, to be constructed from systematic study of historical process. It seems to me in its fascination with Hegelian dialectics that historicism does not adequately capture the dialectic of structure (as theoretically posed) and process (as concrete history).

Nevertheless, historicism, particularly in the work of Gramsci, has contributed greatly to a theory of social classes. A historicist perspective specifies class as a relational process of active subjects; that is, history is a process of class struggle. Moreover, classes are conceptualized within dialectical movement of a historical totality. These contributions, of course, are not easy to disassociate from their roots in a philosophical (neo-Kantian and Hegelian) rather than materialist idea of history (Jones, 1978).

The historicism and dialectical method of the early Mark, Lukács, Korsch, Gramsci, and others situates classes at the center of historical development. For Lukács, the proletariat is object and subject of history. This identity of subject and object presents the central problem of historicist thought: History is subsumed in teleology. Lukács ascribes a self-consciousness to the proletariat and assigns its mission, acts of self-liberation that revolutionize society. Althusser is correct to characterize this essentialist "expressive totality" as Hegelian, not Marxist dialectics.[5] (It might also be asked if the "hidden structures" of structuralist epistemology are not just a static form of theoretical essentialism that invokes its own teleology.) Essentialism and teleological evolutionism have no place in a science of history.

We know that the class struggle is the "motor of history" not because it is a principle of origin and becoming, or because Marx said so[6] and Lukács expressed it as immanent law, but because it has been historically observed again and again. Gramsci was a master of historical observation of class struggle and he made this observation into knowledge by theorizing it. We also know that acting on knowledge, we better understand and transform the world we live in. I believe that this is as true as saying that in knowing the principles of physics, we better understand and transform the physical world (even though a principle of historical sociology hardly has the predictive power of physical "laws"). The "class struggle as motor of history" knowledge is not a doctrine of immanence. It is at worst a sociological ontology; better said, it is a methodological principle for historical/empirical investigation in the practice of a dialectical social history.

One of the most controversial theses of Marxism is the generalization that the central feature of capitalist development is a process of class polarization: at the one pole concentration of production and centralization of control, wealth and power; at the other pole dispossession, proletarianization, and subordination of an ever-increasing proportion of the world's peoples. It is in this context, all historicists assert, that class struggle is inserted. Lukács's classic study, *History and Class Consciousness,* did much to reaffirm Marx and Engels's basic thesis of class polarization emerging from the process of the development of capitalism. Lukács indicated the bourgeoisie and proletariat as the only two "pure" classes of capitalist society. This thesis should again be understood as a principle guiding concrete research, not as teleology.

Combining the two principles we may ask: If capitalist development is a process of class polarization and class struggle is the motor of history, how does one understand the historical formation of nonbourgeois and nonproletarian classes? According to Lukács, and in this he is correct, the social location of the petty bourgeoisie, together with the peasantry, is ambiguous because the existence of both "classes" is not fundamental to the mode of production. Lukács suggests that these classes neither act to promote capitalist development nor support the transformation of capitalism into another social order. Such consciousness as these groupings develop (in contrast to the proletariat whose "ascribed consciousness" negates the "reifications" of capitalism) leads not to a vision of the whole society and its movement but to attitudes of uncertainty toward the established order and to aspirations of return to the status quo ante.

In Europe and North America[7] the peasantry and the petty bourgeoisie were classes formed either within precapitalist modes of production or in earlier premonopoly stages of capitalist development. Whether classes are tied to an antiquated order (as in Lukács's treatment of the petty bourgeoisie and peasantry in *History and Class Consciousness*) or are new formations representing an emerging social order (like the petty bourgeoisie in the stage of competitive capitalism or the "new middle class" of monopoly capitalism) is not the crucial question for concrete historical analysis. The contribution as historical actors of peasants and traditional petty bourgeoisies—classes subjected to historical annihiliation with the process of class polarization—to the vast changes undergone in different areas of the world is well-established. The Chinese, Vietnamese, Cambodian, Laotion, and Angolian revolutions were basically peasant revolutions occurring while the bourgeoisie/working-class polarization was more of a structural tendency (resulting from these countries' insertions in the world-system) than an empirical reality within national social stuctures. The Bolshevik Revolution occurred in backward Russia. Jones says of Lukács: "The Russian Revolution, which fused and *combined* a bourgeois and a proletarian revolution because of the intertwined co-existence of feudal and capitalist relations of production in the Tsarist social formation, is simply unthinkable within Lukács' scheme" (1978:39). Hobsbawm's work on "primitive rebels" (1965) establishes the importance of the movements generated by peoples being forced from the margins of history. Moore's scholarship (1966) portrays the important historic roles of traditional aristocrats and peasants in diverse national contexts. Mayer (1975) has surveyed the changing but always important social-political roles of the petty bourgeoisie in European history from the days of medieval towns through the revolutions of 1848 to the twentieth-century fascist movements. The rise of "progressivism" in early twentieth-century America (Chapter 6, this volume) and the social movements of the "new left" in the United States and Europe (Ehrenreichs in Walker, 1979) during the expansionary decade of the 1960s developed rather clearly from a social base in the middle ranks of society. In the contemporary Caribbean, the "brown middle class" is a governing class (see Volume 3 of this series).

These brief examples illustrate that the bipolarization process asserted so forcefully within the historic tradition may be a necessary starting point, but it is not a basis for understanding the complexities of social history in its empirical variation. O'Connor phrased it well:

> In class society where one class organizes the labor of another class there always exists class struggle in one form or another and with one end or another. The problem is not to prove that classes exist or stand in certain antagonistic relationship but rather to identify the actions, reactions, reconstructions, and reconstitutions (i.e., the concrete element in everyday life) which occur [1975:299].

These "actions, reactions, reconstructions, and reconstitutions" are the social struggles that occur within a historically bipolarizing structure.

The methodological problem, then, is to locate the proper place of historical/empirical research. Framed in terms of the problematics posed by the structuralists' critique of tendencies within Marxism, how is it possible to engage empirical investigation without falling into "empiricism"? How is it possible to pursue historical research without invoking a teleological "historicism"?

With respect to research into the most important intermediate class that has formed with capitalist development, the middle class of the advanced industrial countries, historical/empirical research must be carried out within the premise that middle-class formation is an *expression* of the class polarization process. The concentration of capital and the centralization of corporate power, technological leaps, the forceful incorporation of the petty bourgeois intermediate class formed during the nineteenth-century era of competitive capitalism to the wage labor to capital social relation, and the polarization of industrial capital to industrial labor required the formation of a new class of salaried employees of capital.

Yet the middle class—"called into existence" by the social and technical requirements of development in the era of monopoly and placed squarely between the polar classes—also has a life of its own. From historical observation we know that it has sought a social existence separate from the poles. It forms a culture peculiar to itself and pursues particular lifestyles that give the class a social unity (analyzed in Chapter 7); it has its own interests and separately pursues them (see Chapter 10 on professionalization); it makes alliance with capital in some historical circumstances and workers in others (see Chapter 6 on the progressive movement).

But the social existence of any intermediate formation is always precarious. The middle classes of advanced industrial societies, like the nineteenth-century petty bourgeoisie before it, in the long run is a transitory formation. Different fractions and strata within it are formed and suffer demise. The polar classes are gradually solidified. While the internal structure of the bourgeoisie and working class radically changes, these changes strengthen and consolidate the polar classes as organic social bodies. Intermediate classes, in contrast, are always in a process of fundamental transformation. Changes in internal structure are rapid and may result in qualitatively new formations, as in the case of the transformation of the classic petty bourgeoisie into a salaried middle class. In North America during the nineteenth century, the petty bourgeoisie was a class that encompassed the great majority of the population. By the middle of the twentieth century it had ceased to exist (see discussion of "independents" in Chapter 7). The salaried middle class that displaced the petty bourgeoisie has likewise undergone significant qualitative changes. Doctors and lawyers of the early period were displaced in importance by engineers and the engineers by technicians, administrative cadres, and social workers. These shifts in the internal composition, character, and sheer body count within the salaried middle class are accounted for by the changing forms that the polarizing class relations of capitalist development undergo in specific historical circumstances. That there is so much disagreement about what to term the class is largely a result of not understanding that the middle class is an expression of the polarization process. Use of concepts such as "middle strata" (*capas medias, couches intermédiares*) represent a refusal to deal with the class character of social groupings intermediate between and mediating the social relation capital to labor. The concept of "new working class" applied to the legions of white-collar and technical employees imputes a social character to these groupings that they do not hold. At least this is so until the process of dequalification of professional, technical, and administrative labor has proceeded further than it has so far (Chapter 10). While the new working class concept may have seemed appropriate in the revolt of salaried employees and youthful aspirants to the middle class in the French scene of 1968, things appear quite different in the 1980s. Terms currently in vogue that have an elitist connotation, such as "professional-managerial class" (Walker, 1979) and "new class" (Bruce-Briggs, 1974), reflect opposite political responses to the apparent social-cultural orientations of the middle class in the 1970s and 1980s. In short, different analysts have mistaken specific forms of the insertions of distinct fractions of the middle class into the relations of capital to labor in particular times and places as more generalized class phenomena.

Capitalist development, through its distinct stages and phases, has been and remains characterized by a multiclass complex of class relations in a bipolarizing structure. The specific forms of multiclass relations are an important and proper field for historical/empirical investigation.

Notes

1. Wright would argue that he is placing different groupings within contradictory locations, in that they are simultaneously situated in more than one class within class relations. He locates the discussion in terms of a distinction between class structure and class formation (1978). Wright understands class formation in a quite different way than I do, and his notion of contradictory class locations seems just another way of defining positions out of a class.

2. Terry Johnson (1977: 198) notes: "Carchedi's levels of abstraction ultimately involve an economic essentialism involving the progressive addition of superstructural variables which merely reflect the original abstract divisions."

3. Another prominent "New Left" writer, Stanley Aronowitz (1973), used the term "professional servant class" to refer to middle managers and technocrats. Aronowitz, however, is careful to balance this with an analysis of "white collar proletarians."

4. I have elaborated on bipolarization and intermediate classes elsewhere (Johnson, 1981).

5. The "historicism" of Lukács and other classic writers has been particularly criticized by contemporary Althusserians (see especially Althusser's "Marxism is Not an Historicism," Chapter 5 of *Reading Capital*). Veltmeyer's critique (1974-75) of the structuralist critique of historicism and his substantive contributions on structure and history are important contributions to the debate.

6. Actually, Marx and Engels did not use the metaphor and only implied the motor of history idea in the exhortations of the *Manifesto*.

7. In today's dependent periphery, the questions of mode of production and class formation are quite complex; this is dealt with in Volume 3 of this series and theoretically in Johnson and Chilcate (forthcoming), Volume 2 of this series.

Martin Oppenheimer: The Political Missions of the Middle Strata

Five basic views concerning the political mission of the new occupations that began to take shape in the late nineteenth century are in contention today: An *elite* view sees certain top strata of these occupations as coming to lead society in an enlightened and efficient way, a view harking back to Plato's *Republic* and exemplified by Skinner's *Walden III.* A *stabilizing* view assumes that most people in the labor force will achieve "middle-class" lifestyles based on white-collar and other skilled, educated-level jobs such that they will sustain a consensual, middle-of-the-road democracy with extremely gradual change. A *third force* approach states that these same groups have an inherent interest in gradual, reformist change, conceivably ending in some moderate form of democratic socialism different from the vision of the more Marxist-inclined, class-struggle-oriented, blue-collar proletariat. A *new working class* perspective posits that many members of the white-collar occupations will move leftward to join with, or displace, the blue-collar proletariat as a major lever for fundamental, revolutionary social change in a crisis-ridden capitalist society. Finally, a *contradictory locations* assumption states that different fractions among the middle strata are located in different classes, some in several classes at the same time, so that "white collarites" as a whole constitute neither a single class nor simply an appendage to one other class, but rather a complex of shifting and conflicting segments.

These positions have come down to us in the literature of social science, and of political theory, virtually unchanged for a hundred years. The "Great Debate" concerning the political trajectory of the middle strata, sometimes called "white-collar workers," continues to befuddle us. It is the purpose of this chapter to describe this debate and these positions. My own view, which is the fifth one listed, is also described briefly, with a further discussion in Chapter 11.

Elite Theories

In a world in which social policy appears to be determined by men who act from petty vested interests, who are stupid, crooked, corrupt, or at best inefficient, the intellectual tends to see him or herself as a superior, enlightened being who is surely able to do a better job. For some, if present policymakers are unable to "deal with" mass chaos, with what is termed "anarchy," with the utter corruption of cultural standards, then fascism provides an ideology to rationalize the intellectual's need for an efficient, quick solution. Among other intellectuals, both fascism and communism invoke too great a fear of mass participation, hence further disorder (and possibly an abrogation of certain traditional intellectual rights, such as free speech), an ideology which abjures ideology, a value system which preaches value-neutrality and technicism will develop. Elite advocacy theories insist on the moral quality and efficacy of rule over society by experts who are educated and technically trained to rule and who are selected substantially by processes controlled by their own grouping. These theories, whether aristocratic or modern fascist, or whether they stem from the democratic impulses of European social democracy or the American New Deal or from Stalinism, share one important ingredient: a fundamental mistrust of genuine mass participation in important decision-making.

Given a commitment to elite rule in the interest of efficiency, two political issues divide elitists: First, what shall be the *purpose* of this efficiency—that is, what is the social goal of policymaking? (This question constitutes the political-ideological dimension of the dispute among and between liberals, rightists, and some leftists—that is, shall the purpose be a more equalitarian society? Does this require the elimination of private enterprise? And/or shall the purpose be an orderly society? Does that require the elimination of civil liberties?) Second, who shall be the *agency* of this efficiency—that is, what group shall be the experts? All disputes among those committed to rule by some upper stratum of what today constitutes the technocratic and professional upper white-collar occuntional strata seem to hinge on those two questions. This is true even among those whose rhetorical commitment is to mass participation at the very moment that they defend the rule of some group of party leaders or experts in some other nation on the elitist ground that dictatorship is a necessary price to pay for "progress" or "development."

The logic of this discussion would lead us back at least to Comte and Saint-Simon, if not all the way to Plato. These figures were the forerunners of contemporary "enlightened" technocracy, as well as of the centralized planning agencies associated with the social-democratic conception of "nationalization." Comte and Saint-Simon both saw intellectuals and industrial leaders as the carriers of culture and as heads of society. The connection between this approach and that of Edward Bellamy in *Looking Backward,* an important socialist propaganda tract (1888), or that of sociologist Albion W. Small, particularly in his fictional *Between Eras: From Capitalism to Democracy* (1913, a book which Harry Elmer Barnes compared to Plato's *Republic*), or for that matter of B. F. Skinner in *Walden II* (1948), is not hard to see. All of these are relatively simple elitist views, though sometimes they are couched in socialistic rhetoric; all lacked a theoretical context of a socialism embedded in the notion of democratic participation by the masses in their own liberation.

This is not to say that alternative traditions were unavailable—the debate concerning socialism "from above" versus "from below" had begun with virtually the opening gun of the French Revolution, as Edmund Wilson makes plain in his excellent *To the Finland Station* (1940). It is only to say that the precursors of contemporary elitist theory, until World War I, were scarcely touched by that alternative tradition, and did not bother to defend themselves against it. All shared the belief that philosophers, intellectuals, managers, and administrators could, by virtue of their wisdom (in some cases biologically acquired) and education, rule—and should do so.

Within the field of sociology, one of the leading advocates of this approach was Karl Mannheim (1936). For him, it was essential that intellectuals take a leading role in the reconstruction of society because they are relatively "socially unattached," or classless, and hence can synthesize a progressive politics without dumping, in the process, "the accumulated cultural acquisitions and social energies of the previous epoch." At the same time, they can defend themselves from the attacks of both right and left. Classless, and therefore standing above the petty interests of classes (represented by the right and left), the intellectual represents universalistic progress.

Thorstein Veblen (in *The Engineers and the Price System,* 1921) had nominated technicians, rather than intellectuals, as society's crucial change agents, but the approach is similar. That book, a collection of essays originally published in *The Dial,* "came to be regarded by many as the manifesto of technocracy," reports Henry Elsner (1967).

Veblen's view was simple enough. It had obviously been affected by the Russian Revolution. Engineers "constitute the General Staff of the industrial system, in fact, whatever law and custom may formally say. . . . Therefore any question of a revolutionary overturn . . . resolves itself in practical fact to a question of what the guild of technicians will do. . . . The chances of anything like a Soviet in America, therefore, are the chances of a Soviet of Technicians." A very remote chance, thought Veblen, since such people were a "harmless and docile sort, well fed on the whole, and placidly content with the 'full dinner pail' which the lieutenants of the Vested Interests habitually allow them." Nevertheless, given "harsh and protracted experience. . . ."

It was an attractive view, particularly to engineers and technicians. In 1932, at a point when that harsh and protracted experience had lasted three years, Howard Scott's technocratic movement "exploded" on the public scene. The organizations stemming from Scott's Technical Alliance (later called Technocracy, Inc.) still exist, but the New Deal ultimately drained the movement of mass support. Scott, who used a lot of engineering and physics terminology, called for technologically trained people to form the nucleus of a new revolutionary movement. In 1919 or 1920 he was apparently in touch with the IWW and supplied it with a report on the meat-packing, and possibly other, industries, an interesting forerunner of current "people's research" groups. Two articles by Scott appeared in an IWW paper.

Most members of Technocracy, Inc. were skilled workers or professionals such as engineers. Scott had a "technet" of ham radio operators, a fleet of cars, and by 1938 dressed his cadre in neat gray uniform-suits. Technocracy, like Veblen, was antibusiness and somewhat populist, but was not Marxist, nor did it spend much time attacking Marxism. It was egalitarian in ideology but attacked present-day democracy as inefficient, worthless, and utterly corrupt. Its internal structure was highly authoritarian, and leadership was coopted rather than elected. Elsner's conclusion is that technocracy fits in rather more with the "authoritarian left" than with the right; "in summary, technocracy might be conceived as one specific form of technical-managerial ideology," though it should be viewed more as an *engineering* than an *engineers'* ideology. That is, it did not appeal to self-interest; indeed, members of Technocracy, Inc. who were surveyed in A. W. Jones's study *Life, Liberty and Property* (1941) scored almost as anti-property as did communists and socialists. For Veblen and the technocrats, then, the elitist solution to society's problems (Vested Interests) takes the form of a soviet of technicians—an elite form of socialism, in the interest of the people. For Mannheim, it takes the form of an independent grouping of intellectuals who, it is hoped, will represent in themselves the world's progress.

Strangely, although one would expect C. Wright Mills to come out closer to Veblen, it is ultimately with Mannheim that he stands. While he is better known for his pioneering work, *White Collar,* to which I shall return, we know that he puts little faith in white-collar workers *as a group* in terms of change. In *The Causes of World War III* (1958), Mills isolates one sector of white-collar workers, the intellectuals, and, in a manner highly reminiscent of the philosophical idealist Mannheim, lectures them on their social responsibilities. If only they were honest to the intellectual or cultural "calling," he seems to say, they would reenter politics to "reveal the way in which personal troubles are connected with public issues." They would become "consistently and altogether unconstructive" vis'a'vis the ongoing social order. In short, intellectuals would become a vanguard for change. While this can hardly be termed a radical view (because it is elitist and idealist), we must remember that this was written toward the close of the Eisenhower years, several years before the upsurge of the first mass movement since the 1930s, the Black student movement which began only in 1960. It is also true that Mills, unlike the other thinkers we have briefly surveyed, was not committed to elite *rule* of society—only to intellectuals becoming the vanguard of a movement for change in society. Thus he appeared to differ from both Veblen and Mannheim and to be struggling further in trying to locate a mass base for change and subsequent rule.

Mills's orientation to intellectuals as a potential vanguard was based on the assumption that neither the blue-collar working class nor the white-collar working class would be mobilizable as a force for change in the foreseeable future. Among writers associated with "critical theory" and among some associated with the New Left, university students or intellectuals displace the proletariat as the primary vanguard element. It would seem almost inevitable that intellectuals who, for whatever reason, see no hope for change as the result of mass action must thereupon pin their hope, if they have any, on an intellectual and/or student elite, even while admitting that students alone cannot do the job.

Thus Marcuse, in various writings, particularly *One-Dimensional Man* (1964), pinned his hope for change on an alliance of alienated and "hippie"-oriented students with other alienated sectors of the population, particularly Blacks and the lumpenproletariat. As he stated in an interview during the Vietnam war, "the opposition of American youth could have a political effect. This opposition is free from ideology . . . it is sexual, moral, intellectual and political rebellion all in one. In this sense it is total, directed against the system as a whole. . . . Only in alliance with the forces who are resisting the system 'from without' can such an opposition become a new avant-garde."

Marcuse has been associated, historically, with the so-called Frankfurt School, also sometimes termed the school of "critical theory." A more recent disciple of this school is Jürgen Habermas. Habermas, like Marcuse, holds that class struggle as it was once understood is no longer the chief dynamic of modern society. He believes, as do many liberal theorists, that "state-regulated capitalism, which emerged from a reaction against the dangers to the system produced by open class antagonism, suspends class conflict," so that we are more likely to see open conflict at the "periphery" of society, not among social classes but among the disenfranchised and superexploited (1971). These groups, he states (in opposition to Marcuse), cannot by themselves succeed in a revolutionary struggle. A coalition needs to be made, and at present "the only protest potential" among non-peripheral groups appears to be among students, especially those from privileged backgrounds. "The legitimations offered by the political system do not seem convincing to this group," says Habermas (1971:20): Their protest appears qualitatively oriented (rather than directed toward a larger share of the pie) and hence has the kind of revolutionary implications needed to supply allies to the peripheral forces. While students (the professionals-technicians of the future) cannot by themselves constitute a revolutionary force, in alliance with Third World elements they may succeed, despite the cooptative mechanisms of modern, rational capitalist society.

Norman Birnbaum (1969) shares a similar view:

> As for the proletariat . . . it is neither in its culture nor its politics a harbinger of the future or a revolutionary force. Today's avant-garde in industrial societies will be found among the young, particularly students (that is to say, those without immediate responsibilities or bondages to the existing order), and amongst intellectuals, those with a certain freedom from routine and a certain proclivity to employ their critical faculties.

These ideas are strangely akin to some of those of the "end of ideology" school (Bell, 1960). Marcuse, Habermas, Birnbaum, and other critical theorists disagree with Bell et al. that most fundamental problems have been solved, that ideological conflict is over; but they share with liberals (though not with social democrats) the assumption that masses of the population, particularly the industrial working class and white-collar employees, have been sufficiently coopted (by, among other devices, "repressive desublimation," not to speak of sharing in the industrial nations' wealth at the expense of the Third World) so as to eliminate them as a potentially radical force. This view is related to that of the so-called third worldists (e.g., Debray, Cleaver, Huey P. Newton, Mao, and many others) who hold that the levers of change lie outside the metropole, in the developing world, or among the subproletarians and lumpenproletarians (Habermas's periphery) rather than among the mass of the industrial and white-collar working class in the Western technologically advanced countries. But most third worldists, unlike the critical theorists, do not look to any set of intellectuals or students to be of much more than incidental help, auxiliaries, a la Weatherman.

Still another variant of the view looking to certain upper white-collar strata (particularly students) as a vanguard for change is that of the "counterculturalists." Here Slater (1970) and Roszak (1969, 1973) constitute leading celebrants of countercultural lifestyles as portents of revolutionary change. Slater, who liked to preface his chapters with verses from the Beatles, the Rolling Stones, and Bob Dylan, is actually better known for his work in advanced management theory, particularly around sensitivity training, and the development of new, more flexible structures for business organizations (sometimes termed "Theory Y"). So it is not surprising that his emphasis is on modifications in motivation, on psychic change, on personal liberation. At the same time, he recognizes the need for institutional change. His indictment of our institutions and of the mechanisms through which the Marcusian "One-Dimensional Man" is created is a strong one (as is Roszak's or, for that matter, Charles Reich's in *The Greening of America* [1970], a work along similar but rather more journalistic lines). It is not until midway through Reich's book that one begins to get an inkling of who is going to change all this: the hero of the film *The Graduate,* the alienated, psychic sufferers of the Spock generation—that is, the children of the educated middle class. The Graduate, to make revolution, needs to liberate himself, his libido, his loving essense, Slater (with Norman O. Brown and Wilhelm Reich, and others) seems to be saying. The attempt to do this by many people through music, drugs, and new varieties of sexual expression, among other symptoms (not all positive), constitutes "the cultural revolution" and mounts a fundamental, revolutionary challenge to rationalistic, technological, impersonal, alienated society. The hippie ethic is more radical, says Slater, than the political activist ethic, because the latter still partakes of the stern old code of postponement of gratification, of taskorientation, of rational thought. But the hippie is not realistic. The conflict between the two, both wings of antiestablishment thought, is irreconcilable, and Slater, good liberal that he is, refuses to choose—or, rather, he chooses both, while at the same time implying that in any case the change is coming about, willy-nilly, by gradual permeation of the old culture by the new. In the end, despite the poisonous viciousness of our present system, which Slater details, he backs off from contemplating the kind of power that would be required to overcome it. We are left, one imagines, with playing rock music at management conferences.

For Roszak it is the young, particularly "technocracy's children," who are the hope of the future. In revolt against managerialism and "think-tank" mentality, "technocratic America produces a potentially revolutionary element among its own youth." And the adult radical, confronted with a working class that is allegedly "the stoutest prop of the established order," must make a bid to become guru to alienated youth (e.g., Roszak). As chief gurus, such figures as Norman O. Brown, Allen Ginsberg, Alan Watts, and Paul Goodman (but not Timothy Leary, whom Roszak early recognized as dangerous) are to become for the young what Marx, Engels, and Lenin were to an older generation of radicals. Even the contemporary religious "renewal" we see today among young people is a symptom of "incalculable value" (Roszak, 1973:xvii). The "visionary commonwealth," by which Roszak appears to mean leaving the cities to organize economically sound anarchist communities (to simplify his view just a bit), is opposed to all of the evils of contemporary society. The notion that such a reaction to the evils of rationalism might lead as well to totalitarian spiritualism such as those of Rev. Moon, Rev. Jones, or, for that matter, to the Manson Family, escaped Roszak at that time. The utopians were always solid indictments and beautiful plans, but no inkling as to how to muster the forces, the power to get from here to there.

This view of intellectuals and/or students as a *cultural* vanguard with their allies to be found among other *culturally* alienated elements must be distinguished from the view that intellectuals constitute a vanguard force which actually foreshadows a much more profound social upheaval involving larger segments of society, including the mass of technical and professional workers.

Both these views (the culturalist and the class) have been accepted in a certain distorted sense by the enemies of change: Theorists of the business community have accepted the notion that there is a "new class" of intellectuals and academics which has disproportional power in American society and has influenced governmental policy to the detriment of the society as a whole. If a "new class" of antibusiness intellectuals exists, it can be used as a scapegoat for all of society's failings (particularly in the social policy area). In short, it is not capitalism or the capitalist state (per Marxian theory) that has failed, it is the "new class." The upshot has been an enlarged effort by corporations to influence foundations, universities, and research institutions so that the "new class" can be converted to a more pro-business sentiment (Vogel, 1979).

While on the empirical level this is all nonsense, it must be said that the various theorists arguing one version or another of new class formation in the capitalist West, whether culturally and/or structurally based, have lent themselves to these misuses. They have helped to create what Bell (1979) has rightly called a "linguistic and sociological muddle."

There is actually very little agreement among those who have used new class terminology in recent years. Gouldner (*The Future of Intellectuals and the Rise of the New Class,* 1979) sees it in formation, but not as liberating; Bell denies its existence because it does not have "a community and continuity of institutional interest and an ideology" (1979); the Ehrenreichs, using the term "professional-managerial class," base their definition on the functional identity of "reproducers of capitalist culture and capitalist class relations" and hold it to be a "derivative class" but a class nevertheless, with an independent outlook (1979). Harrington thinks it is synonymous with the new working class but excludes, apparently, the mass of white-collar workers. Hacker (1979) denies that the service professionals and symbol manipulators are a class, and indeed warns against persuading oneself that what one is doing is "essential"—we belong, he says, to a very old class: We work for a living. And Horowitz (1979) throws the baby out with the bath by saying that class as such is becoming a "residual, near passive category." In brief, say the critics of the "new class" approach, the concept is misleading at least for the capitalist West. At worst, it has the conservative implication that this alleged autocertified enlightened elite of welfarists ought to be stopped in its tracks—presumably by laissez-faire supply-siders. (For a further critique of "new class" theory, see Oppenheimer, 1981.)

Stabilizing and Third Force Theories

In *White Collar* (1951), the major American work on the subject in our time, Mills examines the basic political options open to the white-collar occupational strata, which he calls "the new middle class." One of these options is that this grouping will turn into an independent class, displacing other classes "in performance of the pivotal functions required to run modern society," hence becoming the next ruling class. This is the view I have attributed to Veblen, among others, and it is characteristic of the elite approach. A second view, according to Mills, is that the new middle class will become "a major force for stability in the general balance of the different classes," hence will make for the continuance of liberal capitalist society. Alternatively, this grouping can become an independent force for change.

The debate between the "stabilizing" view and more radical visions which saw the new occupations as a force for change, even revolutionary change, began in Germany in the 1890s and has continued to this day. Gustav Schmoller (1897) held that the growing proportion of the labor force which was educated and well-paid would become propertied, and that this social mobility would create an expanding middle class, contented and a force for cultural and moral uplift. Edward Bernstein, on the revisionist wing of the German Social-Democratic Party, argued that the persistence and growth of middle-class groups contradicted the Marxist assumption of polarization between classes and necessitated a moderating change in socialist strategy if these groups were to be won over. Political change would have to be evolutionary rather than revolutionary. His argument remains the basic assumption of European socialists and, indeed, Eurocommunists today. Karl Kautsky, reaffirming orthodox Marxism within the party, predicted that worsening conditions would propel white-collar employees into the proletariat and would revolutionize them. In 1912 Emil Lederer coined the term "inbetweenness" (*Zwischenstellung*) to explain the apparently contradictory position of white collarites who were objectively workers yet subjectively hostile to working-class organization. He saw their heterogeneity, their internal segmentation, and their middle-class consciousness as obstacles to a socialist development. This is the tradition on which the "fifth theory" draws. From 1918 to the middle 1920s in Germany considerable radical organizing among the white-collar occupations took place. Yet it could not be sustained in the face of the growth of more nationalist and proto-Nazi unions. While at least the lower mass of white collarites, contrary to legend, did not disproportionately support the Nazi Party, they also did not disproportionately oppose it as did the blue-collar working class (Hamilton, 1980).

The *stability* approach, while conservative, shares with the Bernsteinian tradition (which belongs to the "third force" school) the assumption that in some way the white-collar strata are a force in their own right; the more orthodox Marxian tradition, exemplified by Kautsky and later in the United States by Corey (1935), assumes either that these strata are part of the working class (or that significant proportions of them are) and/or that they are "marginal," "in-between," "tail-enders," but *not* a force in their own right. Both the stability and the third force assumptions see the white collarites as some form of new class, or new middle class, whether they use these terms or not, while those who argue some version of the more classical Marxist view see them as a "mixed" class, and/or as some form of a new working class.

The typical third force view was posed by Selig Perlman:

> The middle classes, though greatly shaken economically, have stubbornly refused to accept the Marxian verdict that politically and socially they are doomed merely to choose between a capitalist or a proletarian hegemony. Instead, in some countries the middle classes have managed to find expression in an independent political power . . . which . . . may find expression either in Fascism or in a New Deal [1935:632]

The war against Hitler brought relative prosperity to the blue- and white-collar workers of the unoccupied Allied nations. Contrary to many predictions, this prosperity extended into peacetime and, buttressed by anti-Communism and heavy investments, even back into Germany itself. An era was ushered in which many believed would finally lay to rest theories of class conflict and revolutionary change. For Galbraith (1952), white collarites constituted merely another group which would soon "seek to assert its market power." For Bell (1960), this grouping is part of that great American middle class which he sees as educated joiners who have helped us arrive at a "political dead center." Bell's celebration (one cannot call it much less) of American life and American class structure was based on the belief, shared also by Galbraith, that more and more people were living better and sharing an educated culture. They do so, he argues, because inheritance no longer determines access to power, and because technical skill rather than poverty, and political position rather than wealth, "have become the basis on which power is wielded." Hence there is no more ruling class—it is split, today, into an "upper class" and a "ruling group"; the latter is a coalition in which elements of the middle class, particularly managers and the "technocracy," clearly play an impoitant role. This coalition makes decisions largely on technical considerations rather than on substantively political or ideological bases.

The reality for Bell, then, was that a coalition of elite decisionmakers who reflect mass opinion in a general way make *specific* decisions based by and large on technical rather than wider moral-political considerations. There is no ruling class: The only political question is which of our internal groups will bear the costs of any added burden imposed (writing in the late 1950s) by the democratic method of countervalence. As with Galbraith, the notion of the middle class and the main force for stability is present more implicitly than explicitly.

It is David Bazelon (1967) who makes the third force thesis more explicit. "The decisive relation for the future," he posited, "will be that of the New Class and the Under Class." By "new class" he means all the propertyless and educated employees of organizational life, all those whom he terms "working intellectuals" who gain "status and income through organizational position [achieved by] virtue of educational status." While it is not clear where this "class" begins and ends—he seems to exclude clerical and salespeople at one extreme, and owners at the other—it does seem to include virtually the entire college-educated population of the country that works for salaries. This is not just an enlightened or an evil elite—it is a large mass.

The mission of this grouping, according to Bazelon, is to develop a coalition with enlightened businessmen, elements of the "under class" (especially Blacks in the civil rights movement) and New Dealers in politics, to create the completion of the New Deal. This, he suggests, is the first step in developing its own ideology, which is more or less synonymous with liberalism.

Bazelon shares the notion of a "postindustrial society." As Birnbaum has described the theory, "the existence of educational opportunity entails an enlargement and a democratization of opportunity.... The basic issue of stratification . . . has been settled by the technical rationality of the system" (1969:10). And "with the change in the composition of the labor force and the enlargement of the new middle class, the character of the elite

. . . will alter . . . will merge into the new middle class. Meanwhile, the very complexity of the technical operations to be performed at the intermediate levels of the class system, the increasing indispensability of education as a prerequisite for admission to these levels, will inevitably increase the margin of autonomy of those occupying these positions" (p. 37). In short, postindustrial society implies a democratization of society as the vast middle class becomes educated and, at the same time, an "end of ideology" as social conflicts become resolved into technical questions to be solved by an elite which is basically a part of that new middle class. (It should be emphasized that Birnbaum does not share this perspective—the bulk of his book is devoted to an attack on it.)

The hypothesis of a center in which the new middle class plays a crucial political role is shared with only a slight difference of emphasis by social democracy—the European labor and socialist parties (and in recent years even some Western European Communist parties) and the American socialist sects stemming from the Socialist Party of Norman Thomas. The difference may be summed up in the term "moving equilibrium." That is, liberals such as Bazelon and social democrats such as Michael Harrington (1972) obviously do not hold that present society is okay as is, and that the new middle class is well-served to preserve it that way. Rather, the balance of society must be gradually shifted to the left, to progress, in a gradual, evolutionary mode. The idea that this can be done peacefully and piecemeal, the hallmark of social democracy, assumes that the capitalist system is fundamentally capable of dealing with its internal crisis without either collapse or a turn to fascism: Socialism will be achieved qualitatively at some future date, as the sum total of relatively small-scale accretional reforms.

For this reason Harrington, though a socialist, must also be placed among the theorists who believe in a moderate, center-based solution rooted for support in the middle strata of our society. His working coalition is not much different from that of Bazelon, though his final goal sounds more radical. The social reform programs of Debs and Norman Thomas, he argues, have been absorbed, with at least some success, into the mainstream of American culture and politics even while their socialist advocates have fallen by the wayside. The mode of this absorption, and the strategy for its furtherance, is the alliance of the official trade union movement and the Democratic Party, which is, for Harrington, the rough American analog to the European social democratic and labor parties.

While the blue-collar working class continues to be central to social change (precisely because it is not nearly so affluent as Galbraith and Bell wanted us to believe), says Harrington, this is only one element in the "democratization of power" which is required for progress. A second is the new working class, which Harrington seems to limit to the professional and technical stratum and whose members are "middle class in . . . education and income, but often subjected to a production discipline like that of the workers" (1972:442). The third element is college-educated people who are nontechnicians. These three groupings, Harrington argues, form the mass constituency for social democratic politics today and for a socialist movement in the future. This is, incidentally, quite a conceptual muddle: We have a blue-collar working class, a "new" working class, and what sounds like a cultural grouping (college-educated people *in general*); it is not clear where the mass of white collarites fit, or why people can be middle *class* by income and education when those are clearly stratification and not class terms. What makes them new? Class? Working? Middle?

Harrington's position might seem squarely on the fence between a theory which holds that the middle strata will stabilize capitalism and new working-class theories arguing that they will assume the traditional role of a proletarian revolutionary class. This is not so, because of the political *content* of the social democratic programs which he advocates for today, regardless of his commitment to more fundamental change tomorrow. The types of welfare reforms (most of which are not structural—that is, not inherently linked to a drive to raise more fundamental, radical issues), and the organizational context in which to fight for those reforms (the official trade union leaderships and the liberal wing of the Democratic Party) link Harrington's approach far more closely to reform-if-you-would-preserve liberal theoreticians such as Galbraith than to revolutionary exponents of new working-class theory such as Gorz or Mandel (see below).

The point is elaborated by Parkin (1971): European social democracy seeks to change the reward structure of society through "meritocratic" means—that is, to seek fairness in the competition for position in society, to "put the race for privileges on a more equitable footing." Egalitarian socialism, on the other hand, "is concerned with eradicating privileges, not with changing the principles by which they are allocated" (1971:123). "Under meritocratic socialism," Parkin states, "classlessness would be produced by continuous, large-scale social exchange of personnel from one generation to the next. Under egalitarian socialism, classlessness would be produced by the distribution of reward on the basis of need and by the substitution of 'industrial democracy' for traditional authority structures." (p. 123). It is clear that "meritocratic socialism" is basically congruent with liberal reformism, while egalitarian (traditional, Marxist) socialism is fundamentally counterposed to it. Harrington's dilemma is this: Ultimately, like all social democrats, he is committed to the goal of egalitarianism. But practically, today, like all social democrats, he works for meritocratic change. This emphasis on reforms intended to develop "large-scale social exchange of personnel" over a generational period necessarily leads social democrats to measures which are accretional rather than structurally radical. Minute reforms serve to stabilize the system overall when they are not sabotaged by capitalist interests which remain fundamentally undamaged. Thus such changes undermine the chance for short-run qualitative change. The current socialist experiments in France and Greece dramatize this point. Tactically, the attempt is to develop majorities which will force such changes to come about, an approach which indeed prevents the development and espousal of more drastic change because the need to create majorities demands emphasis on minimalist programs.

The role of social democratic theory, therefore, is to provide a leftist, radical rhetoric for the development of majority coalitions (including both blue- and white-collar workers) which will seek out a series of small-scale reforms the function of which is to leave undisturbed "the general balance of the different classes," whence making for the "continuance of liberal capitalist society," to quote Mills. The white-collar strata are numerically essential to this strategy.

This should not be taken to imply that Marxist or egalitarian theories are therefore opposed to majority coalitions or majority rule. Theoretically, Marxist parties are prepared to postpone sharing power and fronting for liberal capitalism in order to develop majorities for a more fundamental, revolutionary change. This change, it is assumed, can come about and be supported by majorities because of the inherent long-range incapacity of even liberal capitalism to function.

New Working Class Theories

"New working class" theories, regardless of other differences, share the assumption that a mass of occupations at the bottom of the "stratification" system constitute a social class which on some basis is in conflict with a minority at the top, and objectively if not subjectively struggles against that minority for social dominance. The term "new" may refer to the newer white-collar occupations, or to the fact that all workers now find themselves in a new technological era; the nature of the conflict may be predominantly cultural, or it may be economic; the leading elements of the new working class may be white collar or blue collar, skilled workers of either collar, or the more proletarianized.

Touraine (1971), at one extreme, views the situation as one in which a rising *technocracy* finds itself pitted against professionals, technicians and other line workers (especially in white-collar occupations), and students. This is the class struggle for him. The contradiction of this society, which is now beginning to absorb capitalism, is not so much economic as cultural, although the workplace is one of the centers of the struggle. The rising technocracy, Touraine argues, constitutes a new ruling class because it controls social resources through power over organization, but it is caught in contradiction between "the technical and cultural realities of modern society and inherited organizational forms" (1971:30). The new class is not capitalist and, indeed, struggles against certain nonrational capitalist institutions. But it is not anticapitalist either: Its dynamic is to strengthen the centers of decision-making and programming, the large, rational organization. This drives it toward a new contradiction: it engenders, by its own dynamic, a revolt against the "commercialization of human relations, feelings, and sexuality," the "manipulation of needs and desires, of leisure" (1971:33), economic and social management of a rationalistic (dehumanizing) kind, and, by implication, the alienation of the educated workers from all significant decision-making.

Touraine points out:

> It is essential to recognize that economic power today belongs, not to private holders of profit, but to large organizations private or public, nourished more by self-financing or public credit than by private capitalists holding the right to make economic decisions [1971:200].

> Thus the conflict is not economic, not against the profit-makers, but against the technocracy—hence "the working class as such is no longer the protagonist *par excellence* of historical evolution" [1971:194].

Rather a "new as yet unnamed sociological formation" including students, but even encompassing some managerial circles, struggles for qualitative change, both for cultural freedom and to "manage industry, and through it, society" (1971:200), but along radical, democratic lines. It is Veblen's vision but with a mass base.

In this "new sociological formation" the skilled, technically trained, professional workers are the most militant and the most likely to raise demands concerning workers' self-management. It is they, not the traditional working class, who are to assume "revolutionary initiative" and raise qualitative as against merely "economic" demands. These upper-level white-collar workers, with students, appear to Touraine ready to incorporate but also to transcend "any purely worker movement in favor of action carried on by all who are subjected to the power of large organizations" (1971:219)—blue-collar workers, technicians, students, marginal elements in the economy, victims of social planning and urban renewal, and the peoples of the Third World as well. "The struggle of revolutionary nations is the strongest condemnation of technocratic domination; because of their common enemy it is united with those who, within advanced capitalist societies, denounce the brutal subjection of certain social groups to the 'requirements' of change, whether . . . by physical or cultural manipulation" (1971:34). Touraine, unlike Marcuse, states that "the struggle is not at the periphery but at the center of this programmed society" (1971:354).

Thus a new stage in the class struggle has been launched (for example, by the events of May 1968 in France). Students and intellectuals symbolize "a class on its way up, struggling against the new managers who are also on their way up." While Touraine does not specifically use the term "new working class," he appears to approve of Mallet's use of the term and, with some other working-class theorists, sees the traditional blue-collar proletariat playing a distinctly subsidiary, dependent, if not actually conservative social role.

A number of other European theoreticians share with Touraine the assumption that many, if not all, strata of the white-collar occupations, including in some cases students (at least as proto-new proletarians), constitute a new social formation, one that will play the critical role in any future leftward social change. Such an assumption is quite different from one that says this grouping will act as a conservatizing, stabilizing force, or a more traditional Marxist view that says under given circumstances it may play a significant role in a rightward, or Fascist, shift.

The pioneer in developing new working class theory was Emil Lederer (1912). While he concluded that the white-collar strata were ultimately too heterogeneous to develop an autonomous politics, as Schmoller had argued, he did posit the hypothesis that within the white-collar grouping two tendencies were in evidence: The upper strata were pro-bourgeois, while the lower strata, "proletarians in false colors," had the potential of aligning with the blue collar proletariat. (Crozier, 1971:35). In the 1920s Lederer predicted such an alignment, coining the term "proletaroids" to indicate the development of a proletarian consciousness among these lower white-collar strata. In 1928, at a general congress of German trade unions, Lederer predicted the decreasing importance of blue-collar workers due to their increasing proportion in the labor force, and consequently an increasing role for white-collar workers. At the same time, he said, employees would ultimately share the fate, of whatever nature, of the entire working class (Neuloh, 1966:33). Several other German writers shared this analysis at one time or another: Kracauer and Dreyfuss are discussed briefly by Crozier (1971); and the early work of Croner (1928) and Engelhardt (1932) are also available in English.

Engelhardt, who also used the term "proletaroid," pointed to the ambivalence of the white-collar employee. The salaried employee on the one hand held to middle-class attitudes and sought (and to a degree attained) a middle-class lifestyle, including the enjoyment of a "social esteem" to which blue-collar workers only aspired. On the other hand he or she suffered from the income limitations of all the employed strata (particularly in the inflation-ridden Germany of the 1920s and in the depression of the early 1930s). One needs to recall that the German salaried employee in the public service lived in a status and prestige system clearly marked by ranks and titles; these titles were also gradually finding their way into the private sector (Engelhardt, 1932).

Croner (1928) went into more detail as to why and how the white-collar employee would develop proletarian consciousness. He argued, first, that the increasing concentration of industry resulted in a need for industry-wide collective bargaining, hence an enlarged group consciousness by workers. Second, the rationalization of work limited the individual's effect over the workplace and narrowed the scope of the job. Third, the white-collar worker was suffering unemployment of "hitherto unknown proportions." All these factors led to increased union activity. Thus, Croner hypothesized, the white-collar employee would move in the stages of his/her consciousness from (1) a person who assists an employer (ideologically a "not yet employer") to (2) new middle class (not a laborer, but a new class "between" the classes) to (3) a salaried employee (not a laborer, but part of the proletariat (Croner, 1928:5).

Croner pointed out that in Germany there had been a 98.2 percent increase in "salaried and civil service employees" from 1907 to 1925, as compared with a 22.3 percent increase in blue-collar workers. He traced the history of white-collar unions, which in 1917 had formed their own federation (the Arbeitsgemeinschaft freier Angestelten-Verbende, AFA) with a socialist orientation. It participated in the 1923 general strike, which caused the collapse of Hitler's attempted coup. By 1927, out of 5,275,000 German white-collar workers, some 1,165,000 were unionized, with 400,000 in the AFA. In 1926, there was an important strike of medical and sanitation white-collar workers in Berlin; even the 460,000-member employees' union oriented to the Christian Nationalists accepted the idea of strikes and was seriously divided on the Hitler question.

The data developed by Croner and others raise some serious questions about the widespread assumption that "it was among the lower levels of the working class, and especially among white collar employees, that Hitler found his best troops," as Crozier states (1971:26). Neuloh (1966) also questions this assumption, as does Hamilton (1980).

German social scientists, mainly of left-wing persuasion, pioneered in analyzing the white-collar strata; no doubt this reflected their very immediate concern with the political potential of this rapidly growing sector of the labor force, in the context of a series of national crises spanning the period from World War I to the rise of Hitler (although some work goes back earlier and involves debates within the powerful German Social Democratic Party). At the same time that some of this work viewed white-collar employees as potentially proletarian (hence, potentially socialist), there was also a clear perception as to the contradictions and conflicts, the "ambiguities" of white-collar life.

In England, the view was apparently not that positive. Lockwood observed:

> The contemptuous term "white-collar proletariat" was coined specifically in the inter-war years to emphasize the pathetic self-deception of the black-coated worker who was seen as indulging in middle-class pretensions on a working-class level of living [1958:14].

This corresponded to unionization figures in England: As of late 1951, only 25 percent of "blackcoated workers" had been unionized (1958:141).

In 1953, Lewis Corey, a Marxist, produced *The Crisis of the Middle Class.* This work constituted the first systematic attempt to update Marxist theory in light of shifts in the labor force and remains the classical Marxist statement on the new working class even today. Corey wrote from the depths of the depression, with fascism a concrete and rapidly rising force. "In New York City, in 1933," he states, "one out of five charity patients in the hospitals were salaried employees"; of urban relief cases in the country in May 1934, 3,134,000 were "workers" and 649,000 were professionals, clerical, and other salaried employees (1935:22). In spring 1933, when there were 17¼ million unemployed in the nation, the blue-collar unemployment rate was 45 percent—and the white-collar rate was 35 percent. But 65 percent of chemists, 85 percent of engineers, and over 90 percent of architects and draftsmen were out of work. By 1934, 20 percent of schoolteachers were unemployed. Of persons seeking relief jobs, 40 percent were unemployed white-collar workers (1935:25). Thus, Corey concludes, the middle class is now largely propertyless; their fight is, or must become, the same as that of all wage workers (1935:25).

Corey argued that while this is true in general, the middle class is, within itself, in ideological crisis. It is an intermediary class split into antagonistic upper and lower layers. The upper layer, or "old middle class," includes "independent enterprisers," and self-employed professionals. The "new middle class" consists of salaried employees, the "result of the profound structural changes in capitalism" (1935:40). But the new middle class is also divided between an upper layer of "managerial, supervisory and technical employees in corporate industry [who] are wholly identified with monopoly capitalism and its reactionary aims" and "the masses of lower salaried employees . . . [who] waver between democracy and reaction." Ideologically bourgeois, the new middle class responds to attempts by the big bourgeoisie to "sell" them security in exchange for a reactionary social order. "But their concrete economic interests drive them into an opposite direction: toward the working class" (p. 148).

The disunity of the middle class, fostered by its heterogeneity, creates "wholly a split personality, tormented by the clash of discordant interests" (p. 151). But the present crisis is "permanent." Thus "if and when their economic interests drive the masses of lower salaried employees (and professionals) to struggle for a new social order, they must necessarily unite with the larger class of the proletariat." There can be no unity of action with upper administrative layers, which "perform the function of exploiting the lower." Strictly speaking, then, the middle class isn't a class at all. "It has no identity of *class* economic interests in terms of a definite mode of production, or economic order" (p. 168).

What needs to happen is that "the lower salaried employees (including the professionals) must split off consciously from the middle class, as they are already split off economically (p. 70). This process will be hastened by their "proletarianization": "a typical large office is now nothing but a white collar factory . . . [also] the proletarization of technicians is marked and inescapable" (p. 51).

Indeed,

> masses of lower salaried employees (including salaried professionals) are *not* members of the middle class . . . [or even of] the "new" middle class. . . . [The latter] can include only the higher salaried employees, the managerial and supervisory, who perform the capitalist functions of exploiting the workers. . . . They are capitalists in the institutional sense and their relation to production is clearly bourgeois. It is otherwise with the masses of lower salaried employees . . .: they are economically and functionally a part of the working class: a *"new" proletariat* [1935:259, italics added].

Here, in perhaps its most explicit terms up to that time, Corey posits new working class theory; the lower white-collar strata constitute a new proletariat, destined, it is hoped, to join the old (albeit as a dependent factor) in the struggle for socialism. Indeed, this is the perspective finally arrived at years later by Mills, though the latter was not so sanguine about the white-collar proletariat's radical potential.

In passing, Corey explicitly denies the old Bernsteinian (and the later Bell-Lipset) view, that the development of a new middle class proves Marx to have been wrong about polarization and that the middle class is becoming a majority. The old middle class is shrinking; the new middle class is qualitatively different, and the lower salaried employees are neither new nor old middle class.

Mills (1951) shared a number of Corey's assumptions. Although radical, his framework was not Marxist in the usual sense. Above all, Mills felt that the white-collar strata ultimately had to align themselves with one or another of the major social classes or directions—capitalist or industrial proletariat, right, or left:

> Nothing in their direct occupational experiences propels the white collar people toward autonomous political organizations. The social springs for such movements, should they occur, will not occur among these strata. . . . The white-collar workers can only derive their strength from "business" or from "labor." Within the whole structure of power they are dependent variables [1951:352].

Which one will it be? "Of what bloc or movement will they be most likely to stay at the tail? And the answer is," says Mills, "the bloc or movement that most obviously seems to be winning" (1951:353).

As Crozier points out, virtually all of the writers who contributed to the early development of new working-class theory shared an approach to the white-collar strata which, while emphasizing the ambiguity of their situation, assumed that in one way or another this ambiguity would be resolved—either by the lower white-collar strata finally joining the proletariat, or by becoming part of a middle class majority, or by supporting its upper layers in an independent bid for power. But time has not served any of these theorists well, and indeed renewed predictions along similar lines may not work better. To this predicament Crozier poses the question "whether, after all, this ambiguity . . . is not on the contrary destined to persist?" While white-collar workers share many characteristics with blue-collar workers, "it is at the same time a situation which facilitates identification with the world of the ruling classes" (1971:33). This persistent ambiguity is reflected in the ambiguity of the evidence available to us, even today.

In the 1960s, in Western Europe, partly as an outgrowth of the student movement but also in response to the collapse of European social democratic and labor parties as the champions of any significant, far-reaching social change (indeed, as these parties functioned to integrate the working-class movement more and more closely with capitalism), a new wave of new working class theory developed, particularly in France (the parallel in West Germany was the popularity of the Frankfurt School, discussed above in terms of Marcuse).

What is significant in this new working class theory, as contrasted, for example, to the work of Corey or Mills, is that the new working class was no longer a minority or dependent partner of this traditional working class. Rather, it becomes co-equal, or even the main force for change. This also contrasts, of course, with theories arguing that the white-collar strata will become, or are, the main force for stability.

Serge Mallet spells out the radical version of contemporary new-working-class theory. The term, he tells us,

> is given to those who work in automated industry. . . . These are of two types: the new factory utilizes two kinds of workers—(a) those who are . . . the human correctors of the machine's failings; . . . (b) the office technicians, who are separated from production itself. . . . The enormous development of offices has created a veritable intellectual unity of production, in which the conditions of work resemble, more and more, a modern shop in which physical fatigue has disappeared [1963:58].

Mallett is saying, then, that the new working class—or better, the new form of the working class—is closely associated with automation, that modern technology creates a new kind of working class (incorporating all highly skilled workers, regardless of collar color) and that it is precisely their *easy* conditions of work (rather than their hardships, their alienation) that enables them to ask deeper questions as to the structure of capitalism. Mallett's view is congruent with that of Touraine but focuses more sharply on the workplace: The new workers "can realize more quickly than other sectors, the inherent contradictions of the system precisely because their elementary needs are satisfied, this new class is amenable to posing other problems which cannot find their solution in the realm of consumption. . . . Their action will tend to be fundamentally in contest with not only capitalism, but with all technocratic formulas for the direction of the economy" (1963:59).

For Belleville (1963), the concept new working class means not so much that *white-collar* workers constitute a new phenomenon, or even that all tertiaries or all personnel in automated industries are a new class, but rather that the form and nature of the *entire* working class has qualitatively changed. "New" working class, for Belleville, is a historical concept to differentiate it—all of it—from an earlier epoch. This new working class consists of

> all the salaried who, by their intervention, of whatever nature, participate in industrial production. But the notion of industrial production must be taken in its largest sense. It is necessary to include, for example . . . indispensable through auxiliary sectors. Maintenance workers in certain automated

factories . . . transport workers . . . workers and technicians in telecommunications . . . repair-service workers. . . . Distribution [today] is a simple prolongation of production into its last stage [Belleville, 1963:15].

In a more general way, "this extension of the notion of industrial production . . . is opposed to a rigid division between production and services, between secondary and tertiary activities" (p. 17).

Opposed to the new working class are their antagonists, the "collaborators" of the bosses: those who participate in authority, those who are responsible for decisions, even though salaried. What we have, then, is a new, integrated working class, quite different from the older, narrower Marxian view limiting the concept "proletarian" to those who *directly* create surplus value, the industrial production workers.

Ernest Mandel, a Belgian Trotskyist, puts this type of analysis into a more formal Marxian context. His analysis begins where Touraine ends: with the students, whom he considers a new kind of social grouping. With Touraine and others, Mandel considers that "the student revolt represents on a much broader social and historical scale . . . [a] colossal transformation of the productive forces" (1969:49). But students are not an independent grouping: They are to be "white-collar employees of the state or industry, and thus part of the great mass of salaried workers." While students are better able to free themselves from bourgeois social conditioning than some other groups, ultimately they must integrate themselves into a genuine workers' movement (that is, apart from "the ossified and bureaucratized structures of the traditional workers' organizations") (1969:51).

In a 1968 talk, Mandel developed the idea of the new working class, in particular in connection with the "growing crisis of the international money system" and the growing proletarianization, as he saw it, of the white-collar strata in response to that crisis. This would produce, he thought, "reduced wage differentials . . . increased unionization and union militancy . . . rising similarity of monotonous, mechanized, uncreative, nervewracking, stultifying work in factory, bank, public administration, department stores, and airplanes," as well as equalization of the "conditions of reproduction of labor power," in the form of mass education extending to the college level (Mandel, 1968).

These theoretical developments coincided with a new outpouring of research, much of which was in German, the mother-tongue of both theory and empirical work on the new occupations. Jaeggi and Wiedemann (1966) clearly approach new working class theory with their view that salaried employees constitute a single grouping with a common, perceived set of interests. Neuloh (1966) is even more concerned with the effects of automation than previous writers and hypothesizes not only that the boundary between office and factory work is quickly disappearing, but that technological unemployment among white-collar workers is likely to reach catastrophic proportions. Other German writers continue the exploration of the political implications of these new strata begun so long ago by Schmoller, Kautsky, and many others, both empirically (e.g., Lange, 1972) and historically (Kadritzke, 1975; Kocka, 1980). Lange (1972) and Witt (1975) both focus on the development of the upper layers of white-collar life and political and trade union developments among those layers.

In the United States, a structural context similar to the European (involving the rapid growth of the student population, especially in the universities) and an immediate political need combined to draw attention to the theory of the new working class. The political need developed when the "old guard" of Students for a Democratic Society, the authors of its 1962 Port Huron Statement and their followers, graduated from college and made their way into the labor force and confronted the need to develop a rationale for political action. By about 1965 or 1966, a Radical Education Project had developed at the University of Michigan among older SDSers, and a series of conferences on "radicals in the professions" were organized. As the authors of a key document, "With a Little Help From Our Friends," put it: "Once we recognize the unviability of an orthodox career line . . . there are three action alternatives open: we can take establishment jobs and seek other outlets for our human and political needs; we can 'drop out' and work for the movement; or we can try to transform our professional roles from ones supportive of the status quo to ones that use their location to undermine it." In the effort to work at the third alternative, a political strategy or ideology was needed: The European new working class theorists filled that void, even though, it is safe to say, few of them were read in depth (especially in their original languages) by the older SDSers. Subsequently, relatively little of theoretical significance has been contributed to new working class analyses by those Americans at that time concerned with the issue.

A rare exception is Becker (1973-74). He argues that in the white-collar strata a replication of what is happening in the production sector is taking place: The proportion of capital to labor is increasing, thus creating the condition for more intensive exploitation of what labor remains.

> The investment mechanism has promoted an enlarged and unproductive circulatory apparatus which is the main abode of the so-called middle class. This class, however, falls into two distinct segments, each of which is in economic opposition to the other. . . . It is in actuality not a social class per se. It is but a divided fragment of the totality of social labor. . . . Its reality is a cleavage between administrative labor and the managers. . . . The contrast is between, on the one hand, the technicians and professionals . . . and at the other pole, the unproductive labor of the managers and the ruling class as a whole. . . . Administrative labor is not a part of managerial labor with which it is so often confused. . . . It is part of the working class, emerging as a definitive portion of that class within the managerial phase of development [1973-74:275-276].

Contradictory Locations

Lederer, Corey, and Mills all made the point that politically as well as structurally, there are profound divisions within that "group" of occupations labeled "white collar" in the United States and "Angestellte" in Germany. Each of these writers described some form of split between the upper layers, which are closer to management and generally to the bourgeoisie, and the lower, which are closer in both condition and consciousness to the blue-collar working class. Becker, quoted above, continues to develop that thesis. It is Wright (1978) who spells out this approach in its most sophisticated form to date.

His analysis, published in earlier forms in the *Berkeley Journal of Sociology, The Insurgent Sociologist,* and the (British) *New Left Review,* occupies only some 60 pages in a larger work (1978). It takes the form, in large part, of a rebuttal to the approach of the French Marxist Nicos Poulantzas (1975), whose argument was that only a minority of workers at the very bottom of the new occupations perform "productive labor," produce surplus value, and can be considered truly a part of the working class. Therefore, the new white-collar workers by and large are antagonistic to the working class, in that the former's source of income is at the expense of the latter, of the surplus value that they generate. Poulantzas's tradition is that of third force theorists. Yet it is a tradition which correctly points to a problem: If the working class consists of *all* wage earners, then virtually the entire population is working class, an obvious oversimplification which obscures real differences and prevents us from understanding why we have not yet succeeded in achieving socialism by majority vote.

Wright sets himself the task of rebutting Poulantzas's third force approach while at the same time examining the real differences not only within the working class but among those occupational layers just "above" the working class. First, he attacks the assumption that surplus value is generated only in the production of physical commodities. He argues that many positions in the labor force "contain a mix of productive and unproductive activities," so that many others besides blue-collar workers in production have unpaid labor "extracted" by their employers. There are indeed, within the contemporary class system, three main classes: the bourgeoisie, the proletariat, and a much smaller traditionally petty bourgeoisie. But between them there are "three clusters of positions [that] can be characterized as occupying contradictory locations within class relations": *managers, supervisors,* and *small employers* (1978:63). The conceptual handle on these contradictory locations is the degree of control one has over *what* is produced, over *how* things are produced, and over the *legal* possession of the means of production. Those within the social division of labor who have at least some control over some of these relations, without having full control, find themselves in contradictory locations. Wright estimates that at least 40 percent of the U.S. labor force is in such locations, although this is probably an exaggeration. Included here are jobs "involving the execution of state policies and the dissemination of ideology"—that is, much of the state sector.

In sum, if we follow Wright's logic, once we strip away those at the "bottom" of the labor force, and those at the "top," we are left with a residue of contradictory, ambiguous, constantly shifting strata and occupations. This residue, if we may call it that, is segmented in significant ways materially, forming obstacles to ideological and political unity either with other classes *or* within itself as a "third force." Within the public and private sectors there are probably three strata of significance: direct policymakers (management), indirect (second echelon) policymakers (administrators, foremen), and policy executors (technicians, semiprofessionals). The first two of these layers fit into the contradictory position between the bourgeoisie and the proletariat; the last is the group Wright calls semiautonomous employees and fits between the old petty bourgeoisie and the proletariat. It is the largest of the "contradictory" groups—much larger than Wright's estimate of 5-10 percent—and includes vast numbers of service professionals and semiprofessionals who participate at least partially in actual production (directly or indirectly) and who often have blue-collar working-class backgrounds.

Wright's argument, then, leads to the conclusion that the failure of the middle occupations to develop an independent politics and also to align clearly with the bourgeoisie or the proletariat (in those countries where party identifications make this possible, such as England or France, where there are clearly defined labor and/or socialist parties), can be accounted for by their contradictory status. Contradictory objective locations imply contradictory subjective politics. The task of a socialist movement is to develop strategies that will overcome the divisions within the working class and between it and its closest "contradictory" allies, who are, according to this analysis, partially workers anyhow. The increasing rationalization of work, the fiscal crisis, the intensification of exploitation all serve to sharpen the "contradictory" position of many people in the middle occupational layers and to place social change on their agendas. What kind of social change is, as always in a crisis, still an open question.

This analysis makes more theoretical and empirical sense, it seems to me, than any of the others and provides us, in addition, with some approaches to the tactics of social change based on democratic assumptions. Elite theories ultimately fail because the elites of the new occupations— managers, administrators of the state sector, upper-level professionals— are not an independent grouping, but are rather part of the higher bourgeoisie order or, to the degree that they find themselves in a contradictory situation, ultimately too close to the bourgeoisie to break with it. Stabilizing theories fail because a stable center cannot continue to exist, to the degree that it has existed in the past, in a capitalist society of crisis. Third-force or new middle class theories ultimately fail because there is no homogeneous middle which can be identified as a separate class—a critical point on which I differ from other contributors to this volume. Likewise, new working class theory is undermined by the fact that there are real differences between many of the "middle" occupations and the traditional working class, and, again, there are too many fragments within the white-collar occupations to allow them a class unity—middle or working. The "contradictory locations" approach is, at this point in the historical debate concerning the political mission of the new occupations, the one that is most persuasive.

David Eisenhower: Unproductive Labor and Crisis

The changes in the American occupational structure which have occurred over the past 30 to 35 years are commonly explained in terms of a response to the imperatives of technology and reason. Legend has it that as American enterprise pursued its goal of the most efficient mobilization and allocation of skills and resources, it brought forth a "knowledge class," a "new class" of scientists, technicians, and specialists who removed the fetters of technological progress. The arrival of the "post industrial," "postcapitalist" epoch was thereupon proclaimed. Under the guiding influence of the "technostructures" this "new industrial state" emphasized the white-collar jobs in finance, commerce, education, administration, and government required to accommodate an open technological frontier. Engaged in producing and processing information (broadly conceived) rather than traditional industrial commodities, this white-collar work force was rapidly equipped with an array of sophisticated instruments which were viewed as evidence of the genius of the American enterprise system.

Efforts to elevate this legend to the level of scientific theory abound. What this essay develops is the scientific theory of changes in the social division of labor which this legend sought to combat—namely, Marxist theory. Within a Marxist framework the occupational and technological changes which occurred over the past generation are not viewed as monuments to the efficiency and ingenuity of the American enterprise system or the American character. Quite the opposite. They represent a capitalism which has entered its "degenerative phase." Owing to the domestic exhaustion of productive investment outlets, capital was forced into a phase of unproductive accumulation; that is, into the multiplication of economic activities which do not result in the production of surplus value.

From the standpoint developed here, technology is not viewed as an imperative shaping occupational changes. Rather, both the social division of labor and technology are developed and transformed in the context of the historical and dialectical process of capital accumulation. The process itself is governed by "laws of motion," the "most important" (Marx) one for understanding capitalist development being the tendency for the rate of profit to fall. Falling profits signal the end of distinct historical phases through which the capitalist mode of production can pass in the course of its development. In each phase capital accumulation is concentrated in a particular department, so much so that eventually "overaccumulation" takes place, triggering a fall in the rate of profit. By shifting departments accumulation can proceed. In the process the technological effort is redirected to complement a new phase and the social division of labor is reshaped.

Having tumultuously progressed through its productive phases, U.S. capital was forced by the 1950s to emphasize the unproductive consumption of surplus value. This not only resulted in the proliferation of financial, commercial, administrative, and governmental employments, but it also redirected the technological effort toward developing the equipment used by these unproductive workers. In addition, it led to the neglect of domestic productive capitals, their facilities falling into disrepair or becoming obsolete.

The political-economic basis for this unproductive phase was provided by the unrivaled position of U.S. capital following World War II. It was from this dominant position that the international division of labor was reshaped. Unproductive personnel were concentrated in the United States and engaged in activities which transferred surplus value from productive sectors located increasingly overseas.

As long as the United States maintained its hegemony and the international pattern of unequal exchange compensated for the domestic unproductive consumption of surplus value, the degenerative effects of the unproductive phase were camouflaged and/or delayed. But the longer they were delayed, the larger the unproductive sector grew, requiring even greater tribute. Inevitably international political and economic forces emerged to contest the flow to the United States of value necessary to neutralize the regressive effects of the unproductive phase. The result was a secular decline in the rate of profit and chronic inflation. Around 1965 the extended reproduction of the unproductive establishment threw capitalism into crisis. By preempting the surplus which could be utilized productively to increase the rate of surplus value, the unproductive sector not only consumes the basis for its existence but in the process threatens the reproduction of capitalism itself. It denies the value-producing departments—that is, industrial capitals—the sustenance needed for their regeneration. At the same time, however, the dismantling of the unproductive establishment (the current target is "big government") not only has obvious political implications but also has serious consequences. While inflation may be curtailed, unemployment will likely reach permanently high levels. For U.S. capital therefore, the search for compensatory sources of surplus has reached a desperate stage.

The Empiricist Vision of the Middle Class

Social theory rooted in the empiricist tradition offers a most cheerful account of the far-reaching changes in the class structure which have occurred in the United States over the past generation. The implicit aim of empiricist theory as it seeks to explain the development of the "new middle classes" is to reassure the public that the specter of class polarization culminating in a struggle to replace the capitalist mode of production with socialism has its source more in the carbuncular dispositions of Marxists than in any inherent tendencies at work in society. Empiricists view the mechanisms which allocate social labor as neutral, essentially free from contradictions, and governed by reason rather than by tendential forces of historical necessity. Changes in the social division of labor are seen as part of a universal process of "industrialization" (Dahrendorf, 1959), which liberated rationality from the constraints of both superstition and greed, establishing the dominance of reason over economic and social affairs. Capitalism was a quaint nineteenth-century form of industrialism whose main characteristics were said to be the private ownership of the means of production, the principle of profit maximization, and conflict between capitalists and workers (Dahrendorf, 1959:40). By the twentieth century, however, the empiricists claim that "revolutions" in technology, in combination with the concentration and centralization of the means of production, brought an end to capitalism. Industrialism could no longer be managed by entrepreneurial whim and avarice. So under the impulse of "economic rationalism" (Dahrendorf, 1959:68) it broke with capitalism. Private enterprise gave way to professionally managed joint-stock companies. Control of the means of production was separated from ownership. Indeed, the influence of ownership became increasingly "tenuous" (Galbraith, 1967:50); ownership gradually degenerating into a mere "legal fiction" (Bell, 1973:294). The nineteenth-century capitalist, Galbraith (1968:188-189) writes, accomplished "his act of conception at the price of his own extinction." Economic power shifted to "functionaries without capital" (Dahrendorf, 1959:43), to a "technostructure," "an association of men of diverse technical knowledge, experience or other talent which modern industrial technology and planning require" (p. 59). Access to the technostructure is achieved through education; specialized knowledge and information are its stock in trade. As Galbraith sees it, "Effective power of decision is lodged deeply in the technical, planning and other specializing staff" (p. 69). This view is quite popular with the Ivy League professoriate. Daniel Bell, for instance, claims that knowledge replaces private property as the "axial principle" (1973:115) shaping society. Technical skills and information are the "source of power" and "central resource" of an organization (1973:128). Promoting his academic interests, Bell adds that the university as the fount of knowledge has become society's key institution, its so-called axial structure (p. 26).

For empiricists, then, capitalism quietly faded into history as control of the means of production ceased to be a function of ownership. Its grave digger was the "engineer" rather than the working class. In the process class conflict is seen as institutionalized; differences between management and labor became subject to rational negotiation and compromise. The "technostructure" could contain class conflict because presumably it is no longer bound by considerations of profit. Corporate management is free to pursue the goal of social harmony. "Never has the imputation of a profit motive been further from the real motives of men than it is for modern bureaucratic managers" (Dahrendorf, 1959:46). Instead, the technostructure is seen as striving for order, consensus, and predictability (Galbraith, 1968). It seeks a balance between the various interests and constituencies it confronts (e.g., regulators, environmentalists, consumers, employees, stock holders, etc.). It seeks to tame the vagaries of the market through planning. It directs the self-sustaining process of technologically induced economic growth, not only ensuring a steady stream of innovation but guaranteeing it a favorable reception.

The entire social division of labor develops to facilitate the generation and application of technocratic rationality to the problems of fine-tuning socioeconomic progress. The corporation is "subordinated" (Bell, 1973) to the tasks of overall social development. Narrow economic concerns are replaced by concerns "of the communal society" (1973:366). White-collar and service and service workers multiply, filling the bureaucratic positions through which reason is realized and providing the personal, corporate, and social services demanded by an "affluent" society.

Seeking to document their claims, empiricists point to the following phenomena: By the mid-1960s roughly 50 percent of the labor force represented "information workers" engaged in producing technical information, or processing information, or applying information in bureaucratic tasks (Porat, 1977). By 1965 roughly 55 percent of the people employed worked in the "service sector," a response to the rising standard of living of an increasingly middle-class society (Fuchs, 1968). By 1975 white-collar and service workers would account for 62 percent of the labor force (Bell, 1973). Such data, empiricists claim, testify to the triumph of reason, thus confirming their thesis.

Whether this is their true significance is, of course, open to question. "Facts" are not neutral but theory laden: Their significance changes when conceived from another theoretical perspective. "Reason" detached from a historically developing totality makes "sense" for the framework of empiricism, which in general treats social practices as autonomous phenomena. The question is, does it make scientific sense? Does it help us understand social development.

Anomalous circumstances, particularly the recent political and economic crises, compel us to rethink the explanation empiricists give for the rise of the "new middle class." The effort here is guided by a dialectical conception that insists on treating social practices, such as the development and allocation of social labor, as part of a complex totality of contradictory practices (Althusser, 1970a). Each practice is viewed as governed by general laws of motion of a historically unique mode of production (in this instance, capitalism), while simultaneously each is seen as contributing to and conditioning the realization of general historical tendencies.

We turn now to a consideration of the general laws of capitalist development which account for the growth of the "middle classes." Subsequently, the effects of their growth on capitalist development will be analyzed.

Laws of Capitalist Development

Official accounting practices which limit themselves to considerations of "value" measure in prices (e.g., GNP is the total dollar "value" of goods and services) grossly exaggerate the efficiency and productivity of capitalism. By considering every economic activity equally productive economic progress is virtually guaranteed by definition, despite cyclical fluctuations. The Marxist tradition *does not* consider every economic activity productive. Some labor is engaged in unproductive activity from the standpoint of capital as a whole. For Marx (1969:396),

> the distinction of [unproductive labor] from other kinds of labour is . . . of the greatest importance. Since this distinction expresses precisely the specific form of the labour on which the whole capitalist mode of production and capital itself is based.

The distinction between productive and unproductive labor is critical to understanding capitalist development, changes in the social division of labor, and economic crisis.

Marxists also employ a different standard to measure value in keeping with the labor theory of value—namely, units of "simple socially necessary labor time."[2] This does not mean prices are ignored, or that prices necessarily reflect the value, measured in units of labor time, embodied in a commodity. For the sake of theoretical convenience, Marx initially assumed (in *Capital I*) that the "law of value" obtained, that goods and services exchanged for "each other in ratios determined by the value of the labor powers expended within each of them in the course of their production" (Becker, 1977:98). But he dropped this assumption (in *Capital III*) when the discussion shifted to the consideration of the uneven development of capital from sector to sector. In the historical process of capital accumulation, the law of value is suspended and prices deviate from value in a process governed by the "law of unequal exchange." In this context the pricing mechanism reflects and in turn influences the uneven process of capitalist development by assigning prices in excess of value for the more developed sectors and prices below value for the less developed sectors. The significance of this will be developed later.

With a different theory of value and a theory of unproductive economic activity, together with a theory of capital accumulation, Marxism not only accounts for the tendency for the rate of profit to fall, but also envisions a stage of economic "regression" (Becker, 1977:86-89). To appreciate this and its relation to changes in the social division of labor we need to consider these theories more thoroughly.

For Marx,

> *Productive labour,* in its meaning for capitalist production, is wage-labour which exchanged against the variable part of capital (the part of the capital that is spent on wages), reproduces not only this part of the capital (or the value of its own labour-power), but in addition produces surplus-value for the capitalist. It is only thereby that commodity or money is transformed into

capital, is produced as capital. Only that wage labour is productive which produces capital. (This is the same as saying that it reproduces on an enlarged scale the sum of value expended on it, or that it *gives in return more labour than it receives in the form of wages.* Consequently only that labour-owner is productive which reproduces a value greater than its own [1969:152; italics added].

Productive labor creates surplus value (S), the difference between the value of the variable capital which employs it and the value of total commodity production.

The rate of surplus value is the ratio of surplus labor time (surplus value) to remunerated labor time (variable capital), or S/V. Competition and a drive for greater profits force capital to try to increase this ratio. Historically this has been generally accomplished through the development of productivity by means of the technological intensification of labor power, through means which increase what Marx called "relative surplus value."[3] In the process of increasing relative surplus value there is a tendency for progressively more of the surplus value to be reinvested in the instruments of labor and raw materials (constant capital) and less in labor power itself (variable capital). In other words, there is a tendency for the ratio of constant to variable capital (c/v), or what is called the organic composition of capital (OCC), to rise.

Unproductive labor is viewed as labor which does not produce surplus value. "It is labor which is not exchanged with capital, but directly with revenue, that is wages and profits" (Marx, 1969:157). Its reproduction depends on its (or its employer's) ability to secure a share of value produced elsewhere. For example, engineers hired to help build an F15 Eagle are paid out of tax revenues garnished, in the main, from workers' wages. No surplus value is realized from production. No fund to rehire the engineers' labor results. Other workers' wages must be continually garnished if this unproductive form of economic activity is to continue. While McDonnell Douglas makes a "profit," it tends to reduce the profits of capital as a whole.[4] It shares in the profits available to all capitals despite the fact that it did not directly contribute to the profit pool.

For Marxists, unproductive activity is not limited to government spending. It is also employed by commercial capital, banking capital, and administrative capital. In addition, the services provided by the self-employed are treated as unproductive. The category of unproductive labor is not used pejoratively. It has a strict definition. It is labor which does not add to the pool of surplus value from which all capitals, productive and unproductive, draw.

Marxist theory in general is guided by the principles of dialectics, by the law of the unity of opposites. Lenin (1972:359-360) defined this law as the

recognition (discovery) of the contradictory, mutually exclusive opposite tendencies in all phenomena and processes of nature (including mind and society). The condition for the knowledge of all processes of the world in their 'self-movement' . . . is the knowledge of them as a unity of opposites. Development is the 'struggle' of [inherent] opposites.

In keeping with this "recognition," the historical process of capital accumulation is viewed as the progress of the movement of opposites. As the capitalist mode of production develops, the productive utilization of the surplus gradually ceases to play the decisive role. It gives way to a stage where the unproductive consumption of surplus becomes the principal economic force, the productive use of the surplus relegated to secondary importance. The very success of increasing relative surplus value creates the necessity for its increasing unproductive accumulation. Stages of productive accumulation result in a stage of unproductive accumulation, where unproductive capitals shape the forces and relations of production, multiplying the quantity of unproductive labor.

Interestingly, this unproductive stage feeds a number of illusions. Academic economists hail it as an era of the "New Economics," a stage of managed prosperity. Even some Marxists succumbed to the heady days of the 1960s. Baran and Sweezy (1966), for example, claim that the laws Marx discovered regulating capitalist development have been transformed. They erroneously argue that a tendency for the surplus to rise has displaced the tendency for the rate of profit to fall.

Stages in Capitalist Development and the Law of the Tendency for the Rate of Profit to Fall

Stages I and II

In order to avoid falling victim to illusions, it is useful (and necessary) to place the era of unproductive labor in a historical context. As Marx noted:

> On a low level of development of the social productivity of labor, where therefore surplus labor is relatively small, the class of those who live off the labor of others will in principle be small in relation to the number of workers. This class can grow to significant proportions to the degree that productivity i.e. relative surplus value, develops [Nicolaus, 1967:43].

Following a pattern of uneven development, relative surplus value "took off" after the Civil War. Although economic historians dispute some of the details, the general outline of the course of capital accumulation in the United States is more or less established. American capitalism was able to move in the 1880s and 1890s from an essentially small and local manufacturing stage (Stage I), servicing an agrarian economy, into a stage of "big business (Stage II) where the leading department of production was the producers' goods sector. Despite some noticeable exceptions (e.g., Swift, Armour, American Tobacco), "by the beginning of the twentieth century many more companies were making producers' goods, to be used in industry, rather than on the farm or by the ultimate consumer" (Chandler, 1965:279). The forces and relations of production were being shaped by capital to produce the machines and raw materials for industry. Technological innovations were adapted for industrial use. Table 5.1 gives an indication of the preponderance of department I production around the turn of the century.

Labor-displacing mechanization in department I was facilitated by the development of joint-stock companies and an American security's market on Wall Street, institutionalized in response to the enormous capital requirements of the railroads.

With the development of joint-stock companies, corporate ownership began to be separated from control (DeVroey, 1975). This permitted the more rapid mobilization of capital, resulting in greater increases in productivity than would otherwise have occurred under single ownership. Just as Marx (1974:387-388) envisioned, the industrial capitalist was being replaced by managers, by "functionaries" *of* capital.

Wall Street was also instrumental in promoting the centralization of department I, being a force behind the industrial combinations of the 1890s in those industries experiencing an accelerating growth rate (Nelson, 1959). These industrial combinations were quickly consolidated into a single operating unit, giving rise to a growing office staff to coordinate and plan extended operations and a sales staff to vend the increased product.

Accompanying the concentration and centralization of capital was a growing share of labor's surplus product being invested in constant capital (C), in machines and instruments which intensify labor power, relative to investment in labor itself (variable capital, V). Department I was mechanizing itself, resulting in a rising organic composition of capital.

As the OCC moved above the social average, the terms of exchange with other sectors moved in favor of department I. The pricing mechanism assigned prices in excess of value,[5] resulting in the realization of above-average profits. Additional capital accumulation in department I was thus encouraged. This, incidentally, runs contrary to Sweezy's claim that "from the point of view of the capitalist there is obviously no inherent virtue in increasing the organic composition of capital" (1974:45). From the stand-point of *individual* capitalists it is the belief that a rising OCC pays a dividend.

Tendency for the Rate of Profit to Fall

In Marxist methodology a rising OCC (C/V) is related not only to increases in relative surplus value but also to a tendency for the rate of profit to fall.[6] The rate of profit is defined as the mass of surplus realized divided by the constant and variable capitals invested. "It is conceived of as an average or general rate obtaining among a more or less large number of lines of production comprising the economy in its entirety" (Becker, 1977:55). The effect of a rising OCC on profits is perhaps easier to see after a little algebraic substitution:

$$P = \frac{S/V}{C/V-1}$$

TABLE 5.1   The Fifty Largest Industrials*

Consumers' Goods Companies

Agricultural Processing	Extractive	Manufacturing
3. Am. Tobacco	2. Standard Oil	4. Int'l. Harvester
8. Armour & Co.	26. Va.-Carolina Chem.	10. U.S. Rubber
9. American Sugar	35. American Agri. Chem.	12. Singer Mfg. Co.
13. Swift & Co.		
30. Nat'l. Biscuit		
32. Distillers' Securities		
50. United Fruit		

Producers' Goods Companies

Agricultural Processing	Extractive	Manufacturing
6. Central Leather	1. U.S. Steel	7. Pullman
18. Corn Products Co.	5. Amalgamated	15. Gen. Elec.
21. Am. Woolens	(Anaconda) Copper	16. Am. Car & Foundry
	11. Am. Smelting &	19. Am. Can
	Refining	22. Westinghouse
	14. Pittsburgh Coal	24. DuPont
	17. Colo. Fuel & Iron	29. Am. Locomotive
	20. Lackawanna	36. Allis-Chalmers
	23. Consolidation Coal	44. Int. Steam Pump
	25. Republic Steel	46. Western Electric
	27. Int'l. Paper	
	28. Bethlehem Steel	
	31. Cambria Steel	
	33. Associated Oil	
	34. Calumet & Hecla	
	37. Crucible Steel	
	38. Lake Superior Corp.	
	39. U.S. Smelting & Ref.	
	40. United Copper	
	41. National Lead	
	42. Phelps Dodge	
	43. Lehigh Coal	
	45. Jones & Laughlin	
	48. Am. Writing Paper	
	49. Copper Range	

SOURCE: Chandler (1965: 305).
*Numbers indicate relative size according to 1909 assets.

It is clear from this calculation that the rate of profit falls if the OCC increases more rapidly than the rate of surplus value (S/V). The assumption that the OCC tends to advance more rapidly than the rate of surplus value rests on the following theoretical arguments.[7]

(1) The limit to the amount of surplus labor per worker is the length of the workday. The portion of the day which can yield additional surplus labor constantly decreases as productivity increases. To the degree productivity is already developed, the more difficult and expensive it is to increase surplus labor through additional increments of constant capital. Marx explains this as follows:

The smaller the already established fraction of the working day which provides an equivalent for the workers, so much the smaller is the increase in surplus-value which capital can obtain from an increase in productivity. Surplus-value increases, but in ever diminishing proportion to productivity [Mage, 1963:146).

(2) Technical improvements in the means of production which increase the productivity of labor power and reduce the portion of the workday required to produce the equivalent of the workers' wages are "labor saving." Marx writes:

However much the use of machinery may increase the surplus-labour at the expense of necessary labour by heightening the productiveness of labour, it is clear that it attains this result, only by diminishing the number of workmen employed by a given amount of capital. It converts what was formerly variable capital, invested in labour power, into machinery which, being constant capital does not produce surplus value [Yaffee, 1973: 186-187].

As there is an inverse relationship between the rate of surplus value (S/V) and the number of workers, the mass of surplus value (number of workers multiplied by their rate of surplus value) tends to decline.
Marx writes,

It is impossible to squeeze as much surplus value out of 2 as out of 24 labourers. If each of the 24 men gives only one hour of surplus labour in 12, the 24 men give together 24 hours of surplus labour, while 24 hours is the total labour of the two men [Lebowitz, 1976:243].

(3) Fewer and larger centers of capital each producing more are the inevitable results of capital accumulation. This requires the diversion of increasing amounts of value from productive to administrative/ circulatory tasks. Marx writes:

The more developed the scale of production, the greater . . . the commercial operations of the industrial capital, and consequently the labour and other costs of circulation involved in realising value and surplus-value. . . . This necessitates the employment of commercial wage-workers who make up the actual office staff. The outlay for these, although made in the form of wages, differs from the variable capital laid out in purchasing productive labour. It increases the outlay of the industrial capitalist without directly increasing surplus-value. Because it is an outlay for labour employed solely in realising value already created. Like every other outlay of this kind, it reduces the rate of profit. . . . If surplus-value s remains constant, while advanced capital C increases to $C + \Delta C$, then the rate of profit s/C is replaced by the smaller rate of profit $s/C + \Delta C$ [Marx, 1974:299].

(4) Working-class resistance to the pace of mechanized production as well as struggle for greater pay and benefits have the effect of reducing the rate of surplus value.

These factors place inexorable pressure on the general rate of profit. But this is not to imply that capital passively accepts its fate. To the contrary, it constantly schemes to check or counter the tendency for the rate to fall. Marx discusses a few of these countertendencies in *Capital* (Vol. III, Chapter 14). Some arise from the economic process itself, requiring only limited bourgeois intervention. For example, there is a tendency for the value of constant capital to lag behind its physical accumulation as the result of improvement in the productivity of department I. In addition, the pool of surplus value is augmented with the development of new lines of labor-intensive production, employing, at minimal wages, segments of the "relative surplus population" thrown up by a rising OCC. Other counter-tendencies, quite significant from the standpoint of social development, require the active intervention of the bourgeoisie or their agents. *Indeed, the pressure of falling profits should be viewed as a force which directs bourgeois class struggle,* determining the development of the various patterns of social activity. The articulation of technical, scientific, and administrative practices, for instance, took place in the context of "revolutionary changes in higher education" introduced by "men of great wealth" (Hofstadter, 1961:563). The university was transformed into a center for technocratic learning, producing graduates with the scientific, technical, and administrative skills needed to improve capital's control over the workers, develop cheaper designs and materials, engage in research and development for the sake of diversification, and to rationalize the production process (Noble, 1977; Braverman, 1974). In the realm of political practice the thrust of foreign policy has traditionally been interventionist and imperialistic—facilitating and protecting the international projection of capital, which in the second phase of capitalist development tended to be aimed at securing cheap raw materials. The domestic political line, in addition to being directed at securing bourgeois hegemony and organizing capital's ruling bloc, has generally provided public support for private profit, serving in effect to socialize many of the costs of production.

Stage III

Despite these and other countertendencies, falling profits eventually slowed accumulation. The economic prospects of the producers' goods sector began to decline after the depression of 1907, through the war and into the 1920s. Moses Abramovitz (1965:390) observed that this decline "reflect [ed] the increasing maturity of this type of investment expenditure."

If accelerated capital formation was again to occur, a new investment frontier had to be invaded. The wage or consumer goods sector (department II) provided the outlet needed to free the fettered process of accumulation. Launched by the automobile, "a new phase of capitalism in the form of consumer asset formation" (Hession, 1970:616) was consolidated between 1922 and 1929 (phase II). By the 1920s the automobile industry emerged as the largest single manufacturing industry, stimulating the petroleum, steel, machine tools, chemical, and tire industries, among others, and altering living patterns by encouraging the initial period of suburbanization. In addition, electricity was adapted for consumer use as GE, Westinghouse, and RCA diversified into new lines of "consumer durables" for example, radios, refrigerators, and toasters. The radio in particular came to play a significant role in shaping the consumer era. As an instrument of marketing, it, and later TV, added to the ideological power of capital, fashioning a hedonistic consciousness (Ewen, 1977).

By the 1920s there was a marked acceleration in productivity as capital, together with new "capital-saving" techniques ("Fordism"), flowed into the consumer goods sector. The physical volume of the means of production applied to department II increased, as did its OCC.[8]

Accompanying the accumulation of this capital was its centralization, with a new wave of mergers occurring between 1925 and 1929.

Management responded to the inevitable administrative pressures of concentration and centralization by becoming ardent practitioners of bureaucratic rationalization.

Planning was removed from the shop and assigned to the office. The unity of conception and execution was shattered, generating in the process mountains of paperwork.

An army of overseers, engineers, supervisors, clerks, accountants, administrators, and managers was required to initiate and carry out planning, serving in addition to deepen social divisions by enforcing capital's power over workers[9] (Braverman, 1974; Edwards, 1979).

In the early 1920s General Motors put together the prototypical general office charged with coordinating the different divisions and integrating them into overall corporate strategy (Chandler, 1968). A white-collar staff filled the expanding number of positions in purchasing, marketing, production planning, forecasting, accounting, R&D, public relations, and legal sections, meeting regularly to coordinate their efforts and provide the data on which investment decisions were made (either by an executive or finance committee). Monthly, weekly, and daily reports of production, sales, inventories, expenditures, profits provided the uniform data required to appraise performance and make adjustments. By elaborating its bureaucratic techniques, capital was creating places of employment for white-collar personnel. In the process the ratio of administrative to productive wage earners began to rise (Melman, 1951).

By 1929 the consumer stage demonstrated its incapacity to usher in the capitalist millennium. A crisis of overproduction materialized, fettering further accumulation. Official doctrine (Keynesian) described the crisis as the result of underconsumption, of inadequate demand. The problem of effective demand became the focus of political-economic concern; its solution—the multiplication of unproductive consumers—was given a theoretical foundation. What was required, however, was a material foundation. The unproductive administrative/circulatory labor which had grown together with the development of the means of production was decimated in the depression (Corey, 1935). Its permanent expansion required that capital move into a new phase, which emphasized the development of unproductive forces and relations of production (department III). This "solution," we will see, solved the problem of effective demand by sacrificing economic growth, ultimately introducing not the millennium but economic regression (Olsen, 1975). The consequences of this strategy were at first masked by the very conditions which made it possible—the U.S. victory and the destruction of its competitors in World War II. American supremacy provided the basis for the permanent war economy and a fundamental transformation of the internal division of labor. The postwar pattern of unequal exchange between the United States and other social formations, plus the activities of U.S. multinational corporations, provided the fuel for the rise of unproductive capital and boasts of the "American Century."

Stage IV: Unproductive Development and the Middle Classes

World War II was the historic event which marked (and accommodated) the transition from the third to the fourth phase of capitalist development, just as World War I and the Civil War before it ushered in the previous transitions. In the wake of World War II, as in the previous world war, conditions existed which supported successful socialist revolutions, first in Russia, then in China. The threat to international capitalism presumably posed by the USSR and the People's Republic provided the pretext for what Seymour Melman calls a "permanent war economy." Vast quantities of the social surplus were used unproductively to build up a military capacity which employed a growing number of engineers, scientists, and technicians, producing military equipment and material and constructing military installations throughout the world. Equipment and installations, Melman reports, "reached a total money value of $214 billion by 1970, an amount equivalent to 38% of the assets of all U.S. industry" (1974:237).

The military industrial complex employs nearly half of all engineers and scientists and commands more than half of the R&D funds spent in the United States. In this manner innovation and new technology is shaped by the leading department of capital, which in phase IV is unproductive capital.

Total military spending increased from $13 billion in 1950 to $47 billion in 1961, $82 billion in 1972, $100 billion in 1975, and to over $120 billion in 1978. Serving to keep these figures inflated is the fact that military-related industries (ordnance, aircraft, shipbuilding, communications equipment, and electronic components) have exceptionally high "administrative overhead rates." While industry as a whole has a current administration/production ratio of about 33 percent "military industrial complex" (MIC) industries average 70 percent, or seven administrative workers for every 10 production workers (Melman, 1974:36).[10] This high ratio not only means a greater number of places for white-collar workers, it also permits MIC industries to divert more surplus to themselves because of the above-average salaries of administrative/technical personnel.

During phase IV the problems of overall social reproduction fall more heavily on the state. This is reflected in the amount of the national product commanded by the state, as well as in the quantity of unproductive labor directly or indirectly employed by the state. Government employment doubled between 1950 and 1978, from approximately 6 to 12 million. For the same period, government spending as a percentage of GNP increased from 21 to 32 percent.

Paralleling this expansion of an unproductive machinery of state and the capitals dependent on it (e.g., aerospace, shipbuilding, construction, heavy equipment) is a pattern of investment which tended to concentrate unproductive economic activity domestically, assigning an increasing proportion of productive activity throughout the rest of the world. In the process the U.S. labor force was more and more engaged in administrative and circulatory tasks. Office buildings, shopping malls, and credit facilities multiplied. The leading civilian technological innovations (e.g., computers, xerography, communications) of the period were increasingly devoted to servicing the unproductive administrative/circulatory apparatus. It is not an accident that "as far as important new consumption goods are concerned we do seem to be suffering from a profound technological depression" (Renshaw, 1976:34). Technology is adapted to the stage of capitalist development. In its unproductive stage the prevailing technology predictably serves unproductive capital.

It is within the context of this fourth phase that we can begin to make some historical sense of the data cited by empiricists. The growth of "service" or "information" workers is really a rise in the ratio of unproductive to productive workers (U/P). Elsie Olsen (1975:15) has charted this ratio for the period 1900 to 1970 and found that the U/P ratio stood at 7:10 in 1970. My own calculations, more in keeping, I feel, with Marx's method of classifying productive and unproductive labor, result in a U/P ratio of roughly 4:3 for 1970, or 4 unproductive workers to every 3 productive workers. In Table 5.2 workers are classified productive or unproductive on the basis of whether industrial capital or commercial, bank or administrative capitals or revenues set the labor to work, not on the basis of specific occupations.

The economic importance of the rise in the U/P ratio is even more significant when the *total* value absorbed unproductively is taken into consideration. In Stage IV, science and technology are increasingly devoted to developing the machines and technology for unproductive labor. These range from electronic banking to automatic checkout counters, inventory-taking cash registers, computerized accounting and planning processes, sophisticated diagnostic machines, electronic

TABLE 5.2   Workers on Private Nonagricultural Payrolls, 1970 (in thousands)

Employing Industry	Productive	Unproductive
Government	—	12,535
Mining[a]	472	150
Construction[a]	2,400	945
Manufacturing[b]	15,033	4,336
Transportation and Public Utilities[a]	3,908	596
Wholesale/retail trade	2,321.9	12,600.1
1. eating and drinking places	2,321.9	
Finance, insurance, real estate	708.7	2,981.3
1. insurance[d]	708.7	
Services	5,558.0	6,072
1. hotel/motel[c]	626.6	
2. personal	992.3	
3. motion pictures	203.4	
4. misc.: business[e]	1,390.0	
5. medical[f]	654.0	
6. auto repair[g]	281.8	
7. misc. services	638.0	
8. misc. repair	182.0	
9. amusement	419.9	
10. agricultural	170.0	
Total	30,401.5	40,215.4

SOURCE: *Employment and Earnings, United States, 1909-1971.* (Washington, DC: Bureau of Labor Statistics, 1971).

a. From Table 3 Productive workers on nonagricultural payroll, p. XV. Conservative adjustment in construction for government-contracted employment.
b. Calculated on the basis of one unproductive worker for roughly every three productive workers.
c. Nonsupervisory workers.
d. Nonsupervisory workers in fire, accident, and life insurance.
e. Workers in advertising and credit reporting and collection, deducted from total employees in this category.
f. About 15% of hospital workers are employed by private capital (*Business Week*, June 25, 1979). These are deducted from the total because they are employed for their use value.
g. From Table page 657 of source.
h. Workers in nonprofit research agencies deducted.

battlefields, satellites, executive jets, and computerized teaching aids. Therefore, in calculating the social surplus consumed unproductively, consideration must be given not only to the wages and salaries[11] of the unproductive workers themselves but also the growing volume of instruments with which they work. All this technological gadgetry provides the physical basis for a rise in the OCC of unproductive capitals. As they rise above the social average, the pricing mechanism generously rewards them, thus encouraging the accelerated accumulation of unproductive capitals. The vaunted efficiency of the market results, in fact, in the inefficient (from the standpoint of capital as a whole) accumulation of capital. Productivity (relative surplus value) is sacrificed to reproduce a bloated unproductive sector.[12]

Countertendencies

Given a rising OCC, an estimate of the total value consumed unproductively would be a multiple of the 4:3 ratio—8.3 would represent a conservative estimate. Because this unproductive consumption functions socially as constant capital, and was treated as such by Marx, such a large proportion of value consumed unproductively would have a serious effect on the rate of profit $(P = S/V // C/V + 1)$ if it were not compensated for. To postpone its effect, labor-intensive industries were shifted to countries where the industrial wage was 10 to 30 times less than in the United States. Not coincidentally, "most of the[se] low wage industrial enclaves have a politically repressive state apparatus which supports the maintenance of low wages" (Chossudovsky, 1978:67). American corporations operating abroad not only earn high profits there, they export to the United States and other "affluent" markets. One study showed that by 1970, 34 percent of U.S. imports came from U.S. multinationals operating abroad (Barker, 1972:20). As phase IV developed, the tendency of the rate of profit to fall, compounded by the general shift to unproductive consumption, dictated that corporate strategy be conceived and rationalized on an international scale in order to tap the external sources of surplus as fully as possible.[13] Questions such as where to produce component parts, where to assemble the final product, which affiliate and what amount to charge on intracorporate sales and services, where to purchase raw materials, and where to declare profits in order best to take advantage of local tax laws were answered in corporate headquarters. A worldwide plan for market coordination and money management was implemented. In addition, strategic control over the development, licensing, sale, and distribution of R&D was exercised through central corporate planning. A corps of international representatives drummed up business, bribing foreign officials where necessary, in order to secure an external source of surplus value. U.S. foreign policy was fashioned to buttress this new international order. The international operations of multinational corporations resulted in the repatriation of profits and offered the opportunity to transfer the costs and administrative/circulatory activities onto foreign affiliates. Although Bell is dead wrong in almost all of his major theses, he is correct to observe that the United States was increasingly becoming a "rentier" society (Bell, 1973:159).

Another source which defrayed the expense of domestic unproductive consumption was the premium which U.S. exports tended to receive due to a social composition of capital well above the international average and the pattern of unequal exchange which resulted (Becker, 1977: chap. 7, "Unequal Exchange"). For capitalism as a whole, as an *international* mode of production, the result of the uneven accumulation of capitals up and down the "imperialist chain" resulted in the terms of trade favoring social formations high on the imperialist chain and characterized by a high organic composition of capital, disadvantaging social formations low on the imperialist chain, charaterized by a low OCC. The prices paid by "underdeveloped" countries for imports from "developed" countries tend to rise substantially higher than the prices underdeveloped countries generally fetch for their exports. This phenomenon encouraged and supported the technological and administrative development of social formations with a high organic composition of capital, with the result that their OCCs rose even higher, in the process establishing terms of trade even more to their advantage. The "free market" left *unchecked* systematically transferred economic value from poor countries to rich countries, structuring the international division of labor with the following commonly observed characteristics:

High OCC	Low OCC
highly skilled / technological labor	less skilled labor
high wages / salaries	low wages / salaries
exporters of scientific management skills	importers of scientific management skills
exporters of advanced scientific machines, instruments, and weapons	importers of advanced scientific machines, instruments, and weapons
prices above value	*prices below value*

The advantages of a high OCC tend, however, to be neutralized in time. Cartels (such as OPEC) can be arranged to counteract the deleterious effects of "free trade." Where possible, the states of impacted countries intervene politically to protect and support native industry, encouraging its development. Where successful (as in Germany and Japan), the flow of value can actually be reversed—not, of course, without triggering counterresponses (currency depreciation and trade restrictions). Where partially successful, the rate of transfer can be slowed. In many cases, however, social formations low on the imperialist chain become so depleted that they are brought to the brink of bankruptcy, dependent on the credit extended by either private banks or the IMF and other international financial institutions.[14] Because of the severe "austerity" conditions attached to IMF loans in particular, the investment opportunities and import prospects of the recipient countries tend to be reduced. The exception to this is investment which exploits the low wages that are enforced by the draconian measures demanded as a condition for IMF loans. In this situation political instability and repression are heightened, which in turn fuels struggles for change.

Thus the pattern of unequal exchange, which feeds the unproductive development of the forces and relations of production, provokes both political and economic responses, ultimately reducing the external sources

TABLE 5.3   Debt and Gross National Product

	(1) Net Additions to Public and Private Debt – Billions of $ –	(2) Gross National Product	(3) Net Additions as a Percent of Gross National Product (Col. 1 ÷ Col. 2) × 100
1960	38.5	506.0	7.6%
1965	78.1	638.1	11.4
1973	238.0	1,306.6	18.2
1974	209.2	1,412.9	14.8
1975	196.5	1,528.8	12.9
1976	265.3	1,706.5	15.5
1977	378.3	1,889.6	20.0

SOURCE: *Monthly Review* (June 1978: 2).

of the surplus required to counteract the effect of unproductive consumption of surplus on profits. In Mage's words, "imperialism becomes progressively less able to offset a falling tendency of the metropolitan rate of profit" (Mage, 1963:96).

To buy time, production is floated on a sea of debt, preparing the basis for a monetary crisis. The quantity of debt is striking. Total U.S. debt stood at $400 billion in 1946. By 1974 it had reached $2.5 trillion (*Business Week,* 1974). Total debt as a percentage of GNP has also been growing, as Table 5.3 indicates. Consumer debt reached a record of 15.4 percent of disposable income during the first quarter of 1978 (*Business Week,* 1978:16). This expansion of credit, however, eventually creates a barrier to its further expansion, at which point the tendency for the rate of profit to fall begins to exert itself more forcefully.

Crisis

Around 1965 countertendencies to declining profit rates became less effective. External sources of surplus did not increase fast enough to counterbalance falling profits in the United States. Internal unproductive consumption began to place a drag on productive investment. Becker writes: "The entrance . . . of advanced capitalism into its degenerative phase [phase IV] places the rate of unproductive consumption in curious and deadly juxtaposition to the law of the falling rate of profit" (Becker, 1977:87).

The economic stagnation which results with the reduction of external sources of surplus, and the progressive inability of productive capitals to increase their rates of surplus value, given the magnitude of unproductive consumption, triggers "countercyclical" fiscal and monetary policies

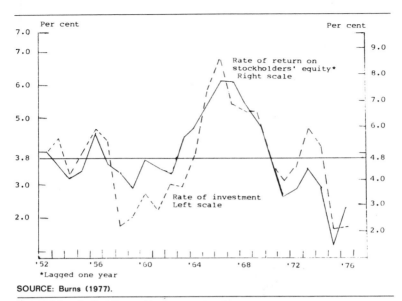

SOURCE: Burns (1977).

Figure 5.1   Profitability and Investment (nonfinancial corporations)

(Mattick, 1969). These result in rising unproductive expenditures and debt, compounding the problem. More precisely, they add the scourge of inflation to the curse of stagnation, financing consumption while tending simultaneously to reduce the general rate of profit and hence the rate of growth. The weakness of capital spending in the 1970s (see Figure 5.1) is a reflection of this tendency (Burns, 1973), just as the dramatic increase in the national corporate and personal debt is its consequence (*Business Week*, 1974). At a certain point a vicious cycle begins to operate. Profits fall. Accumulation declines. The reproduction of the class structure is threatened. Therefore the state pumps up spending, reducing profits and, as a consequence, accumulation, even further. This triggers more unproductive state expenditures, and so on—all within a general context of the development of unproductive forces and relations of production which tend to diminish the rate of profit.

Thus, the rise in the ratio of unproductive to productive labor plunges capitalism into crisis. It erects an obstacle to continued capital accumulation which even the decimation of the places in the social division of labor occupied by unproductive labor cannot remove. Nevertheless, capital is moving to reduce its parasitic progeny: taking aim at social spending by fanning the fires of a taxpayers' revolt; calling for balanced budgets; and crimping credit through high interest rates. These policies, together with a more aggressive interventionist policy overseas (*The*

Nation, June 9, 1979) and an antilabor policy at home, can only be expected to create a charged political situation both domestically and internationally.

Notes

1. The subtle prepositional change from Marx's "functionaries of capital" allows empiricists to conceive economic development outside the context of capitalism.
2. This section is deeply indebted to James Becker, particularly his recent book *Marxian Political Economics: An Outline* (1977).
3. Increases in the length of the work day result in what is called "absolute surplus-value."

HIGH OCC		AVERAGE OCC	LOW OCC
$\dfrac{P1}{V1}$	$\dfrac{P2}{V2}$	$\dfrac{P3}{V3}$	$\dfrac{Pn}{Vn}$
price above value		price = value	price below value

4. This tendency can be momentarily neutralized *if* the rate of surplus value happens to increase. However, the relationship between unproductive spending and increases in the rate of surplus value runs contrary to Keynesian expectations. See Mattick (1969) for a discussion of this issue.
5. For a more detailed explanation of the pricing mechanism, see Becker (1977) and Marx (1974, Vol. III, especially Part 2).

The formation of the general or average rate of profit among the various branches of production is accomplished through the market which transforms value (V) into price (P) in the context of capital accumulation. The price/value relationship tends to depend on where the composition of a particular capital stands relative to the average OCC.

Unable to realize the value of its production, capitals of a low OCC, which swell the pool of surplus value given the large number of productive workers employed, contribute to the increasing profits of capitals of a high OCC. This process has historically been disadvantageous to certain sectors, such as agriculture.

6. Marx called the tendency for the rate of profit to fall "the most important law of modern political economy and the most essential one for understanding the most complicated relationships. It is the most important law from an historical standpoint" (Yaffee, 1973:200).
7. It has also been established empirically by Mage (1963).
8. Specific data on the OCC in department II are not available, but it is safe to assume it rose as part of the general increase in the OCC which occurred between 1919 and 1932. Mage calculated the rise in this period to be from 3.87 in 1919 to 6.58 in 1932 (1963:208).
9. The mode of organization cannot be separated from class domination. The adoption of the practices of bureaucratic rationalization must be viewed as a part of an overall struggle on the part of the bourgeoisie to reproduce its hegemony.
10. Melman correctly views the capital and labor employed in the MIC as "unproductive" and "parasitic." He is wrong, however, to assume that the technical personnel employed in the MIC are drawn "away from civilian industry" (1974:28). Civilian (productive) industry simply could not employ the technical people.
11. Recall that the salaries and perquisites of college-educated labor tend to be above average. And in the case of managers and some professionals (doctors, lawyers), this tendency is exaggerated in the extreme.

12. The debate on the "slowdown" in productivity should be seen in this light rather than as a result of a shift to a service economy as it is commonly explained (Nordhaus, 1972).

13. Nabudere (1978) argues that imperialism is the mechanism capital uses to overcome the tendency of the rate of profit to fall.

14. The debt of the "LDCs" is reported to have doubled between 1973 and 1977 to a total of $170 billion.

Michael Heffren: Ideology and Hegemonic Projects: The Alliance Between Corporate Capital and the New Middle Class in Early Twentieth-Century United States

Ideology is one of those odd problems in Marxist thinking. In a few sentences Marx provided insights into the nature of ideology which still stand as the basis for any serious discussion of the concept. And yet, Marxists have failed to advance this knowledge much beyond the point at which Marx left it. This is unfortunate, not only for science, but for political progress as well. Happily, considerable interest in ideology has been developing in contemporary Marxist circles.

Marxism is unique as a theory of historical development in that it has a dual basis. Marxists have always understood social change as a product of both the economic process (capital accumulation, forces and relations of production) and the class struggle. This creates a definite requirement that research reflect this dual core. The purpose of this chapter is to investigate the relationship between ideology and the class action of the bourgeoisie. Much attention has been given the bourgeoisie, but this has been rather narrowly focused. Mainly, the question has been: Who are the bourgeoisie? Studies have estimated size, social base, composition, and power; there have been many attempts to show how the capitalists rule but few to see how they struggle. Here I focus on one particular form of that struggle: the hegemonic project (a concept developed by Johnson in this volume and elsewhere). The bourgeoisie struggles constantly and in a variety of ways. Class struggle is business as usual for businessmen. But hegemonic projects are unique. They usually represent an intraclass power struggle as well as movement in relation to the struggles of the subordinate classes. The hegemonic project is an exceptional form of struggle in that it is a response to crisis. Often this crisis is the result of a period of transition from one stage or phase of capitalist development to another. In this case the project is the means by which the transition is carried through and realized throughout the social formation. Successful projects are usually led by that fraction of capital most likely to benefit from the transition. However, hegemonic projects can be a response to other types of crises as well. They can be carried out to break a stalemate in the class struggle or to fill a power vacuum. Crises which result from the failure of some significant institutional order, such as the state, can be resolved through a hegemonic project.

In any case, a hegemonic project is always a necessary but desperate measure. It is aimed at a transformation of the state and the subordination of rival projects and the class interests behind them, thus endangering the stability of the society. The project aims at changing the balance of power in society as a whole, and this provides an opening for revolutionary and counterrevolutionary force. Projects imply an alteration of basic social relations which risks social disintegration.

Hegemonic projects involve a reconstitution of "the power bloc," an alliance of classes and class fractions that constitutes the social bases for the exercise of state power (Portantierro, 1974; Leal, 1975). The new alliance aims at transforming the state in order to overcome the crisis and effect a redistribution of power within the bloc and between the major contending social forces. The nature of the hegemonic project is defined by the nature of the crisis and the social composition of the power bloc.

This chapter, then, will view ideology in light of the hegemonic project. To further specify, I shall focus particularly on those projects which involve an alliance between fractions of the bourgeoisie and the new middle class (NMC). The NMC is defined as that class which takes the role of capital in the systems of class exploitation and class domination (Carchedi, 1976, and this volume, Chapter 3). The role of capital, in this sense, is central. Thus, the NMC are those who exercise control in the corporations (managers), in the state apparatuses (bureaucrats), and in the ideological apparatuses (scientists/professionals). The NMC is a contradictory force, in that it neither owns the means of production nor augments surplus value. It derives its independence from its special relation to the apparatuses of domination and control. Since these apparatuses play the role of capital, the NMC has a special relation to the bourgeoisie. However, since the NMC is itself subject to work relations of domination and exploitation, they share a common interest with the proletariat. At the same time, since these apparatuses enjoy a relative autonomy, the middle class has a unique self-interest in maintaining and expanding their position within them. This triple allegiance gives the NMC a rather unstable political posture. For this reason they are an extremely important target of any hegemonic project as well as to any revolutionary movement. Those who ignore the NMC do so at their peril.

Finally, theoretical discussion is structured around a concrete historical analysis. It is hoped that this will ensure some degree of theoretical realism and curb any tendency to extreme abstraction. The situation to be studied is the United States from 1880 to 1920. This period was chosen both because it has received considerable attention from "revisionist" historians and, more important, since its shadow lies across the current situation in the United States. Studying this period will tell us a good deal about our own struggles. The method employed involves developing theory and presenting analysis simultaneously. While this may prove more awkward than first presenting theory, then application, it is hoped this will ensure that theory and analysis form an organic whole, each informing the other.

General Considerations on Ideology

When Marxists speak of ideology, they usually take one of two tacks. One might be described as the philosophical position. Ideology for these writers is alienated consciousness, reified through the externalization and objectification of human labor. People's products stand above them as though independent and dominate them (Lukács, 1971:150-155).

The other approach, which might be called instrumentalist, sees capitalist control over certain institutions as the source of bourgeois ideological hegemony. This position states that ideology "is the way in which one concept of reality is diffused throughout society in all its institutional and private manifestations. This involves propagation of ruling class values through privileged access to institutions censoring heterodox values and setting the parameters of legitimate discussion" (Sallach, 1974:41).

Both these positions are useful but incomplete. The philosophic position abstractly explains what ideology is but fails to explain either the content or the means of transmission. The instrumentalist approach explains how ideology is transmitted without telling us why or what it is. Neither position brings us much further than Marx's famous statement that ruling ideas of a society are the ideas of the ruling class.

Ideology can be defined, from another point of view, as a socially determined, imaginary conception of the relation of subjects to their conditions of existence (adapted from Althusser, 1971:173). Ideology always contains some assumption about the social order and one's relation to it. The term "imaginary conception" refers to the fact that social relations appear as objective reality. They exist independent of one's will and demand that the individual relate to them on their terms. Insofar as the individual is a self-aware, self-creating subject, he/she must make sense of these relations. He/she imagines or mentally creates a relation to them which includes his/her own subjectivity. Obviously, it is not necessary that each individual do this him/herself. Rather, each simply rethinks what has been thought before (Mannheim, 1936:42). Each internalizes ideology.

It is here that we locate the first contradiction in ideology. Ideology is an imagined relation, it is a created connection to objective reality. But reality is constantly in flux, constantly changing, constantly contradicting one's fictional relation to it. When this occurs, the imaginary relation becomes problematic. It loses its "taken for granted" status. In this instance the subject must redefine his/her relation to the conditions of his/her existence. This provides the opportunity to see beyond the imaginary relation to the objective social relations behind it. Further, it allows the subject to "imagine" a critical relation to the conditions of existence. In other words, it becomes possible to escape the given ideology and to embrace a revolutionary one. Ideology, then, implies a dialectical process of mystification being transformed to liberation. By keeping this general character in mind, we avoid a static, hopeless view of ideological domination.

Individuals as subjects take part in all the social relations of a given society. Thus, all social relations are infused with ideology. Each social relation contains within it an imaginary explanation to reconcile the participants to their existence within that relationship. It is clear, then, that all that is social is in some measure ideological. If this is so, then it is possible to speak of ideology as a structural force implicit in all social relations. The ensemble of these relations and practices which reflect this structural force make up the ideological region of the social formation.

The Crisis

Hegemonic projects are always a response to crisis. What brought on the crisis of nineteenth-century America?

Economic

From the end of the Civil War, capitalism developed rapidly but unevenly. Competition was fierce and thousands of new enterprises were wiped out every year. A succession of increasingly severe economic panics hastened the course of the concentration and centralization of capital. By 1904 nearly half the industrial output was the product of one percent of the firms. Capitalism was entering a new stage, the period of monopoly capital. Those who owned and controlled this highly concentrated capital represented a new fraction of the bourgeoisie, corporate/finance capital. It was clear that this type of capital was attaining a dominant position within the American economy.

However, there was a problem for corporate/finance capital at the turn of the century. The American economy was structured as if competitive capitalism was still the order of the day. For the huge monopolistic firms, traditional price-slashing competition was too costly. It led to severe depressions and political instability. For the big corporations it was wiser to fix prices to ensure an adequate profit rate and to compete solely through the sales effort instead of increasing production and lowering prices. Profits were also increasingly better invested in high return overseas ventures than in overproducing for the home market. Gradually, informal mechanisms for price regulations, such as the Gary dinners of the steel industry, were developed by monopoly capital. However, with the economy still designed for competition, there remained the temptation to grab a higher share of the market. Cooperation and good faith were insufficient to eliminate this threat. It was necessary to find some means to regulate competition. In the transition to the new stage of monopoly capitalism/imperialism, that meant the state. State regulation of competition became a necessary feature of the systems (Kolko, 1963).

Political

The American state which was well suited to facilitating primitive accumulation, granting land, and building transportation was not designed to interfere in the free play of the market. To be more precise, the state was structured for nonintervention and to reproduce the social relations of the stage of competitive capitalism.

Clearly, the state structure and functions were inappropriate for the new circumstances; this was a period of transition from one stage of capitalist development to another. The state must intervene effectively in periods of transition if the relations of production are to remain intact (Poulantzas, 1973). If the state is not designed to intervene, then it must be restructured. This was a main reason for a new hegemonic project, spearheaded by the corporate fraction of capital, at turn-of-the-century America. But there were great political difficulties in this period. Extremely important was the intensification of class struggle which accompanied the growth of the working class. Long, bloody strikes polarized the nation; the Socialist Party grew more rapidly than the established parties; and class politics seemed the wave of the future. Immigrant workers brought Marxist and anarchist ideas to the labor movement.

Since the hegemonic project is aimed at transforming the state, it is potentially quite dangerous. Since the state is the guarantor of the existing relations of production, to change the state is to risk an opening to those who would revolutionize these relations. It makes the state, and thus society, vulnerable to the forces of deeper, more comprehensive change. This presents a grave danger to the established order. In a period of intense class struggle, as transitional periods usually are, this danger is increased. The hegemonic project must have a strategy for defusing any potentially revolutionary force as it carries out its necessary transformations.

Another political danger in this period was the farmer. America had been largely a nation of farmers; the frontier held out the possibility of cheap land and an independent existence. But the 1898 census announced the end of the frontier. No longer could a person pull up stakes and start a homestead in the West. The American safety valve was closed, but the majority of the population was still tied to the land.

The age of monopoly capital was not kind to the farmer. Small farmers could not compete with the growing number of larger, capitalized farms. Monopoly pricing of inputs, and marketing controlled by big grain companies depressed the farmers' standard of living. The development of railroads, high freight costs, and market instability enabled the big producer to expand while the local farmer was shut out. These factors, in conjunction with monetary policies and tariff regulations favorable to business, gave rise to an antimonopoly, populist movement which sought to protect the little man. The easy credit and liberal monetary policy demanded by the populists would allow the farmer to keep his head above water. Breaking up the monopolies would protect the independent entrepreneur. Neither populist goal was acceptable to monopoly capital.

Finally, the nature of American politics itself contributed to the crisis. Throughout the 1870s, '80s, and '90s, American government was only as good as money could buy. Pervasive corruption contradicted the needs of monopoly capital. This was a state of capitalist vested interests, not of capital, since it responded far more to the immediate interests of its patrons than to the long-range needs of capital as a whole. This was not an acceptable state of affairs for the class of the future—the corporate/finance fraction of capital. If the state was to push capitalism through the period of transition into a stage in which this now economically dominant fraction would wield an effective hegemony, it had to go against the immediate interests of many individual capitalists, especially of competitive capital and, of course, the numerous petty bourgeoisie. But a government that deviated from laissez-faire principles only when bribed to do so could not accomplish this and threatened the legitimacy of the state as well. It was difficult to see the state as representative of the common good when the legislators were the hired hands of business titans and numerous behind-the-scenes interests. If the state was to intervene effectively it had to be rationalized. In such a corrupt atmosphere this rationalization was politically difficult to bring about.

Ideological

The ideological dimensions of the crisis had their roots in the values of the small town America and the legitimations of competitive capitalism that stood in stark contrast to emerging realities. The problems brought on by urbanization and industrialization seemed incomprehensible to nearly everyone. Pious sentiments about hard work and virtuous living could not make sense of this new and foreign world. The old verities no longer held. Many Americans either looked back in the populist vision to the independent yeoman or forward to the socialist utopia. The problem was to convince the general population to share the monopolists' vision of a new corporate industrial America.

Just as the laissez-faire state was inadequate in the political sphere, so too was Social Darwinism as an ideology. The virtues of competition and the survival of the fittest were the watchwords of this creed. Government regulation, trade unionism, and social welfare seemed crimes against nature. If the cities were cauldrons of despair, it was the fault of the ignorant immigrants. If the factories were dangerous, wages miserable, and hours inhuman, it was the just reward for a shiftless life. If workers had a bit of enterprise, they could start their own businesses. And so went the myths of the time. Under the conditions of competitive capitalism and an open frontier, the hypocrisy of this ideology was perhaps somewhat tolerable. But that time had passed. In the early twentieth century, the new conditions and old ideology seemed blind, cruel, and irrational. More important, the old creeds were dumb enough to be dangerous; they played into the hands of populists and revolutionaries. Dangerous and useless to the rationalized world of the monopolies, this moribund ideology had to be replaced with a modernizing vision.

The Modal Ideology

With a clearer view of this multidimensional crisis of the early twentieth century, I return to theoretical considerations.

This crisis was not really anything unique to the system, it represented business as usual under capitalism. Capitalism develops through crises: Crisis is its recurrent state.

Theoretical tools need to be grounded in an understanding of their connection to the capitalist mode of production (CMP). If we are to understand ideology, it is necessary to conceptualize the point of connection between the mode of production and the deepest layer of the ideological region. This concept is the modal ideology.

Perhaps Marx's greatest achievement was his identification of modes of production. Modes of production are defined by a given level of the forces of production and a particular means by which surplus labor is appropriated and used (Hindness and Hirst, 1975:9-10). Mode of production refers to the common definitive characteristic of a number of very different types of societies (ancient, feudal, capitalist) within the context of a fairly long historical epoch. Marxian science seeks the laws of motion of different modes of production as a means of analyzing the development of concrete social formations. Marxism is unique in postulating that social laws are specific to modes of production. Any attempt to produce theoretical knowledge of social phenomena must first locate their place in the mode of production.

The deepest level of the ideological region, then, must be that level which is linked to the mode of production. For that reason, we speak of modal ideology. Each modal ideology is specific to a mode of production and goes beyond its concrete manifestations. It might be helpful to look at it as a particular type of skeleton or framework. There can be considerable variation as to what covers this frame, but the nature of the beast is fixed. The point to remember is that there is a basic identity between that which defines a given set of social relations and a given ideological region.

What, then, more specifically, are the roots of capitalist ideology? Lichtman (1975) provides an opening when he invites us to consider the following quotation from Marx:

> The specific economic form in which unpaid surplus labor is pumped out of direct producers, determines the relationship between rulers and ruled, as it

grows out of production itself and, in turn, reacts upon it as a determining element. Upon this, however, is founded the entire formation of the economic community which grows out of production relations themselves, thereby simultaneously its specific political form. It is always the direct relationship of the owners of the conditions of production to the direct producers—a relationship always corresponding naturally to a definite stage in the development of the means of labor and thereby its social productivity which reveals the innermost secret, the hidden basis of the entire social structure, and with it, the political form of the relation of sovreignty and dependence, in short, the corresponding form of the state [1975:55].

For Lichtman it follows that as the state is determined, so is ideology. Both are part of the entire social structure. In its modal aspect, ideology involves the conceptualized relationship of dominance and subordination. Ideology develops as an intrinsic aspect of the production of surplus value. Lichtman states that if it is always the "relationship between exploiter and exploited that determines the . . . hidden basis of the social structure and if falsification is an inseparable aspect of this exploitative relationship, then . . . the concrete form of ideology embedded in the extraction of surplus value will permeate and determine the nature of consciousness in the entire social structure" (1975:57). Bourgeois hegemony does not stem merely from their control over the media and institutions; rather, it is part of exploitative relations and becomes generalized in other institutions. This occurs because of commodity fetishism. Under capitalist relations individuals are formally independent, free to sell labor power or to buy it. Of course, some must sell and others can buy. But the exploitative nature of the purchase of labor power is hidden in ideological mystification. The fact that this is a social relationship recedes into the background. What is apparent are relations between things. Capital yields profit; labor brings wages. The relations of domination and exploitation are submerged. This fetishism establishes the requirement of mystification in other institutions. Thing-like relations prevail in all aspects of society. It could not be otherwise without laying bare economic exploitation and the relations of class domination that surrounds it. The labor relation is the paradigm for all other social relations, whether in the family, the school, or the state (Lichtman, 1975:64).

We see, then, that the modal ideology is not merely certain ideas. Rather, it becomes an aspect of the way in which people relate to each other. It lends a particular structure to practice. Viewed dialectically, it defines the same social relation of which it is a product. At the same time, it is a particular structure of thought.

The modal ideology is composed of two elements: cognitive style and conceptual field. Cognitive style refers to a characteristic way of thinking, acquired socially (Berger and Luckman, 1967). The cognitive style of the capitalist modal ideology reflects fetishism in thought. It is atomistic, mechanistic, and measurable. Reality is seen as made up of components: self-contained units which can be manipulated, brought into relation, or replaced. Components relate in given sequences which are rational and predictable. Thinking takes an implicit abstraction. Social relations are seen as anonymous, and people are defined in terms of their functions. One's own self becomes compartmentalized into home self, work self, leisure self. Eventually one begins a process of self-anonymization where being disappears into functions (Berger et al., 1973: 20-31).

The conceptual field is that universe of unexpressed elements wrapped up in the relations of productions. In other words, it is those key ideas tied up in the sale of labor power. Those elements and their origins include the following:

Individualism—this stems from the mode of appropriating surplus and the way in which labor is sold and wages are distributed.

Dominance/subordination—these relations stem from control of the capitalist over the labor process.

Formal freedom—an effect of the absence of formal constraints on the worker and the freedom of the capitalist to do whatever he/she likes with profits.

Formal equality—the result of the elimination of modes of relation other than the cash nexus.

Acquisitiveness—a result of accumulation process.

Competitiveness—a result of struggle for profit.

Separation of thought and action—a result of the division of those who direct production and those who execute it.

Reification—an effect of fetishism.

As well as being characterized by a cognitive style and conceptual field, modal ideology serves two functions: It limits and selects. The limiting function denies the rationality of ideas critical or inimical to capitalism. Commodity fetishism creates a mental world in which capitalist relations seem natural and inevitable. This makes anticapitalist ideas seem questionable or opposed to common sense and restricts the conceptual universe to ideas that are sensible and realistic within the limits of the existing order. The other function of the modal ideology, that of selection, ensures that, of the millions of ideas produced, only a certain number are widely embraced—those that have a good fit with the modal ideology. These ideas become the means by which the modal ideology is brought into consciousness. In this way the modal ideology can be expressed and used to relate people to their conditions of existence.

But this is only one aspect of the ideological region, the deep structure which reflects the fetishistic character of capitalist social relations. Yet, since Marx, we have known that the CMP is inherently contradictory. If this is so, then the modal ideology must necessarily embody contradiction. The modal ideology and consequently the entire ideological region are contradictory, and a number of interesting conclusions can be drawn from this fact.

The modal ideology, like the relations of production, is experienced differently by different classes. The same special rewards which tie the capitalist to his position in the relations of production, encourage his commitment to the modal ideology. It all seems so right, so natural to the capitalist. And of course, it pays. The contradictoriness of the modal ideology is more apparent to the worker because so often it hurts rather than pays. Even more important, when it is working best it hurts most and pays least. Also, the worker is closer to the mystification. After all, the worker is the one being exploited.

The contradictions of the modal ideology go beyond this class difference. I have spoken of the elements of the modal ideology: cognitive style and conceptual field. The cognitive style of capitalism is contradictory, in that it is at one and the same time hyperrational and irrational. This cognitive style can be characterized as instrumental rationality, a calculating type of thought which seeks efficient means to predetermined ends. This would be fine if the ends of capitalism were not always so irrational and contradictory. The ends of pursuing profit and maintaining the given set of social relations necessarily come into contradiction. The danger is that the instrumental thinker will be forced to question and eventually reject ends which so often confound rational calculation and adopt rational ends. Moreover, the conceptual field contains elements which reflect different aspects of the relations of production. These aspects can and often do contradict one another: Formal freedom contradicts dominance relations; individualism is contradicted by the increasingly social nature of production; material ends, even individual acquisitiveness, can often be best served by collective, noncompetitive means.

The functions of the modal ideology are contradictory as well. If the modal ideology limits what is seen as reasonable, it can do so only when reality itself remains reasonable. In situations where food rots while thousands starve, the limiting capacity of the modal ideology is neutralized. The selecting function has definite limits as well. Ideas selected in periods of general stability seem inappropriate in times of crisis. As the mode of production develops and changes, ideas promoted in earlier periods are delegitimated. Selected ideas reflect different aspects of the modal ideology and can contradict each other. Clearly, the modal ideology is not as solid as may seem in periods of economic and political stability.

Modal Ideology and the Hegemonic Project

The relation between a hegemonic project and the modal ideology is also a contradictory one. Consideration of that project known as "Corporate Liberalism" (Weinstein, 1968), which was carried out in the United States at the turn of the century, bears this out. As noted previously, a transitional crisis situation prevailed, precipitated by the development of the monopoly stage of capitalism. This created the need for a general social transformation. Changes in the economy, in the state, and in ideology were necessary. How could these be carried out?

Consider the class forces active in that situation. First, of course, we have the bourgeoisie. But this class was divided into two significant fractions—competitive and corporate/finance capital. Competitive capital was threatened by the development of monopoly and even more threatened by the regulation demanded by the monopoly and even more threatened by the regulation demanded by the monopolists. Competitive capital was in a strange position. It had lost its economic dominance; but it was still the most powerful fraction politically. Its ideology held sway. If the project was to succeed, these remaining prop bases had to be usurped.

Corporate/finance capital was the spearhead of the hegemonic project; it dominated the economy. However, existing social arrangements acted against its expansion. Before any changes could occur, it was necessary to redistribute power. Monopoly capital sought to establish its hegemony by forming new class alliances, forging a new "power bloc," fostering new ideologies, and restructuring the state.

In order to achieve these aims, the project was particularly directed toward forming a new social basis for the exercise of state power and toward creating an interventionist state which would complete several tasks. First, the state had to begin to regulate competition to ensure a stable economy. Second, it had to neutralize class conflict and rechannel the protests against monopoly. Third, the state needed to be employed to solve some of the social problems which threatened social stability. Finally, in the age of imperialism the state had to advance the international ventures of American capital, as versus European capital.

Other class forces active in this conjecture had either to be brought around and allied with or politically subordinated. Farmers and other petty bourgeois forces were allied with competitive capital in opposition to monopoly. The working class was divided between militant anticaptalist elements and sectors more inclined to accommodation, as monopoly capital seemed to offer a better bargain than low-wage competitive business. However, this could only be a brief marriage of convenience with manageable unions, as neither class could really trust the other.

The most important class in this conjuncture was a newly formed one: the new middle class. Its development had accompanied the rise of monopoly capital, industrialism, and a steady increment of state activity. The concentration of capital had created a great mass of surplus which required handling and utilization. This created a need for various managers, accountants, lawyers, and economists to tend to the realization and reinvestment of these great profits. Scientists and technicians were necessary to open up new avenues of accumulation and create better production techniques. As competition shifted to the sales effort, new positions in sales and advertising were created.

The new needs of the corporation were accompanied by corresponding needs in the society. The most obvious of these was the need for educators to provide trained personnel. This meant that new high schools, colleges, and graduate and professional schools were opened. With more schools, more people were literate. Newspapers, magazines, and book publishing became going concerns with large staffs of writers, editors, and other functionaries. Growing city populations created the need for doctors, nurses, social workers, architects, planners, and various other professionals (see Chapter 7, this volume).

The people to fill these positions came from the ranks of the bankrupt entrepreneurs, younger children of capitalists and farmers, sons of native white workers; all those who might have once tried their luck on the frontier now joined the middle class. The middle class became the new frontier.

This class made a good potential ally for monopoly capital. Its members shared a common rise to prominence, rested on similar social bases, and their future paths seemed to run together. In the new world of monopoly capital the middle class could anticipate security and expansion. From the point of view of the corporate fraction, the nature of middle-class work, thinking, and pretensions made them a very desirable ally.

Perhaps the most attractive characteristic of the NMC grew out of its close connection to the means of ideological production. The NMC in a real sense lived by ideology, and this made its members valuable allies in a struggle which would require considerable transformation in the sphere of ideas.

This has brought us back to the central problem: ideology. However, before exploring the relation of the modal ideology to the hegemonic project, it will be well to delineate the ideological tasks to be carried out through the project. Popular thinking about public issues had to be altered. The new ideology in the making had to justify monopoly as a natural and necessary development of the economy; social intervention was to be rationalized as human and useful and unbridled competition and laissez-faire portrayed as irresponsible and anarchic; political conflict should be seen as amenable to collaboration and compromise; the general interest, it must be explained, is best served through rational, nonpartisan management; the country had a "manifest destiny" as a great power with global responsibilities.

While all of these requirements could be fulfilled without transcending capitalist relations, hegemonic projects are, by their nature, dangerous. Beyond the fact that, by aiming at transforming the state and redistributing power, they leave an opening for revolutionary forces, hegemonic projects have ideological dangers as well. I have explained that ideology relates people to their conditions of existence. It makes comprehensible to them why they live as they do. A new hegemonic project changes that explanation. It provides a new relation to the conditions of existence. People must be convinced to give up their old way of thinking. But what is to prevent them from going too far in their rejection of outmoded ideas? Why should they not reject the basic social relation with which their old ideology was associated? In a sense, an ideological vacuum is created which may be filled by ideas which are completely opposed to the purposes of the project.

A related danger lies in the fact that in discrediting the old ideology, its commonsense character is destroyed. Much of the resilience of an ideology comes from the fact that it has always been around. It is taken for granted. A new ideology is subject to scrutiny and discussion and cannot claim the hallowed privileges of tradition or common sense. It is much more likely to be perceived as merely a vulgar ideology. It is easy to attack and hard to accept. Choice is required, and choice allows the possibility of rejection.

Finally, the new ideology itself may have contradictions lurking within it that will bring it into conflict with the basic social relations. The populist ideologies of the period with their mix of old and new visions had this problem. The project of the corporate fraction had to pay a great deal of attention to avoid discrediting of the modal ideology in the process of ideological replacement.

But the modal ideology of nineteenth-century capitalism in many ways helped to circumvent the ideological dangers of the project. For instance, the limiting function of the modal ideology to a large extent prevented the formation of a new ideology which contradicted capitalist social relations. Ideologies like anarchism seemed alien and populism a bit anachronistic. The selecting function worked here, too, to make acceptable many of the ideas of the "progressivism" of the era, which seemed to embody a good deal of common sense.

Concretely, monopoly capital had to be aware of the dangers implicit in their project. In attacking the Social Darwinist ideology they were cutting close to the bone of the modal ideology. The old ideology represented the idealization of the competitive capitalist. It had popular appeal because it implied that everyone was at least potentially an entrepreneur: Social mobility was the reward and result of individual initiative whether one set up shop, farm, or factory. To attack this ideology came very close to attacking capitalism itself.

But in crisis lies both danger and opportunity. If the old ideology idealized the entrepreneur, it did so very obviously. It was, plainly, a class ideology. As long as this class remained relatively open, this ideology was inoffensive. However, the precise factor which identified the stage of monopoly capital was that the club was closed. The thriftiest worker imaginable could not save up and buy a railroad or steel mill; artisans had to close shop; small businesses failed. The frontier was closed. The old ideology had already begun to acquire that hypocritical self-satisfied tone that one associates with Chamber of Commerce luncheons. Rather than an all-embracing world view, the old ideology began to seem more and more apologetic for a bygone era.

The opening was there for a new, more universal set of ideas. But how could such an exclusive group as monopoly capital provide one? Obviously, by themselves they could not. But at least one actor on the social stage could: the new middle class. I have already pointed out the structural affinity between the corporate fraction and the NMC, but their relations went further than this. They had a similar way of thinking, one which was congruent with the cognitive style of the modal ideology.

The NMC was unique in one very important characteristic: They were highly educated. This had tremendous significance for their world view. They had boundless faith in science and rationality. Even further, they saw no hindrance to applying these powerful tools to every aspect of life. They saw education itself as the solution to many, if not all, of the problems confronting the society. Education would cure disease, crime, unemployment, and overpopulation. If only people were educated the cities could be renovated, corruption eliminated, and social harmony would prevail. Closely related to this was a great fascination with expertise. Those with special knowledge were best suited to deal with problems. This approach is a specialized, piecemeal one which avoids broad speculative visions in favor of very limited but detailed views.

These characteristics meshed very well with the monopolistic need for rationalization and intervention. Here was a way out of the dilemma of how to develop a new ideology with universal appeal without violating the conceptual field. Where the entrepreneurs idealized themselves, the monopolists would idealize the middle class.

How would this affect the modal ideology? At first glance it would seem that the middle-class world view fit quite well with the modal ideology. Certainly the middle class reflected the cognitive style of capitalism in their thought even better than the competitive bourgeoisie. There was something a bit too romantic about the entrepreneurial figure which reflected the market more than the factory. Middle-class thinking reflected the severe rationality of the modern production process.

There was a contradiction here, however, which would not become apparent for some time. Viewed in parts, capitalism is the most rational of systems; viewed as a whole, the most irrational. The capitalist class reflects this contradiction in their thinking. They were acquisitive ascetics who used the most rational means in a frantically irrational pursuit of profit, even when that pursuit would ruin them. The NMC did not encompass all these contradictions. If they were acquisitive it was in pursuit of the good life. They had no desire to throw their wealth back to gain new profits; better that they should enjoy it themselves. Certainly their rationality was narrow, but quite often it was genuine and could not be discarded easily. Really, the NMC stressed only one side of the modal ideology. This was sufficient for a period in which capital was growing. In another time it might be a problem.

Ideological Apparatuses

I have stressed that the form of modal ideology grows out of the basic social relations and thus out of particular social practices. The content of ideology is the product of social practices as well and is expressed through particular mediating institutions known as ideological apparatuses (IAs).

The origin of this concept is Louis Althusser's (1971) idea of the ideological state apparatus. Althusser's identification of these apparatuses with the state seems unwise in that the state becomes so broadly defined as to mean nothing. As Anderson (1977:34) points out, this concept is based on a misreading of Gramsci. However, this conception does have the virtue of reminding us that ideology ultimately stands on power. To forget that is to forget everything.

Ideological apparatuses are the means by which the modal ideology is realized and brought into everyday life. Specifically, they are those institutions that work by and with ideology. They are those institutions which create a relation between people and their conditions of existence. We have already suggested that all societal institutions are marked by the modal ideology. The reasons for this are these: (1) Since the relations of production are primary, other social relations take a complementary form, and (2) since mystification is a requirement of the relations of production, it is introduced into other social relations and concretized in institutions. For those institutions which function mainly by ideas to diffuse ideology this is doubly true, since the modal ideology structures those ideas. Major IAs include the family, schools, churches, the military, political parties, and trade unions. By participating in these institutions, people participate in the modal ideology.

Institutional apparatuses can be considered in three lights. The first is that of function. The primary function of the IAs is to make provision for the reproduction of classes equipped with the proper skills and attitudes to ensure the expanded reproduction of capitalism. By participating in the IAs, people acquire these things and are exposed to the modal ideology. Also, the IAs ensure that even those outside the production process participate in the modal ideology. This is not as smooth a process as it may seem. Insofar as the IAs embody the contradictory modal ideology, they are themselves contradictory. Different apparatuses stress different aspects of the modal ideology. Sometimes they are self-contradictory; often they contradict each other. For example, "bread and butter" trade unions transmit the modal ideology by stressing acquisitiveness, but at the same time they promote cooperative modes of struggle; rational thinking learned in schools is contradicted by the dominance relations of the classroom.

Second, we must view the IAs in light of the class struggle. The IAs constitute a fertile field of class struggles, as so much of the antagonism of classes is expressed vividly in the institutions of everyday life. For the bourgeoisie, the object of struggle is to keep the IAs in line with the modal ideology and responsive to the expansion of capital by complementing the accumulation process. If they fail to keep pace or contradict the needs of capital, the bourgeoisie struggles to bring them into line. The IAs are not simply instruments of capital, since they have a history and dynamic of their own, but capital constantly struggles to make them so.

The IAs are the targets of working-class struggle as well. The working class attempts to make the IAs the vehicle by which to improve their conditions of life. This is the impetus of grass-roots reform movements and fights for institutions responsive to community needs. The third active force in this field of struggle are the functionaries of the IAs, the new middle class. Their struggle is for self-maintenance and expansion as well as for the realization of their professional ethos. This is expressed in funding battles and struggles for greater institutional autonomy and growth. These prerogatives place the IA functionaries in an intermediate position in the class struggle. They come into conflict with the bourgeoisie when the IA expansion and operation hamper capital accumulation or seem to diverge from their defined missions. The working class comes to oppose them when their mode of operation is seen as reinforcing existing class relations.

Finally, we must view the IAs as historical entities with unique historical origins and development, which often brings them into conflict with capitalist social relations. (The Catholic Church in Italy is a good example of this). Even those IAs which are unique to capitalism develop an internal logic of development which can make them antagonistic to capitalist relations. This may occur on the level of institutional developments, such as the growth of unwieldy bureaucracies with entrenched special interests. Or it may take the form of an ideological development, such as the existence of an egalitarian or critical spirit in higher education. In any case, it is impossible for the ruling class of any social formation to dictate the form of institutional development in the long run.

The IAs do not usually create and transmit ideas; rather, their ideology is contained in the practices of the institution: (1) in the actions of the functionaries toward the participants (e.g., teachers' treatment of students) and (2) in the nature of participation. By acting a particular way continually one begins to create ideas which correspond to this action. Also, the explanation for one's actions bears this out (e.g., the student who constantly competes for grades, honor, and prestige soon gets the idea that competition is human nature). But if the message of the IAs is contradictory, or it is possible to participate in alternative practices, then other conclusions are likely.

Although the IAs present a fairly standard message to the whole population, their effects on the classes are differential. In other words, different classes experience the IAs differently. This effect occurs for three reasons: (1) different classes participate in different IAs (different churches, social activities, cultural experiences); (2) the IAs are internally stratified to accommodate each class (e.g., high school tracking systems); and (3) the milieu of the IA is more congenial to one class than another, so that one class succeeds in the IA while another class receives discriminatory treatment (e.g., the academic environment seems more natural to the middle-class student).

Ideological Apparatuses and the Hegemonic Project

Returning now to the corporate capital/NMC alliance of the early twentieth century, two things are clear: The IAs were a necessary target of the hegemonic project and the NMC occupied the strategic positions in the IAs. If for no other reason, it was necessary that monopoly capital bring the NMC into the alliance in order to transform the IAs. Note should be taken of the word "transform." To discredit, attack, or eliminate the IAs would be too dangerous to the reproduction of capitalist relations. This made the NMC doubly valuable. From their position within the IAs they could carry out a quiet revolution in the ideological region.

In making an alliance with NMC, corporate capital appealed to the special interests of this new class. Social intervention was cast in terms of expertise; regulation was described as rational management; the movement was draped in the cloak of science. Progressivism was the name of the movement which cemented this alliance, a name which exuded the naive self-confidence of the middle class.

But the bargain went beyond merely couching corporate capital's ends in terms congenial to the NMC. It was necessary to provide some concrete payoff to enlist NMC cooperation. First, it was made clear that a social order dominated by corporate industrialism would allow those middle-class occupations which had already grown to expand astronomically. The IAs would be given a middle-class character and would serve as the center of middle-class life. The expanding state would be a middle-class preserve of technocratic talent. This would allow the class to expand with no forseeable limits. Education would be the new means of upward mobility. The social transformation necessary would be carried out by middle-class people using middle-class means. Only the end result would accrue to monopoly capital.

The necessary transformations first involved the IAs. For many apparatuses little change was necessary. Graduate and professional schools, scientific institutes, magazines, and welfare organizations were new and already characterized by their middle-class character. Once their functionaries were committed, little manipulation was necessary to bring them in line with the needs of the project. Some other apparatuses had been caught up in what has been called the "status revolution" brought on by the ideological crisis (Hofstadter, 1955).

A certain devaluation affected many of the older IAs, such as newspapers and traditional colleges. In losing prestige, these institutions were forced to reevaluate their basic premises. As a result, they were far more amenable to change than they would otherwise have been. Since they were not all that dissimilar in structure to the newer IAs, it was easier to redirect themselves in conjunction with the general line of the project.

However, it was still necessary to transform the IAs to some extent. Perhaps the most significant move toward this end was the movement toward professionalization (Bledstein, 1976). This was the NMC's method of self-transformation. Jobs in the IAs were defined as professional or technical with certain educational prerequisites and achievement requirements. NMC professionals formed groups which controlled accreditation. By making education the primary basis of participation in the IAs, it was assured, given the new methods and content of education, that the ideas of expertise, science, and social intervention would become the message of the institutions. These ideas had a basic affinity with the project's goal of an interventionist state. Thus the IAs were brought into line with the needs of the interests in question. To further cement the relationship, bureaucratic organization was transported from the corporation to the IAs. The IAs now shared organizational structure with both the firm and the proposed interventionist state. This added to the acceptability of the project's aims. In form as well as content, the IAs were linked to the project and thus secured.

Once the IAs were brought into the project, they began to work for its fulfillment. In newspapers and magazines like *McClures* the attack on the old order began. This was the age of the muckrakers and the politics of exposé. Novels detailed the effects of unprincipled competition (*The Financier*), irresponsible business practices (*The Octopus, the Pit*), and the horrors of urban life (*Sister Carrie*).

In the schools, the doctrines of progressive education made NMC thinking seem most natural and democratic. Reform movements began in the political parties. Colleges abandoned the old liberal curriculum for the elective plan. Pragmatism became the philosophical basis for much of public life. In concert, this assault discredited the old ideology and paved the way for acceptance of a new one, a hegemonic ideology—the main features of which constitute the ideological means of domination in the United States to this day.

Hegemonic Ideology

In discussing the modal ideology and IAs the structural components of the ideological region were established. Now the focus shifts to that part of the region more definitely identified with class struggle.

Hegemonic ideologies exist in two senses. In the first, they represent the ideological position of the power bloc struggling to implement its project. The second sense of the term is roughly the equivalent of dominant ideology. This refers to a successful project which has established its ideology as the most important ideology of the social formation. This dominant ideology structures the ensemble of ideologies in a social formation. For the sake of clarity I use "dominant ideology" to refer to this second sense.

Hegemonic ideologies are, first of all, general. They relate the individual to the totality of social relations in that formation. These ideologies are designed to explain, direct, and justify the arrangement of social relations demanded by the project. The hegemonic ideology functions to cement the alliance of the power bloc, to give it an ideological unity, and to represent the aims and interests of the project, both to its participants and to the rest of the population. Usually the hegemonic ideology takes the form of a guiding principle which subsumes a number of particular ideologies.

Just as the IAs have their functionaries, the hegemonic ideology has its complementary social group: the organic intellectuals. Organic intellectuals are those individuals, either members of a class or attached to it, who fashion ideology and represent its action to itself and to the other classes of the society (Gramsci, 1971). Organic intellectuals play a special part in the hegemonic project: They must create and see to the implementation of the hegemonic ideology. Also, organic intellectuals direct the struggle against alternative ideologies. Once the project is successful, organic intellectuals have the responsibility to develop, propagate, and defend the dominant ideology. Part of this task includes overseeing the new arrangement of particular ideologies as determined by the new dominant ideology and introducing that ideology to the IAs. Organic intellectuals belong to one of three groups: the dominant fraction of the power bloc, a completely subservient fraction, or a more autonomous class or class fraction.

Some of the contradictions of the hegemonic ideology spring from the origins of its propagators. Membership in the dominant fraction can compromise the universality of the hegemonic ideology (The pronouncements of "robber barons" were viewed with suspicion.) An organic intellectual's attachment to a different group creates the possibility of a split with the dominant fraction. Other contradictions also exist; most important, this is a capitalist ideology and is thus beset with the contradictions of the modal ideology. Because the hegemonc ideology aims at a social transformation, it may go too far and endanger capitalist relations. Also, insofar as it must unify divergent class factions, it may slight some fraction and cause the alliance to fragment. In that the hegemonic ideology is one of struggle, it may mobilize and unite those classes outside the alliance in opposition to it. Finally, because the hegemonic ideology is a response to crisis, it may be discredited by a rapidly changing conjuncture.

One final point must be stressed. All struggles of the bourgeoisie do not take the form of hegemonic projects. A hegemonic project is an exceptional form of struggle defined by its nature as a response to crisis and by its object, state power. The hegemonic project always aims to transform the state through the redistribution of state power and its restructuring. In this way the hegemonic project can be distinguished from other forms of bourgeois struggle, just as the revolutionary movement is distinguished from trade union struggles, by its object, state power (Poulantzas, 1968:42-49). This creates the most dangerous contradiction of the hegemonic project. The state is the central mechanism for the maintenance of capitalist social relations. In aiming their struggle at the state, the power bloc risks creating a crisis of the state which would make capitalist relations vulnerable to revolutionary forces. It is this, more than any other factor, which makes the hegemonic project such an exceptional form of struggle.

The Hegemonic Ideology of Corporate Liberalism

The hegemonic ideology advanced by corporate/finance capital has been called "corporate liberalism." It asserts the necessity for state regulation of competition and for state intervention to solve social problems; the scientific method, or at least applied rationality, are the accepted means of governing; politics should be replaced by management; class harmony can be established through responsible trade unionism; knowledge is power. Problems should be approached piecemeal, dealt with by experts, and tinkered with like an engineering problem; education is the means to social mobility. This is a kind of technocratic utopia where conflict is eliminated and every aspect of life is rationally managed and controlled.

This hegemonic ideology was fairly unique to American capitalism of the early twentieth century but quickly spread to Europe and is today the dominant ideology of Western capitalism. Since then it has continued to represent the self-glorification of the middle class. It is attractive in its Promethean self-confidence. It is frightening in its totalitarian presumption. But at base it is hollow. All that rationality, all that science, all that management is for profit over social ends. Monopoly capital pursues profit after its own fashion. But now it does so more efficiently.

Corporate liberalism was successful because it held out the promise that, as a Boston paper put it in 1904, "Everyone in America is middle class" (Goldman, 1955:56). For the first time a class as a whole formed what might also be called a collective organic intellectual. As the middle class celebrated itself, it swept all before it. No reform movement has ever been so overwhelmingly middle class (Hofstadter, 1955:148).

There are a number of important points here. By allowing the NMC to carry out the ideological struggle, the corporate fraction had gotten its way without ever having to appear directly in the matter. The new relations of power were effectively disguised. The Progressive Movement was perceived as antibusiness. This was quite helpful for carrying out the changes demanded by the project. With the IAs broadcasting the new ideology, it was much easier to carry out the necessary reforms. Through such policy groups as the National Civic Federation, the project advanced a number of causes aimed at rationalizing the social order. Legislative initiatives were advanced for managerial city government, civil service, workman's compensation, party reform, the Federal Trade Commission, and the Commission for Industrial Relations (Wiebe, 1962). By the onset of World War I, the project was successfully implemented. Corporate liberalism became the dominant ideology.

Particular Ideology

The most narrow, specific, and common level of the ideological region is that of the particular ideology (Mannheim, 1936:34). Particular ideologies are specific in both object and social base or origin. Its object is specific, in that it concerns a limited area of a person's experience. For example, a particular ideology might say that blacks are inferior to whites. This would refer only to that limited portion of an adherent's experience which refers him to blacks. The particular ideology is quite close to an idea. The difference is that particular ideology has a social basis and relates specifically to the conditions of existence. The specificity of particular ideology does not necessarily derive from its limited nature. Indeed, a particular ideology may constitute a whole world view. In this case it is particular because those who hold it form a specific referent group such as a social movement or religious cult. Regardless of the origin of the particularity of an ideology, it always has a specific class nature. The class nature of an ideology does not necessarily reflect the class origin of those who hold it. Rather it is derived from the modal elements which structure the ideology.

Particular Ideologies in
the Hegemonic Project

In carrying out a hegemonic project, the power bloc must deal with existing particular ideologies. Some are the property of the class allies. These are contained in the hegemonic ideology. This is useful for cementing the alliance. Of course, some are incompatible and must be excluded. It is desirable to include particular ideologies, if possible; otherwise, they may create contradictions in the alliance and fracture its unity. Particular ideologies of the old power bloc must be attacked and discredited. This can be done without endangering capitalist relations if the opposing particular ideologies are identified with opponent fractions as special interests. Thus certain people or groups and not the system are condemned. The particular ideologies of revolutionary forces must be attacked and discredited, or coopted or eliminated and their adherents subordinated.

We can see these processes occurring in the corporate liberal project. Socialist ideas were repressed by legal and extralegal action by capital and the repressive arm of the state. Reformist labor leaders were recognized and encouraged. The particular ideology of responsible trade unionism was embraced by the project and integrated into the hegemonic ideology; the ideologies of the political machine were portrayed as corrupt; those of the competitive capitalist were described as cruel and irresponsible.

Of the particular ideologies embraced by the project, perhaps the most important was Taylorism. In its original context, Taylorism meant the application of scientific principles to management and the labor process. However, in the hands of the NMC ideologists, this had a much broader application than the workplace. For these visionaries "the factory was a temple in which citizens could be freed of the doubts and uncertainties of their secular lives to achieve salvation through unity with the absolute rationality of the machine" (Noble, 1971). Politics, social life, and culture could profit from this rationalization. This coalesced in a vision of a scientific community, the Total Society of Cooley or the Technocracy of Cawley of the New Republic. In practice this meant efforts to legislate conformity with middle class values and cultural standards. It was by no means a democratic vision.

Another particular ideology of the project might be described as educationism. This was a faith in individual social mobility through participation in education. This was closely tied to the belief that education would solve all problems, would improve health, prevent crime, and make for class harmony as well as helping one get a good job and get the most of one's leisure time. Related ideologies included the worship of science and the cult of expertise. That these ideologies fit together in a sort of package should be no surprise, considering their common class origins and their organization under the hegemonic ideology.

Conclusion

I have developed a general theory of the ideological region and utilized it to illuminate a particular hegemonic project. To conclude I may say:

1. The concept "hegemonic project" is fundamental to understanding the history of bourgeois class struggle.

2. While the political dimension of the project and its roots in economic transition and crisis is most important, its ideological side is indispensable, if the project is to succeed in defusing crisis and creating a new order.

3. In the current situation in which the now dominant ideology is subject to challenge, the NMC plays the pivotal role in the outcome of impending social struggles. Any new bourgeois project and the struggles of progressive social forces must take it strictly into account.

4. The NMC is particularly tied up with the ideological dimension of any potentially new project as a result of the nature of their work. Further, it will be susceptible to the ideological approaches, such as visions of a new technocracy, whether that be a new authoritarianism of the Right or a technocratic socialism.

5. The unique class position of the NMC must be recognized by opponents of the bourgeoisie if any class alliance is to be successful. This alliance will best be achieved by stressing the progressive aspects of NMC ideology.

6. Only by developing the understanding of the nature of ideology can the power of the bourgeoisie be shaken.

With the hegemonic project, the bourgeoisie takes history in its hands. Perhaps, soon, the bourgeoisie will find itself in the hands of history.

Part Three: The Middle Classes of
Advanced Capitalist Societies

Dale L. Johnson: The Social Unity and Fractionalization of the Middle Class

Such unity as the middle class displays is based on the particular insertions of administrative, scientific, technical, and professional labor in the class relations of a polarizing social order and an always changing social division of labor. This unity is cemented in the sphere of class culture and lifestyle. But this is a unity-in-division.

There are four main groupings within the middle classes of advanced capitalist societies (the middle classes of dependent countries have a different internal structure; see Volume 3 of this series). Each "fraction" performs particular functions (normally divided, as Carchedi argues, between those of capital and the collective worker); each has a distinct pattern of conflictive relations with workers or clients on the one hand and the bourgeoisie on the other hand; each is situated in a different set of relational positionings that are in constant historical change; each is an expression of a different form of the bipolarization process:

— *The administrators*, including supervisors and middle-level bureaucratic functionaries. They perform the "line" and "staff" authority functions in the technical division of labor and are directly enmeshed in the antagonisms of capital to labor.

— *The service professionals* are mainly state employees who produce use values in the sphere of social services.

— *The semiautonomous employees*, such as scientific and technical personnel and many professionals. The "semiautonomy" refers to their place in the labor process, which has historically evolved to fragment and routinize "workers' work", while elevating coordinative and developmental activity to work conditions that are more creative and freer of direct controls.

— *The independents*. The old petty bourgeoisie has been, as the twentieth century progressed, entirely transformed, if not liquidated, as an independent class and the remnants incorporated into the middle class and working class.

The Social Unity of the Middle Class

While the middle class is divided, it is also the case that administrators, scientific and technical personnel, professionals, and small entrepreneurs share a common relationship to the fundamental social relations that form the foundations of society in its present stage of development, and this is what makes them a class rather than simply strata occupying "contradictory locations" or a series of residual groupings arbitrarily aggregated. Their occupational roles have been defined such that they become directly enmeshed—each fraction in a distinct manner—within the polarizing relations of capital to labor. Their defined roles fix them in antagonistic relations with the working class. Moreover, they have not suffered the direct exploitation and work regimentation of workers. At the same time, the middle class experiences its own forms of class subordination in respect to the bourgeoisie, and this also brings the fractions together as a class. As Burris argues: "If classes are ultimately defined by their relation to other classes in the process of class struggle, then such intermediate positions should be interpreted as constituting a distinctive social class and not, as some have suggested, as positions 'between' classes" (1980:19).

The basic social unity of the middle class is established in terms of the various forms of insertion of its different constituent elements directly into the *middle* of the social relations of exploitation and domination. This creates distinct patterns of sectional and broader class interests. Yet these relations, shaped in a bipolarizing structure, and therefore the interests of the middle class, are never fixed. For example, the movement of the forces of production or a shift in capital accumulation patterns may transform the positioning of a particular occupation, a stratum within a fraction, or an entire fraction, impinging on the class situation and interests of those affected. The extent and intensity of struggle between the two major classes of society changes the place of large sectors of the middle class. Or the dominant class may attempt to transform existing social relations by evolving a new "hegemonic project" (Chapter 6) in which the place of the middle class is redefined. Moreover, the positioning of the *entire* middle class may change from one phase of historical development to another.

It is also important to understand that an intermediate class, formed in the primacy of the relations between the polar classes, has a life of its own. Constituent elements of the class struggle to consolidate their positions and privileges. Later (Chapter 9) we emphasize the importance of the historical process of professionalization of different occupations as a means of "enhancing their market power and preserving their status and autonomy from encroachments by either employers or clients" (Burris, 1980:27); that is professionalization is a principal vehicle in the formation of the middle class.

Another basis of the social unity and interests of the middle class as a class is provided by their positional insertion in the relations of exploitation and domination as this is both experienced and reinforced in the sphere of class culture and lifestyle. These are facilitated by the operations of ascriptive and distributional social inequalities (social stratifications).

Social stratifications form a basis for social unity and cultural cohesion within the middle class while also, contradictorily, operating to promote a highly competitive class culture that atomizes individuals, nurtures narcissism, and inhibits collective action. For the middle class, shared educational attainments, higher income levels and affluent consumption patterns, more desirable residential locations, shared patterns of social intercourse and marriage, and generalized styles of life are means by which the diverse fractions achieve their social/culture unity as a class, however fragile that unity may be given the salience of intraclass invidious social distinctions and the competitive culture. Superior placements in the various socially defined hierarchies provide the material and social bases for the social interaction of professionals, technicians, administrators, lesser businessmen, and private practitioners. In the process of intimate social interaction, forms of consciousness and conceptions of interests peculiar to the middle class are established. The middle class is a principal social base for cultural and political movements that proceed from the consciousness and interests of the class, and which also reinforce certain forms of consciousness. The "countercultural" and New Left movements of the 1960s and the cultural fads of the 1970s largely proceed from a social base in the middle class, as do various right-wing political movements.

The seemingly contradictory, bewildering array of cultural manifestations and political behaviors proceeding from the middle class has caused some analysts to throw up their hands in desperation. They retreat from class analysis to an empiricism of time-bound appearances; to "interest-group formations, which gather around ascriptive societal features, such as race, ethnicity, gender, religion" (Horowitz, 1979:62); to culture as class (Bell in Bruce-Briggs, 1979) rather than class culture; or to the secular religiosity of modernity (Berger in Bruce-Briggs, 1979).

To be sure, entirely too much can be made of the unity of a class that is formed and transformed into something other than what it was in the course of social development. But rapidly changing appearances of complexity and disunity should not allow one to fall into a rejection of class analysis in the manner of Horowitz: "New classes, stratum, sectors, segments, are indeed constantly being formed and reformed; but more pointedly, their explanatory power is limited by the extraordinary degree to which American society, and postindustrial societies generally, have become integrated along political lines and correspondingly disintegrated along class lines" (1979:62). Of course, the middle class contains a fragile unity of diverse social elements in which various social stratifications enter; of course, the middle class can be viewed as a constellation of strong occupational subcultures, each with its particular ideologies, professional associations, sectional interests, values and norms, and associational patterns; but these understandings need to be theoretically placed as particular manifestations of multiclass relations in a bipolarizing structure.

The Fractions of the Middle Class

The problem of unity and fractionalization of classes is one of long standing. The working and capitalist classes have been seen as divided along identifiable lines, even though there is no general agreement on how the problem should be approached. In the main, approaches to the "fractionalization" of classes have proceeded on the basis of examination of the place of particular groupings in the social or technical division of labor. Viewing class divisions in terms of the division of labor often results in a sectoral or scale of operation breakdown of the fractions of classes. For example, the bourgeoisie is divided between commercial, industrial and finance capital, by monopoly and competitive capital, by "comprador" and "national" bourgeoisies, and/or by large-scale, medium-size, and small-scale producers. The working class has been seen as divided between production and tertiary sector workers; or between workers in primary (unionized, high-paying monopoly) sector and secondary (nonunionized, low-paying competitive) sector (see Edward's [1979] application of "dual labor market theory" to working class fractionalization); or by a stable working class and an "underclass" of unemployed underemployed, "marginalized," or "colonized" peoples (Johnson, 1971; Cockcroft, forthcoming). The theory of productive and unproductive labor, criticized in Chapter 2, has also been used to identify fractions of classes. Viewing class divisions mainly in terms of the technical division of labor yields a breakdown of the functions of occupational categories in industrial or bureaucratic hierarchies (within the bourgeoisie: owners, managers, top staff, and line personnel; within the working class: technical, office or mental workers, shop or manual workers; etc.)

C. Wright Mills's classic study, *White Collar*, posited a basic rift in the middle class between old and new segments. Many authors still see the middle class divided according to the distinction between the "old" petty bourgeoisie and the "new" middle class of "white-collar" salaried employees. Yet today the old class of self-employed persons constitutes, at best, a residual category of leftovers from a bygone era. Recent literature takes a different approach to division among intermediate formations. Poulantzas's main effort in *Classes in Contemporary Capitalism* is to distinguish the petty bourgeoisie from the working class. One problem is that he lumps all sorts of working-class categories into the new petty bourgeoisie, so that the class becomes a vast array of groupings united by being unproductive, mental, supervisory employees. Wright (1978) posits "contradictory class locations" and places various occupational groupings, here considered middle class, into limbo. These are not "fractions" of an intermediate class, since Wright's approach comes down to a notion of classless strata. Poulantzas unifies too many diverse groups into a class; Wright has no criteria by which to identify the makeup of an intermediate class.

Many authors (including Oppenheimer, Chapter 4) point to the diverse character and disunity of the middle class, but they do not attempt to make sense of the diversity. Among the few who have addressed this problem, social function is emphasized. Szmanski, for example, has examined the divisions within the "petty bourgeoisie" in these terms:

We can perhaps usefully sub-categorize the petty bourgeoisie by two dimensions: 1) *their social function*: whether their role is to, a) reproduce capitalist culture and indirectly capitalist class relations (e.g. social "scientists," literary apologists, social studies teachers, social welfare workers, etc.), b) directly administer and reproduce capitalist class relations through supervising and directing labor power (i.e., managers, managerial consultants), c) produce goods or add to productivity e.g., small farmers, artisans, engineers, d) sell goods or provide non-professional services (e.g. high level salesmen, small retail businessmen), or e) provide professional services (e.g. doctors and lawyers); and 2) *their employment status*; whether they are, a) self-employed, b) employed by private corporations, or c) employed by the state. Each of the possibilities on these two dimensions (five on the first, three on the second) has different consequences in terms of the life experiences, and hence, politics, of the various sectors of the single petty bourgeoisie [Walker, ed. 1979:55].

Social function and employment status are indeed important criteria in identifying divisions within the middle class. But to avoid a static, functional analysis or a mechanistic formalism, it is necessary to place these criteria within the dynamic of capital accumulation, class formation, and polarizing class relations.

In the preceding chapters a general historical approach to the interrelations of accumulation and class formation was established. Historical/ empirical studies applying this approach are needed of the ways in which the places of the traditional petty bourgeoisie of craftsmen, small businessmen, and independent professionals have been entirely transformed with the mature development of the monopoly stage. And those studies need to be linked to others that examine the formation of segments of the "new" social groupings of administrators and professionals that come to form part of the system of class domination within corporate enterprise and by agencies of the state; similarly, new segments were formed, as the growth and concentration of the economy proceeded, to assume coordinative and technical tasks in an increasingly complex, differentiated, and integrated economic process.

In historical/empirical research, care has to be taken to view the formation of these segments in relational terms; they are not simply composed of administrative and technical agents of the bourgeoisie. The places of the diverse occupational groupings in the division of labor cannot be reduced to a single factor, and the forms of their "intermediations" in class relations are many and tend to shift over time. It is these variations that present the problem of "fractionalization" of the middle class—and it is these shifts that make any classification of "fractions" necessarily time bound.

Perhaps the most important social division with the middle class is located at the level of relations of production: the division between those fractions directly bound up with administering the relations of exploitation and domination (the "administrators," "social control professionals"), those that are located outside the direct relations of capital to labor (the "semiautonomous employees"), and those fractions that produce use values in performance of necessary social services (the "service professionals"). The work of an assistant manager for personnel of a large corporation, a chief of a local FBI office, a judge, an official of the Internal Revenue Service—all involve a daily round of activities in administering or upholding existing social relations. The work of a teacher, a salaried physician in a new health maintenance organization, a family counselor, a community mental health specialist, a researcher in a governmental social service agency, while also institutionally defined to uphold existing relations, is mainly to provide a service to meet human needs. Similar divisions that bind specific occupations to existing social relations, in contrast to work activities that contain an opening to a future society organized to produce and equitably distribute and consume use values, permeate the other sectors of the middle class. The creations of an advertising copy writer are specific to the sales effort of corporations in the stage of monopoly capitalism, while a staff writer who creates for *Rolling Stone* magazine or *The Village Voice* is, in Gramsci's sense, an organic intellectual of a middle class that strives to establish its independence from the bourgeoisie in the sphere of cultural ideology. These divisions are important in social struggles of the present phase of capitalist development.

Added to these divisions, that appear to widen with each successive phase of development, are those brought about by great structural transformations. The semiautonomy in the work situations of many salaried employees is being eroded by the extension of the rationalization of the labor process into technical and administrative spheres. Layers of administrators themselves become more and more administratively subordinated to the managerial bourgeoisie as organizational rationalization and institutional centralization of power proceed. These trends, in the present period in the United States at least, tend to polarize the middle class into strata whose labor power is devalued and pushed in the direction of the working class, while the technocratic strata whose work is increasingly defined in terms of control functions thereby move closer to the bourgeoisie (Chapters 9 and 10).

The approach to the fractionalization of the middle class adopted here includes consideration of (1) the identification of the places of different occupational groupings in the social and technical division of labor; (2) the analytic perspective necessary to locate the occupational groupings into class fractions in the relations of exploitation and domination; (3) the historical formation of the fraction and its numerical presence in the United States in 1970; (4) the divisions and strata within the fraction; (5) the principal structural forces impinging on the class position of the fraction in recent years; and (6) the predominant forms of class relations between the fraction and the working class on the one hand and the bourgeoisie on the other. Space does not permit analysis of each distinct fraction in terms of all these factors. Therefore, I have presented this approach by emphasizing one factor with respect to one fraction and another factor with respect to another fraction, and so on.

Empirical Configurations of the Middle Class

Concretely, the middle classes of advanced capitalist societies are here presented as formed of four fractions: administrators, service professionals, semiautonomous employees, and independents. In the United States in 1970, administrative employees (excluding upper-level managers and lower-level supervisors) numbered 5.4 million, an increase from 3.9 million in 1960 and 1.6 million in 1940. Semiautonomous employees are mainly engineers, scientists, researchers, and higher level technicians; they were 4.6 million in 1970, an increase of 59 percent from 2.7 million in 1960. The service professionals numbered 4.3 million in 1970 (of which 3 million are state employees), an increase from 3 million in 1960. The 1970 census lists 5.9 million self-employed persons, a substantial decrease from 9.8 million self-employed in 1940. This study posits that the old petty bourgeoisie has been destroyed as a distinct social class, with sectors (here termed "independents") being absorbed into the middle class now composed largely of salaried employees; that is, 2.7 million proprietors, professional practitioners, self-employed cultural workers, and some salespersons are no longer properly seen as a petty bourgeosie in the classic sense; while other sectors of the self-employed such as craftsmen and own-account workers in services, constitute an unstable fraction of the working class.

Thus, 17 million persons, or 21 percent of the U.S. labor force in 1970, were employed in middle-class occupations. The administrative, technical, and professional labor force has grown at a considerably faster rate than the labor force as a whole throughout this century, but the increase was particularly rapid during the decades of the 1950s and 1960s. The 1980 census data on occupational distribution are not available at the time of this writing, but limited data since 1970 indicate that the growth of the middle class has slowed in recent years.

The Administrative Fraction of the Middle Class

An analysis that begins with function in the social division of labor usually ends with a view of middle- and lower-level administrative and supervisory personnel as agents of capital. The beginning is appropriate, but the ending is not, as it downplays the relational aspect of class analysis and tends to foreclose an analysis of transformations of the labor process.

A functional analysis proceeds along these lines: There is a double aspect to the positions of an important fraction of the middle class—lower-level managerial, upper-level supervisory, corporate staff employees and technocrats, and the like—that shapes their class location. Considering first the "pure case" (which, I note below, does not empirically exist), (a) they work as agents of capital in control tasks and, for this reason, (b) they are paid a salary out of profits. (The same would be the case for certain categories of state functionaries, who are paid from revenue.) Thus their functions in the social division of labor are those of capital as delegated by the bourgeoisie. However, they, like the bourgeoisie, owe their privileged social existence, defined by their activities as appropriators of the value of labor of producers, to the continuation of the system of exploitation and domination, in which they occupy administrative places.

If middle-class employees have a real hand in controlling the economic process and, in relational terms, of administering the system of exploitation and class domination, while deriving their superior incomes from profit redistributed to them, then their class experience would condition a fundamental class interest in the maintenance of the existing system. If the middle class was composed entirely of administrative agents, and if this pure case were the only structural determination bearing down on its existence, the middle class would only be differentiated from the bourgeoisie by its inferior position in bureaucratic hierarchies and the scale of appropriated income—that is, by gradations of power and privilege. They would be, if these were the only determinations of class, an inferior fraction of the bourgeoisie itself.

Some analysts of the middle class (e.g., the Ehrenreichs in Walker, 1979) attribute administrative functions and conservative class interests to the middle class as a whole. The middle class, however, is a distinct historical formation that first eclipsed and finally absorbed the traditional petty bourgeoisie to form a broad and historically expanding sector of society. Administrative employees, as a major component of the middle class, are not purely agents of capital. Following Carchedi (1978), we posit that a principal fraction of the middle class is constituted by those who combine a *mix* of the functions of capital and of the "collective worker" in their work activity. This fraction includes administrative and supervisory personnel employed by corporations and by those of equivalent positions within the different agencies of the state. The administrative fraction, as distinct from other groupings within the middle class, comes closest to the "pure case" analyzed above. Yet, in fact, all but the highest level of administration combine a mix of control and productive labor activities in their work. Like other workers dispossessed of any other means of survival, they have only their labor power to sell on a labor market. They are paid a share of profits to exercise control and they are paid from wage funds to produce use values—a flow of paper that governs the labor process and ensures profitability.

Yet administrative labor is concerned with the technically and socially necessary work of coordination as well as with control. Becker notes the extensive enlargement of administrative work in the "managerial phase of capitalism" and observes:

> This technical utility of administrative labor does not, of course, account for the extent of its accumulation under capitalism... Even though demands and supplies of administrative labor are governed by considerations of profit, rather than by technical coefficients of coordination of production, the utility of this labor for the work of coordination is implicit within it [1973-74:442].

Becker's concept of "administrative labor," however, is much broader than that employed here; he seems to be referring to the middle class as a whole. The same is the case for Carchedi, who rests his conception of the "new" middle class on an analysis of the functions of capital and of collective workers, with the new middle class being defined as that class which shares both functions.

While Carchedi's idea provides an objective means of identifying a sizable segment of the labor force that is neither bourgeoisie nor working class, it is not a sufficient basis for analysis of the middle class as a whole. Other segments—semiautonomous employees, service professionals, and independents—can be identified as forming fractions of the middle class by criteria that will be explored shortly.

Administrators of all categories have increased by leaps and bounds, especially during the post-World War II period. In 1970, the U.S. census listed 6,224,647 "managers, officials, and proprietors, except farm." If we include certain occupations listed by the census as "professional and technical" that are actually administrative (e.g., 296,000 personnel and labor relations workers and 12,321 judges), and exclude the self-employed and bourgeoisie from the census category (e.g., 913,000 proprietors and perhaps 200,000 top corporate managers and higher state bureaucrats), the administrative fraction of the middle class numbered about 5.4 million employees in 1970. This is a considerable increase from 1960, when the administrators were less than 4 million. In 1910 and 1940, administrators in all sectors numbered approximately 1 and 1.8 million, respectively. The fastest-growing occupations in the administrative fields during the 1960s were categories not engaged in "front-line class antagonisms" of the corporate sector—namely bank officials and financial managers (who increased from 24,106 in 1960 to 311,907 in 1970) and health administrators (increasing from 7,190 to 84,966 during the decade).

The administrative fraction constituted 6 percent of the labor force in 1970 and 30 percent of the middle class. There were 900,000 administrators (exclusive of top officials) within the state bureaucracy in 1970, or 17 percent of the administrative fraction. Administration is predominantly a male pursuit—only 14 percent of the fraction was female in 1970 (22 percent female among state administrators).

What is really important about administrators is not their function as agents, even when modified by the observation that they also assume coordinative and "collective worker" functions: Many administrators are front-line contestants in the relations of exploitation and domination. They are a historically formed fraction of an intermediate class that intervenes directly in class antagonisms not of their making, but in which they are paid a salary to intervene. Yet other administrators—for example, bank officials—are less "line authorities" in bureaucratic hierarchies that encapsule and condense class antagonisms than they are technical functionaries.

There are, of course, different strata within the administrative fraction of the middle class, ranging from middle management to line supervisors further down bureaucratic hierarchies (as well as different categories of functionaries in state agencies). In general, the higher the placement in the administrative hierarchy of corporate enterprise, the greater the mix of functions carried out shifts toward those of capital—overall control. The exercise of control functions places the higher category of administrators more directly on the side of capital in its antagonistic relations with workers. The lower the placement in the hierarchy, the more coordinative and production tasks are performed. Relations with workers become more cooperative and relations with higher managers and bosses more antagonistic. However, the mix of functions itself, together with relative positioning in class relations, is continually redefined by the direction of transformations of the accumulation process and economic organization with their resultant effects on the labor process.

These transformations will be subject to closer scrutiny in Chapter 10. Here I note only that they present two basic contradictory tendencies, affecting the administrative (as well as other fractions) of the middle class. Development of the monopoly stage of capitalism has, as a consequence, the continual formation of new occupational groupings within the middle class that require skill levels superior to average labor. In the sphere of administration, the ratio of administrative employees to production workers in the United States increased from 8 per 100 at the turn of the century to 21 per 100 by the middle of the century (Braverman, 1974:240; see also Melman, 1951). However, the quantitative increase in administrators says nothing of the qualitative aspects of administration as a labor process. Again, even though administrators can be more clearly defined in terms of their functions as agents than other middle-class occupational categories, this emphasis can close an analytic eye on transformations in the labor process that radically change the position in class relations of different occupational groupings. For example, while demand for educated labor skilled in manipulating symbols increases, the contrary tendency is for organizational rationalization to reduce work, including administrative work, to simplified, routine tasks and thereby to devalue skilled labor to average or even unqualified labor. The functions may continue to be defined by corporate organizational charts and the Census Bureau as administrative, but the actual movement may be toward "proletarianization." Especially in the latest phase of development in North America and Europe, the coordination and control elements and the technically creative aspects of the work of administration (and that of middle-class employees generally) is reduced, whenever technically feasible, to fragmented tasks performed by employees who more and more resemble clerical workers. This process of subordination of middle-class employees in the labor process has, as an outside limit, the "proletarianization" of sectors of the middle class, but more commonly the end result is a greater component of routine workers' work in middle-class jobs.

The tendency toward stripping jobs of increasing amounts of control and coordinative and creative activity has borne down on the middle classes in the Western capitalist countries in recent years, but its impact is selective among the different occupational groupings. However, it does appear that middle-range administrative employees in private corporations and government bureaucracies are increasingly divested of authority, subordinated to managers, and subjected to deteriorating conditions of work. Becker notes: "The split between the managers and administrative labor divides the ranks of white collar labor and marks an ineradicable schism within the middle class of modern society" (1973-74: 437).

The Service Professionals

Poulantzas (1975) and several others who employ the theory of productive/unproductive labor to the problem of class determination conclude that *all* state employees are "new petty bourgeosie" (or that there is no working class representation among state workers). Because state employees do not engage in the process of producing surplus value and are paid from revenue, they are unproductive workers who are not exploited. To lump office workers and postal clerks with teachers, bureaucrats, and cabinet ministers in the same social class is absurd. As was argued in Chapter 2, the theory has no relevance to class determination.

Carchedi analyzes the collocation of state employees in the class structure by proposing a distinction between capitalist and "noncapitalist" state activities. Capitalist activities are defined as "those that spend money in order to increase it" (1978:105). Noncapitalist activities are defined as those that provide use values independent of the process of producing surplus value. He argues that the class determination of state employees engaged in capitalist activities proceeds in the same way as for employees of private firms engaged in producing surplus value. Employees who perform a mix of managerial and collective worker functions within state enterprises or agencies are middle class. The criteria of social class determination of employees in noncapitalist state activities are the same as those applied to employees in unproductive private enterprises. This is the case because noncapitalist activity "takes place in a structure dominated by the capital producing process and relations. . . It produces use values just as capitalist commodities are produced, i.e. by the extraction of surplus labor" (1978:111). While not exploited, state workers are "economically oppressed" because surplus labor is appropriated from them in return for a wage less than the value of the services produced. While Carchedi's logic is different (depending as it does on a distinction between productive and unproductive labor), he arrives at the same conclusion as I do in this chapter. State employees can be placed in the class structure by the same criteria as private sector employees, taking into account the primary functions of state agencies.[1]

These functions (generalized and simplified) include (1) facilitating the process of private capital accumulation; (2) promoting the system of exploitation and class domination through repressive and legitimizing activities; and (3) providing minimum services to meet elementary human needs not otherwise met, for social reproduction, and for essential social coordination. These functions, carried out to greater and lesser degree by all agencies of the state, bear on the class collocation of state employees. Here we consider only those employees with the third function, service professionals.

A sizable segment of state activity is organized primarily (but by no means exclusively) to produce use values, rather than to directly facilitate the process of private capital accumulation or to exercise class domination. The most important category of use values produced are those that meet elementary human needs in complex societies (health services; assistance to the needy, aged, infirm, handicapped, and children; fire protection; sanitation; social insurance provision; and other social and community services), those that provide for social reproduction (education), and those that provide a modicum of social coordination (planning and environmental agencies).

The class collocation of employees in state service, reproductive, and coordinative agencies must be undertaken with these considerations in mind: (1) They do not participate directly in capitalist production relations, yet they are caught squarely in the middle between public demands for social services and their institutionally defined roles as agents of social control. (2) By producing use values geared to social need, they perform service functions universal to complex societies, capitalist or socialist. (3) Like scientists and higher level technical personnel in both private and public sectors, they enjoy semiautonomy in their work activity.

The bulk of state employees in the service and reproductive agencies are professionally trained workers. "Service professionals" perform very different functions than "social control professionals." The special, universal nature of their activity makes their labor productive; yet since the use values they produce are not commodified, they are not directly exploited. They relate to the system of exploitation and class domination in quite distinct ways, as compared to state employees in the sphere of capital accumulation or in the sphere of the repressive agencies of state, or as compared to administrative, professional, and scientific and technical employees in the private sector. The service professionals constitute a distinct fraction of the middle class.

The service professional fraction in 1970 consisted of 4.3 million persons, including 3 million state employees or 70 percent of the service professional fraction as a whole. (The 4.3 million figure excludes 500,000 self-employed service professionals, who are classified as independents, and about 500,000 health workers who are nonprofessional technicians, here classified as working class). Service professionals constitute 5.4 percent of the labor force and 26 percent of the middle class.

In many ways social work exemplifies the service professions. In the United States in 1970 there were 267,000 social workers. The rate of growth of the profession has been extraordinarily high, but only since the 1920s. In the nineteenth century, communities and families performed the service functions later to be usurped by professionals. At the turn of the century only charitable relief activity existed. But by the 1920s several schools of social work had been established and professional organizations founded. In 1940 there were 77,000 credentialed social workers; and in 1960, 121,000. Social work exploded in the 1960s. No less than 250 accredited institutions gave degrees in the field. The number of social workers grew by 121 percent between 1960 and 1970. Paraprofessional workers in social work bureaucracies also increased dramatically.[2]

College teaching is also a major component of the service professions. As the professional, technical, and administrative labor force grew at rates faster than the total labor force over several decades, higher education expanded dramatically. The professorate grew from 16,000 in 1910 to 77,000 in 1940 and 193,000 in 1960. In the 1960s, college teaching grew even faster than social work, by 152 percent, reaching 486,000 in 1970.

In 1950, 8.9 percent of the GNP was expended on welfare, social security, unemployment insurance, public housing, education, and public health programs. The figure climbed to 20.4 percent of GNP in 1976, its high point. The process of formation of service professionals reached its maturity in the 1960s. The major social services—education, health, welfare, and religious services—employed 70 percent more workers in 1970 than in 1960. The number of librarians, counselors, writers and, entertainers also increased substantially. While the ministry actually declined during the decade, of the major professions only medicine and dentistry experienced a slower rate of growth than the labor force as a whole. Physicians and dentists numbered 152,000 in 1910, 168,000 in 1940, 463,000 in 1960, and 541,000 in 1970. Physicians and dentists also account for the great majority of self-employment among professionals.

Between 1960 and 1970, the service professional fraction of the middle class expanded 38 percent, compared to 18.6 percent for the labor force. As we stated elsewhere: "A 'war' on poverty was declared and the decade was a period of conflict over whether these services were to be strictly control-oriented as in prior years, or to be more widely and equitably available, genuinely service-oriented and subject to community control" (Johnson and O'Donnell, 1981:15).

Since 1976 government spending on social services has dropped precipitously, even declining as a percentage of GNP. In 1979, before Ronald Reagan's massive budget cuts of the early 1980s, absolute dollar allocations to social services in real terms fell. People who need social services and the professionals that provide them today find themselves in defensive positions.

Identifying the place of service professionals in the social division of labor and in the class relations of advanced capitalism depends on an adequate view of the state. In Chapter 3 I sharply criticized the Ehrenreichs and others who pose middle-class employees as mere agents performing prescribed system reproduction functions. The nature of the intermediate formations that owe their existence to state employment is immediately redefined if an alternative concept of the state is entertained:

The state is an institutional expression of the class relations of civil society.
Correspondingly, activities of persons who exercise the machinery of state
are expressions of class relations. Employees of the state in positions of
responsibility are intermediaries in a very precise sense: They intervene
directly within the social relations of which the state is an expression. It is
not surprising, therefore, that 43 percent of all state employees are, by
occupational criteria (technical, administrative and professional labor),
middle class, as compared to about 15 percent of private sector employees.

Chapter 9 is devoted to analyzing different kinds of professionals as
components of the middle class, so here I will but touch on the salient
features of these professions, in the main employees of the state, that
provide social services. (We have also treated service professionals more
extensively, and in relation to accumulation crisis, elsewhere [Johnson and
O'Donnell, 1981]. There are three features that define service professionals
as a distinct fraction of the middle class. (1) The wide range of social
services administered by the state is in part an outcome of capitalist
development and what Braverman terms the "universalization of the
market." (2) The provision of social services is also the historical result of
popular struggles; while the form of administering these services represents
efforts by the dominant class to turn popular social gains into means of
social control. (3) Social services are islands of decommodification in a sea
of commodified production and exchange; they represent socialized
production of use values.

Human Needs Laid Bare

In mid-nineteenth-century America, small town and rural life prevailed
for the majority. In the main, people in these communities were able to
work cooperatively to meet their individual and collective needs. They
produced and exchanged most goods on local markets; they assisted each
other in home construction; gardens and domestic animals provided a
good proportion of people's diets; families were meaningful social-
economic units of producers of use values for self-consumption; people
generally had a variety of useful skills and craftsmen of exceptional skill
abounded; the social arts of healing, midwifery, music, and entertainment
were cultivated by folk practitioners; and the few professionals (doctors,
lawyers, ministers, and teachers) lived on a basis of equality with the
people.

A century later practically nothing of this existence remained. The
process of capitalist development has been one of destruction of communal
bonds and the atomization of individuals. Dispossessed of their prior
means of existence, people turned to labor markets for their livelihoods
and commodity markets to try to meet their needs. Commodity markets
proved particularly niggardly in one area: social services.

This presented especially difficult conditions for many, as by the early
twentieth century the need for social services had exploded: rapid
industrialization depending on millions of impoverished immigrant labor-

ers; the great crowding of peoples from abroad and from rural American into urban slums; unemployment; old people without families to care for them; sickness without means to obtain medical assistance, and so on. The most elementary human needs had been exposed to conditions of deprivation. In the initial stages, some services necessary for the satisfaction of these individual and social needs became commodified—they could only be purchased for a fee. In these activities, with the community or family basis of production of use values destroyed, commodification of the servicing of human needs presented opportunities for professionals to become successful independent practitioners. Physicians, for example (almost entirely males from privileged class backgrounds), seized opportunities to appropriate the healing arts from folk practitioners (mostly women of popular class background) and to monopolize medical practice. Medical practice became a distinct and privileged profession (Ehrenreich, 1978; Ehrenreich and English, 1973).

The early petty bourgeois organization of professional service and the charitable relief that women of the bourgeois class organized proved inadequate to contend with the growing needs of the population. There was a pressing social need for service provision in areas of extreme deprivation and for decommodification in spheres that proved unprofitable for private practitioners or market-oriented businessmen. In effect, since the market did not extend to the provision of an increasing range of essential services or people could not afford to purchase them, the state stepped in to provide them. This had the effects of socializing the production and distribution of an increasing range of services and of creating an expanding group of salaried service professionals recruited into state agencies or tax-supported institutions.

The Dialectic of Social Services

It was not exactly that the Prince, seeing the plight of his people, opened his treasury. The social services increasingly provided by the state were *demanded* by the dispossessed, the poor, the workers—and to a certain degree by an emerging class on the make, a middle class that saw its future in social amelioration.

There is a dialectic of social-historical process here in three senses. First, the objective conditions presented to people in trying to live their lives generates social demands. Second, these social demands bring people into conflict with established class power. Third, an intermediate class is formed that intervenes in this conflict, a class that develops a set of social interests distinct from either pole.

We do not have space to present this as a dynamic process of social development. What can be concluded is that the modern "welfare state" (see Gough, 1978; Castells, 1980), the main employer of service professionals, is an outcome of the dialectic between the economic transformations propelled by the accumulation process and the social struggles impelled by the conditions presented to people on the one hand and by the need of dominant interests for social control on the other. The welfare state represents a social gain of popular struggle—and an instrument of domination over people. The service professionals who minister to social need are caught within this contradiction. Their intermediate class determination proceeds first from location within relations of antagonism.

In the uneven development of the social struggle, the provision of social services as means of social control has predominated. The roles of service professionals are defined as agents of social control. "Professionals see themselves as liberal and humanistic. They are bureaucratic and techno-logical in practice" (Reiff, 1971:63). This is shaped by the organizational context within which they work. As we stated elsewhere:

> A needy consumer must face the bureaucracy and enter into a subservient relation with the service provider. Service professionals mainly work in bureaucratic structures that have the coercive power to enforce the professionals's decision *vis a vis* his/her client. Professional expertise and largesse are reinforced and constrained by bureaucratic power. State organized production of human services produces not only the needed service but the mode of the objective and subjective dimensions of its consumption as well. Concretely, in the day to day contacts between ordinary people and professionals, the objective structures of social relations are those of marked dependent inequality: social worker/client, teacher/student, doctor/patient, bureaucrat/applicant. . . . The client's subjective response may be one of submissive deference to what may appear as the natural order of the social world or, as is the main feature of the present period, of hostile acquiescence to authority. The professional's attitude may be one of professional (often patronizing) concern or of contempt for dependence and ignorance. In either case, the social relations are those of latent or manifest antagonism [Johnson and O'Donnell, 1981:45].

In a later chapter on the professions, we analyze a process of "deprofessionalization" that is current to the emerging phase of develop-ment. In the 1970s, perhaps the principal factor affecting the personnel of the service institutions was that the semiautonomy characteristic of professional activity was eroded (see especially Patry, 1978). Also, popular movements began to challenge the "cult of expertise" and place demands for professional accountability on clients and citizens. Professionals are under assault from both sides in the class struggle. It is from the side of the managers of the state and the dominant class, however, that the threat to the semiautonomy—as well as to a wide array of social privileges of the professionals—mainly proceeds. Professional (as well as administrative and technical) labor today is subject to devaluation as the labor process is reorganized, computers brought in, and paraprofessionals hired; institu-tional power is centralized in the hands of the managerial bourgeoisie; and efficient methods of bureaucratic accountability of professional, technical, and administrative labor are imposed. And these trends take place within a conservative backlash to servicing human need and the fiscal crisis of the state. On the other side, many people no longer defer to the professional/ client relationship of inequality; and they are no longer trusting of the self-serving and often bungled expertise of elitists seemingly divorced from human concern and unresponsive to popular demands for accountability. "The upshot of the technological assault on knowledge claims and the ideological assault on service claims is that professionals no longer have the relatively unchallenged autonomy they often enjoyed in a former period" (Haug, 1973:205).

Decommodification and Socialization

There is a further angle from which to view the service professions from a dialectical perspective. Service professions are involved in the socialized production of use values (i.e., they produce socially necessary services rather than marketed commodities). As a historical process, decommodification and the socialized production of use values that meet the needs of individual and collective social needs represent one basis for the birth of a new society within the old society. Capitalism creates incipient forms of socialism, understood as a society that suppresses private accumulation and organizes the economic and social order to produce, distribute, and consume use values in an egalitarian form. Moreover, there is another dimension to this dialectic that has to do with the very foundations of capitalism—labor power as a commodity. While reproductive and service institutions are designed to channel and control labor, they also evolve to threaten the link between the imperatives of worker subsistence and the exigencies of the labor market. Unemployment insurance, social security, welfare, and income transfers and social services of many types are incipient forms of the eventual decommodification of labor power itself.

This does not mean, of course, that incremental social gains in decommodification of the means of satisfying human need, and to some degree of labor power, and the socialization of social services and necessary social reproduction will one day add up to socialism. A socialist society does not emerge as the end result of an evolutionary process out of the welfare state. It certainly does not mean that the professionals who provide social services are the harbingers of the new, socialist order. It does mean that service professionals have a clear *class* interest in maintaining, even extending, the process of decommodification and socialization of the production of use values.

Decommodification and the socialization of human services and social reproduction that creates the basis for an eventual new, rational society geared to production of use values also simultaneously, particularly in the latest phase of monopoly capitalism, become means for extending, reinforcing, and reproducing the system of class domination. The dominant social interests and the managers of the state constantly attempt to move these activities away from servicing social need toward social domination. Social welfare is organized, as Piven and Cloward (1971) put it, "to regulate the poor." Education works, following Bowles and Gintis

(1976), according to the "correspondence principle"; that is, attempts are made to gear schools to the manpower needs of monopoly capital, to ideological indoctrination, and to the creation of a disciplined and docile labor force. Service professionals also have a clear *class* interest in system maintenance.

These are the kinds of contradictions that service professionals live. In the present fiscal climate and conservative political moment, social services are under sharp attack. Equally deep contradictions shape the lives of other categories of the middle class. And this is why the middle class in an advanced industrial society cannot be written off as an insignificant social force. We turn to larger questions of incipient crises of the emerging phase of development in advanced capitalism, and the changing place of the middle class in class relations, in the concluding chapter.

The Semiautonomous Fraction

With the mature development of monopoly capitalism in the post-World War II era, the rationalization of work in factories, offices, and bureaucracies polarized the work force into a hierarchy of administrators and experts and an army of executors. Such control as was exercised by the great majority of workers over their work situation and their skill levels were progressively reduced. The direct relationship between skill levels and control over the work situation, determined within the evolving division of labor, meant the fragmentation and routinization of ever-widening spheres of work activities. This process of "rationalization" defined each task, often reducing a job to easily learned mechanical movements that had to be performed with exactitude and according to a carefully prescribed rhythm. In the historical process of development, those who gained employment in the upper levels of the hierarchy in administrative, technical, and scientific activities tended to gain skills, to engage in creative work, and to assume whatever levels of control over their work situation that higher echelons of management delegated, according to the imperatives of the technical division of labor (and within the limits of the social division of labor). This process formed the structural basis of the semiautonomous fraction of the middle class.

The semiautonomy of many professionals, technicians, researchers, and various categories of staff employees in corporations and government agencies is a major factor in defining their position as middle class. Workers enjoy no such autonomy. This semiautonomy is based on the coordinative and developmental tasks that are by technical necessity delegated by managers to technically skilled employees. Capitalists and managers are not capable of producing technological innovations; they hire a staff of scientists to think and invent for them and a larger technical staff to implement and operate innovations. The complexity of administration is such in large corporate units that management even has to hire specialists to devise systems of management; and they fill offices with other specialists to analyze the data on which informed management decisions can be made. Of course, in time other experts are employed to convert each of these scientific and administrative processes into an industrial-type division of labor with their own fragmentation and hierarchical ordering of labor in process of dequalification.

Unlike the administrative fraction of the middle class, the labor of scientists, technicians, and staff employees is directly productive: They do not regularly perform supervisory roles or exercise control functions in the system of exploitation and class domination. They exercise only such bureaucratic authority as is necessary to their coordinative and developmental activity. As educated, skilled labor they are exploited by capital for the contribution their activities make to facilitating the further development of the material forces of production, to augmenting the productivity of the labor force, and to improving the technical or organizational efficiency of the production process so as to promote profit maximization. Their class position differs from workers in that their work *requires* at least a limited autonomy. They are hired to carry out technical and creative tasks that capital has not yet been able to transform into routinized tasks performed by unskilled or semiskilled detail workers. They are able to escape entire subordination in the system of class domination and earn incomes that contain a premium for their skilled labor.

Wright describes the position of semi autonomous employees well (though he does not quite consider them a fraction of the middle class):

> In their immediate work environment, they maintain the work process of the independent artisan while still being employed by capital as a wage labourer . . . many white-collar technical employees and certain highy skilled craftsmen have at least a limited form of this autonomy in their immediate labour process. Such minimal control over the physical means of production by employees outside of the authority hierarchy constitutes the basic contradictory location between the petty bourgeoisie and the proletariat [1976:36].

In discussing planners, systems and production analysts, and the like, a group of Italian technicians notes that "the fundamental criterion that defines their special status is the degree of autonomy arising from the nature of their jobs and the influence that this exerts over the process of production" (Il Manifesto, in Gorz, 1976:126).

The semiautonomous fraction in the United States included 4.6 million scientific and technical employees in 1970. This represents a 60 percent increase in numbers employed in the period 1960 to 1970. A number of technical pursuits have grown at an astounding rate. Engineers, for example, increased from 77,000 in 1910 to 297,000 in 1940 to 1.2 million in 1970. Accountants and auditors were hired by the thousands every year to check and double-check corporate ledgers; they numbered 39,000 in 1910, 238,000 in 1940, and 713,000 in 1970. In the decade of the 1960s computer specialists, operations and systems analysts, social scientists, public relations employees, and advertising agents multiplied at faster rates than other scientific and technical personnel. On the other hand, occupations such as chemist, draftsmen, forester and conservationist, and life or physical scientist have grown at a much slower than average rate. Eight percent of all professional, technical, and kindred workers are self-employed. Self-employment among scientific and technical personnel is less than 5 percent, with somewhat higher percentages among architects, accountants, and social scientists. Twenty-three percent work for government. Scientific and technical careers remain largely male dominated; only 23 percent of the semiautonomous fraction are female, and they are disproportionately located in the census category "other professional and technical" (this includes a variety of mainly lower level technical activities the census does not deem worthy to specify). Between 1940 and 1970, the proportion of the male labor force in professional, technical, and kindred occupations doubled, while the proportion of the female labor force employed in these occupations remained constant over the three decades. This began to change as sectors of technical work became dequalified and feminized in the 1970s.

This fraction of the middle class is divided between an upper level of "technocrats" and a mass of technicians. Engineers, scientists, and highly skilled technicians do not constitute a large proportion of the labor force. Braverman estimates that "the technical knowledge required to operate the various industries of the United States is concentrated in a grouping in the neighborhood of only 3 percent of the entire working population — although this percentage is higher in some industries and lower in others" (1974:242).

In the course of their occupational careers, this upper stratum of scientists and staff professionals often move into administrative positions, sometimes climbing to higher managerial levels. The legions of technicians, on the other hand, tend to experience a decline in their conditions of work and are subject or potentially subject to deterioration in their work situation as semiautonomous employees.

The paradoxical character of the position of semiautonomous employees as a whole is that their own activity in the invention and operationalization of new techniques and organizational innovations can have the effect of devaluing their labor power. This is true to the extent that technical and organizational initiatives are applied to the fragmentation and routinization of technical and developmental activities. This has already resulted in a considerable downgrading of the labor power of certain technical and scientific pursuits, such as drafting and chemistry. These activities have been transformed into a division of labor of dequalified work performed by technicians of narrow, specialized skills. "In applying the Taylor system to others, the mental worker is obligated to apply it to himself" (Glucksmann, 1976:82).

There is another important aspect emphasized by Carchedi. Since technicians can be trained in large numbers at low cost in comparison to skilled professionals and scientists, these professions are also subject to what he terms "wage goods devaluation:"

> The possibility is always open for those agents who are exposed to devaluation through dequalification (e.g., technicians whose operation is fragmented and who thus lose part of the global function of capital) to be subjected also to wage goods devaluation (when, e.g., their technical training and education can be produced more cheaply) [1975b:390].

There is a whole body of literature on the postindustrial society thesis (see especially Bell, 1973) that posits the semiautonomy of an increasing range of occupations as the trend of the future. Guildlike structures of occupations with a monopoly on specialized knowledge and expertise are said to be reemerging and undermining—even replacing—the traditional prerogatives of management to organize the division of labor (see especially Friedson, 1973). This is entirely false. The trend is not toward a revived guild form in occupations, but in fact an accelerated reassertion of managerial prerogatives in the reorganization of the division of labor. The semiautonomy of scientific, technical, and professional labor, as we demonstrate in Chapter 10, is being whittled away and labor power in these spheres dequalified.

Only a few words need be said at this point concerning the relations between this fraction of the middle class and the bourgeoisie and working class. Gorz says of this relation:

> They have a monopoly of technical and intellectual skills required by the production process and they *deny* these skills to the workers. Their role is to dequalify workers and to reduce work to manual work pure and simple. They represent the skill and knowledge of which workers have been robbed, the separation between intellectual and manual work, between conception and execution. They enjoy significant financial, social and cultural privileges. They are the workers' most immediate enemy [1976:175].

But this overstates the case. Unlike the administrative fraction, which is directly bound up in relations of exploitation and domination, scientific and technical personnel are relatively isolated from the sharpest class conflicts. Historically, their antagonistic relation with the managerial bourgeoisie as hired employees has been softened by the semiautonomy of their place in the production process, their socially respected position as experts, and their higher incomes as skilled, productive workers. Their location at the margins of corporate or governmental authority structures does not bring them into as deep an antagonistic relation with workers as Gorz believes. However, to the extent that more recent changes in the labor process have the effect of devaluing the labor power of scientific and technical employees and subordinating them in a controlled labor process, the structural basis for sharper antagonistic relations with the bourgeoisie emerges.

The Independents

What is conventionally defined as the petty bourgeoisie is composed of distinct strata of self-employed persons: small businessmen in commerce and services, independent professionals in private practice, craftsmen and servicemen, a variety of self-employed people in the cultural sphere (entertainers, artists, writers), and farm proprietors. To these strata might be added persons unaccounted for by the census, the self-employed in illegal activities.

Until well into the twentieth century, the petty bourgeoisie in North America and Europe was a social class of major social weight. Today, the traditional petty bourgeoisie has been eliminated as an independent class with its own economic base because the small-scale production and distribution of goods and services characteristic of the competitive stage of capitalism has been submerged into the interstices of the structure of the corporate economy. While the petty bourgeoisie no longer exists as a distinct class, the numbers of own account workers, while in continual decline, are still significant (1 in 14 in the U.S. labor force was self-employed in 1970). The thesis developed here is that over the course of this century, the "new" middle class of salaried employees first eclipsed and finally absorbed major segments of the old petty bourgeoisie as part of itself, while the other strata have been absorbed into the working class.

In 1970, 5.9 million persons (7.7 percent of the labor force) were self-employed in the United States. This is a considerable decrease since 1940, when 9.8 million persons (18.9 percent of the labor force) were self-employed.

Apart from dwindling numbers of small farmers, business proprietors are the largest grouping within the independents, numbering over one million in 1970. However, there were also nearly one million self-employed professionals and technicians. Together with 150,000 independent cultural and intellectual producers and about 400,000 insurance and real estate agents, manufacturing sales representatives, and certain other salespeople, they constitute a fraction of the middle class that numbered about 2.7 million persons (3.4 percent of the labor force in 1970).

The working class also has a fraction that pursues self-employment. While this may seem in contradiction to the formal definition of a working class (those who have only their labor power to sell), the actual economic and social circumstances of craftsmen, service repairmen, and other self-employed workers with specialized skills are distinctly working class. Their social origins and social ties are within the working class. Historically, the artesanal basis of production has been destroyed and the craft sectors of the old petty bourgeoisie have been largely proletarianized. Independent craft activities, teamstering, and servicing remain highly unstable and precariously situated in the face of corporate intrusion into all areas of production, distribution, and services. While in 1970 there still remained 835,000 independently employed craftsmen (7.9 percent of the labor force in the sector), the trades are highly fluid. A small number of workers gain skills in industry and open shops of their own. Many such ventures fail, and workers, their dreams of independence shattered, return to the labor market. The crafts with the largest proportion of self-employed workers (between 12 and 20 percent) are mechanics and repair, construction crafts, apparel and upholstering, and cabinetmaking. Self-employment in the service sector stood at 487,000 in 1970 (5.5 percent of all service workers).

One of the chief sources of livelihood for the most oppressed sectors of the population, the "underclass" fraction of the working class, is self-employment. A substantial segment of the working class is excluded from stable employment within corporate or state spheres and is reduced to irregular employment in low-wage sectors of the economy (especially services), unemployment, welfare, and crime. The Census Bureau does not provide data on those persons self-employed in criminal activity. But this unofficial sector of the labor force contains an unknown, but undoubtedly significant and probably increasing, number of entrepreneurs. Persons who derive their livelihoods in whole or in part from the sale of drugs in the United States must number in the tens of thousands. Gambling, prostitution, theft and fencing, and various hustles are important sources of employment for sectors of the population marginalized from the mainstream of the economy, though not secure or renumerative work for the great majority engaged in criminal activities.

Perhaps a case could be made that the petty bourgeoisie has been more transformed than eliminated, or "absorbed into" the middle class or working class as I put it earlier. Development liquidates sectors of the petty bourgeoisie, but it also opens up opportunities for entrepreneurship in other sectors. The historical process of market extension into all spheres of social existence provides numerous opportunities for entrepreneurs of all types to expand their range of activities, providing services not previously marketed. Yet the case is not a very strong one, as these activities are gradually subsumed or reorganized by large-scale capital. For example, an increasing proportion of small businessmen are *de facto* managerial employees of large corporations, in that they depend on franchises or contracts with large corporations. Their class position is thus similar to the salaried administrative employees of corporations (except that the interests in private property and profitability of the independents are more salient). The independents of today are much more dependent than the small entrepreneurs of old.

Among professionals there is still considerable self-employment, but the circumstances of practicing a profession have substantially changed. More than half of physicians and lawyers and 85 percent of dentists operate entirely or in part from private offices. Ten percent or more of accountants, architects, pharmacists, health technicians, and other registered practitioners are self-employed. Nevertheless, self-employed professionals are no longer the old-style practitioners who simply hang out a shingle on graduation from professional school. The ranks of self-employed professionals are quite fluid. In the course of professional careers many doctors, lawyers, therapists, family counselors, accountants, architects, some Ph.D.s in academic disciplines, and others move from one fraction of the middle class to another. A traditional lifelong, successful private practice is less and less viable for professionals, and much less so for their sons and daughters who join the ranks of the salaried middle class. In general, the professional stratum of the independents tends to decline as services are organized by capital or gradually socialized by the state. The same is true for artists and writers. The salaried middle class is strengthened by their numbers.

Not much need be said about the relations between this fraction of the middle class and the major social classes. Each phase in the development of capitalism further reduces the possibilities for an independent existence outside the wage-labor/capital relation, placing the independents in objective opposition to big business and the welfare state. With respect to relations with the working class, many independents exist in day-to-day antagonistic relations with clienteles. The small businessman and professional practitioner in particular must be, to survive, in a position to obtain a profit. Often several low-wage workers are employed to organize delivery of services so as to enhance profitability. The quality of services rendered inevitably becomes secondary to the profits to be gained. Independents exist either in a relation of exploitation to their clientele in face-to-face situations or of dependence on corporate capital.

Notes

1. Robinson argues: "The state is constrained by cultural, economic and political factors to initiate the forms of work organization found in the private sector. This process of imitation takes two forms: technique-specific imitation; and systematic imitation. The first form dominated state employment until the early '70s, but since then pressure has grown to turn to more systematic forms" (1982:8).

2. Gilbert and Specht's book, *The Emergence of Social Welfare and Social Work* (1981), treats the profession thoroughly, although somewhat conventionally and uncritically.

Sherry Gorelick: Class Relations and the Development of the Teaching Profession

> Schoolteachers, especially those in grammar and high schools, are the economic proletarians of the professions. These outlying servants of learning form the largest occupational group of the professional pyramid.
> —C. Wright Mills, *White Collar*, p. 129.

> There is today an ever-present temptation to suppose that class is a thing. . . . "It," the working class, is assumed to have real existence, which can be defined almost mathematically—so many men who stand in a certain relation to the means of production. . . . If we remember that class is a relationship, and not a thing, we cannot think in this way.
> —E.P. Thompson, *The Making of the English Working Class*, pp. 10-11.

Class is a process in a double sense: It is a set of relationships in dynamic interaction at any one moment, and it is a historical process. These two "senses" are only *analytically* separable: The historical and the relational are really two aspects of the same unity.[1] To understand the class "position" of teachers, we must understand the historical process that has shaped the formation of the teaching profession, and the contradictory forces that continue to buffet teachers within the class system.

The teaching profession took its determinate form at the turn of the century. With the development of a national economy after the Civil War, a nationwide capitalist class drew its work force from the expropriated peasantry and artisanry of Europe and the United States. Economic development, perennial "labor shortage," and the continuing problem of labor discipline led capitalists to recruit ever-new batches of European peasants, who presented continuing problems of labor discipline. The working class organized into the first successful nationwide unions and waged militant strikes that were often marked by violence on both sides. Faced with the political organization of workers, small businessmen, and farmers into such oppositional movements as the socialist, labor, and populist movements, a segment of the business class united with intellectuals and other social reformers in the Progressive Movement. The Progressives' general aim was to combat radicalism, promote social reform, introduce business "efficiency," and secure political control for the members of a business elite and their academic associates.

The teaching profession, like the Progressive Movement, grew out of class struggle. Teaching expanded because schooling expanded, and schooling expanded because of the development of capitalism and class conflict. Workers demanded compulsory schooling and prohibition of child labor. Capitalists promoted schools to control and socialize the children of labor, to "Americanize" immigrant (and socialist) labor, and to teach manual training, substituting publicly taught skill training for union-controlled apprenticeship. Unions fought the imposition of manual training. These forces, and the simple increase in the school-age population through the recruitment of an expanded working class, vastly increased the need for teachers.

As soon as any category of labor becomes large, capital develops an interest in controlling and cheapening it. As the teaching work force expanded, teaching was transformed. The development of the graded school permitted specialization. Women were hired at half the pay. A control structure of male administrators was created, and Taylorism was applied to school organization. The fraction of the bourgeoisie linked to the Progressive Movement took *direct* control of big-city school systems against the opposition of teachers and of local ethnic urban communities. The Progressive bourgeoisie took *indirect* control of schooling across the country through their influence on training and their creation of Teachers College as the "lead institution," defining teaching "professionalism" and training superintendents of schools and other high-level administrators sent out throughout the nation. These control efforts, and the maintenance of low salaries for teachers, encountered and provoked a feminist response within the National Education Association and a unionization movement.

Because the establishment, nature, and control of schooling have been the objects of class struggle, the job of teachers has been at the front line of a clash of ideologies and interests. Teachers are ideological workers, and their position is fraught with conflicting pressures and contradictory forces.

Class Conflict, The Expansion of Schooling, and the Expansion of Teaching

"In 1820, half of the factory workers were boys and girls 'of the tender age' of nine and ten years, who worked twelve to thirteen hours a day" (Foner, 1971:65). For over a century, from the 1820s well into the twentieth century, organizations of labor fought for the restriction of child labor, the shortening of the working day, and compulsory schooling. In the early nineteenth century, workingmen's parties demanded free public elementary schooling, and some local workers' groups set up schools of their own. As had some other organizations before them, the Knights of Labor in the 1880s supported free rudimentary schooling *in the context of their demand for the abolition of child labor*. They stressed *compulsory* attendance because they understood the coercive nature of "voluntary" education where parents were underpaid and industrialists had the option of voluntarily hiring their children for even lower pay. The AFL took a similar stance and became more and more adamant in favor of compulsory attendance and prohibition of child labor as the decades wore on (Curoe, 1926; Hogan, 1978).

In this struggle, business groups sought to prevent, limit, or weaken all laws that tampered with child labor. In times of social crisis, however, when faced with an active and radical working-class movement, or in economic depressions, when unemployed youth roamed the streets, capitalists were more likely to become enraptured by the civic need to inculcate moral discipline by means of expansion of "the common school." They espoused truancy laws that stipulated that children had to be "either at work or at school" (Calcott, 1931:252). In the 1870s and '80s, with the rise of labor militancy, organized labor secured the support of middle-class social reformers in curtailing or modifying child labor by some form of enforced schooling.

From the workers' point of view, child labor laws made schooling economically possible; from a bourgeois point of view, child labor laws made schooling politically necessary. The prevalence of radicalism among foreign-born workers led to a zealous—sometimes frantic—effort to Americanize the immigrants, to use the schoolhouse as "a stronghold of defense against the spread of socialistic and un-American ideas," as New York's Governor Flower said in 1892 (Rudy, 1949:213). And John Buchanan, principal of one of New York City's new high schools, declared in a Progressive magazine: "Compulsory education we must have as a safeguard for our institutions" (1902-688).

An enormous expansion of schooling and therefore of teaching resulted from large-scale immigration and the struggles over compulsory schooling, an end to child labor, Americanization, and manual training. The number of five- to eighteen-year-olds enrolled in school rose from six and a half million in 1870 to fifteen and a half million by 1880, a rise from 57 percent to over 72 percent of the age group (Perkinson, 1968:70). Between 1870 and 1930 the U.S. population doubled; the number of persons engaged in teaching multiplied eightfold, increasing from 126,882 in 1870 to 1,062,615 in 1930. Burritt's study of the professions of the graduates of 37 representative colleges and universities, from 1642 through 1900, revealed that "within [the last] 100 years the profession of teaching has grown from about one-twentieth to about one fourth of the graduates." Teaching surpassed the ministry in 1880 and law in 1890. "Thus at the close of the century it is the dominant profession, with business as its closest competitor" (Burritt, 1912:19,77).

The Development and Transformation of the Teaching Profession

Teaching had always been a modest vocation. Teachers came from poor families and had little more schooling than their students. In rural areas boarding and meals, rotated among the families of their students, comprised part of the wage. In cities the salary was so low as to require odd-jobbing to provide enough for subsistence. As late as 1910, when L. D. Coffman did his dissertation on *The Social Composition of the Teaching Population*, he found to his professional dismay that "most teachers become so out of economic motive," having come from families whose income "can be but little more than a bare minimum" (Coffman, 1911:54,65).

Before the 1860s teachers taught by rote, cookbook style, hearing recitations of prescribed materials. As late as 1910, the nation's teachers had, on average, four years of schooling beyond elementary school. Twenty-one percent of Coffman's sample had had less than a year's schooling beyond grammar school; almost half had less than four years of high school (1911:31-36). Although the years of training were sufficiently short to make teaching a possible profession for youngsters whose families could not dream of sustaining the expense involved in the even longer preparation for medicine or law, it was in itself a severe struggle. Even Coffman, who feared the influence of teachers from the uncultured lower classes, expressed his admiration that such families would "give their children the advantage of four years of school beyond the elementary school" (Coffman, 1911:65; see also Bernheimer, 1905:191; Van Denburg, 1911:46-47, Part 7; Covello, 1970).

The degree to which becoming a teacher was economically difficult for the children of the poor may be gathered from a reanalysis of Van Denburg's data on New York City high school students. Although the majority of high school girls wished to become teachers, only a small percentage would actually succeed; among boys the proportions were even smaller.[2] Those children of the poor who became teachers did so against great odds.

Training of the Teaching Workforce

The expansion of schooling fostered vast changes in the teaching force. Aside from the sheer need for much greater numbers of teachers, teaching itself had to be changed. At minimum the development of the high school meant that some teachers had to be trained to at least the high school level, and some college training began to seem necessary to keep the teacher a little ahead of the students. But the training of teachers began to involve not only the lengthening of their training but a change in its nature. Beginning in the 1860s, teaching began to be seen as more than drumming a prescribed set of facts into children's memories: It came to be a matter of eliciting understanding. As Elwood Cubberly, a major force in the "professionalization" of teaching and the managerialization of educational administration, put it in his extremely influential text:

> [A] real "technique of instruction" was now called for. . . . Class lessons must be thought out in advance, and teacher-preparation in itself meant a great change in teaching procedure. Emancipated from dependence on the words

of a text, and able to stand before a class full of a subject and able to question freely, teachers became conscious of a new strength and a professional skill unknown in the days of textbook reciting [1934:390-391].

The various "Progressives" who created this newly professional teacher were most concerned about the nature of the person who "stood before the class." Coffman, writing from the heart of administrative influence, Teachers College, felt that "certainly the lower the class from which teachers come in social position the more inadequate their rational basis and insight for determining the values of the materials and techniques of education" (1911:54). He feared that they might be "insufficiently Americanized."

There are two obvious solutions to the perceived problem of the cultural inadequacies of the low-born: increased training and increased administrative control. Progressivism produced both.

The number of public normal schools rose from less than 25 in 1860 to over 150 in 1900, and close to 300 by 1930 (Cubberly, 1934:384, Figure 107). But the normal school was to be a relatively transitory phenomenon. First developed to extend the training of teachers in ordinary school subjects beyond the level of the students they were themselves teaching, the normal schools were transformed into schools for the professional study of the art and science of teaching. Later they were either supplanted by college departments of education or retained as a lower level of instruction for teachers when administrators were receiving B.A.s in education or graduate degrees. More recently, they have been transformed once again into general education institutions, offering the Liberal Arts B.A. (Cubberly, 1934:384,400; Whittemore, 1962:65; Anonymous, n.d.; Cremin, 1961:169).

The class nature of teacher-training went through a similar development. Originally, the less impoverished prospective teachers went to the normal schools, the poorest getting by with a few years of public school. But with the development of college and university departments of education, it was the poorer teaching recruits who went to normal school and the more privileged who were trained in the public college departments of education. They, in turn, were overshadowed by those more privileged still: the graduates of Columbia University's Teachers College (Coffman, 1911: 77; Jessup, 1916:112). With the creation of Teachers College, the institutionalization of training was integrally linked to the creation of a professional ideology, an ideology which turned business needs into invisible professional assumptions.

Progressivism and the Development of a Professional Ideology

It was the Progressives who defined professionalism (Cremin, 1961:-175). More than anyone else, it was Nicholas Murray Butler who fashioned the ideology of professionalism. The son of a New Jersey businessman who had been President of the Paterson Board of Education, Butler was personally groomed by Frederick A.P. Barnard, President of Columbia College, to implement Barnard's 1881 plan for "a Columbia University school of education that would provide leadership for the whole of American public education" (Whittemore, 1962:62-63). In the nineties, Butler was to become "the father of the College Entrance Board" and President of the National Education Association. Later still, he was to be a member of the National Civic Foundation, which James Weinstein called "the most important single organization of the socially-conscious big businessmen and their academic and political theorists" (1968:6).

Applying the typical model of educational innovation, Barnard and Butler decided to "build up a teacher's college outside the University, and to bring it later into organic relations with the University" (Cremin, 1961:171; Whittemore, 1961:71). Accordingly in 1887 Barnard and several powerful Columbia Trustees, several of whom were members of the Industrial Education Association, secured the presidency of that association for Nicholas Murray Butler. The executive vice-president of the IEA, Grace Hoadley Dodge, daughter of "one of New York's wealthiest merchants," had built the IEA from the Kitchen Garden Association, "dedicated to the amelioration of a slum living through education for household management," into a powerful force for manual training. She had just secured a $10,000 gift from George W. Vanderbilt in order to set up a training school for teachers of manual training. (Vanderbilt's generosity to higher education was made possible by his labor policies: In 1877 he decreed a wage cut on his railroads. When workers struck, militia killed 26 of them and wounded hundreds more. The strike was crushed, and Vanderbilt's ability to have cheap labor to expand his fortune was protected [Whittemore, 1962:81; Perkinson, 1968:104-105].) Butler and Dodge immediately set up the New York College for the Training of Teachers, later to be named Teachers College of Columbia University, an institution which Butler was to dominate, as president, for 32 years. In 1892 Vanderbilt wrote the college another check, this one for $100,000 (Whittemore, 1962:97-98).

The class content of pedagogy: professionalism for the teacher; vocationalism for the student. Butler outlined the meaning of professionalism in innumerable articles and speeches. Professionalism required high admissions standards, supervised teaching, and educational theory. "On these principles, and on the further one that manual training should be an integral part of the common school course, the New York College for the Training of Teachers has been founded" (Butler, 1889; Whittemore, 1961:86,89).

Manual training was a subject of great controversy between capital and labor. In part, manual training was a response to technological change in industry. But those changes in industrial technology are themselves complex: they are a result of competition among businessmen and of conflict between management and labor over productivity. The continual problem of socializing new waves of ex-peasants and ex-artisans also encouraged manufacturers to mechanize (Gutman, 1973:582).

Mechanization undermined apprenticeship; manufacturers saw manual training as a mode of skill training to replace apprenticeship. From the point of view of workers' organizations, however, employers' interest in the manual training movement, which gained momentum after several expositions in the 1870s, was motivated by the possibility of using public schools to break craft control of apprenticeship and union control over the size of the skilled work force (Cremin, 1961:33).

In 1887 the Knights of Labor supported manual training as an effort to give due dignity to labor and to prepare boys "to become good mechanics, of wider mental horizon than heretofore," but the AFL opposed manual training in the 1890s as an attempt "to turn out botch mechanics who can be used as 'dummies' in time of strikes." With the development and expansion of the high school, the controversy continued, the NAM advocating "giving dignity to labor" through trade training beginning at age nine, and the AFL asserting that "general education is more important than industrial education."[3] (Note that it was primarily the businessmen who spoke of giving dignity to labor and the unions that espoused general cultural education.)

Thus when Butler and Dodge based their Teachers College on the Industrial Education Association, they were integrating the corporate side of a management-labor conflict into the training and professional ideology of teachers. In his first report as president of the IEA, Butler promoted manual training even further:

> The college for the training of teachers is to be founded to give systematic instruction to persons desirous of entering on the profession of teaching. For the present, at least, the instruction given will be almost wholly confined to those hitherto neglected factors in Education which may be included under the name of Industrial Training [Whittemore, 1962:85].

Having integrated manual training into the science and philosophy of professional education, Butler had two tasks: He had to convince the businessmen who supported the Training College that manual training needed pedagogy, and he had to convince the educational administrators that pedagogy implied manual training.

To the businessmen/trustees his explanation was pragmatic:

> "Teachers must be trained so as to view manual training in the light of the history and principles of all education, and not as a special . . . addition to the course of study. . . ." Reluctantly, the philanthropically minded trustees accepted his ideas, convinced by the argument that the cause of manual training could be promoted in a permanent way only by thoroughly trained teachers [Whittemore, 1962:84, quoting Butler, 1899:345].

That is, manual training, which was a most controversial political issue, could best be slipped into the schools if it lost its special character and became seemingly politically neutralized into a professional ideology.

"Persuading" educational administrators, on the other hand, was more a matter of power than persuasion. The principal of the New Jersey State Normal School had taken the pro-labor position, that "teachers for industrial schools should be drawn from the ranks of skilled mechanics." In 1887 he wrote: "Teaching industrial pursuits is beyond the scope of operations of the State Normal School" (Whittemore, 1962:127, quoting Washington Hasbrouck). But in 1887, Butler had secured a political appointment to the New Jersey State Board of Education, which made him also a trustee of the State Normal School. In the 1889 Trustees Report, he is quoted at length in a purely theoretical and philosophical justification of the learning virtues of manual training, and "by 1891 the State Normal School had a new building containing industrial education classrooms, and the course of study required manual training of all students" (Whittemore, 1962:128).

The organizations representing capital and labor struggled for 30 years over the content, direction, meaning, and control of manual training. Labor unions continued to regard manual training as "scab training," even though they eventually confined their opposition to demanding labor representation on boards of supervision. Thus, Butler's version of professionalism (philosophical manual training) gave "scab training" a respectable and even erudite face. Butler's ideology of scientific and "nonpolitical" professional education rationalized the establishment of a business-oriented pedagogy.

The class content of pedagogy: teachers as professional Americanizers. Americanization was a response by the white Protestant bourgeoisie to the political threat posed by immigrant labor. It was the bourgeoisie's attempt to assert (and create) cultural and political hegemony. This cultural hegemony was to be inculcated through the schools with the hope that, through the children, parents would also learn the proper discipline of labor and the proper political attitudes.

Not all workers responded eagerly. Truancy and dropping out were recurrent problems (Katz, 1968:Part I; Greer, 1972). A Polish newspaper in Chicago told its readers:

> Anxiety should furrow the brows of every father and mother concerning those whose children who, because of necessity or some other reason, attend American Schools. These schools . . . cause the children to lose interest in their own languages, the history of their nation and their customs. It . . . makes a typical American out of them.

They demanded that the Polish language be taught in the public schools, and despite their poverty, they created an extensive system of private Polish schools as "a shield against . . . submergence in the boundless sea of Americanism" (Hogan 1978:251). Other Catholic groups did the same, responding, in part, to the rabid anti-Catholicism of "American" Schools. Thus Americanization was the subject, not merely of the imposition of a dominant culture, but of cultural *conflict.*

As a conscious program of Americanization became part of the schools, teachers became professional "Americanizers." Civics lessons in the elementary schools were to emphasize American institutions and love of country. The teacher was extolled to encourage children to be kind to immigrant newcomers, to help them to adjust and "learn our ways." But they were not instructed to teach all the children appreciation (or knowledge) of the immigrants' "ways" (see, for example, Harris, 1920). Accordingly, courses were "designed especially for social workers and teachers doing work with the foreign-born" (College of the City of New York, 1925-26).

Even before the Americanization program entered its most "hysterical" phase, teachers were expected to be (regardless of origin) "American, 100% pure" (Mahoney, 1920:9). Coffman, remember, worried that lower-class teachers might be "insufficiently Americanized." Given the proper ideology, however, their immigrant origins might be a decided asset. At the City College of New York, Magnus Gross argued that City College's new immigrant student population would have special entre in assimilating their younger siblings:

> Who, better than they, . . . will be . . . likely to assimilate the diversified moral and mental habits, the foreign customs and prejudices of a mixed population, of which they themselves have formed a part from childhood? [Gross, 1904:2-3].

Nevertheless, while the children of immigrants were becoming teachers and principals in the public schools, higher administration was being developed (by white Protestants) at Columbia Teachers College. By the 1920s, Columbia had established Columbia House, which "presented a very complete program of Americanization courses, including those that can be regarded as strictly professional in the sense that they prepare for classroom teaching" (Mahoney, 1920:9). In a period of great conflict between a new corporate bourgeoisie and an immigrant working class, the ideological reliability of teachers of poor immigrant origins was sought through the integration of Americanization into teacher training, and through the creation of a structure of administrative control.

Administrative Control: The Sexual Division of Labor, School Centralization, and Scientific Management

Through the "feminization" of the teaching force, the sexual division of labor became the main form of control of the working teacher. Through school centralization the business class took direct control of top educational policymaking for big-city schools. And, through the school management movement, Progressives created a system of indirect, intermediate control through an educational bureaucracy. Both feminization and "school management" involved lowering the teaching wage bill. All three developments provoked teacher opposition in some form.

The sexual division of labor. The expansion of the teaching work force moved school boards to seek ways of lowering the cost of teachers' salaries. The replacement of the one-room schoolhouse by the graded school[4]

rationalized the employment of women in the lower grades. Sexist conceptions of women's greater "natural facility" for dealing with younger children provided the rationale for their employment in the (more numerous
and lower-paid) lower grades, while men's greater strength was presumably
needed to tame the older, high-school-age brutes. But Charles William
Eliot admitted that although "it is true that sentimental reasons are often
given for the almost exclusive employment of women in the common
schools . . . the effective reason is economy. . . . If women had not been
cheaper than men, they would not have replaced nine-tenths of the men in
American public schools" (Katz, 1958:56-62). Meanwhile, the feminization
of teaching led more girls to stay in school through high school, thereby
adding to the expansion of schooling and of jobs for teachers (Davies,
1979:250-252).

Women moved from being less than 30 percent of the teaching work
force in 1871 to over 78 percent in 1911. Women were paid less than half the
salary of men in the same position. But increasingly, they were not hired to
fill the same position.

> There is less difference between the salaries of the two sexes than is com-
> monly believed. The difference in pay is due usually to a difference in
> position, which means a difference in work.

> [The low salary] partly explains why young men are increasingly dissuaded
> from entering teaching. It is claimed . . . that the male recruits in teaching
> come from a lower social stratum than they did a half century ago.[5]

> Practically all of the graded school positions have been pre-empted by
> women; men still survive in public school work as "managing" or executive
> officers [Coffman, 1911:39,82,28].

The men "survived" chiefly by managing to preempt administration.
Throughout the country men became school administrators, high school
teachers, and teachers of special subjects, particularly manual training
(Jessup, 1911: Bronner, 1920). Thus, five processes intersected: teaching
required greater skill and planning; it required longer training; it became a
woman's profession; it became lower paid; and it became subject to an
administrative hierarchy. Administration spread both in extent and degree
of hierarchy, expanded by the centralization of school districts—which was
itself an expression of the effort of the Progressives to control the national
school system—and by the school efficiency management movement.

The centralization of control over city schools. Across the United States
big businessmen organized at the turn of the century to gain control of city
governments from local Democratic "political machines." In most major
metropolises, municipal power was centralized (Weinstein, 1968); and
there the business class mobilized to centralize control over city schools, to
establish high schools (which were generally unpopular), and to wrest
decisionmaking from local, primarily ethnic businessmen. The case of New
York City may be taken as typical (see also Gersman, 1970).

In 1896, the Progressives took control of New York City Schools administratively by wresting control over the public schools from the elected local school boards and centering it in an appointed central School Board for Greater New York. According to David Hammack, the aim of school centralization was "to reduce the principal to a mere record keeper." As for teachers, the Progressives' aim was "to subject these municipal employees to the discipline of a streamlined bureaucracy" (1969:10).

The main organizational force in the seven-year struggle was a Committee of 100, organized by Nicholas Murray Butler. Members of the Committee of 100 were generally big businessmen with direct business interests in the projects involved in "municipal reform"—tenement building, street-widening, subway-building, and other infrastructural projects—as well as class interests in supporting that education "which would inculcate respect for private property and individual liberty" (Hammack, 1969:27, quoting ex-Mayor Hewitt). In seeking to establish mayoral appointment of a small, strong, centralized board, they saw themselves as making education "non-political," implementing businesslike methods, and substituting "intelligent men and women" for foreigners. School board positions had to be "sanitized" by making them subject to appointment by the mayor instead.

Butler had accomplished the same feat of political accumulation in New Jersey on both the state level and in Paterson, Trenton, and Camden. But he and his associates were not unopposed in their effort to "sanitize" public education. Ranged against them in the New York school centralization fight were business and community leaders from Yorkville, Harlem, and the Bronx whose base would be destroyed by centralization, some local politicans, and "nearly everyone connected with the public schools" (Hammack, 1969:4). Virtually *all* teachers opposed centralization vigorously and actively.

The battle was fierce. It took the Progressives seven years to win. In 1895, with the Progressives' attempt to legislate centralization in Albany, 4000 teachers attended a mass meeting sponsored by the New York City Teachers' Association. They accused Butler's "Committee of Five" of "trying to introduce politics into the schools," and lobbied successfully against the bill. The audience at a meeting held by the Women's Association for the Improvement of the Public Schools were so hostile that Thomas Hunter, president of the Normal School, "abandoned the attempt to speak [to their meeting] and [reformer Payson] Merril retired under a barrage of catcalls."

When, despite the vociferous and virtually unanimous opposition of the school staff, the Progressives finally won, teacher appointment began to be subject to a newly formed Board of Examiners which began to compile an "eligibles list." Beginning in 1899, the teachers were appointed in order of their placement on that list. In 1904, the central board took control of the selection of texts, and even the construction of syllabi (Palmer, 1905: 291, 298).

Teachers had formerly been picked by ward bosses who examined them on such inherently political criteria as "manners" and "moral character" (Hammack, 1969:120-122: Palmer, 1905:112). Now they were emancipated from the ward bosses only to be subjected to the Board of Examiners. Their required years of training had been lengthened, and their control over curriculum had been weakened. Their work had been dignified into a "profession," but the meaning of that profession was carefully circumscribed. They were to do manual training; they practiced a nonmanual trade (McGurk, 1934:74).

The school management movement. Centralization gave the bourgeoisie control over top decision-making in big-city school systems. The school management movement created a managerial structure—a hierarchy of control—over the working teacher in school systems throughout the country. The simple increase in the number of schools would have multiplied administrative personnel, but it need not have created a bureaucratic hierarchy were it not for centralization and the desire for accountability, inspection, and control.

Between 1913 and 1925 school administrators, under relentless atack by business and newspapers for the high cost (and high failure rate) in the schools, became obsessed by "school efficiency." Leaders of the top school administrators' organizations insisted on the direct application to the public schools of Frederick Taylor's work in "scientific management" (Callahan, 1962; Braverman, 1974). The school is a factory, they said. School superintendents must become "educational engineers." Teachers are the workers, who must be managed, trained, and commanded. Pupils are the raw materials. The "products" and methods must be measured and standardized. Most important of all, costs must be minutely measured and controlled. School plant must be used with "100% efficiency"—that is, all day and all year. In Gary, Indiana, the "platoon system" was devised, in which students were rotated among classrooms so that no teacher and no portion of the "school plant"—shops, laboratories, playground, classrooms—would remain idle for a moment. The platoon system was also known as "the Gary plan." Attempts were made to introduce it in school systems all across the country.

In 1913 Franklin Bobbitt developed Principles of Management for the schools closely patterned after Frederick Taylor's general principles. Callahan explains:

> Just as Taylor had said that the development of the science of the job was too difficult for the worker in the machine shop, so Bobbitt took the position that "The burden of finding the best methods is too large and too complicated to be laid on the shoulders of the teachers" [Callahan, 1962:87, quoting Bobbitt, 1913:51-52].

In education, as in industry, scientific management involved measurement fetishism and increased workloads for each employee. In industry the speed-up and reduction of wage costs was in the service of maximizing profits; in education it was in the service of minimizing taxes. In education, the efficiency movement was motivated by the desire to control culturally suspect teachers, to appease the critical businessmen who kept the administrators on their toes, to cope with school overcrowding continually aggravated by burgeoning immigration, and to reduce the amount of tax money spent on school buildings and teachers' salaries. In education, as in industry, scientific management was a managerial ideology, legitimizing management's effort to monopolize decision-making power, and implementing that attempted monopoly by means of bureaucratic accounting schemes. Administrators' salaries increased markedly, especially the salaries of those superintendents of schools who were famed for their business orientation and their implementation of school management (Callahan, 1962:216-218).

In New York City the *Journal of the Board of Education* listed charges and reprimands against individual teachers. It noted each teacher's absence, stating whether or not the absence was "excused" and if so, whether it was excused with or without pay (New York City Board of Education, 1910:II:205-1,205-2). Teachers had to have a doctor's note even when absent for a single day.[6] These rather demeaning regulations cast a rather strange light on Cubberly's grand portrait of the professional teacher who "stood before the class." Rather, these rules express the age of the professional administrator.

Beginning around 1905, the center of "professional" educational administration was Teacher's College. There men like Ellwood Cubberly and George strayer promulgated the business model of educational administration.

[Strayer] wrote a book on quantitative studies in educational administration with Thorndike, numerous survey reports, and textbooks on the teaching process and on elementary school arithmetic. He also produced . . . a series of materials to assist schoolmen with their business and building problems such as score cards and check lists for school buildings, standards for elementary and high school buildings, record books for high school and elementary school principals, . . . monthly reports for principals to keep track of the attendance of teachers, inventory record books for high schools and payroll forms.

And since he was the leader in the institution which trained by far the greatest number of persons in the field—persons who not only went into important superintendencies all over the country, but also went into teachers colleges and universities and taught courses in administration—his ideas, as they were translated into courses, programs and research, had a tremendous influence on the development of the school administrator in American education [Callahan, 1962:186-187].

Beyond their direct influence and their specific programs, the men at Teachers College had a profound, general cultural impact in establishing the idea of the school administrator as a professional (see Karier, 1967). Teachers College influence included the work of Coffman, whose concern over the social origins of teachers was expressed in his dissertation; and Van Denberg, whose 1911 dissertation united measurement-fetishism, worship of school efficiency, and a manual-training-oriented critique of the public schools (Van Denburg was to become a member of the New York City Board of Examiners in 1927. This is the board which, ever since centralization, has controlled teacher certification throughout the city [New York City Board of Education, 1927].

Through Teachers College, the "lead institution" in education, the Progressive bourgeoisie was able to create and train a network of male administrators, organizing hierarchies of management in school systems throughout the country, attempting to control their line supervisors—the (largely male) principals—and, through them, a work force of female and teachers of working-class origin.

The Teachers Fight Back

Taylorism in education objectified not only the worker (the teacher) but the future workers (the students.) The fact that the "raw material" and "product" of the school factory was human—children—provoked parents as well as teachers and gave teachers an ally in combating the platoon system. It also gave them a counterideology with which to fight the managerial ideology of the administrators—and fight they did. In New York City, the Gary plan was defeated by the opposition of the teaching and administrative staff and the rioting of the Lower East Side and Harlem communities, including some vandalism on the part of high school students. In other major cities similar coalitions prevailed. And the fact that the plan bore the name of Judge Gary, of U.S. Steel, only made the relationships clearer and the rage stronger, in an era when entrepreneurs were hated as "robber barons."

Efforts to control teachers' salaries and to minutely supervise their work provoked various forms of opposition. As early as 1897 New York teachers expressed sufficient "unrest," "agitation," and "discontent" about the low level of their salaries that the state legislature increased and rationalized teachers' salaries in New York City over the strong opposition of its Board of Education and mayor (Palmer, 1905:281-283). And within the National Educational Association, of which Butler was also president, a group of teachers associated with the movement to unionize teachers in Chicago organized an insurgent group.

In 1897 the insurgents mounted a successful campaign to wrest appointment to the Nominations Committee "that for all practical purposes, chose the N.E.A.'s officers" from the control of the president, in favor of the appointment of delegates selected by a majority of the members from each state. At the 1903 convention, in the face of Butler's attempt to restore appointive power to the president, Margaret Haley, "militant president of the Chicago Federation of Teachers [affiliated with the AFL], charged Butler with attempting to centralize power and shut out the women who made up 90 percent of the membership." At the 1907 convention, "a

California woman went so far as to attack the trustees as 'people who could be bought and sold'" (Whittemore, 1962:216-218;220).

The thirteen-year struggle between the movement of unionists and the increasingly exasperated Butler and his "old Guard" culminated, in 1910, in the election to the NEA presidency of Ella Flagg Young, candidate of the insurgents, and "a fighter for teachers' rights to organization and higher salaries."

> To Butler, the movement to organize teachers was unprofessional, dangerous, and little short of criminal. He told a Chicago audience in 1906 that if he were on the school board, he would "insist upon the passage of a bylaw that would dismiss any teacher that affiliated herself with a labor organization [Whittemore, 1962:224].

Many a school board did just that, but by 1906 the movement to unionize teachers was well under way. The AFL had started an organizing drive in 1902 in response to the application of Chicago Teachers for a charter. In 1916, the American Federation of Teachers became the first group of professional public servants to affiliate with the AFL.

In the period following the teachers' rising in the NEA, and in the New York centralization fight, the movement to introduce business efficiency, Scientific Management, Taylorism, the Factory Model, into the schools can only have fueled the teachers union movement. After all, if, as scientific managers claimed, the school was a factory, with children as the raw materials and products, the administrators as the managers, and the teachers as the employees, then the teachers were indeed not "free professionals," but employees.

And since they were employees, it was not so extraordinary that they thought of forming unions to defend their rights as employees. Indeed, where they were organized they were better able to fight not only for better salaries but against the very introduction of the factory model which overtook the school systems of less organized cities.

Contradictions Within the Teaching Profession

Teachers' unions were very much professional unions: They demanded the right to organize but eschewed the right to strike. (It was undignified; and besides, they were servants of the *whole* public [Curoe, 1926:137-142].

And yet they did organize. Salaries were extremely low and further depleted by inflation. A 1914 national survey showed teachers' annual salary to be considerably lower than that of "other skilled workers" (Jessup, 1916:110), such as plumbers, bricklayers, plasterers, painters, and, in some cities, molders and machinists. In Cleveland, plumbers averaged $1219 per year; elementary school teachers got $791 (Jessup, 1916:30,31). In 1890, the average annual salary of U.S. teachers was a little more than half that of all wage earners in manufacturing, and a little more than a quarter that of clerical workers and postal employees. In 1910, when coal miners received, on average, $558 per year, teachers received $492. In *each* year between 1890 and 1926, farm laborers and domestic servants were the only categories of worker earning less than did teachers. These were the two occupations most common for women from 1870 through 1920, when teaching supplanted farm labor as one of the two most common women's occupations (Historical Statistics, 1976:167,168; Baxendall et al., 1976: 406-407).

In view of the poor alternatives open to women, and in view of the fact that male and female teachers were predominantly persons of proletarian or small farm origins, teaching was probably a step up for most teachers, a step up in potential security and status which might have prevented them from feeling "proletarianized" by the low salary or the loss of control over textbooks and syllabi. Certainly there was much in their situation and in their job itself which might produce an anti-labor outlook. Their training as "professionals" embodied anti-labor ideologies regarding manual training, Americanization, and control of the laboring class. Moreover, on a subtler level, Van Denburg pointed out that teachers often instill contempt for manual labor by warning students that those who do not do well in school will be relegated to mere manual work. Considering the severe struggle that staying in school involved, one may conjecture that it would be common for those who made that struggle to internalize such a view.

It was partly to counteract this view that the other AFL unions supported salary increases for teachers. Although they gave that support on general principles, they were also well aware of the antiunion biases in social studies texts, particularly in high schools and colleges, and they hoped that unionizing teachers might help keep teachers in touch with the viewpoint of manual labor (Curoe, 1926:137-150, esp. p. 142).

Insofar as becoming a teacher or a school principal may have meant internalizing the ideological conceptions of professional pedagogy, that process contained a certain irony. For the rise of the teacher was made possible by the militancy of labor, which created the problems of worker control and political strife which inspired the business class to solve those training and social control problems by expanding the schools and hiring the sons and daughters of immigrant workers to socialize the sons and daughters of immigrant workers. The class consciousness of immigrant labor became the condition for the "upward mobility"—and *embourgeoisement* of the children of immigrants.

And yet the teachers reacted by no means gullibly or gratefully to "Progressive" efforts within the NEA and the cities to reduce their power while increasing their prestige. Teachers were subject to contradictory forces.

The tastes of the teachers might be those of people in refined economic leisure, but the salaries, being those of mechanics and day-laborers or even less, prevent the enjoyment of these higher things. Between what they ought to do, and what they can do, there is a wide gulf [Coffman, 1911:83].

And no matter how much "upward mobility" might have led teachers to share the tastes and prejudices of their "betters," they were also subject to conflicting everyday forces other than those of their previous training and their current administrative superiors. Particularly important was the community itself, even when teachers and principals no longer lived in the community in which they taught. Leonard Covello, for example, petitioned for permission to teach Italian under the determined prodding of his Italian high school students. Ravitch notes that some of those marching against the Gary plan carried posters boosting Socialist Congressional candidate Morris Hillquit, although the Socialist Party claimed no role in the matter (1974:224). And no matter what went on inside the schools, the labor movement and political conflict continued to help create the milieu outside.

Conclusions: Theoretical Implications of the Development of the Teaching Profession

Placing teachers in the U.S. class structure presumes a theory of class. From the point of view of Poulantzas (1973), teachers would be part of the new petty bourgeoisie because their function is ideological, their work is nonmanual, and their labor is unproductive (see also Finn, 1977). According to other analysts, teachers would be part of the "new working class" because they are dependent for their livelihood on the sale of their labor power. For the Ehrenreichs (1977), they are part of the professional managerial class. For C. Wright Mills (1951), they are white collar, somewhere at the bottom of the middle class. For bourgeois analysts they are "middle class," perhaps suffering from "status inconsistency" (Nagi and Pugh, 1976).

The trouble with all of these efforts to nail teachers into a "place" in "the class structure" is that the classifications are insufficiently dialectical. They fail to take into account the fact that the class "position" of teachers is, historically and at any moment, a product of a contradictory historical process. And they fail to deal adequately with the full complex of contradictory forces acting on teachers as a result of the fact that they are ideological workers.

Class as Process

As Braverman has shown, the class structure has changed dramatically as a result of forces inherent in capitalism itself. As the foregoing analysis demonstrated, the expansion and transformation of the teaching profession has been a result of the expanded accumulation of capital and of (immigrant) labor, and of the class struggles which accompanied that accumulation. Class struggle—over child labor, compulsory schooling, discipline of labor, manual training, and Americanization—expanded the schools, the length of the school year, the number of years of school attendance, and hence the number of teachers employed. The bourgeoisie's desire to use the schools for ideological indoctrination—discipline and Americanization—also made the schools an arena for ideological conflict, sometimes explicit, as in the development of parochial schools, and sometimes subterranean, as in high dropout and truancy rates. Thus, the bourgeoisie had to ensure the ideological reliability of the newly expanded teaching force through longer, ideologically based training, greater administrative control over top decision-making in school systems, and the development of a management control system based on the sexual division of labor and Taylorism.

We cannot exactly say that the teacher's job was "degraded." Unlike the clerk of early capitalism, the early teacher did not share in the profits of enterprise and did not marry the boss' daughter.[8] But he was part of a very small middle class, and in small towns probably had considerable prestige. Nor can we say that the teacher of the mid-1920s was fully a proletarian, even though she may have been a union member, and by the 1970s she may well have gone to jail for waging illegal strikes.

But certainly something had changed. The nature and structure of the teaching profession had changed with the development of U.S. capitalism. Although the important overall features of the organization of teaching were formed at the turn of the century, the processes we have examined continue until today: Educational expansion (and contraction) reflects the class struggle in the political economy outside the school and contains, often explosively, myriad forms of class struggle within the classroom.

Class Contradictions

Erik Olin Wright says that teachers "occupy contradictory locations within class relations: . . . While teachers may be *functionally* organic intellectuals of the bourgeoisie, *structurally* they are generally not members of the bourgeois class" (1978:6, italics in original; see also Gramsci, 1975:118-125). We must go further: There are contradictions on both the functional and the structural levels for both the bourgeoisie and for teachers.

Teachers' work is reproductive work. Their job is (1) to help to reproduce capitalism as a system and the conditions for continued accumulation by dealing with the ideological and cultural problems which a system of exploitation inevitably creates, and (2) to provide "skill-training," thereby helping to endow labor power with its technical usefulness. The work of the reproduction of labor power is not only generally not well-paid; most of it is *unpaid*, being performed by women in the household (Beneria, 1978). Capital has succeeded in passing the costs of reproducing "its" labor power onto the laboring class itself, partly collectively through the state, and partly privately and individually through individual families' daily labor and their "investments" in their own children's education. Capital expects to find labor power already reproduced, free and easy, on the labor market. Capital expects teachers who, ever since the "feminization" of the teaching force, are most often women engaged in the private reproduction of labor power in the home for *no* pay to reproduce labor power in the schools for *low* pay.

But low pay recruits teachers from the very class which capital must attempt to control, and it reminds teachers that they are wage labor. On the structural level, therefore, capital faces the problem that attempts at efficiency and control inspire unionism and other forms of resistence—that is, further problems of control. These forces are not peculiar to teaching: They are general characteristics of the relations between capital and labor and hence applicable to teachers as wage workers. This conflict inspires the *general* problem of the loyalty of the work force; the general problems of ideology.

But the loyalty of teachers is of special importance to capitalists, because teachers are ideological workers. Much of their job is to inculcate loyalty in the rest of labor. Hence, the *structural* contradiction for capital is intertwined with the *functional* contradictions for capital. To maintain the loyalty of teachers, the bourgeoisie is moved to emphasize the prestige of teaching as a middle-class, clean "profession" superior to manual work. Yet in a system in which money is the measure of all value, prestige and low wages mix like oil and water. The pressure to reduce the wage makes prestige less convincing. Moreover, capital tends to distrust its ideological agents, and moves to control them. Control, "efficiency management," and low wages undermine prestige, "professionalization," and, perhaps, ultimately loyalty.

The creation of bourgeois ideological hegemony is not automatic; it is a struggle. Ideological hegemony had to be established originally, and it continually has to be corrected to deal with changing times. That is, rapidly changing cultural issues thrown up by the national and international class struggle make the old ideological solutions obsolete and call urgently for new cultural pronouncements and a new content to "professionalism." If teachers, principals, and administrators were simple automatic agents of the bourgeoisie, the bourgeoisie would not have to continually take a directing hand, as did Butler, Dodge, Carnegie, and Vanderbilt at the turn of the century, or as do their counterparts in our own day.

The contradictions for teachers reciprocate those for the ruling class. As I discussed these quite extensively above, a quick summary should suffice. On the structural level, teachers—especially upwardly mobile teachers— experience a contradiction between the "prestige" of teaching and its low wages and lack of autonomy. On the functional level, teachers must inculcate a contradictory ideology in a changing and conflict-filled world. Teachers stand on the front line of the clash of ethnic and class ideologies and interests. Even when working-class consciousness is politically undeveloped, teachers face working-class culture, "the problem of motivation," and the various forms of passive and active resistance of a population which feels that school culture misrepresents them and school does not serve them.

In addition, teachers face the contradictory expectations of the school: that they create equality—and "selection" (inequality); that they produce (in classes kept too large by penny-pinching budgets) motivation—and order; that they apply an idealized pedagogy to a school system based on social control; that they miraculously create social harmony in a system based on conflict; and that they infuse young labor power with the skills which *might* be useful to capital in the proportions which *might* be useful to capital, when the essence of capitalism itself is such cyclical instability and continual change that skills are often either obsolete or over-abundant by the time children graduate and offer them to capital.

Pushed and pulled by these contradictory pressures, teachers' behavior in the class struggle may have a greater tendency to vacillate than that of other workers, but it is determined by specific historical circumstances, a condition they share with all other workers. Teaching was not created in a vacuum and teachers do not work in a vacuum. They work, and have always worked, on the front line of struggles in a class-divided society.

Notes

1. In Karl Marx, *Grundrisse* (1973). Marx shows how production, distribution, exchange, and consumption are each determined by the others, and determine them; are identical, yet separate, in multiple complex ways. Yet all form a unity (an economic system) determined, ultimately, by production. In *Capital* he demonstrates the complex interactions whereby the capitalist class and the working class determine each other's formation and, in the process, transform both capitalism and themselves.

2. Van Denburg's data are based on a 1906 questionnaire survey of high school freshmen. I have used his data here, basing my calculations on those with definite occupational aspirations and on brothers and sisters with known occupational destinies. Although 64 percent of the girls wished to become teachers, only around 9 percent of older sisters taught. Teaching was 78 percent female at the time. Five percent of boys wanted to be teachers; only 0.8 percent of their brothers were. One caveat as to this procedure is in order: Girls who stayed in school tended to be older daughters with dead fathers; they stayed in high school in order to become teachers and support their families. Boys who stayed in school tended to be the youngest brother; their older siblings had gone to work that they might stay in school. Consequently, the boys might not have uniformly followed the paths of their older brothers.

3. Curoe (1926:84), quoting *Journal of United Labor*, May 14, 1887 (editorial); p. 163, quoting *American Federationist*, 11 (1895), p. 82; p. 164, citing a 1908 speech by Van Cleane; and pp. 112 and 164 citing a 1909 speech by Gompers.

4. There is considerable variation in U.S. educational structure. In some rural areas, one-room schoolhouses survived into the 1970s. There were 1111 one-room schoolhouses in the U.S. in 1977, according to *The Wall Street Journal* (1979).

5. Several recent studies show that this pattern persisted into the 1970s. Male elementary school teachers tend to be sons of blue-collar workers; female teachers are of more mixed-class origins. This recruitment pattern is explained by the limited professional options available to working class youth, and to *all* women (see Lortie, 1975; Schwartzweller and Lyson, 1978). The latter study showed a strong tendency for rural youth to aspire to teaching, as Coffman had found to be true 60 years before.

6. I am indebted to Ms. Cathryn O'Dea, librarian of the New York City Board of Education, for this information.

7. Evidence that this contradiction is actually experienced today may be seen in the study by Nagi and Pugh (1976).

8. This is one of Braverman's indicators of the early clerk's quasi-integration into the capitalist class, as compared with the modern, more proletarianized clerk.

9. Note that Butler implicitly made room for future changes in the content of profession-ialism when, in announcing the curriculum of the Training College, he said, *"for the present, at least,* the instruction given will be . . . confined to . . . Industrial Training."

Dale L. Johnson and Christine O'Donnell:

The Dequalification of Technical, Administrative, and Professional Labor

In the latest phase of development in North America and Europe, the labor process as it affects professional, administrative, scientific, and technical personnel is undergoing changes. We argue here that the principal change is an extension of the rationalization of the labor process, such that previously complex technical and skilled mental labor functions in the division of labor are simplified, routinized, and deskilled. Since the mid-1970s there may well have been an acceleration in the pace of this rationalization. Following Harry Braverman (1974) and his pioneering work on the labor process and the formation of the working class in the United States, this may be referred to as the process of "dequalification."

We also suggest that accompanying this process is a removal of the semiautonomy previously enjoyed in work by professional, administrative, and technical employees and a bureaucratic centralization of power in the hands of higher managers. Dequalification of work, erosion of work conditions, and centralization of power within institutions are contributing to a changing positioning of intermediate formations in class relations and to a deterioration in the class situation of the heretofore rapidly expanding and privileged sectors commonly referred to as the middle class. Substantial strata of the middle class are being pushed in the direction of the working class, while a few elements are being elevated to the position of the technocratic staff of the managers. Thus, over the course of its development as a class, the middle class is not only fractionalized (Chapter 7) but also bifurcated into strata that are pushed or pulled toward one pole or the other in the relations between working class and bourgeoisie.

In this chapter we pursue a dialectic of the qualification/dequalification and professionalization/deprofessionalization of the higher orders of labor, providing the groundwork for an analysis in the succeeding chapter of the implications for class relations in the 1980s. This dialectic moves in the context of other contradictory social-historical phenomena: capital accumulation as a process of unfolding class relations, the introduction of

Author's Note: Our thanks to Martin Oppenheimer, who assisted on this chapter.

technical and organizational innovations to the labor process, and the contrary development of decentralization of function and centralization of power within institutions. The interrelations of these factors are examined in particular occupational spheres. Emphasis is placed on the professions in general and the computer field in particular.

In examining the dequalification of the higher orders of labor, we are painfully aware of a problem Johnson repeatedly raised in the theoretical chapters. The identification of a determined historical tendency, in this case the dequalification inherent within the capitalist labor process, is not equivalent to its actual uneven course of development. It is a dual and uneven process of qualification/dequalification. It is too easy to conflate tendency with outcome. In the absence of substantial empirical study we have perhaps too often substituted "the logic of the process" for actual development in the complexity of emerging realities. The logic of this process, we contend, is that the qualification tendency formed an intermediate class in tempo with the deskilling of the working class. The qualification tendency in recent years has been reversed: Technical, administrative, and, to a certain degree, even professional labor is now being fragmented, routinized, and deskilled. Our theoretical perspective does allow a reinterpretation of various studies in the sociology of occupations that point toward current trends appearing to threaten the very existence of the middle class as an intermediate and mediating formation. If this is so, then the 1980s will be years of increasingly polarized class relations.

The Dequalification Process in Administrative, Technical, and Professional Labor

Capital Accumulation and Dequalifications

In Chapter 3, the various historical sources of capital accumulation in the development of the monopoly stage of capitalism were identified. These included the incorporation of increasing sectors of the working population into the waged labor to capital nexus (i.e., proletarianization), the great "epoch-making" technological and organizational innovations, colonialism and imperialism, and the development of the interventionist, "welfare-warfare" state. It was also suggested that (with the exception of the first which provides the basis of all forms of accumulation) these historical avenues of accumulation may be reaching their limits as sources of dynamism. Since in the decline or absence of continuing sources of accumulation the system slips into crisis, there is a structural and corresponding political imperative to explore the potentialities of all available means of accumulation. We believe that a principal means of this accumulation, beginning with the economic instabilities of the early to mid-1970s, is an accelerated pace in the rationalization of the labor process.

This takes a number of forms. One is a quickened pace in the incorporation of new workers into productive activities that are being organized as low-wage sectors of production. This occurs internationally and within the advanced industrial countries and contributes to a continuation of the process of class polarization on a world scale. Within the United States, incorporation of new workers swells the working class and changes its internal structure. Since the late 1960s in the United States, women have been massively incorporated into waged work—but nearly half of working-age women are still out of the labor force and only 43 percent of women who work hold full-time jobs, offering still further possibilities of incorporation. The high degree of internalization in the mobility of both capital and labor achieved in recent years also expands the sources of exploitation that generate profits and investment capital. Transnational corporations opened up substantial production facilities in countries like Mexico, Brazil, Taiwan, South Korea, and many other locations in the Third World, drawing on cheap, previously unproletarianized labor there (Vuskovic, 1980). There is a seemingly inexhaustible supply of surplus population in the dependent periphery and peoples have migrated by the millions: Southern Europeans as "guest workers" in Western Europe, Latin American and Caribbean immigrants to the United States, and Asian workers to the construction booms and oil fields of the Middle-East. But continued proletarianization of new entrants into the orbit of capital has its limits: It depends on the development of new sectors of production, new avenues of accumulation.

Another form related to incorporation that the rationalization of the labor process has assumed is an acceleration and extension of the dequalification of work. This is accomplished by extending to ever-greater absurdities the technical division of labor and the hierarchization of organization and by subordinating widening spheres of work activity to more "efficient" technologies. First we should say something of this as a historical process.

In general, we agree with Braverman (1974) that the primary tendency in the evolution of the division of labor in the monopoly stage of capitalism has been the separation of "manual" from "mental" labor; technological and organizational innovations were then adopted to fragment, specialize, and subordinate manual labor. The original impulse to the evolution of mental labor was the separation of the conception of work from its execution. We suggest that this applies especially to the earlier phases of development of the monopoly stage. In the more recent phases of development, the separation of conception from execution has been applied to mental labor as well. The transformation of the great bulk of office activity into routine clerical work is a prime example of its earliest development. The issue pursued here is to what degree this separation now affects the preexisting spheres of mental labor that have been primarily concerned, in one way or another, with the process of conception—that is, to what degree is administrative, scientific and technical, and professional labor subject to dequalification?[1] To address this question, we broadly trace the dequalification process to then turn to the specifics of mental labor.

The labor process of modern-day corporate capitalism did not come to be organized as extensively fragmented activity organized in vast bureaucratic hierarchies for reasons of technical superiority. "The social function of hierarchical work organization is not technical efficiency, but accumulation" (Marglin in Gorz, 1976:14). When the conception of work is separated from its execution, mental work is made to seem superior to manual work; and when both are subjected, organizationally and by new technologies, to extensive rank gradations, control becomes centralized and workers atomized and pitted in competition against one another. Historically, it was not enough that independent producers were dispossessed of their productive means and proletarianized; they had also to be made into servile appendages of the machine, glued there by the watchful eyes of foremen. By detailing the technical division of labor, ordering it in hierarchies, and spinning off control as a separate function, the process of production was set up "as an alien, autonomous power that exacts the worker's submission" (Gorz, 1976:57).

Gorz also suggests: "As a whole, the history of capitalist technology can be read as the history of the dequalification of the direct producers.... The power of control which [workers] carried ... is transferred to nonworkers as a separate function" (1976:57). In this process, Glucksmann has noted that "the intellectual worker is the product of the disintellectualization of manual work under the law of profit. Even the technician has a repressive function, his 'competence' always presupposes the incompetence of the worker and tends to reinforce it" (1976:81).

Rationalization of the labor process in the monopoly stage has always involved continuing incorporation to waged labor and an increased subordination of workers to machine technology and bureaucratic hierarchies of control. But today there is a new dimension: Rationalization now also involves a reorganization and increased subordination of the former controllers—the administrators, scientists and technicians, and professionals. Dequalification of these substantial sectors offers a new source of capital accumulation.

Before elaborating on this thesis, we hasten to point out that the evidence to substantiate it is impressionistic, fragmentary, and illustrative, rather than definitive, except in the case of lower-level office work. The evolution of the division of labor in "white-collar" clerical activity has been well studied. Braverman's account of the organization and reorganization of work in this sphere is extraordinarily sound and lucid. A good empirical study is Glenn and Feldberg:

> Proletarianization is said to occur as clerical work loses the features that have traditionally placed it among middle-class, white collar occupations; as narrow, largely manual skills displace complex skills and mental activity; as

close external controls narrow the range of worker discretion; and as impersonal relationships replace social give and take. The extent of proletarianization varies among organizations. The larger organizations are leading the changes by developing technologies and organizational techniques for proletarianized clerical work. . . . . It is argued that structural changes promoting proletarianization may seriously impair the very efficiency that the changes are claimed to promote [1977:52].

Gorz, Braverman, and others who have studied the development of the division of labor and the dequalification of workers have not given a great deal of attention to the way in which control and related functions of capital may be subject to a similar dequalification process. However, at one point, Gorz gives a clue to what for us is the key process in dequalifying higher orders of labor: "Accompanying mechanization, which dequalifies and fragments production tasks, automation dequalifies and fragments control itself. After mechanization has dispossessed workers of all power of control and transferred it to separate agents, automation transfers the function of control to machines, which now control their former supervisors" (1976:57).

A group of Italian technicians undertook an extraordinary study of "technical experts" (published in *Il Manifesto,* translated in Gorz, 1976). They analyzed the "all pervasive extension of the Taylorism of the shop floor to include all the operations undertaken within the enterprise:"

The fragmented, simplified and repetitive nature of assembly-line work is well-known, but many people will be surprised to learn that about 90 percent of administrative employees also do nothing but repeat strictly predetermined tasks that, in the majority of cases, preclude any personal initiative; that among white-collar workers in production departments about 60 percent of all personnel follow a rigidly defined procedure. . . .

The great majority of employees have become passive participants in a thoroughly rationalized economic process. *Capital has less and less need of a stream of trustworthy representatives to whom it can delegate some of its authority. Under modern conditions it organizes the labor process primarily by objectifying all existing tasks and functions.* The great majority of employees no longer exercise power on behalf of the owners [Gorz, 1976:125].

They continue, however, that the Taylorizing of the technical labor process is not complete; the planner, the systems and production analyst, and others are yet distinguished from the "proletarianized" technicians, employees, and workers by income levels, academic credentials and, most of all, the "the degree of autonomy arising from the nature of their jobs and the influence that this exerts over the process of production" (Gorz, 1976:126).

On the basis of these kinds of ideas and the fragmentary evidence available to us we would formulate this generalization: The historical tendency toward the formation and proliferation of technical, administrative, and professional labor is accompanied by a countertendency, which seems to be increasingly pronounced in the most recent phase of development in the industrial countries, particularly the United States. The labor power of these categories of historically qualified employees is dequalified by rationalization of the administrative and technical labor processes. This process is uneven, complex, and multisided. The root of dequalification of labor power resides in the accumulation process—capital is accumulated only through the appropriation of the surplus labor of workers and not by employing huge numbers of unproductive (of surplus value) agents of capital. Corporations strive to reduce the range of activities devoted to performance of the functions of capital and enlarge the proportion of the labor force engaged in activities that permit the appropriation of surplus labor.

Yet the very process of this attempt to be more "rational" engenders its own contradiction: The rationalization of work also requires resources devoted to social control of the work force, for dequalified labor tends to be dissatisfied labor. Moreover, the technical overqualification ("over-education") of sectors of qualified labor undergoing dequalification contributes to employee alienation. Thus capital is involved in a constant conflict between the imperative of rationalization—which is required both for capital accumulation and for control of the overall labor process—and the need to expend resources for social control over alienated labor.

Nevertheless, in the latest phase of the development of monopoly capitalism, the main tendency appears to be that the functions of capital, including that of direct supervisory control, are themselves subject to rationalization. Complex functions such as planning, coordination, innovation, and supervision are, with the aid of technologies, divided, subdivided, and codified; the labor dequalified; the work fragmented and routinized. The conditions of work within those sectors of the middle class subject to dequalification begin to change from relative independence to dependence, from varied, sometimes interesting, and creative activity to routine task, from superordination to subordination, from job security to job insecurity, from employment as educated and skilled labor to underemployment in terms of education and skill levels attained, and from economic well-being to relatively reduced levels of income. As a consequence, the class position and class privilege of sectors of the middle class are eroded. They become less managements' agents and more like workers as their work is stripped of its control or coordinative or creative functions and their salaries held down commensurate with their new functions as detail workers collectively engaged in facilitating the production of surplus value and the appropriation of profit.

This is, of course, a tendency. As such, it proceeds at an uneven pace and affects different middle-class occupational groupings at different times and to different degrees. It can also be counterbalanced to some degree by the development of new social positions appropriate to the middle class resulting from the introduction of a new technological process, or a resurgence of capital accumulation in a particular activity, or the need for expanded systems of social control. It can be slowed or modified by the resistence of the employees affected. Proletarianization is the outside limit to this tendency. Formally, the structural basis for proletarianization exists when the mix of capital and collective worker functions characteristic of administration and the developmental and coordinative work of technicians and professionals is reduced entirely to collective worker functions[2] (Carchedi, 1975a).

The various studies of the dequalification process among technicians and administrators and deprofessionalization among professionals tend (like our own study) to be rather generalized observations of apparent trends rather than carefully designed empirical research. Carchedi examines changes in the division of labor in a few fields and cites Italian studies of other occupations. He notes of the "devaluation through dequalification" process:

> This type of devaluation of labor power is due to the fact that agents with certain qualifications, whose labor power has a certain value, must—for whatever reasons—fill positions which require lower qualifications and thus a lower value required. This is what seems to have happened in the field of chemistry in the last 10-15 years: what used to be the job of a chemist with a university degree has now become the job of a technician with only a high school diploma . . . . This lower value, this devaluation, has been achieved by introducing into the labor process new instruments which can now be handled by a technician. The operation changes, the technical requirements decrease, and new agents (the technicians) now occupy the dequalified positions [Carchedi, 1975b:379].

In examining labor dequalification, Carchedi divides the production process into three phases and studies the changing "social and technical content" of labor in each phase: design of products, production proper, and control and maintenance. He cites as examples of changes in the design phase, for example, the situation of technical designers and draftsmen:

> A recent research in four major metal-working enterprises in Italy, shows that the work is extremely heavy; the pay low; the possibility of making a career almost non-existent; the subordination to the computer increasing in the sense that (a) the computer gives all the initial data, (b) the computer determines the ever increasing fragmentation of the work, (c) the computer, when the fragmentation has reached a suffecent degree, tends to take over that function; the possibility of creativity and invention has disappeared [1975b:399].

Terry Johnson provides an interesting study of changes in the "control and maintenance" phase of production. Accounting as an activity has undergone considerable differentiation; much of it reduced to clerical activity in bookkeeping. New functions "are proliferating at the margins of accountancy work with the establishment of new systems of management information gathering and distribution made possible by computerization.

. . . Functionaries find themselves on the lower rungs of the bureaucratic hierarchy" (1977:218).

Turning to the third phase, "production proper," Crompton's (1976) study of the available empirical literature on production technicians in Great Britain can be cited. She closely follows Carchedi's formulation of technical work as combining the functions of labor and of capital: "The effect of the rationalization of the technical workforce has been to split the technicians' occupational role between, on the one hand, the graduate manager, and on the other, manual workers, whilst downgrading the remaining elements of the technicians' work role. In other words, the extent to which technicians participate in the labour function has been made more explicit, and their participation in the capitalist function drastically reduced" (1976:421).

At the same time, the contradictory nature of this process should be stressed.[3] For example, in a study of two factories in the same industry that differed in organizational structure, Low-Beer reminds us that the rationalization trend is by no means universally applicable. "Even within the category of technicians, there is . . . a fairly sharp division between those doing routine tasks and those doing varied and involving tasks. . . . Opposing tendencies exist in social reality as well as among various theories"[4] (1978:13).

Dequalification of technical, administrative, and professional labor is not confined to the direct sphere of corporate capital. In recent years it is a process which seems to be moving with potentially devastating impact in many spheres of work. This has been especially the case after the mid-1970s with the public sector budget cutbacks. These cutbacks, particularly severe in New York and decaying Midwestern industrial cities, have been accompanied by bureaucratic restructuring which has greatly affected professions like teaching, nursing, social work and services such as libraries and recreation. Professionals, who used to have a reasonable work autonomy, employment security, and a manageable workload, suddenly face threatening changes. The resources and organizational basis for acting on professional commitments to a service ethic have been sharply eroded. We cite just one example of great familiarity to us at this point, higher education (other examples, especially in the professions, are cited later).

In institutions that more closely emulate the bureaucratic hierarchies of corporate work places, managers of higher education are busy devising ways to cut costs and increase faculty productivity: Student-to-faculty ratios are increased, teaching workloads augmented, class sizes bloated, operating budgets and supporting services cut, administrative controls tightened, senior professors set against junior colleagues, and part-timers hired to replace full-time faculty.

The latter trend is increasingly important in rationalizing the labor process and dequalifying the professorate in community and state colleges, and even to some degree in universities. According to the National Center for Education Statistics (NCES), the 1970s have seen an increase by almost

50 percent of part-time faculty while full-timers have increased by less than 9 percent. By the 1976-77 academic year, part-timers represented 27 percent of all faculty at four-year schools and 51 percent at two-year institutions (Tuckman et al., 1978; Van Arsdale, 1978).

Empirical analysis of part-timers suggests that on all criteria they are deprofessionalized compared to their full-time counterparts. Part-timers are hired at lower ranks than full-timers with similar credentials; they are financially compensated considerably less for equal work; they are much more likely to be excluded from fringe benefits (e.g., retirement plans, medical insurance, workmen's compensation, sabbatical leaves) and from the material means to pursue their work (e.g., office space and supplies, grants, and institutional support of professional development); they are rarely promoted, offered a full-time position, or eligible for tenure; the "contracts" for their semester-by-semester coursework are subject to cancellation if enrollment is inadequate (cancellations and changes of both course and schedule are not infrequent) so that dismissal can occur without appeal or protection of a formal grievance mechanism. Beyond these material disadvantages, there are less tangible but equally significant amenities denied to part-timers. They have little if any say, let alone control, in the colleges, departments, and classrooms they work in. The data indicate few part-timers have a vote at department and college faculty meetings, few are consulted on curriculum matters, and in fact most are discouraged from developing new courses or having any input on old ones. Part-timers, as Van Arsdale (1978:198) notes, experience "severe restrictions upon the academic freedom of professionals to develop course materials, choose appropriate texts, and direct their classroom teaching as they choose." They are also not often covered by collective bargaining.

Within academia then we see the increasing bifurcation of faculty into two strata—full-timers and part-timers. While one might argue that full-time faculty are themselves mildly experiencing a tendency toward dequalification via increased subordination to centralized administrative decision-making, increased specialization and decreased work autonomy, and so on, it is certainly clear that the pretense of professional status is not even afforded part-time faculty. Part-timers are "proletarianized" from the start of their careers. As Phillip Kraft, a full-timer, notes:

> As long as we pretend that because we are "professionals" we are not also employees, as long as we prefer to deal individually with our employers rather than collectively, as long as we condone the existence of a permanent under-class of badly paid, overworked, dead-ended, and disenfranchised colleagues, then we will join their ranks before they join ours [1979:208].

Dequalification and Computers

The dequalification of technical, administrative, and professional labor is a complex and contradictory process. Nowhere is this more evident than in the examination of the application of computers to the labor process.

Computer technology can be viewed as a means (1) of increasing productivity while also producing the need for some categories of unskilled and semi-skilled labor; (2) of effecting further rationalizations of work at all skill levels; and (3) of achieving greater management control of the labor process. We illustrate these points with data and generalizations from recent studies, of which there are surprisingly few with sound empirical appreciation of recent trends.

There is no question that the machines, where introduced in ever wider spheres of work, have enormously increased output per labor unit. Workers equipped with such powerful machines are highly productive. Computers greatly cheapen capital stock and save labor time. Moreover, an unknown though substantial proportion of increased productivity in the economy as a whole proceeds from the elimination of labor; in the United States in particular this comes at the cost of persistent structural unemployment. The immediate impact of computers has been to displace routine labor, especially in the clerical field, but increasingly in computer-controlled automated production as well. A study of the impact of computers on employment in England found that, in 1970, the United Kingdom economy lost 37,336 jobs that had been directly replaced by computers; the author estimated the direct job loss up to 1978 as over 230,000 (Stoneham, 1975). A 1979 report by *Dollars and Sense* cited a recent study in France, concluding that in the "previous five years 30% of the white collar jobs which would have otherwise developed in banking and insurance had been 'rationalized' by computerization." The same study indicated that the United States' largest employer, American Telephone and Telegraph, "used computerization to reduce its workforce from 1 million to 900,000 between 1974 and 1977." Still, in the United States, "from 1957 to 1977, the total of analysts, programmers, key punch operators and other employees directly involved in data processing increased from 100,000 to 2.5 million" (*Dollars and Sense*, 1979:15).

An unpublished paper by Devey and Devey (1979) surveys the available literature on the employment impact of computers. According to these authors, the trend seems to be (a) large-scale displacement of female clerical labor, only partially compensated for by the rapid growth of sex-typed labor in keypunching and routinized data processing operations; and (b) an increase in (mainly male) employment in programming and operations that does not nearly compensate for jobs lost. In the United States in 1970 there were about 630,000 employees in the computer field; 272,600 of these were keypunch operators (90 percent female); 117,200 operators (29 percent female) and 161,300 programmers (22.6 percent female) were already being rapidly ordered in a specialized division of labor, while management functions were being concentrated in the activities of about 79,300 systems analysts (14.7 percent female; see Gilchrist and Weber, 1975).

On the surface, the displacement of many categories of routine labor by computer technology would seem to point to an upgrading of the skill levels of the labor force as a whole and thus contradict our thesis of the dequalification of the higher orders of labor. This is not, when contradictory effects are balanced, at all the case, as we will argue in discussing how computers are used to further the rationalization of work in ever-widening spheres.

The advent of computers evoked a considerable body of literature in the 1960s and early 1970s that asserted a complete transformation of the industrial division of labor. In particular, semiskilled employment and minute specialization of jobs would be banished as capital-intensive, continuous process, automated production displaced the labor intensive assembly line. Blauner (1964) thought the new character of work would mitigate worker alienation and lead to an even more thorough social integration of the working class into the established order. Mallet (1975) came to the opposite conclusion: Technical workers in the advanced sectors were emerging as a militant "new working class." Bell (1973) constructed a theory of "postindustrial society" (critically analyzed in the introduction to this volume) that had eclipsed the class divisions of industrial capitalism.

Automated production has restructured the old industrial division of labor to some extent. Gallie's study of the labor process and workers in French and English oil refineries (1978) indicates both the impact of high-technology industrial processes on the organization of work and the implications for broader political questions. But the extent and impact of automation should not be exaggerated. Technological development seems to have altered the forms within which the labor process unfolds more than the content of that process. Edwards's study of high-technology corporations like IBM, AT&T, GE, Polaroid, and other giants indicates that "rather than producing qualitative differences, the new technology simply expanded the potential in the concept of technical control" (1979:122). Edwards concludes that "workers find even less opportunity to exercise any control over their work lives. . . . Control becomes truly structural, embedded in that hoary old mystification, technology" (1979:125). Further, in the most technically advanced corporations, an unprecedentedly elaborate system of bureaucratic controls over the entire labor force, top to bottom, has been devised. Under the combination of sophisticated technical and bureaucratic control systems the specialization of labor has reached new absurdity. Edwards notes, for example, that Polaroid has 18 different "job families," 300 job titles with highly specialized operations encompassing the jobs, and 14 different pay grades, each with seven pay steps. The 300 job titles are divided between salaried technical, supervisory and professional, and waged production and office work. The higher-level technical jobs are, within the technical limits, every bit as specified and routinized as the lower category.

Much of the literature on new technologies deals with their impact on occupational structure. These studies are mainly guided by a technogenic perspective that tends "to fetishize technology as an extra-social, quasi-natural evolutionary force" (Burris, 1980:20). Technologies are not independent of the social relations in which they are adopted. In fact, technological innovations are designed, modified, widely adopted, or not adopted in the context of the ebb and flow of the conflict between capital and labor. (Edwards's work [1979] is particularly adept in utilizing this perspective.) That is why the net impact of computer technology has not been—in spite of reductions of semiskilled labor in a number of categories—to eliminate the working class but to augment its ranks. While some jobs are eliminated, technologies permit control systems that deskill previously skilled labor and create new categories of working-class work. Nor has, as was argued elsewhere in the book, a new kind of socioeconomic order, postcapitalist or postindustrial, in which the majority are "middle class" been fashioned out of technological progress.

The primary impact of computers, then, has been to further rationalize the labor process and subordinate labor. To return to our main thesis on dequalification, what is perhaps somewhat unique about computers is that the technology permits rationalization and subordination to be extended into the "higher" orders of labor.

In the contemporary phase of development, the implication of machine information processing for the work of scientists and technicians, administrators, and professionals are weighty indeed. Obviously, at one level, computers are a powerful tool to assist these employees in their jobs. Once conceptualized and programmed, complex technical problems can be solved almost instantaneously; huge quantities of information can be gathered and ordered so that the administrative or research processes can proceed more or less efficiently (or at least according to prevailing standards of efficiency). But the other side of this dialectic of technological innovation is that information and problem-solving procedures that were once stored and framed in the minds of employees are now located in the electrical circuits of the machines. The overall impact of computers is to remove knowledge, skills, and responsibility from people and to place greater levels of control in the hands of the systems analysts and managers who command the machines and the specialized workers appended to them. As Devey and Devey put it, "information handling changed from a process of interaction between people and paper on all levels within white collar work to a process of interaction between management and machines" (1979:7). While it is also true that technical and organizational innovation before computers had the effect of subordinating and dequalifying labor, they also tended, as great new historical avenues of capital accumulation, to increase overall employment and to form groupings of scientific, technical, administrative, and professional employees that grew at rates exceeding the growth of the labor force as a whole. Though data are lacking to demonstrate it, this latest innovation seems, in net impact and through the medium of technical subordination, to dequalify more labor than it qualifies.

The programmed dequalification of labor is as yet less clearly the case in the professions as in the technical and administrative processes in large corporations and government agencies. Yet computer technology has a considerable implication for the future of the established professions. Haug (1973) makes the excellent point that the monopoly of technical knowledge by the various professions is being eroded by computers. While she does not look at computer technology as a sophisticated means by which the managers rationalize the labor process at all levels, she does note the implication for the erosion of the knowledge claims of experts:

> To the extent that scientific professional knowledge can be 'codified,' it can be broken into bits, stored in a computer memory, and recalled as needed. No longer need it be preserved in the professional's head or in books alone. . . . And what is put into the electronic machine can be extracted by anyone who knows the output procedures. Command over the stored knowledge is not because one knows it but because one *knows how to get it* [1973:201].

There are already places where physicians' assistants record patients' symptoms into a computer for diagnosis; legal assistants can instruct the machine to locate precedents; teaching assistants monitor students in front of teaching machines; and so on. Computers can also be used in systems of professional accountability to check whatever judgments professionals still are allowed to make, in the exercise of the more artful side of their craft, against standardized norms and procedures. In other words, the delivery of professional services is probably on its way to being reorganized as a labor process of large numbers of machine-assisted narrow technicians commanded by elite professionals who more and more resemble managers. Working-class ranks are augmented by "paraprofessionals," while the number of professionals shrinks and those remaining are elevated toward the managers.

The computer field itself, because of the rapidity and extent of its development, is a prime example of the dequalification of scientific and technical labor. From its infancy in the 1950s to its explosion in the mid-1960s, a craftlike division of labor existed among programmers, operators, and repair technicians with a high level of job interaction and interchange of skills. Computer people were in short supply, salaries rose rapidly, and work conditions facilitated independence and creativity. By the late 1960s, management was able to begin an accelerated and continuing effort to effect significant changes in the division of labor. Operators became specialized feeders and attendants; analytic functions were separated from those that required only translation into programming, resulting in systems analysts being differentiated from programmers; programmers in turn were subdivided into single-skill technicians, with many programming functions eventually downgraded to simple coding.

By the early 1970s, most work had been substantially dequalified within a hierarchy of job classifications.[5] As one worker in the industry from the early days notes: "The rigid hierarchy was created to reinforce the effects of standardization. Job categories were minutely defined so that tasks could be performed at the lowest rate of pay. The resulting hierarchy reflected the class and race positions obtaining in society as a whole" (Greenbaum, 1976:42). Higher levels of technical skill and creative work became largely concentrated in the positions of data-processing managers, systems analysts, and high-level specialists in the manufacturing and servicing ends and university computer science departments. By this time, too, the supply of school-trained or experienced computer workers began to reach demand levels. While real salaries increased rapidly in the 1960s, between 1970 and 1977, according to a survey by *Datamaton,* there was no increase in real incomes among systems analysts and a decrease in real salary levels of 10 percent or more among the different categories of programmers and "class A" operators (Cashman, 1977). At the beginning of the 1980s, demand for computer labor had again exceeded supply, and salaries are high in comparison to other technical trades.

Hierarchy in the computer field is also reflected in what Kraft (1977) terms "the programming academy." The 300 educational institutions which train "programmers" (using the term to include coders, programmers, analysts, and other computer specialists) are organized to "track" students into specific levels of the industry; junior colleges and technical institutes are at the bottom (graduating chiefly coders) and research institutions and schools of management at the top (graduating supervisory and managerial personnel and analysts). Kraft notes:

> Software training, in summary, is apportioned to different kinds of institutions which prepare people for different kinds of software occupations.... They are also likely to differ in the kind of student who attends them [so that] ... the sons and daughters of the less affluent [are channeled] into low-level technical and clerical positions, while directing the children of the comparatively more prosperous to positions in the field which offer considerably more in the way of interesting work, material rewards, career opportunities, and high social standing [1977:46].

The changes in the economic organization and division of labor in the computer field are so rapid that it is difficult to identify trends and make valid generalizations. It may be we are overstating our case here. But we do not foresee a whole new augmenting of the technical (i.e., "semi-autonomous") fraction of the middle class propelled by the new industry.

Unlike the scientific professions of earlier phases of development (excellently discussed by Larson [1977]), employees in the computer field have not been able to "professionalize" (except among "computer scientists" in academic settings). Finerman (1975) argues that programmers and other computer technicians have been increasingly forced to specialize; they are not molded by schools and employers as "professionals," but are given technical training and are hired as technicians. Computer people will probably struggle to professionalize as the technology leaps forward. But as yet the absence of professionalization and the extremely rapid implementation of a specialized technical division of labor in the field is a marked departure from the earlier historical formation of new "professional" sectors of the middle class with the opening up of a vast new avenue of technological innovation and capital accumulation. This is explored in a later section on professionalization/deprofessionalization. For now we turn to a discussion of decentralization/centralization, the institutional context of the qualification/dequalification of technical, administrative and professional labor.

The Rationalization Process
Through Institutional Centralization

Labor dequalification is most conveniently effected by assertion of firm organizational and managerial control over the labor process. The chief factor in the formation of a dependent, deskilled working class was the stripping of all vestiges of workers' control over work by means of management's authority (a) to innovate organizational changes and introduce technologies that tied work rhythms to the tempo of machines and (b) to separate the conception of work from its execution—mental from manual labor. To accomplish this subordination and deskilling of workers, it was necessary to disperse high-level technical skills and delegate developmental, coordinative, and creative functions in new categories of scientific and technical, administrative, and professional labor—that is, to form a class of people related to the economic process in new ways. Middle-class employees found very comfortable and privileged niches in the great bureaucracies that sprawled throughout the private and public landscapes. We suggest that this somewhat uncoordinated sprawling, and with it the perquisites of the middle class, is today being curtailed.

At the institutional level of power and decision-making within bureaucracies (corporations, government bureaus, social service agencies, universities, school systems), it appears that a recent tendency is for centralization to supersede decentralization. In earlier phases of development, the basic changes associated with the accumulation process that formed the administrative and semiautonomous fractions of the middle class required a real delegation of authority and responsibility over a considerable range of tasks within a generalized structure of hierarchical authority. Development of the giant monopoly corporation required legions of staff and line personnel to plan and effect the extremely rapid growth of organization and productivity. Expanding public institutions, in education and a variety of public agencies, accorded professionals considerable control over institutional functions and development. Of course, this control, as we emphasize later on, was not just "given"—it was achieved through struggle by professionals themselves; and these struggles were a part of the historical formation of the middle class. The point here is that the actual historical course of the concentration and centralization of capital was one of a certain degree of decentralization and dispersion of function and organization. This was true in the private sector and was even more the case for a number of public institutions that required a disproportionate quantity of professional labor and that grew by leaps and bounds with the process of development, especially in the post-World War II period.

Although, again, our evidence is fragmentary and illustrative, it seems that decentralized institutional development is now being superseded by strengthened centralized control of the great bureaucracies.

In the public sector nowhere is the broad outline of the shift more in evidence than in the greatly strengthened control systems that have accompanied budgetary cutbacks occasioned by the fiscal crisis. In cities like New York, control over the many municipal services have been centralized, and a financial control board, within which the banks exercise predominance, insists as much on new forms of control as on austerity. Changing budgeting systems also reflect this shift. In the 1970s, program budgeting (PPBS) and zero-base budgeting were widely adopted. These systems, which have given rise to great intrabureaucratic power struggles, are designed to concentrate greater power in the hands of institutional managers (Straussman, 1978; Hammond and Knott, 1980).

Space does not permit an analysis of the vast literature on transnational corporations from the perspective of centralization/decentralization and its implications for the qualification/dequalification of labor on a world scale. Obviously, the transnational corporation is an administratively centralized institution with geographically dispersed production units that require a certain degree of local autonomy. Financial controls are the chief instrument of centralized decision-making, and computer and communications technology assists in coordinating worldwide activity. A higher proportion of administrative, technical, and professional employment is located in the home offices and plants, while production labor is predominant in subsidiaries located abroad. Financial and investment decisions, the organization of labor, and other global planning functions tend to be centralized, while home-office-established parameters provide guidelines for local managements on decentralized subsidiary decisions on production and sales.

While these are extraordinarily complex issues, we maintain the existence of a real trend in the main institutional spheres. Heightened control systems within a process of institutional centralization, seemingly pronounced in some spheres, lagging or strongly resisted in others, has meant that powers previously delegated—by historical convenience or necessity or by successful struggles by employees—are reappropriated to higher administrative levels. Thus, the hand of the managers in the spheres of corporate capital, the state, and other institutions is considerably strengthened; in this process substantial sectors of the scientific and technical, administrative, and professional labor force are administratively subordinated, while smaller sectors are elevated to the higher levels of the technocracy. This has, as Johnson discusses in the next chapter, enormous implication for the multitude of sharpening social struggles of the present period and a broad structuring effect on the emerging class relations of the 1980s.

Relatively decentralized institutional development and the growth of a middle-class of "experts" of some kind or another never had (as we emphasize elsewhere) the effect of forming a "postindustrial" society, or of shifting power from the bourgeoisie and institutional managers to middle-class experts. The notions of "post-industrialism," "technostructure," and the like, while dubious enough in their time (the late 1950s to the early 1970s), are today, with the pace of centralization of institutional power, more out of place than ever. As an example we take just one aspect of this argument, John Kenneth Galbraith's thesis of the "technostructure" (1968). We have emphasized the contradictory organizational developments prior to the present phase of industrial capitalism; that is, concentration and centralization of economic and public sector activity came about by way of the growth of relatively decentralized corporate and governmental institutions. This never resulted in the formation of anything approaching a Galbraithian "technostructure" of experts who appropriated power from the managers (just as managers are said to have appropriated power from the legal owners of corporations). On the contrary, the rise of technocrats is a more recent development associated with the stripping of planning and coordinative and creative activity from middle-level managers, professionals, and scientists and technicians (heretofore dispersed in somewhat decentralized institutional settings) and the centralization of these activities (and the power they carry) at higher organizational levels. In this emerging shift in institutional power structures, the technocrats do not usurp power from managers. This power is grasped by managers from administrative, technical, and professional labor and reorganized at higher bureaucratic levels; the managers in turn develop a technical and administrative support staff, the "technocrats," directly responsible to and dependent on management, whose major functions are research and development, the gathering and systemization of information, and advising management on policy options.

While Galbraith's concept of technostructure is seriously deficient, Straussman's recent treatise on the "limits of technocratic politics" is very interesting. Straussman postulates the emergence, especially since the late 1960s, of a restructured bureaucratic order of "princes and counselors" (managers and technocratic staff). His study of the "new economics," applied to government policy formation, the adoption of program budgeting (PPBS), and the social indicators movement, suggests that these innovations are closely linked to centralization of institutional power:

> One of the major efforts of program budgeting was to facilitate the centralization of power for executive managers. This was also true for social indicators. . . . Even when interest in improving managerial rationality was less important as in the case of the "new economics," the centralization of

decision-making power was also a by-product of information flow. Often euphemistically described as "rationalizing the policy process," "making the policy process more efficient," or "controlling the bureaucracy," such symbolic proclamations frequently hide institutional conflicts in which technocratic counsel often serve as catalysts to the eventual centralization and coordination which executive managers strive for. Under these conditions the allocation of resources (knowledge) is not only based on preferred policy goals or "outputs," but it is also directed toward the readjustment of institutional power relationships [Straussman, 1978:36].

Institutional centralization of power and the consequent administrative subordination of professionals, technicians, and administrators goes hand in hand with the process of dequalification of their labor. While there is a clear correlation of the two, this is neither a direct cause and effect relationship nor do the dual processes proceed evenly; and both are often strenuously resisted by the people whose lives are affected. Moreover, the relationship is mediated by technological innovation, especially the introduction of computers, into the spheres of administrative and technical labor. As Neagius (who makes a distinction between the "administrative" and "technical" divisions of labor that is not pursued here)[6] notes: "An increasing subjection to and loss of administrative authority may not proceed at the same rate, nor in the same form as the 'degradation' of technical skill and the loss of technical authority" (1978:18). Though unevenly proceeding, one might in general suggest that administrative centralization is a necessary first step in reorganizing the division of labor in such a way that organizational and technological innovations may be increasingly applied to fragmenting the division of labor, with the principal effect of labor dequalification. Though Edwards's study (1979) of the conjunction of technical with bureaucratic systems of labor control in high-technology corporations is excellent, he does not relate these systems to the dequalification process.

Education can be cited as an example, even though dequalification has not gone as far as in other spheres. We have already pointed out encroaching deprofessionalization in the most professionalized of locations, academia. Part-time employment as a new form of dequalification of the professorate cannot be effected without a prior administrative centralization within colleges and universities and the displacement of power from local to higher system levels. For example, Marcoantonio Lacatena, President of the Council of New Jersey State College locals (AFT, AFL-CIO), has sharply attacked the chancellor of higher education (a former chairman of the National Center for Higher Education Management Systems) for his and the state board's imposition of management systems in New Jersey's higher education system. The union head analyzed events in higher education: "Productivity is the name of the game, and cost effectiveness is the Bible." Colleges have become "knowledge factories." External controls and monitoring have meant that "decision-making authority on even the smallest of matters has moved upward from the institutional level to the system level" (Lacatena, 1980:1).

Much of the thinking behind this analysis of institutional centralization and what is happening to the professions has been stimulated by our own direct experience in academia. One of us is employed by and the other is a recent alumnus of Rutgers—the State University of New Jersey. Rutgers developed as a highly decentralized system of undergraduate colleges, professional schools, and a unified graduate school. After some years of strenuous effort and against widespread resistance by faculty and students, the university administration by 1980 had succeeded in imposing a centralized structure on the institution. Power is now much more concentrated in the hands of the higher administration and their allies among the conservative senior professorate, while the university is more subject to the controls of state authorities. The consequence for students, faculty, and something resembling a decent educational process have already been great and will be greater in the future. Similar centralizing tendencies are very much in evidence at many other educational institutions.

In the absence of extensive empirical studies of different institutional settings that are guided by a perspective which interrelates institutional centralization with technological innovation and dequalification in the labor process, we cannot offer definitive demonstration of the centrality of centralization. However, after first turning to a discussion of the process of professionalization and deprofessionalization in general, we analyze several institutional spheres where deprofessionalization appears to be associated with centralization.

NOTES

1. Our Rutgers University colleagues Lourdes Benaría and Bruce Steinberg have also raised this question: "But as soon as the mental work is separated from the manual work, the former is subjected to the same principle of separation of conception from execution" (1979:13).

2. Once stripped of control and coordinative functions, formerly middle-class employees may nevertheless, for historical or political reasons, retain some of the symbols of class privilege attached to their prior social positions.

3. Singelman and Wright (n.d.) examined tendencies and countertendencies in the proletarianization of "semiautonomous employee" positions. The net tendency is for these positions to be reduced. However, during the decade 1960-1970, sectors (such as social services) where proletarianization does not advance as rapidly expanded faster than the sectors (such as durable manufacturing) most subject to the process, resulting in a relative expansion of semiautonomous employees during the decade. In a private communication Wright has indicated that "it is quite reasonable to expect that the trends have been reversed in the 1970-1980 period."

4. Low-Beer (1978:119) indicates that worker dissatisfaction is linked to incongruence between the nature of the task and the organizational structure: Where the task is involving or encouraging of participation while the organization is "confining," or vice versa, higher levels of strike activity can be predicted.

5. Pettigrew (1973) studied work place conflicts over time between programmers and systems analysts as a result of specialization.

6. Distinctions between the technical and social, and perhaps "administrative," division of labor do have a considerable implication which we have chosen not to elaborate here. Walker gives a good synopsis of how the technical and social division of labor relate to the process of social reproduction and to the place of the middle class in that process (Walker, 1979:xv-xviii).

Martin Oppenheimer, Christine O'Donnell

and Dale L. Johnson: Professions and

the Middle Class: Professionalization/

Deprofessionalization

In the preceding chapter we argued that dequalification of labor is inherent to the capital accumulation process. Without bringing labor into the orbit of capital, without increasing the scope and intensity of exploitation of labor, without centralizing control, and without technological innovation applied to the labor process, there is no forward surge to capitalist development. But as a historical phenomenon during the stage of development of monopoly capitalism, dequalification carried a very specific contradiction: There could be no dequalification of the lower echelons of the division of labor, no increase in the rate of exploitation, without a corresponding qualification of other categories of labor. We have also emphasized a parallel contradiction: Centralizing control of the labor process required a certain degree of decentralized institutional development. The formation of large numbers of highly skilled engineers, scientists, technicians, accountants, administrative personnel, and professionals of all types, located in dispersed institutional settings and exercising a certain autonomy in work, formed the basis of a middle class that mediated the capital to labor social relation. This class was formed, not just in direct response to the accumulation and class polarization processes, but also through its own self-interested assertions. Professionalism was not simply given, it was struggled for and gained.

Insofar as the position of the middle class is concerned, in the emerging phase of social development, the other side of the contradiction is forcefully emerging: Institutional centralization is superseding decentralization, skilled work is being deskilled, and the labor process is being reorganized, leaving less space for work autonomy. We believe that this has proceeded further in technical and administrative spheres, but it also, as we argue here, bears down on professional labor.

Since the concept of "professional" has become almost coterminous with that of "middle class" we turn first to an evaluation of the concept and an examination of the process of professionalization. We argue that professionalization as a historical process of formation of segments of the middle class also carries, especially in the current phase of development, its specific contrary tendency: deprofessionalization. This involves both dequalification of professional labor and erosion of work autonomy.

We survey a range of recent studies of particular professions that document our thesis. The interrelations between professionalization/ deprofessionalization and centralization/decentralization in different institutional spheres are given attention and the effects on these processes of the introduction of technologies into the labor process are considered in a variety of contexts.

In the emerging phase of development in the United States, and probably in other industrial countries, there appears to be a process of bifurcation of the middle class. Significant segments of the class are being pushed in the direction of the working class, while other segments are being elevated to the status of technocratic staff of the managerial bourgeoisie. This process points to the need to maintain the historicist perspective developed in Chapter 3. The continuing polarization of class structure through the different stages of development makes intermediate class formations unstable and transitory phenomena.

Defining Professionals

What is true of salaried employees generally is even more pointedly the case when it comes to "professionals": No grouping of occupations has been assigned so many contradictory functions, political missions, and cultural outlooks. No grouping has been so diversely labeled and so ill-defined as to its boundaries. No set of occupations has been greeted with so many different prognoses as to their demographics, life chances, and working conditions. From "new class" to "lackeys of capital," from leaders of a "service society" to misleaders of a dismal bureaucratic future—all these labels and many more have been laid at the doorstep of a grouping the very labeling of which is historically determined. Thus, as in the case of "white collar," the expression "professional" serves to mask a host of contradictory phenomena and glosses over fundamental class divisions, and within classes, important fractional distinctions.

The "professions" include, depending on the authority consulted, every occupation from upper management to store-front lawyers, from surgeons and priests to student nurses and computer programming coders, from astronauts, athletes, and authors to technicians, therapists, and veterinarians. And while some professions can be traced to the Old Testament, other occupational titles subsumed under the label appeared (literally) only yesterday.

Among theorists, one's view about the role of the professional strata in society is probably more revealing of the self-conception of the theorist than of the realities of "professional" life and its prospects, politically as well as culturally. So it is not surprising that intellectuals who see themselves as among the "best and brightest," waiting (together with the likes of Walt Rostow, Arthur Schlesinger, and John Kenneth Galbraith) the call from the White House, view professionals as a "new class"; or that those who see themselves as leaders of working-class revolt (the French new working class theorists) view their stratum as part of the working-class; or that those who hold the life of the mind as sacredly above mundane struggle (as, for example, Peter Berger in *The Pyramid of Sacrifice*) see themselves and their like as philosopher-kings. Similarly, one's definition of what professionals are, in class terms, will tend at least in part to be dependent on one's overall view of social class in capitalist society—a denial of the existence of class contradictions in the Marxist sense will lead to a definition along *cultural* lines (as Bruce-Briggs, 1979); a view of stratification in functionalist terms will lead to a conception of professionals which differentiates them according to *specific function* within a spectrum of strata (the sociology of occupations literature); a political-economic approach to classes will lead to an approach dividing professionals according to their *general function* in capitalist economy (Ehrenreichs, in Walker, 1978).

The term "professional" is itself partly a function of *reification*: the term is not a neutral, objective description of a reality, but is, rather, a label which has developed in response to specific social context and which functions in turn to create a reality which becomes part of the social context. Thus, as Lasch puts it:

> Recent studies of 'professionalization' by historians have shown that professionalism did not emerge, in the nineteenth and early twentieth centuries, in response to clearly defined social needs. Instead, the new professions themselves invented many of the needs they claimed to satisfy. They played on public fears of disorder and disease, adopted a deliberately mystifying jargon, ridiculed popular traditions of self-help as backward and unscientific, and in this way created . . . a demand for their own services [1977:19].

Lasch goes on to attack several studies which do not take this into consideration, charging them with "ignoring the connection between the rise of modern professionalism and the rise of industrial management. . . The new historian of professionalism, by treating professionals as a separate class with their own interests and identity, repeats the mistake made by earlier students of the 'managerial revolution', who argued that managers constitute a 'new class' " (1977:17).

Most sociological discussion defines "professionals" by criteria which are historically determined, in part by professionals themselves: An occupational grouping defines itself as a "profession," declares membership limited to those meeting qualifications (including educational levels and certification) set by itself, and creates for itself a "rationale"—for example, a code of ethics for behavior and a jargon which in turn further excludes nonmembers. In this manner various "professional" groupings have struggled to dissociate themselves from the status of ordinary working folk and to establish the occupation as a privileged sector of what they explicitly define as the respectable middle class. The outside world then accepts this set of (self-) definitions and *reifies* the concept: The label becomes a reality as the rest of society finds itself excluded from knowledge or skills over which the profession has declared a monopoly; and the profession, for a time at least, gains a privileged position.

In the actual historical circumstances in the United States, this process of quasi-class self-identification became an important component of the subsequent development of a "real" class. Johnson's prior arguments imply that this is the case here. Classes are formed in part through the "objective" movement of the accumulation and class polarization processes, in part through self-conscious activity of class formation (Chapter 7).

Larson's account of the rise of professions in the United States (1977) implicitly recognizes professionalization as class formation. On the other hand, a good example of blind acceptance of the reifications of the notion of professionalism is in Ginzberg. In a discussion aiming to demonstrate the growth of professionals in the labor force, he counts the total of "professional, technical and kindred" labor at 13.7 million for 1977; from this figure, he says, "one can substract 1.078 million technicians in engineering, science and other fields who *by definition* are not professionals" (Ginzberg, 1979:49, italics added). By whose definition?

The excuse for the monopoly of know-how claimed by professionals is often said to be the "knowledge explosion" which, theoretically, forces specialization and prevents the "layman" from commanding the details of *any* profession (except the one she or he practices, and then only a subdivision within it). And, not incidentally, the monopolization of an area of knowledge, skill or technology, protects that particular labor market in a guildlike fashion: so long as the supply of labor can be limited by the guild itself, the price of labor (especially of the self-employed type) can be kept relatively high.

This brings us to the question of how some occupations are able to define themselves as professions and others not. Occupations which are not officially labeled "professional" but in which workers take some measure of pride (that is, see themselves as doing a "professional" job, meaning an expert job not readily doable by people outside the field) seek to professionalize by emulating existing professions—they organize trade associations, publish journals (there is, for example, a journal for mercenary or "professional" soldiers), and create structures for admission and certification. This is known as "upgrading the profession." Thus social workers actively seek to be licensed by the state: Licensing will tend to exclude "nonprofessionals" and will legitimize those passing the examination as "professionals." In this way, just as some professions (as will later be analyzed) are undergoing downgrading, fragmentation, and "proletarianization," other occupations are struggling (though against increasing odds) for upgrading, broader spans of control, and professional status.

One of the key variables in professionalization is higher education. There appears to be a "halo effect" at work: Certain occupations define higher education as one of their characteristics. As this occurs in more professions, it becomes a generalized social assumption that all educated people (meaning university-trained and certified) are per se professionals, so that anything they do is therefore "professional."

The development of the professions has gone hand in hand with the establishment of superior market positions for their labor. Mechanisms were instituted to regulate entry into these occupations so as to perpetuate favorable market conditions. Some professions—for example, medicine in the United States—have been able to maintain the supply of professionals well below either the market demand or social need for their services, while the state, under pressure from the professional associations, sanctioned licensing enforcement so that uncertified practitioners cannot practice. In this way, high incomes and privileged working conditions remain assured.

The professions also evolved so as to reproduce the class structure along with the professions themselves. For a time, the professions became almost the exclusive prerogataives of the sons of professionals. Institutions of higher education adopted admission standards (and tuition fees) that discriminated against working-class applicants whose oppressive class situation frustrated achievement of the requisite standards. Culturally biased tests screened out persons of a different social background and mode of intelligence than the class-bound, instrumental rationality measured by the tests. The steady growth of demand for educated labor, operational control of universities and professional schools by elite professionals, and control of funding necessary for expansion by private foundations and governments pursuing policies designed primarily to reproduce the existing social order combined, in most instances, to create equilibrium or supply shortages in the markets for professional labor.

This situation began to change in the 1950s and 1960s, especially in the United States. Demand for educated labor escalated so rapidly in this period that a system of mass education was introduced and the doors were opened to increasing numbers of working-class youth. During the 1960s, higher education became a principal site of class struggle. Sharp social struggles were waged during the decade for easier access to higher education and professional and technical careers. The middle class, having reached considerable size and maturity, sought to ensure their sons and daughters the same, or better, opportunities than they enjoyed. Trade unions and working people pressured for greater social democratization. Racial minorities and women demanded access to opportunities closed by discrimination. Under pressure, universities stepped up recruitment of "non-traditional" students, and graduate and professional schools began to admit more women and minorities.

In recent years the situation has changed dramatically. The supply of a growing number of types of educated labor has run ahead of demand in the United States and even more so in many other countries. The Third World exported scientists, engineers, doctors, and other professionals in ever-increasing numbers to the metropolitan countries. The rapid expansion of the U.S. economy during the post-World War II decades culminated in the economic difficulties and relative stagnation of the 1970s. Unemployment reached into the ranks of the middle classes for the first time since the 1930s. The expansion of higher education accompanied by the social gains of easier access to it increased supply just when the workings of the economy contracted demand. It is now no longer possible for middle-class families to ensure their children middle-class careers; higher education faces cutbacks rather than growth budgets, with the effect (among others) of contracting educational opportunities for working-class and minority students; and an elitist academic traditionalism reminiscent of the pre-1960s is being foisted on higher education by the educational managers and conservative senior professors, destroying the openness and innovation in education won during the 1960s.

We have not yet fully established the social definition of the professions. Professions do exist: they are real enough (as the result of the process described above, plus others to be discussed below) and can therefore be described, sociologically, in ideal-typical terms. Professionalization is a process by which persons in an occupational category struggle to gain the advantages of being professional. Deprofessionalization is a process by which the characteristics of professionalism are eroded.

Until recently, "professional" meant work involving discretion and judgment so that it is difficult or impossible to standardize or mechanize; work in which the worker produces an entire product, be it a painting, a surgical operation, a book, a bridge, or an idea; where the worker's pace, workplace conditions, product, its use (and even to a degree its price) are largely determined by the worker; where ideally the source of income is an individually regulated sale of a product or service under fairly loose market conditions established by face-to-face bargaining rather than sale of labor time in advance of the creation of anything; and where the bulk of the income goes to the worker without any bureaucratic intermediary except perhaps an agent (as in the case of an artist). Finally, by implication, professional activity is work involving high levels of training, apprenticeship, or other forms of formalized education. Of course, many of the ideal-typical terms of professionalism were either never gained or lost along the way in a spectrum of professions. For example, the absorption of social services by the state and private corporations to a large extent has undermined an independent practitioner and fee-for-service organization of the newer professions, and steadily whittled away at medicine and law as well. Professional associations have had to come up with other ways to maximize income, establish perquisites, and defend prerogatives.

The ideal construct of the term "professional" implies the existence of its opposite, the "proletarianized" employee for whom an extensive division of labor exists. He or she typically performs only one or a small number of tasks in a total process. The pace of work, the characteristics of the workplace, the nature of the product, the uses to which it is put, and its market conditions are determined not by the employee but by higher authorities (private or public management). The employee's primary source of income is a salary, which is determined by large-scale market conditions and economic processes. The employee, in order to defend this situation from deterioration of living standards or working conditions, moves toward unionization.

Again, as Braverman and many others have forcefully argued, there is nothing *inherent* in knowledge or technology to create "proletarianized" conditions any more than "professionalized" conditions: They are products of specific political-social processes, especially struggles of class assertion, within social structures shaped by the dynamic of capital accumulation and class polarization. But these conditions become real enough. As such, they provide us with another concept, that of *deprofessionalization*, or at the extreme *proletarianization*. We suggest that such a process is now under way.

Many professions are now moving, selectively and unevenly, away from the ideal-typical conditions described above toward their opposites—that is, toward conditions typical of the classical working class. Note that we say *toward*. We do not say that some professions have now become synonymous with "blue-collar" labor, or that there are not many fluctuations, or that, like other forms of labor, the professions do not attempt to prevent this process, often with degrees of success. We say only that there is a deprofessionalization process.

The varying impacts of contradictory forces, rooted in such factors as changing technology, the relative strength of contending forces in struggle, fiscal exigencies, and the role of the profession itself (as a pressure group) shape the extent and rapidity of deprofessionalization.

In general, the process of deprofessionalization is rooted in the need of capital, and the state, to rationalize and cheapen the cost of production and to assert the domination of management over all forms of labor, including professional labor. Yet this process forces the professional employee to protect her or his traditional prerogatives through unionization, political lobbying, ideological pronouncements, and other means. At the same time, the segmentation of professional labor and the creation of a growing lower-level "professional," increasingly unionized, and resistant labor force (in the U.S. economy, the administrative center of world capital, this is particularly important), generates the need for supervision and high-level technocratic staff. We suspect that the following trend now holds: Those professionals who are able to "upgrade" themselves (including an increase in formal certification requirements and education) are forming, within professional ranks, a supervisory/administrative or technocratic upper layer, while the rest become downgraded and their work deskilled, to form a proletarianizing element within professional ranks.

Within many professions, then, a new hierarchy is developing: at the bottom, a large mass of less-educated employees engaged in fragmented labor; at the top, a small group of more highly-educated technocrats who are engaged less in traditional professional labor than in the jobs of conceptualizing the labor process and coordinating, supervising, and controlling employees on behalf of capital and the state.

Thus, the tendency is for professions to bifurcate into strata that begin to approximate class contradictions. What is the process by which those at the bottom find themselves deskilled and administratively subordinated in a technified labor process, while those at the top find their professional skills being transformed into higher administrative activity?[1]

As we noted in the prior chapter, over the scant years of computers there has been an extensive division of labor, undermining the generalist and creating separate training tracks into careers in systems analysis, programming, and coding. "Programmers," says Kraft, "have not been reduced to quite the same level of fragmented activity as auto workers. . . . But the social and individual consequences have been remarkably similar" (1977:61). Managers, in turn, are drawn from the upper levels of the computer field, either from among technical experts or from those trained more generally in "software sciences." Thus creative work is separated from the increasingly detailed labor at the bottom and is used to control that labor.

A similar picture has developed in pharmacy. In 1970, there were 19,820 small independent retail pharmacies in the United States, most operated by professional pharmacists. This number had been cut by two-thirds by 1980! The pressure of large chains, combined with changes in the manufacture and dispensing of drugs, has made the traditional pharmacist obsolete while expanding employment opportunities in hospitals and nursing homes. Thus pharmacists have sought to become upgraded in order to maintain their prerogatives, particularly those honorific ones associated with being a "professional." In an attempt to share authority with doctors, pharmacists will strive for a Doctor of Pharmacy (still relatively rare). The field, Birenbaum (n.d.) predicts, will become segmented between that group, largely supervising others and in charge of the standards of the profession, and the many licensed bachelor's degree pharmacists whose main job regardless of professional rhetoric about providing an essential service, will be to move drugs from a larger to a smaller container and type a label.

In the health field generally, three trends can be discerned that provide the structural framework for the development of the health care professions. First, most notable in the recent period is the enormous expansion of the numbers of people employed in the sector. By the 1970s, health services employed about five percent of the civilian labor force. Second, increasingly the entities that produce health care are no longer storefront private offices but large institutions: big hospitals, clinics, and large-scale health maintenance organizations (HMOs). In health care institutional centralization supersedes decentralization. Third, this institutional labor force is becoming more and more fragmented and stratified. This trend has reached rather extreme proportions. Greater New York Blue Cross, for example, sent its member hospitals a form requesting the number of people in different jobs. The form listed 280 titles, excluding physicians.

In general, this increased employment, fragmentation, and stratification of the labor force is primarily due to the concentration, over time, of health care services in the institution of the hospital, the centralization of operational control and financing, the specialized technologies introduced that "require" technical labor, and the extraordinary degree to which hospital administrators have been able to grasp and wield institutional power and thereby structure the labor process.

After World War II, with the growth of medical technology and the move away from solo practice to complex health institutions, the need for categories of allied health professionals expanded well beyond the original foursome of physicians, dentists, nurses, and pharmacists. Each new category of worker attempted to follow the doctors' pattern of establishing itself as a profession by organizing to claim control of particular tasks; associations were formed to establish entry requirements, to certify practitioners, and to seek codification of professional functions in state law through licensing. There are major differences, however, between doctors and other allied health professionals. Each seized what it could in terms of power and territory without encroaching on the more established and powerful profession of physician, and their associations joined the AMA in guarding the borders of the new profession. In the contemporary period there are as many as 22 different licensed health occupations.

The greatest concentration of hospital workers is in nursing, and these services run the gamut from skilled RNs with a Bachelor of Science or even higher degree to unskilled orderlies and attendants. Concerned with increased costs of professional nursing and with control of this sector of the hospital work force, hospitals and doctors have moved to support differentiation within the field. As a consequence, three training programs currently exist for registered nurses: the four-year BSN program, the two- or three-year community college AD program, and the hospital-based diploma program. The BSN program emphasizes theory over floor practice and hence trains people for supervisory roles; the other programs are "bedside" oriented and attract disproportionately women of working-class backgrounds and minorities.

Today the nursing profession is being restructured by the explosion of "new careers" and the government has gotten into the act through manpower training programs which turn thousands of technical and paraprofessional health workers onto the job market. Many of the functions originally a part of registered nursing have been usurped by these "new careers." One of these that is a dead-end job is disproportionately nonwhite male and pays better than nursing is the physician assistant (PA).

The hospital work force, perhaps more than other work settings, is a rigid caste system. It reflects divisions between job categories on the basis of class, sex, and race stratification, and most persons remain at their entry-level job. For the workers who have strived for "professional" licensing, this status has provided them with some degree of job security and higher wages, but at the expense of reinforcing the monotonous, fragmented, alienating nature of the work and rigidifying the job hierarchy within hospitals.

The social work profession is likewise segmented; the Masters in Social Work is widely regarded as the prerequisite for supervisory positions, while state licensing will serve further to prevent non-MSWs and MSWs untrained in professional argot from attaining upper-level jobs. The vast mass of social workers working at lower-level, semiclerical jobs, as in public assistance, will obtain only an Associate's degree. The segmentation of public sector social work—for example, the division of labor between those who "determine eligibility" for public assistance and those who do home visits or deal with clients face to face—enables the state to settle for a lesser-educated employee who earns, correspondingly, less pay. The MSW, on the other hand, will alone be eligible for supervisory roles and for the kind of social work practice that pays—state-licensed private clinical practice.

With pressures of severely contracted job markets, even Ph.D.s are forced into either "proletarianizing" activities in their fields, such as part-time work or into other fields that may have less "professional" standing. One example is the authors' own profession, sociology. A new specialty, "clinical sociology" (i.e., sociology applied in action settings such as therapy, planning, and law enforcement so that it overlaps, hence challenges, professions currently licensed to practice in those fields) is now seeking governmental licensing so that it can effectively compete for the professional jobs now monopolized by social workers, clinical psychologists, counselors, planners, and others. One reason for the growth of new specialties like clinical sociology in a variety of professions is straightforward: Academic posts in all the disciplines in the 1970s and 1980s have failed to expand to absorb new Ph.D.s, and the increasing number who are denied tenured positions, under redefined "standards" for the traditional sinecures, are forced out of academia.

There are not enough studies across a range of professions to build a complete, documented case for generalized dequalification. One macro-level, empirically based model is consistent with our thesis. Pampel, Land, and Felson (1977) devised a social indicator model of changes in the occupational structure of the United States between 1947 and 1974. The ten-equation dynamic model attempts to explain and predict rates of mobility into higher-status occupations. They found that rates of mobility, rapid in the postwar period, decreased in the first years of the 1970s. They suggest further decline "in the absence of counterbalancing structural trends" (1977:963). But models based on aggregate data do not explain how and why the occupational structure is tightening. Studies of specific professions employing an adequate methodology need to be undertaken.[2]

It could also be argued, persuasively in some cases, that the "knowledge explosion" has forced a certain division of labor in some professions and that this is not inherently related to the development of hierarchy, with a few managerial professionals at the top and a mass of deskilled pseudo-professionals at the bottom. In the older professions (medicine, law, and the clergy) this may be true: The division of labor remains more horizontal than vertical. But there are several important qualifications to this truth. First, it is true only insofar as the profession has been able to stay "closed," as in the case of physicians. This closure and horizontal specialization of expertise of course stands on a vast hierarchy of differentiation in lower-level medical personnel. If physicians were trained in numbers proportional to the illness produced by the stresses and turmoil of our society—that is, in numbers exceeding what society can at the time "afford"—a vertical segmentation would probably develop. Second, it is true only insofar as the profession is relatively free from the compulsions of the labor process within capitalism: Engineers, computer specialists, and many others are subordinated to the imperatives of market economies or, like librarians and nurses, to the constraints of state tax structures. In the face of these imperatives and constraints, very few professions indeed are able to maintain true independence. In the case of physicians, it is in part because they *control* the organizations (hospitals), hence their own labor conditions; nurses do not. Third, it is true only insofar as the subordinate profession has not (yet) been subjected to technological changes (in the main, information processing technology) which would undermine the practitioner's traditional skills. Professors survive only because they have not yet been displaced by teaching machines. In both the fields of law and medicine, computer diagnosis is already making inroads on the traditional skills, real or imagined, of the practitioners. In occupations that are subordinate to the dynamic of capital (as practiced in large corporate bureaucracies particularly), in which there are labor surpluses, where much labor can be and is being displaced by machines, the profession is doomed to the bifurcation described above.

Professionalization/Deprofessionalization and the Transitory Nature of Intermediate Classes

It is inconceivable to talk of a process of dequalification or deprofessionalization, much less of proletarianization, if one believes that professionals "really" exist in some inherent form growing from the very nature of modern knowledge, technology, and cultural life. There is nothing "inherent" in a presumed knowledge-based or technological social order. The question is how knowledge and technology are organized in a political economy of capital accumulation, augmented in the case of the formation of professions, by the historical possibility of an occupation in a position of relative power (due to this political economy and through its self-assertions) being able to define itself in a particular way. The fact that a process is under way which undermines or transforms professional conditions means that those conditions are not inherent and that that grouping is not unique—it is, like other groupings, subject to the dynamic, not of some mythical "postindustrial society," but of capitalist development as it moves into qualitatively new phases. This is a dynamic which *tends* to drive some professionals *toward* working-class conditions of existence, and in some sense toward being proletarian, while the same or other forces drive others toward or into the managerial bourgeoisie.

It is the proletariat which is unique (under capitalism), together with its contradiction, the bourgeoisie. These are the antipodes of capitalist class relations: All other "middle-class" formations tend over the long run and in the process of their continuous evolution to be pulled toward or coopted into the bourgeoisie or pushed in the direction of or into the working class. Capitalist development has always been and remains, in the contemporary phase more than ever, a process of class polarization. Nonbourgeois and nonworking class groupings constitute either vestiges of past class relations (e.g.) independent farmers, small proprietors, and privately practicing professionals) inserted in new ways in the changing relations of exploitation and domination, or they are groupings historically formed in particular stages of development that are in transition from one social location to another; they are more or less constantly in the process of becoming something other than what they were, of joining some other class.

This is different from the changes that occur with capitalist development in the nature of the working class and bourgeoisie. The process of class polarization changes the internal structure (the "fractionalization") of the two main classes and the *forms* of relation between them, but the *essential* relations, those of exploitation and domination, remain constant. This is not at all the case for any intermediate class (e.g., eighteenth-century merchants, nineteenth-century petty bourgeoisie, or the middle classes of the twentieth century) which are, with the process of development, fundamentally *transformed*, in the sense of their rise and demise, changing social functions, and shifting positioning within the main class relations.

The class polarization tendency of capitalist development must always be studied in its historical specificity. And it is amply evident that capitalist societies at all stages of development have been, with considerable variation in different times and places, characterized by *a multi class complex of class relations in a bipolarizing structure*.

In the case of advanced capitalist societies, the formation of a substantial array of intermediate groups was a necessary concomitant to the transformation of the population into a vast mass of dependent proletarians. These groups were instruments of that transformation: They became integral expressions of that very process of class polarization.

The process of class polarization in the currently emerging phase of capitalist development, which is one of an incipient crisis of capital accumulation, is being turned against professional, technical and administrative employees as one-time necessary intermediate and mediating formations, subordinating increasing sectors to the discipline of a rationalized labor process and elevating others to the position of tail-enders of the managerial bourgeoisie.

It can be concluded that the concept of "professional" as applied to any particular occupation or to a whole range of occupations, is a *process*: Occupations come and go, they are nonprofessional today, semiprofessional (as measured by sociologists, relative to the time required for training, etc.) tomorrow, and "fully" professional (i.e., even more training) later on. Other professions, meanwhile, lose ground; they lose control and autonomy over their work, become fragmented so that their lower layers "require" less training or education, and become technically dequalified and thoroughly subordinated in the labor process. To view this agglomeration of shifting formations as the main basis of an important social class may indeed seem sociologically very spongy. But what is important is not the label of class but the process of formation and transformation of the social relations that the different occupational structures and work activities express.

Notes

1. There are fundamentally opposed points of view on professionalization/deprofessionalization in the literature. Friedson states: "It seems to be implicit in discussions of the prototypical worker of the postindustrial society that knowledge-based work, the work of middle class experts, professionals, and technicians, is by its very nature *not* amenable to the mechanization and rationalization which industrial production and commerce have undergone over the past century" (1973:55). Haug, on the other hand, argues that "deprofessionalization rather than professionalization is the trend of the future" (1973:197). In the main Haug is right. But neither she nor Friedson nor other authors have attempted to systematically develop the argument or to survey a range of professions and present empirical documentation.

2. In the absence of a wide range of studies of what is happening to the professions, how can one concretely grasp the transformation of the professions, their movement toward one or the other of the main classes? One method is to examine what happens to the semi-autnomy characteristic of professional activity, which sharply differentiates professionals' work from that of workers'. Studies of the interrelations between eroding work conditions and unionization would be important.

Dale L. Johnson: The American Middle Class in Crisis

The 1980s are likely to be years of acute economic crunch and accelerating social degeneration and political turmoil. In the United States the economic indicators of "stagflation" have been accumulating since 1971. The year 1980 opened with an unparalleled inflation and a sluggish economy that slid into a 1981 recession. High levels of structurally induced unemployment are expected to persist; the dollar's low value abroad, high energy costs, and deteriorating real incomes of the great majority will probably continue unabated.

The problems of the 1980s are not simply economic ones (nor are they specific to the United States). It is almost certain that the growing American social ills of the past decade will become more serious (if not raging pathologies) in the 1980s: vicious crime; rampant narcissism; rupturing of remaining social bonds; increased antagonism between races, sexes, and generations; deteriorating quality to all aspects of life.

The immediate political consequences will doubtless be less dramatic than these economic and social problems: Policy failures of the Reagan administration; confusion on all sides; law and order rhetoric; surely a continuing decline in the people's faith in established institutions and, most of all, in the capacity of government to solve problems. The year 1984 is more likely to be the year of Hobbes than of Orwell: a chaotic war of all against all rather than highly organized oppression.

But these hard times and bitter social conditions, together with threatening international situations, may well begin to take socially constructive, if anarchic, forms of organized social struggle as the decade proceeds: organized protests against massive budget cuts in social programs; movements against militarism and American intervention abroad; heightened movements against sexism, against a resurgence of racism in both its vicious and institutional forms, and against a surge of right-wing reaction and government repression. There should be expanded rank-and-file agitation for the revival of democratic and militant trade unionism and for its extension to unorganized workers and middle-class employees. The 1980s will also see movements for alternative energy sources, consumer protection, and the environment; perhaps the traditional political parties will decline as there is halting movement toward new political groupings on the Left and Right.

These projections for the United States are at once dismal and hopeful. If they are on mark, whether the actual course of events turns toward a more chaotic, bitter Hobbesian world or toward a more hopeful scenario of people's organized struggle to confront their circumstances and to come together to build new social bonds and thereby to strive for a better world, depends on a variety of international and national forces and the actual outcomes of unfolding events.

This descriptive summary of the situation at the turn of the decade adds up to a catalogue of symptoms of an incipient *crisis* of the economic and social order. This, of course, runs totally counter to the prevailing doctrine of postindustrial society. In this new social order, marked by an "end to ideology," knowledge and the knowledgeable are said to exercise benevolent guidance; the social structure is one of greatly ameliorated class divisions; economic problems are manageable; and the political system functions by technical rationality. The United States is not a postindustrial order—it is entering a qualitatively new phase of capitalist development in which new, sharper forms of antagonistic class relations are both consequence and cause of an incipient structural crisis of the prevailing order. This crisis is mainly rooted in the limitations of the current modes of capital accumulation.

This statement promises more than a concluding chapter can deliver. To fully establish what is meant by "crisis" and a "qualitatively new phase of capitalist development" would require many additional pages in an already heavy book. Here analysis is confined to drawing out some of the findings and arguments of the book, concluding that the middle class is squarely at the center of this crisis.

The Middle Class in Crisis

Class Situation

What people do in relation to their circumstances depends in the first instance on immediate matters that visibly press on their lives and consciousness—on their "class situation." The economic problems and social-economic trends of the present phase of development have already had a measurable impact on the immediate class situation of the middle class: There is growing unemployment and underemployment and an increasing tax burden, together with an end to the benevolence of the state with respect to supportive measures for the class; social service cuts aimed at the needy take the jobs of the middle class; there are stagnating or declining real incomes and increased subordination on the job; and, in general, the middle class suffers a demise of assured privileges. As everyone knows, a college degree is no longer the ticket to a secure, comfortable sinecure in a corporate or administrative hierarchy. Public sector budget reductions force salary cuts, increase workloads, deteriorate work conditions, and raise the specter of unemployment for even the established professionals.

The conventional data on class situation are clear enough. In the aggregate, real income levels in 1979 were only one percent above 1967 levels for "professional, technical, and kindred" employees, a sharp relative decline from income growth in previous periods and far below the real growth in national income during the period. In a variety of specific occupations, incomes that once outspaced inflation now often lag behind the cost of living. Maintenance of a socially defined and economically feasible middle-class family lifestyle requires two incomes—and women from middle-class families have entered the labor market, in largely proletarianized sectors, in unprecedented numbers. The traditional salary differentials between blue-collar and white-collar workers are disappearing. In the mid- to late 1970s, "higher-level" middle-class occupations gained some in real income, but middle and lower levels lost to inflation.[1] Blumberg's detailed study (1980a) of income trends among different occupational groups between 1967 and 1978 found that only workers in strong unions made increases in real incomes during the inflationary period, with the sharpest losses among technical and professional employees.

Perhaps even more significant than income trends is what appears to be a substantial slowdown in the historic rate of increase of middle-class occupational positions. Our preliminary data indicate this, but we are awaiting the availability of the 1980 census data before completing a thorough study. Burris (1980) generalizes on the basis of his data that between 1970 and 1978, "the proportion of the new-middle class positions within the labor force increased by an average of less than one-fourth of one percent per year—a rate less than half the average for the previous decade and lower than that of any decade since the 1930s. Of the developments which might reverse this trend, none appear likely at the present time" (1980:31).

We will later argue that declining labor markets for technical, administrative, and professional labor is first a consequence of the limits of the accumulation process. Burris notes: "Many of the structural transformations which contributed to the growth of this class during the early part of the century are effectively completed, while the expansionary trends which have supplemented these in the most recent period are beginning to reveal their own limits and contradictions" (1980:29).

We will also argue shortly that the social relations of the 1980s and beyond in the United States will be those of a more polarized class structure, encompassing relations which are less and less cushioned by intermediate and mediating formations. This does not mean that the full gamut of social structures will be any the less complex than at present. One question of particular import is the fate of the lower echelons of the middle class as income levels and employment possibilities decline—as they are pushed toward the working class.

The push toward the proletarian pole is in fact not simply a given result of labor markets and the dequalification process we analyzed in prior chapters. It also involves a social process of stratification and re-

restratification of the population. In looking at data over time on labor force composition, the impression (1980 census data are not yet available) is that the internal structure of the lower strata of the middle class is undergoing change. The social demands for equality of opportunity and "affirmative action" and the cooptation of large numbers of people from working-class origins to paraprofessional status and to technical vocations to some degree undermines the intergenerational inheritance of class position for the offspring of both the working and middle classes. Significant in the United States is the changing sexual and racial composition of technical, lower-level administrative, and paraprofessional sectors of the labor force which were (except for nursing and teaching) previously bastions of white, male privilege. Such expansion of lower-level technical, administrative, and paraprofessional employment as occurred in the 1970s seemed to be related to the increasing participation of women in the labor force and to a diffusion of minorities in the occupational structure. This may well be associated with the dequalification of labor power in a number of occupations. As scientific work is broken down into fragmented technical tasks, as administration is converted into clerical-type operations, and as paraprofessionals assume many of the tasks of professionals, women and minorities are brought into these employments in increasing numbers. Kraft has observed about the computer field:

> The reappearance of large number of women in programming, largely at the lowest skill levels—as applications programmers or coders—is an indication of the rapid routinization and deskilling of programming as a whole. Women have traditionally been used as a pool of cheap labor allowed into skilled occupations only during acute labor shortages or when an occupation has been drained of skill through technological and social innovation [1979:16].

This incorporation of marginalized sectors of the population into previously more privileged occupations undergoing devaluation may reflect an old ploy by employers to effect changes in the labor process, but it may also signify a qualitative change in sexual and racial stratification of the social order.

The declining class situation and restratification of the middle class occurs in the context of a more difficult class situation of a highly stratified working class. One scenario suggested by Blumberg is a kind of Hobbesian 1984:

> What we may expect as Americans begin fighting over the scraps is not only what used to be called an "intensification of the class struggle,' but the intensification of the struggle among all competing groups in the society: racial, sexual, generational, regional and so on. Whatever natural fissures or cleavages already exist may become the basis for social conflict. At the end of the 1970s, after a generation of unprecedented postwar prosperity, America finds itself paradoxically undergoing a revolution of falling expectations [1980b:10].

The economic underpinnings of people's social existence and the dynamics of stratification is *not* what is intended—to clarify in this analysis. This we leave for later work. The more challenging question is the place of the middle class in the larger context of changing class relations in the 1980s. For in the long run, this is more important than the short-run facts of class situation or the restratification of the population. In reality, the incipient crisis of the 1980s is, in one of its most fundamental expressions, a crisis of the middle class in the larger class relations of the social order.

The Limits of the Accumulation Process

The crisis of the middle class is a deeply structural one. This is so in at least two senses. First, the very sources of capital accumulation that once formed proliferating sectors of the middle class are now either increasingly constrained or no longer operating. Second, the most recent shifts in processes of rationalization of the labor process, institutional centralization, and technological innovation have contributed to a sharpening structural polarization between the dominant and working classes in which the middle class (as we analyzed in Chapters 9 and 10) is less and less in the middle and more and more bifurcated into upper and lower strata, the one pulled closer to the bourgeoisie, the other pushed toward the working class.

Chapter 3 argued that the process of accumulation—while it has an economic appearance in investment decisions, capital movements, and paths of historical development—is fundamentally one of formation of classes and transformation of relations between classes. A number of specific historical sources of accumulation were identified: technical and organizational innovation, the internalization of capital, the development of the state, and the incorporation of increasing proportions of the population into the waged labor to capital social relation. Each source had the effect of forming new sectors of the middle class and increasing the structural polarization between capital and labor, while propelling overall economic and social development. In recent years, most of the historical avenues of accumulation that once swelled the middle class seem to have nearly reached the limits of their expansion.

(1) Innovations.[2] New technological accomplishments are not significantly revamping the labor process in such a way as to rapidly expand middle-class occupations. While technical innovations, especially in the energy and military fields, are likely, and new products will expand some markets, no epoch-making innovations appear on the horizon. In fact, the overall impact of the latest technological marvel, computers, has been to rationalize the labor process so as to eliminate or reorganize and downgrade technical, administrative, and professional work.

Expenditures for research and development in both public and private spheres have been in relative decline since the 1960s. Worried editors of *Business Week* (1977) noted a decline in growth of R&D expenditures from an annual rate of 5.6 percent in 1961-1967 to 1.8 percent between 1967 and 1975. While there is a lot of rhetoric about "reindustrialization" and the high technology potential of the American economy, the reality is that private sector spending for R&D remained relatively stable in real terms between 1970 and 1979. (Of the $38 billion spent by business for R&D in 1979, 40 percent went for new products, 22 percent for new processes, and 38 percent to improve existing processes; *New York Times,* 1980). Straussman notes: "If Daniel Bell's axial principle of postindustrial society—the codification of theoretical knowledge—has an empirical reference point, it would be entered in the amount and content of basic research" (1978:6). Straussman goes on to point out that only 5 percent of private sector R&D money is devoted to basic research, rising to 12 percent of federal government R&D expenditure. Public support of R&D "reached its zenith" in 1967. Moreover, 78 percent of government expenditure in R&D (in the early 1970s) was for defense and space. The defense budget dwarfs the combined total of private and public R&D. As we pointed out above, employment of scientific and technical personnel in the 1970s receded from the high rates of previous decades. This is associated with the decline in technological research and achievement.

> By the late 1970s, the initial research, design and installation phase of the third technological revolution began to draw to a close as new forms of technology became generalized throughout industry and their construction and installation became increasingly routinized. While further research and development has continued beyond this stage, the exaggerated demand for scientific and technical personnel associated with the first feverish burst of automation has tended to return to its preautomation levels [Burris, 1980:30-31].

Moreover, unlike many previous technological innovations (e.g., electronic machines) fugure developments (e.g., nuclear energy) are not likely to cheapen capital but to greatly increase the cost of production—and prove politically expensive as well (e.g., the antinuclear movement). Similarly, huge areas of potentially dynamic investments (e.g., rebuilding decaying cities) are not likely, given great political constraints, to open up the possibility of what O'Connor (1973) called the "social-industrial complex."

(2) Declining empire. While the internalization of capital, with the transnational corporation as the principal productive force on a world scale, proceeds apace, the United States is no longer the exclusive administrative center of international economic activity. The American administrative apparatus of world empire is largely consolidated, even in decline; this means that the demand for middle-class labor to man the machinery of empire is also in decline. Transnational corporations are moving many of their North American operations overseas; this exports technical and administrative jobs as well as production labor. U.S. exports of sophisticated industrial products and technologies are losing out to

Japanese and European competition; this limits opportunities for scientific and technical employees in the United States.

(3) The attack on social services. The historical expansion of state activity in public service activities is receding under structural, fiscal, and political constraints. This directly affects middle-class employment, especially in social services. Beyond direct employment effects, the relative contraction of the growth of state activities impinges on the entire development process, constraining the kinds of class formations of previous periods. Of course, it greatly affects the class situation of the working and underclasses, exacerbating social tensions.

The current political attack on social services goes far beyond the negative effects on the needy and the jobs of the service professionals. It may, in fact, represent a vehicle for a disaccumulation process in the larger political economy. Hirschorn (1979) has developed a provocative analysis of what he terms the "rationalization" of the social services sector (by which he means primarily cutbacks, but also centralization and labor dequalification). His analysis complements the thesis developed in Chapter 7 on social services as the most advanced form of production of use values. In the advanced stage of industrialism, he contends, the expansion of social services is necessary, not just as a complement to capital accumulation but as a primary vehicle of accumulation. Nevertheless, capitalists and the state resist expansion of the sector "because these services represent the new and most socialized form of productive forces" (1979:163). The dominant interests cannot so easily control and directly profit from social services, so expansion is resisted and, as the fiscal crisis deepens, cutbacks are imposed. Hirschorn's conclusion is worth quoting at some length:

> Insofar as services are rationalized, production and marketing cannot be transformed. But in that degree that the latter are not transformed, disaccumulation takes place. Labor is displaced in industry and in services through the application of classical Taylorist techniques. Surplus labor and hidden unemployment become endemic, the web of social life unravels, and services are pushed to comply with the contradictions of this decay. Schools become warehouses for misplaced and displaced youth, welfare bureaucracies become the loci for maintaining subsistence incomes, hospitals medicate men and women who face blocked careers and a decaying family life, and marketing channels the consequences of social decay along consumerist lines, e.g. the spread of alcoholism among youth and the dissemination of pornography. . . . to the degree that services do not become developmental, to the degree that they do not transform production, marketing and job allocation, then to that degree do services become unproductive, wasteful and irrational [1979:165].

The implications of these trends for class structure and class relations in the 1980s are considerable. If the traditional sources of accumulation are constrained and if development of what O'Connor (1973) called the "social-industrial complex" as a new source of economic dynamism and social amelioration is not politically feasible, then generalized social and resultant political tensions can only increase.

(4) Intensified proletarianization. We previously argued that capital accumulation by means of incorporation of increasing sectors of the population into the waged labor to capital relation has not, unlike the other avenues of accumulation, yet approached its limits. In fact, this incorporation is taking place on a sizable scale through the international activities of the leading productive force, transnational corporations. The process of proletarianization is extensive in underdeveloped countries, especially those suffering under "modernizing" military dictatorships: Brazil, Uruguay, Argentina, Chile, the Philippines, South Korea; Mexico's vast peasant and "marginal" population is also drawn into this orbit, and to a lesser degree in many other countries. This process also throws up hundreds of thousands who immigrate to the metropolitan centers, especially the United States. In the United States, therefore, new waves of immigrants potentially constitute nearly limitless new sources of exploitation for accumulation. Women are also still available in great numbers. Yet in the absence of an economic dynamic of great new investment avenues, incorporation of new workers can be only accretional. Insofar as the middle class is formed in consort with rapidly increasing incorporation of persons to the waged labor to capital relation, one basis of middle-class expansion is stymied.

Perhaps the greatest advance in increasing the quantity of labor for accumulation in the contemporary period is not direct incorporation of labor previously outside the orbit of capital, but the *intensification* of exploitation of the existing labor force. While this takes a number of national and international forms affecting the working class, a principal means of effecting intensification, we have suggested, has been to rationalize the labor process, with the effect of dequalifying technical, administrative, and professional labor. The dequalification process, we argued, is inherent to capitalist development. It is thus not surprising that it is now being applied to technical, administrative, and professional labor; that labor which in its origins was itself an instrument of dequalification of workers is now the object of dequalification. Perhaps this dequalification even takes an *imperative* form when other sources of accumulation reach their limits or suffer constraints. That seems to be the situation in the emerging phase, which is simultaneously a crisis of accumulation and of the middle class.

Crisis, Dequalification, and Class Formation

Eisenhower (Chapter 5) analyzed the embodiment of unproductive activity in middle-class labor at the level of macropolitical economy. Recent occupational and technological changes "represent a capitalism which has entered its 'degenerative phase.'" Having exhausted the potential of productive investments by the 1950s, American capital entered a phase of investment in the unproductive consumption of surplus. "This not only resulted in the proliferation of financial, commercial, administrative and governmental employments but it also redirected the technological effort toward developing the equipment used by these unproductive workers. In addition, it led to the neglect of domestic productive capitals, their facilities falling into disrepair or becoming obsolete."

I differ from Eisenhower in his view of the formation of the middle class as linked to "unproductive consumption of surplus." Middle-class employees are hired in part to carry out the functions of capital and are maintained in the exercise of those functions only when their activity will promote profitability and accumulation. The activities of some categories of these employees increase the productivity of the labor force: They devise and implement new technical or organizational innovations in the labor process, permitting more efficient production and increasing exploitation of workers. Other categories in the service sectors work to extend or intensify markets. State employees are involved in the overall facilitation of the accumulation and reproduction processes. While none of these activities is *directly* productive (of surplus value), all contribute to overall profitability and accumulation. However, I agree with Eisenhower that there are limits to "unproductive" investment and employment. If and when the aggregate of middle-class employment in unproductive tasks is at the point where the cost of their maintenance (and reproduction) exceeds the contribution they make by improving the productivity of the labor force, extending markets, facilitating accumulation, and so on, they will not be hired or they will be laid off; or the state will reduce support for their reproduction; or, to get to the heart of rationalization and dequalification, the unproductive activities they are engaged in will be reorganized so as to reduce or eliminate them or, at the very least, to lessen costs.

There is, of course, no way to quantify the contribution of middle class labor and derive a net cost-benefit to the larger political economy. We suspect, though, that the costs began to exceed benefits in the mid-1970s. There is no other satisfactory way to explain the contraction of state subsidies and incentives in widening spheres of reproduction, or the declining demand for and the unemployment and under-employment, and dequalification of technical, administrative, and professional labor that has taken place since that time. And here we confront two other contradictions.

If "unproductive" activity no longer contributes in the way it did in prior phases of development, investments in these areas as a dynamic source of accumulation is stymied. Further, these areas contract, then the accumulation process faces the problem Hirschorn raised: This may cause a cycle of disaccumulation in sectors that depend on "unproductive" service activities.

We are somewhat uncertain of the above propositions.[3] But we are certain, in this phase of incipient crisis, that class structure and class relations are undergoing significant transformation. The limits of the accumulation process, fiscal problems of the state, and other factors affect the class situation of the working class and underclass even more than the middle class. But what the middle class loses and the working class suffers the managers gain. Mills's "power elite" become more powerful; "white collars" are tinged blue; and the most oppressed do without.

In generalized terms, the class structure at the upper reaches shapes up as a strengthened managerial cadre. The power elite of the major institutions are a managerial bourgeoisie. This fraction of the dominant class has its origin in an earlier phase of corporate development in which the demise of the day-to-day operational significance of legal ownership in large corporate enterprise (as well as rapid growth of large scale quasi-autonomous public institutions) strengthened the position of managers vis-a-vis owners. The managerial bourgeoisie came to form a leading fraction of the bourgeoisie as a whole, subordinate only to centralized finance capital—that is, to the David Rockefeller category of corporate president, member of N corporate boards, major stockholder in a range of large companies, and guiding figure in the making of government policies, cabinet officials, and presidents. As the position of the managerial bourgeoisie is strengthened by centralization of institutional power, it becomes more integrated with the core fraction of the dominant class, corporate-finance capital, and in greater degree of structural antagonism with all other classes.

The managerial bourgeoisie has a double class interest in continuing and accelerating, where possible, the process of labor dequalification affecting the middle class, the accompanying centralization of power within institutions, and the selective introduction of technological innovation to further both these ends. To the extent that the various dimensions of the global function of capital are delegated, the managers have less than full control of the means of production, the process of capital accumulation, and, especially, the labor process. The conversion of the positions of middle-class employees to positions of specialized, technical workers producing only as an organized collectivity therefore returns the control functions of capital to the managers, especially those at the very pinnacles of bureaucratic hierarchies. At the same time, this permits a cheapening of the costs of unproductive activity and a greater degree of appropriation of the value of the dequalified labor power of sectors of the middle class, since more of their labor time is spent productively (i.e., in activities other than control), while the remuneration of their labor power and cost of formation as technical workers are reduced.

The trend toward dequalification of technical, administrative, and professional labor and the reassertion of higher administrative pre-rogatives over the labor process corresponding to these activities signify more than a strengthened managerial bourgeoisie and the decline of the general class situation and positioning of increasing sectors of middle-class employees. As we pointed out in the previous chapter, another impact of these trends is to bifurcate the middle class into two kinds of strata— defined by their specific functions and changing place in class relations— which have less and less in common. Counterposed against the lower strata of technical and administrative employees and paraprofessionals, strata that are increasingly feminized and with more than token minority representation, and whose labor is increasingly subordinated and dequalified, whose security is constantly threatened, and whose place in the social order is downgraded, are upper strata composed of staff technocrats, a lesser managerial grouping, elite professionals, systems analysts and the like—all tied to the managerial bourgeoisie. This is a "technocracy" of sorts, and its formation strengthens the hand of the managers while it widens the gulf between "bourgeoisified" technocrats and "prole-tarianized" technicians, thus undermining the structural basis of the social unity of the middle class as such.

The emerging main line of class relations in the 1980s is thus shaping up as a growing tight alliance of corporate-finance capital, the managerial bourgeoisie and the technocracy, at the one pole, with a highly fractionalized and stratified working class at the other pole. Segments of the middle class move toward this pole. In this tendential relational polarization the remaining strata of the various fractions of the middle class have a declining social weight and receding mediating place in class relations as they, too, are pushed or pulled toward one pole or the other.[4]

The Probable and the Possible

The 1980s will be ripe for political appeals to middle-class anxieties. This is all the more so as the crisis deepens and the structural trends we identified unravel. We hold no crystal that mirrors the future; and we cannot pursue an in-depth political analysis of the middle class in the context of the 1980s. A structural analysis such as that undertaken throughout this book cannot result in reliable political predictions. There is no direct correlation between changing structure and changing consciousness, or between consciousness and political behavior, especially in the short run.

Trends in the transformation of social structure and configurations of class relations only define the parameters of the improbable, the probable, and the possible. It is improbable that the deepening crisis and sharpening class antagonisms of the United States in the 1980s will be so severe as to lead to a fascist dictatorship and highly improbable that there will be a revolution of any kind. It is probable that the decade will be one of increased strife and turmoil. It is probable that conditions within middle-class occupations will further deteriorate and that sectors will unionize and politicize. It is probable that large numbers of people will be politically mobilized on both the right and left, and that middle-class people will be militants in both mobilizations. Structural developments, then, only define limits: What comes to fruition depends on events that unfold, the depths to which the emerging crisis sinks, what social forces mobilize, and what large numbers of people do in relation to their changing circumstances.

Some of the political conclusions of this analysis are obvious. As the incipient crisis of a new phase of development deepens, the class situations of the poor and oppressed, the working class, and substantial sectors of the middle class deteriorate. The political responses of the state, at least through 1984, will exacerbate the difficulties of the great majority. This class situation and political alienation will necessarily increase the level of social conflict. Its intensity depends on the actual course of the struggle. "Objective conditions" are less important in shaping struggle than struggle itself. The 1970s was a quiet decade in spite of adverse circumstances for many; there was no forward surge of struggle which builds on itself.

With respect to our principal object, the middle class, the political implications are several:

—The 1980s will require a good deal of "crisis management." Whatever policies that result from the probable demise of Reaganism will require both a source of political support and functionaries who implement the changing formulae. The elements now being constructed as technocratic staffs of the managerial cadres are likely to compliantly involve themselves in "system maintenance."

—Those sectors which as yet remain in the middle will undoubtedly scramble individually to elevate themselves toward the technocrats if they can and to hold their own if they cannot. They are a timid and conformist lot, but many may collectively (through increased unionization and professional associations) fight against being downgraded.

—The service professionals, except for an elite singled out for promotion to the technocracy and the independent practitioners, have a vested interest in promoting the expansion of state activity and in opposing the political attack on social services. However, the competitive subcultures of bureaucratized professionalism strongly foster weak and individualistic responses to changing conditions. This class fraction also harbors the intelligentsia who forge ideologies out of structural trends. The class will produce a new crop of mandarins, perhaps some "organic intellectuals" of a middle class in decline, and a group articulating reformist and revolutionary ideas (see Wolfe, 1981, and Johnson, 1981).

—The logic of our analysis also points toward the possibility of a more progressive role for those strata of the middle class being pushed toward the working-class condition, perhaps the more so as these strata are increasingly made up of persons recruited from the traditionally oppressed sectors—women and minorities. Perhaps. But this may not result. The squeezing of intermediate classes has often been associated in historical experience with their growing mobilization in reactionary or fascist movements. The emergence of fascism in Germany and military dictatorship in Chile are but two salient examples in which the bulk of the middle class, under pressure from economic difficulties and heightened class struggle, moved decisively to the right.

The character of the responses of sectors being pushed downward may well be a principal ingredient defining the temper of the times. The social interests of intermediate classes are, in the first instance, contradictory, and when threatened, especially by being downgraded in the social order, many cling desperately to respectability, while others take to the streets to defend the privileges that set them apart from their social inferiors. Only minorities of the class, in other experiences, have located the sources of their difficulties in the system itself.

But the incipient crisis of the 1980s in the United States has the mark of a qualitatively new historical phenomenon. It is here one encounters the limits of structural analysis. Of course, structural trends define the context of struggle. In the long run a class that is qualitatively transformed forms new patterns of consciousness and constellations of social interests that broadly correspond to its changed positioning. But in the shorter run, consciousness is much more shaped by the varying course of struggle than the impositions of structure. And, in the first instance, the potential and direction of struggle is limited by lingering consciousness. Among the great American middle, the hardening realities of the day cannot be separated from the myths with which people confront these realities. In these social spheres, obliterated consciousness is summed up in the popularized sociological expression of the "hidden injuries of social class": the myth of Horatio Alger still stands; the idea of the individual as exception to the rule, of the capacity of each American to attain higher status if only he or she will work hard at it persists. This old myth seems today to have a new life in the cultural psychology of the middle class and in the competitive impulse of careerism. Individuals are normatively enjoined to accept individual responsibility for personal failure, as opposed to a social awareness of the collective roots of failure. Within the middle class this individualization has even taken the form of a collective social movement of large numbers, each searching inwardly and with each other in group encounters for what is wrong. It is this social definition, one rooted in the persistent class culture of the petty privileged, in competitive occupational substructures, in the infinite hierarchical gradations of the bureaucratic cultures in which they work, in social personality or character structure which stand as obstacles, in the face of the hardening realities of economic and social existence, to seeking collective solutions to personal troubles.[5]

We do not know whether, in deepening crisis, the consciousness of middle-class people will become more aligned with the structural forces operating, or whether the panic of being downgraded and the distortions of preexisting consciousness will cause middle-class people to misperceive the systemic roots of crisis and their class situation. Our analysis does suggest that the great American middle will no longer be the more or less favored and content, stable, and gently reformist force that it has been. It will likely break into several large fragments moving in contradictory directions.

"The unity of any middle class depends on the stability of the social order; any crisis breaks it" (Glucksmann in Gorz, 1976:73). This is surely the more so in the uniqueness of the present incipient crisis in which a principal ingredient is the transformation of that very class into something qualitatively distinct from what it was. The actual course and duration of this transformation is shaped by the structural trends identified here. These trends lay down the parameters of the probable and possible within which people, in living out their lives under changing circumstances, create their social world. "Classes are made, unmade and remade in the course of class struggle" (Przeworski, 1978:131). And so, too, is social development a process shaped by struggle, within the limits defined by structures.

The vaunted middle class of advanced industrial capitalism, like older intermediate formations of history, in all probability is entering a period of permanent eclipse as a class. Its rise and decline, the forms of changing relations with the main classes, is one more study in multiclass relations in a bipolarizing structure. Its passing, perhaps even more than that of the classic petty bourgeoisie, is likely to leave indelible marks on the history of social development.

NOTES

1. A Department of Labor study among professional, administrative, and technical employees (1979) indicates that salary increases between 1961 and 1979 were greater for "higher occupational levels" than for middle and lower levels. From 1966 to 1971 middle-level salaries increased at the fastest rate; and from 1971 to 1976 the lowest group gained; between 1976 and 1979 gains among the higher occupational levels outstripped the other categories. These data are consistent with our thesis of the bifurcation of the middle class into two strata in recent years, the lower strata of labor undergoing devaluation and the other strata being elevated.

2. The lack of productive dynamism deserves more space than we can give it here. The productive base of the American economy is in very serious trouble, while the financial superstructure is dangerously heavy. Sweezy analyzes the economic basis of the current crisis in the interrelations among stagnation, inflation, and financial expansion and instability. His main point is that the financial sector has ballooned "out of all proportion to the underlying base of production and real capital formation" (1981:1). The rate of debits to demand deposit accounts at banks stood at $68 trillion compared to a GNP of $2.7 trillion. "Those who talk about capital shortages, lack of savings and so on, as the cause of the present economic troubles should ponder this fact" (p. 3). He goes on to note: "The hyperexpansion of the financial sector . . . [is] . . . pathological and parasitical, as proved by the fact that it has occurred simultaneously and in step with the deterioration of the underlying productive economy. And, as on many previous occasions in the history of capitalism, the swelling financial bubble is developing weaknesses which may give way and lead to a chain-reaction financial collapse and panic" (p. 3).

3. There may be a logical contradiction between Eisenhower's, Hirschorn's and my own analyses; it is also possible that all three views capture different sides of the same contradictory reality.

4. A dissertation that generally confirms our findings came to our attention after completing this book. Sobel analyzed a mass of empirical data from 1945 to 1977 in relation to proletarianization of white-collar employees. The long-term trend is away from self-employment and toward wage employment ("simple, class proletarianization"). Other indices of proletarianization include "loss of supervisory employment" and "condition proletarianization" ("movement to narrowly delimited job situations"). "There has been a trend away from supervisory status in the 1970s. In some cases structural conditions on the job

have declined; in others they have been upgraded" (1981:xi). Both conclusions are consistent with our theses of dequalification and bifurcation of the middle class. He also notes that "both theoretically and empirically there is strong evidence for a close, and in many cases, growing link between white collar labor and the working class. This connection exists both in theoretical analysis, cross-section, longitudinal changes and educational levels" (1981:xii).

5. Moreover, as Low-Beer (1978) has argued in his empirical study of Italian technicians, there are a range of factors that impinge on consciousness, attitudes, and political behavior among sectors of the middle class. These include the social background and current lifestyles of people making up the class, the social and political dynamics of the particular society, and a number of variables in the actual organization and conditions of work.

Citations

(Note: general references and works cited in more than one chapter; see also chapter citations.)

Althusser, Louis
1970a For Marx. New York: Vintage.
1970b Reading Capital. New York: Pantheon.
1971 "Ideology and ideological state apparatuses," in L. Althusser, Lenin and Philosophy. London: New Left Books.
1976 Essays in Self-Criticism. London: New Left Books.
Anderson, Charles H.
1974 The Political Economy of Social Class. Englewood Cliffs, NJ: Prentice-Hall.
Anderson, Perry
1976 Considerations on Western Marxism. London: New Left Books.
Appelbaum, Richard
1979 "Born-again functionalism? a reconsideration of Althusser's structuralism." Insurgent Sociologist 9 (Summer): 18-33.
Aronowitz, Stanley
1978 "Marx, Braverman and the logic of capital." Insurgent Sociologist 8 (Fall): 126-146.
Baran, Paul and Paul Sweezy
1966 Monopoly Capital: An Essay on the American Economic and Social Order. New York: Monthly Review Press.
Becker, James F.
1973-74 "Class structure and conflict in the managerial phase." Science and Society, Part I: 37 (Fall): 250-277; Part II: 38 (Winter): 437-453.
1977 Marxian Political Economy: An Outline. Cambridge, MA:
Bell, Daniel
1973 The Coming of Postindustrial Society. New York: Basic Books.
Best, Michael H. and William E. Connally
1979 "Politics and subjects: the limits of structural Marxism." Socialist Review 48 (November-December): 75-99.
Bowles, Samuel and Herbert Gintis
1976 Schooling in Capitalist America: Educational Reform and the Contradictions of Economic Life. New York: Basic Books.
Braverman, Harry
1974 Labor and Monopoly Capital: The Degradation of Work in the Twentieth Century. New York: Monthly Review Press.
Bruce-Briggs, B.
1979 The New Class? New Brunswick, NJ: Transaction Books.
Buraway, Michael
1980 "Toward a Marxist theory of the labor process: Braverman and Beyond." Politics and Society 8 (Nos. 3-4).

Burris, Val
    1980   "Capital accumulation and the rise of the new middle class." Review of Radical
           Political Economics 12 (Spring): 17-34.
Canning, Jane and James D. Cockcroft
    1979   "Althusser: strengths and weaknesses." Monthly Review (January).
Carchedi, Guglielmo
    1975a "On the economic identification of the new middle class." Economy and Society 4
           (November 1): 1-75.
    1975b "Reproduction of social classes at the level of production relations." Economy and
           Society 4 (November): 361-417.
    1978   On the Economic Identification of the New Middle Class. London: Routledge &
           Kegan Paul.
Castells, Manuel
    1980   The Economic Crisis and American Society. Princeton, NJ: Princeton University
           Press.
Corey, Lewis
    1935   The Crisis of the Middle Class. Covici, Friede.
Cueva, Agustin
    1979   "La concepción marxista de las clases sociales." Tareas (Panamá) 45 (July-Septem-
           ber): 76-102.
Edwards, Richard
    1979   Contested Terrain: The Transformation of the Workplace in the Twentieth
           Century. New York: Basic Books.
Ferrarotti, Franco
    1979   An Alternative Sociology. New York: Irvington.
Frank, Andre Gunder
    1969   "Functionalism and dialectics," in Latin America Underdevelopment or Revolu-
           tion. New York: Monthly Review Press.
Friedson, Eliot
    1973   "Professionalization and the organization of middle-class labour in postindus-
           trial society," pp. 47-60 in P. Helmos (ed.) Professionalization and Social Change.
           University of Keele.
Galbraith, John Kenneth
    1968   The New Industrial State. New York: New American Library.
Geras, Norman
    1972   "Althusser's Marxism: an account and assessment." New Left Review 71 (January-
           February): 57-86.
Giddens, Anthony
    1975   The Class Structure of Advanced Societies. New York: Harper & Row.
Glucksmann, Andre
    1972   "A ventriloquist structuralism." New Left Review 72 (March-April): 68-92.
Gorz, Andre
    1976   The Division of Labor. Atlantic Highlands, NJ: Humanities Press.
Goldman, Lucien
    1976   Cultural Creation in Modern Society. St. Louis: Telos Press.
Gramsci, Antonio
    1971   Prison Notebooks. New York: International Publishers.
    1975   The Modern Prince and Other Writings. New York: International Publishers.
Haug, Marie R.
    1973   "Deprofessionalization: an alternate hypothesis for the future," pp. 195-212 in P.
           Helmos (ed.) Professionalisation and Social Change. University of Keele.
Hindess, Barry and Paul Hirst
    1975   Pre-Capitalist Modes of Production. Boston: Routledge & Kegan Paul.
Horowitz, Irving Louis
    1979   "On the expansion of new theories and the withering away of old classes." Society
           16 (January-February): 55-62.

Insurgent Sociologist
1979   "Marxism and structuralism." Special Issue, Vol. 9 (Summer).
Johnson, Dale L.
1978   "Strategic implications of recent social class theory." Insurgent Sociologist 8 (Winter): 40-44.
1981   "Intermediate classes in a bipolarizing structure," in R. Rubinson (ed.) Dynamics of the World System. Beverly Hills, CA: Sage.
forthcoming-a Intermediate Classes: Historical Studies of Social Class and Social Development on the Periphery. Beverly Hills, CA: Sage.
forthcoming-b "A Post-Braverman study of the labor-process." Science and Society.
Johnson, Dale L. and Ronald Chilcate
forthcoming Mode of Production or Dependency? Alternative Perspectives on Peripheral Social Formations. Beverly Hills, CA: Sage.
Johnson, Terrence
1977   "What is to be known? the structural determination of class." Economy and Society 6 (May): 194-233.
Kraft, Philip
1977   Programmers and Managers. New York: Springer-Verlag.
1979   "The industrialization of computer programming: from programming to 'software production,'" in A. Zimbalist (ed.) Case Studies on the Labor Process. New York: Monthly Review Press.
Laclau, Ernesto
1977   Politics and Ideology in Marxist Theory. London: New Left Books.
Larson, Magali Sarfatti
1977   The Rise of Professionalism: A Sociological Analysis. Berkeley: University of California Press.
Levine, Andrew and Erik Olin Wright
1980   "Rationality and class struggle." New Left Review 123 (September-October): 47-68.
Lichtman, Richard
1977   "Marx and Freud: Marx's theory of human nature." Socialist Review 7 (November-December): 37-78.
Low-Beer, John R.
1978   Protest and Participation: The New Working Class in Italy. Cambridge, MA: Cambridge University Press.
Lukács, Georg
1971   History and Class Consciousness. Cambridge, MA: MIT Press.
Mallet, Serge
1975   Essays on the New Working Class (D. Howard and D. Savage, eds.). St. Louis: Telos Press.
Mayrl, William W.
1978-79 "Science and praxis: a sociological inquiry into the epistemological foundations of structural and phenomenological Marxism." Berkeley Journal of Sociology 23: 183-199.
McNall, Scott G. (Ed.)
1972   Theoretical Perspectives in Sociology. New York: St. Martin's.
Mills, C. Wright
1951   White Collar. London: Oxford University Press.
Nicolaus, Martin
1967   "Proletariat and middle class in Marx: Hegelian choreography and capitalist dialectic." Studies on the Left 7 (January-February): 22-49.
Noble, David
1977   America By Design. Science, Technology, and the Rise of Corporate Capitalism. New York: Alfred A. Knopf.

O'Connor, James
 1975   "Productive and unproductive labor." Politics and Society 5 (No. 3): 297-336.
 1973   The Fiscal Crisis of the State. New York: St. Martin's.
Poulantzas, Nicos
 1969   "The problems of the capitalist state." New Left Review 58 (November-December): 67-78.
 1973   Political Power and Social Classes. London: New Left Books.
 1974   Fascism and Dictatorship. London: New Left Books.
 1975   Classes in Contemporary Capitalism. London: New Left Books.
 1976   "The capitalist state: a reply to Miliband and Laclau." New Left Review (January-February): 63-83.
 1977   The Crisis of the Dictatorships. London: New Left Books.
 1978   State Power, Socialism. London: New Left Books.
Przeworski, Adam
 1978   "El proceso de la formación de clases." Revista Mexicana de Sociología 40 (E78): 109-141.
Rosenberg, Samuel
 1977   "The political sociology of government intervention: the United States in the post World War II era." Ph.D. dissertation, Rutgers University.
Skotnes, Andor
 1979   "Structural determination of the proletariat and the petty bourgeoisie: a critique of Nicos Poulantzas." Insurgent Sociologist 9 (Summer): 34-55.
Stolzman, James and Herbert Gamberg
 1973-74   "Marxist class analysis versus stratification analysis as general approaches to social inequality." Berkeley Journal of Sociology 18: 105-125.
Straussman, Jeffry D.
 1975   The Limits of Technocratic Politics. New Brunswick, NJ: Transaction Books.
Sweezy, Paul
 1974   "Some problems in the theory of capital accumulation." Monthly Review (May): 38-55.
Therborn, Goran
 1980   The Ideology of Power and the Power of Ideology. London: New Left Books.
Thompson, E. P.
 1978   The Poverty of Theory and Other Essays. New York: Monthly Review Press.
Universidad Nacional Autonoma de México
 1973   Las clases sociales en América Latina. Mexico: Siglo XXI.
Veltmeyer, Henry
 1974-75   "Towards an assessment of the structuralist interrogation of Marx: Claude Levi-Strauss and Louis Althusser." Science and Society 38 (Winter): 385-421.
 1978   "Marx's two methods of sociological analysis." Sociological Inquiry 48 (No. 2): 101-112.
Walker, Pat (Ed.)
 1979   Between Capital and Labor. Boston: South End Press.
Williams, Raymond
 1973   "Base and superstructure in Marxist cultural theory." New Left Review 82 (November-December): 3-16.
 1977   Marxism and Literature. London: Oxford University Press.
Wright, Erik Olin
 1976   "Class boundaries in advanced capitalist societies." New Left Review 90 (July-August): 3-41.
 1978   Class, Crisis and the State. London: New Left Books.
Zaret, David
 1978   "Sociological theory and historical scholarship." The American Sociologist 13 (May): 114-121.

Zimbalist, Andrew
   1979   Case Studies on the Labor Process. New York: Monthly Review Press.
Zimmerman, Marc
   1978-79   "Lucien Goldman: from dialectical theory to genetic structuralism." Berkeley Journal of Sociology 23: 151-182.

General Bibliography

Introduction

Bell, David
    1960   The End of Ideology. New York: Free Press.
Chomsky, Noam
    1969   American Power and the New Mandarins. New York: Pantheon.
Davis, Kingsley and Wilbert E. Moore
    1945   "Some principles of stratification." American Sociological Review 5 (November): 242-249
Gartman, David
    1978   "Marx and the labor process." Insurgent Sociologist 8 (Fall): 97-108.
Gilbert, Dennis and Joseph Kahl
    1982   The American Class Structure. New York: Dorsey Press.
Gouldner, Alvin W.
    1979   The Future of Intellectuals and the Rise of the New Class. New York: Seabury Press.
Hill, Judah
    1975   Class Analysis: United States in the 1970s. San Francisco: Synthesis Publications.
Lane, Robert C.
    1966   "The decline of politics and ideology in a knowledgeable society." American Sociological Review 31: 649-662.
Lipset, Seymour Martin
    1980   The Third Century. America as a Postindustrial Society. Stanford, CA: Hoover Institution Press.
Miliband, Ralph
    1970   The State in Capitalist Society. New York: Basic Books.
Price, D. K.
    1965   The Scientific Estate. Cambridge: Harvard University Press.
Touraine, Alain
    1971   The Postindustrial Society. New York: Random House.
Vallas, Steve
    1980   "The Marxist theory of skilled labor and the shaping of the labor process." Unpublished paper, Department of Sociology, Rutgers University.
Walzer, Michael
    1980   "The new masters." New York Review, March 20.
Westergaard, John and Henrietta Resler

Chapter 1

Abercombie, Nicholas, Bryan Turner, and John Urry
    1976   "Class, state, and fascism: the work of Nicos Poulantzas." Political Studies 24
           (November 4): 510-519.
Lefebvre, Henri
    1971   Everyday Life in the Modern World. New York: Harper & Row.
Luporini, Cesare
    1975   "Reality and historicity: economy and dialectics." Economy and Society 4
           (August): 286-331.
Miliband, Ralph
    1973   "Poulantzas and the capitalist state." New Left Review 82 (November-December):
           83-93.
Szmanski, Al
    1978   "Braverman as a neo-Luddite." Insurgent Sociologist 8 (Winter): 45-50.
Vallas, Steven
    1980   "Marxism and the labor process: a review essay," Socialist Review 54 (November-
           December).
Vuskovic Rojo, Sergio
    1978   "Polémica en torno a 'El Capital.'" Desarrollo 13 (May): 17-23.
Walker, Jill
    1981   "Markets, industrial processes and class struggle: the evolution of the labor process
           in the United Kingdom engineering industry." Review of Radical Political
           Economy 12 (Winter): 46-49.

Chapter 2

Appelbaum, Richard
    1978   "Marx's theory of the falling rate of profit." American Sociological Review 43
           (February): 67-80.
Baran, Paul A.
    1957   The Political Economy of Growth. New York: Monthly Review Press.
Baran, Paul and Eric Hobsbawm
    1961   "The stages of economic growth." Kyklos 14 (No. 2): 234-242.
Berthoud, Arnauld
    1974   Travail Productif et Productivite du Travail chez Marx. Paris: Maspero.
Careaga, Gabriel
    1970   "Sociología y estructuralismo." Revista Mexicana de Ciéncia Política 16
           (October-December): 55-61.
Carrión, Juan Manuel
    1978   The Petty Bourgeoisie in Puerto Rico. Ph.D. dissertation, Rutgers University.
Cohen, G. A.
    1978   Karl Marx's Theory of History: A Defense. London: Oxford University Press.
Eisenhower, David D.
    1977   "The political economy of the middle classes in a period of permanent crisis." Ph.D.
           dissertation, Rutgers University.
Evanson, John
    1977   "Workers and imperialism: where is the aristocracy of labor?" Insurgent Sociologist 7
           (Spring): 54-63.
Fine, Ben and Laurence Harris
    1977   "Surveying the foundations," in R. Miliband and J. Saville (eds.) The Socialist
           Register. New York: Monthly Review Press.

Godelier, Maurice
    1978   "Infrastructure, societies and history." New Left Review 112 (November-December): 84-96.
Gonzalez Casanova, Pablo
Forthcoming "System and class in Latin American studies." Latin American Perspectives.
Gorelick, Sherry
    1977   "Undermining hierarchy: problems of schooling in capitalist America." Monthly Review 29 (October): 20-38.
Gough, Ian
    1972   "Marx's theory of productive and unproductive labor." New Left Review 76 (November-December): 47-72.
Gutierrez Garza, Esthela
    1978   "La determinación económica de las clases sociales en el Capitalismo." Cuadernos Políticos (México) 16 (April-June): 104-117.
Hodgson, Geoff
    1977   "Papering over the cracks," in R. Miliband and J. Saville (eds.) New York: Monthly Review Press.
Holloway, John and Sol Picciotto (Eds.)
    1978   State and Capital. Austin: University of Texas Press.
Horton, John and Manuel Moreno
    1978   "Alienation and class struggle in advanced capitalist society." Synthesis 2 (Spring): 1-30.
Johnson, Dale L.
forthcoming "Chile: before, during, after." Science and Society.
Johnson, Dale L. and Christine O'Donnell
    1981   "Accumulation crisis and service professionals," in Economics Education Project (ed.) Crisis in the Public Sector. New York: Monthly Review Press.
Kellner, Douglas
    1978   "Ideology, Marxism, and advanced capitalism." Socialist Review 42 (November-December): 33-66.
Korsch, Karl
    1972   Three Essays on Marxism. New York: Monthly Review Press.
Lebowitz, Michael A.
    1978   "Marx's falling rate of profit." Socialist Review 38 (March-April): 3-97.
Luporini, Cesare
    1975   "Reality and historicity: economy and dialectics in Marxism." Economy and Society 4 (August): 206-231.
Miliband, Ralph
    1973   "Poulantzas and the capitalist state." New Left Review 82 (November-December): 83-93.
Przeworski, Adam
    1978   "El proceso de la formación de clases." Revista Mexicana de Sociologia 40 (E78): 109-141.
Resnick, Stephen and Richard Wolff
    1979   "The theory of transitional conjunctures and the transition from feudalism to capitalism in Western Europe." Review of Radical Political Economics 2 (Fall): 3-22.
Sanchez Vasquez, Adolfo
    1975   "El teoricismo de Althusser (notas críticas sobre una autocrítica)." Cuadernos Políticos (México) 3 (February-May): 82-99.
Wolff, Richard D.
    1978   "Western Marxism." Monthly Review 30 (September): 55-64.

Wood, Ellen Meiksins
   1981   "The separation of the economic and political in capitalism." New Left Review 127 (May-June): 66-95.

Chapter 3

Aronowitz, Stanley
   1973   False Promises. New York: McGraw-Hill.
Hobsbawm, Eric J.
   1965   Primitive Rebels. New York: W. W. Norton.
Jones, Garth Stedman
   1978   "The Marxism of the early Lukács," in New Left Review (ed.) Western Marxism: A critical Reader. London: New Left Books.
Lasch, Christopher
   1978   The Culture of Narcissism. New York: W. W. Norton.
Mayer, Arnold
   1975   "The lower middle class as a historical problem." Journal of Modern History 47 (September): 409-436.
Moore, Barrington, Jr.
   1966   Social Origins of Dictatorship and Democracy: Lord and Peasant in the Making of the Modern World. Boston: Beacon.
Veblen, Thorstein
   1964   An Inquiry into the Nature of Peace and the Terms of its Perpetuation. New York: Sentry Press.

Chapter 4

Bazelon, David
   1967   Power in America: The Politics of the New Class. New York: New American Library.
Bell, Daniel
   1962   The End of Ideology. New York: Free Press.
   1973   "The new class: a muddled concept," in B. Bruce-Briggs (ed.) The New Class? New Brunswick, NJ: Transaction Books.
Belleville, Pierre
   1963   Une Nouvelle Classe Ouvriere. Paris.
Birnbaum, Norman
   1969   The Crisis of Industrial Society. Cambridge: Oxford University Press.
Croner, Fritz
   1928   The White Collar Movement in Germany Since the Monetary Stabilization, translated from Archiv für Sozialwissenschaft u. Sozialpolitik, v. 60. Columbia University, New York State Department of Social Welfare and Columbia University Department of Social Science 1937.
Crozier, Michel
   1971   The World of the Office Worker. Chicago: University of Chicago Press.
Elsner, Henry Jr.
   1967   The Technocrats. Syracuse, NY: Syracuse University Press.
Engelhardt, Erich
   1932   "The Salaried Employee," translated from Kolner Vierteljahrschefte für Soziologie. New York: Columbia University, 1939.
Galbraith, John Kenneth
   1952   American Capitalism. Boston: Houghton Mifflin.

Gouldner, Alvin W.
  1979 The Future of Intellectuals and the Rise of the New Class. New York: Seabury Press.
Habermas, Jürgen
  1971 Toward a Rational Society (J. Shapiro, trans.). Boston: Beacon.
Hacker, Andrew
  1979 "Two 'New Classes' or None?" in B. Bruce-Briggs (ed.) The New Class? New Brunswick, NJ: Transaction Books.
Hamilton, Richard F.
  1980 "Germany's white collar employees and national socialism: some comments and hypotheses." Paper presented at Z.I.F., University of Bielefeld.
Harrington, Michael
  1972 Socialism. New York: Bantam.
Jaeggi, Urs, and Herbert Wiedemann
  1966 Der Angestellte im Automatisierten Buro. Kohlhammer.
Jones, Alfred W.
  1941 Life, Liberty, and Property. Philadelphia: J. B. Lippincott.
Kadritzke, Ulf
  1975 Angestellte—Die geduldigen Arbeiter. Europaische Verlagsanstalt.
Kocka, Jurgen
  1980 White Collar Workers in America, 1890-1940. Beverly Hills, CA: Sage.
Lange, Hellmuth
  1972 Wissenschaftliche Intelligenz: Neue Bourgeoisie oder neue Arbeiterclasse? Pahl-Rugenstein Verlag.
Lederer, Emil
  1912 Die Privatangestellten in der modernen Wirtschaftsentwicklung. Tubingen. (Arno Press, 1975)
Lockwood, David
  1958 The Blackcoated Worker. London: George Allen & Unwin.
Mallet, Serge
  1963 La Nouvelle Classe Ouvriere. Paris. Also see Essays on the New Working Class (D. Howard and D. Savage, eds. St. Louis: Telos Press, 1975.
Mandel, Ernest
  1968 "The working class under neo-capitalism." Guardian (September 28).
  1974 "Where is America Going?" in the Revolutionary Potential of the Working Class. New York: Pathfinder.
Mannheim, Karl
  1936 Ideology and Utopia. New York: Harcourt Brace Jovanovich.
Marcuse, Herbert
  1964 One Dimensional Man. Boston: Beacon.
  1969 "On Revolution," in J. D. Cockburn and M. Black (eds.) Student Power. New York: Penguin.
Mills, C. Wright
  1958 The Causes of World War III. New York: Random House.
Neuloh, Otto
  1966 Die Weisse Automation. Grote.
Oppenheimer, Martin
  1981 "The PMC." Insurgent Sociologist 10 (No. 3): 95-103.
Parkin, Frank
  1971 Class Inequality and Political Order. New York: Praeger.
Perlman, Selig and Philip Taft
  1935 History of Labor in the United States 1896-1932, V of IV. New York: Macmillan.
Roszak, Theodore
  1969 The Making of a Counter Culture. New York: Doubleday.
  1973 Where the Wasteland Ends. New York: Doubleday.

Schmoller, Gustav
    1897   Was verstehen wir unter dem Mittelstande?
Slater, Philip
    1970   The Pursuit of Loneliness. Boston Beacon.
Touraine, Alaine
    1971   The May Movement. New York: Random House.
Veblen, Thornstein
    1921   "The technicians and revolution," in The Engineers and the Price System. New
            York: Kelley.
Vogel, David
    1979   "Business' 'New Class' Struggle." The Nation (December 15).
Witt, Gunter
    1975   Leitende Angestellte und Einheitsgewerkschaft. Europaische Verglagsanstalt.

Chapter 5

Abramovitz, Moses
    1965   "Large swings in American economic growth," in R. Andreano (ed.) New Views on
            American Economic Development. Boston: Schenkman.
Barber, Betty
    1972   "U.S. foreign trade associates with US multinational companies." Survey of
            Current Business (December).
Becker, James
    1971   "On the monopoly theory of monopoly capital." Science and Society (Winter).
Bettleheim, Charles
    1976   Class Struggles in the USSR: First Period 1917-1923. New York: Monthly Review
            Press.
Boretsky, Michael
    1975   "Trends in U.S. technology: a political economist's view." American Scientist
            (January/February).
Burns, Arthur
    1977   "The need for better profits." Paper presented at Gonzago University, Spokane,
            Washington, October 26.
Business Week
    1974   "The debt economy." October 12.
    1977   "The slow investment economy. October 17.
Chandler, A.
    1965   "The beginnings of 'big business' in American industry," in R. Andreano (ed.) New
            Views on American Economic Development. Boston: Schenkman.
    1968   "General Motors: creating the general office," in A. Chandler et al. (eds.) The
            Changing Economic Order. New York: Harcourt Brace Jovanovich.
Chossudovsky, Michael
    1978   "Orthodox economics and the formation of contemporary bourgeois ideology."
            Review of Radical Political Economics (Spring).
Dahrendorf, R.
    1959   Class and Class Conflict in Industrial Society. Stanford, CA: Stanford University
            Press.
Delahanty, G. E.
    1968   Nonproductive Workers in U.S. Manufacturing. Amsterdam: Elsevier-North
            Holland.
Denison, Edward
    1974   Accounting for U.S. Economic Growth, 1929-1969. Washington, DC: Brookings
            Institution.

DeVroey, Michael
    1975   "The separation of ownership and control in large corporations." Review of Radical
            Political Economics (Summer).
Ewen, Stuart
    1977   Captains of Consciousness: Advertizing and the Social Roots of the Consumer
            Culture. New York: McGraw-Hill.
Fuchs, Victor
    1968   The Service Economy. New York: Columbia University Press.
Giddens, Anthony
    1973   The Class Structure of Advanced Societies. New York: Harper & Row.
Hession, Charles and Hyman Sardy
    1970   Ascent of Affluence: A History of American Economic Development. Boston:
            Allyn & Bacon.
Hofstadter, Richard and W. Smith (Eds.)
    1961   American Higher Education: A Documentary History. Chicago: University of
            Chicago Press.
Kendrick, John
    1973   Post-War Productivity Trends in the United States, 1948-1969. New York:
            Columbia University Press.
    1976   "Productivity, trends and prospects," in U.S. Economic Growth From 1976 to
            1986, Vol. 1. Washington, DC: U.S. Joint Economic Committee, October 1.
Kuznets, Simon
    1964   Post-War Economic Growth. Cambridge, MA: Harvard University Press.
Lash, Scott
    1978   "Productive Labor, class determination and class position." Science and Society
            (Spring): 62-81.
Lebowitz, Michael
    1976   "Marx's falling rate of profit: a dialectical view." Canadian Journal of Economics
            (May).
Lenin, V. I.
    1972   "On the question of dialectics," in Collected Works, Vol. 38. Moscow: Progress
            Publishers.
Mage, S.
    1963   "The 'law of the falling tendency of the rate of profit': its place in the Marxian
            theoretical system and relevance to the U.S. economy." Ph.D. dissertation, Colum-
            bia University.
Marx, Karl
    1969   Theories of Surplus Value, Part I (E. Burns, trans.). London: Lawrence and
            Wishart.
    1974   Capital, A Critique of Political Economy, Vol. III. (S. Moore and E. Aveling,
            trans.). New York: International Press.
Mattick, Paul
    1969   Marx and Keynes: The Limits of the Mixed Economy. Boston: Porter Sargent.
Melman, Seymour
    1951   "The rise of administrative overhead in the manufacturing industries of the U.S.:
            1899-1947." Oxford Economic Papers (January).
Monthly Review
            "Review of the Month." June 2.
Nabudere, D. Wadad
    1978   The Political Economy of Imperialism. New York: Monthly Review Press.
Nelson, Ralph
    1959   Merger Movement in American Industry. Princeton, NJ: Princeton University
            Press.

Nordheus, William
  1972   "The recent productivity slowdown." Brookings Papers on Economic Activity, III. Washington, DC: Brookings Institution.
  1974   "The falling share of profits," in A. M. Okun and G. L. Perry (eds.) Brookings Papers on Economic Activity, I. Washington, DC: Brookings Institution.
Olsen, Elsie
  1975   "A Marxian model of growth." Master's thesis, New York University.
Porat, Marc
  1977   The Information Society. U.S. Dept. of Commerce, Office of Telecommunication Publication No. 77-12. Washington, DC: Government Printing Office.
Renshaw, Edward F.
  1976   "Productivity," in U.S. Economic Growth from 1976 to 1986: Prospects, Problems and Patterns, Vol. I. Washington, DC: Joint Economic Committee, October 1.
Solow, Robert
  1957   "Technological change and the aggregate production function." Review of Economics and Statistics (August).
Survey of Current Business
  1973   Vol. 53, No. 2 (February).
Yaffee, D.
  1973   "Marxian theory of crisis, capital and the state." Economy and Society II.

Chapter 6

Anderson, Perry
  1977   "Antinomies of Antonio Gramsci." New Left Review 100 (November-January): 5-80.
Berger, Peter and Thomas Luckman
  1967   The Social Construction of Reality. Garden City, NY: Doubleday.
Berger, Peter, Brigitte Bergen, and Hansfred Kellner
  1973   The Homeless Mind. New York: Random House.
Bledstein, Barton I.
  1976   The Culture of Professionalism. New York: W. W. Norton.
Goldman, Eric F.
  1955   Rendezvous with Destiny. New York: Random House.
Hirst, Paul
  1976   "Althusser's theory of ideology." Economy and Society 5 (No. 4): 385-412.
Hofstadter, Richard
  1955   The Age of Reform. New York: Random House.
Kolko, Gabriel
  1963   The Triumph of Conservativism. New York: Free Press.
Leal, Juan Felipe
  1975   "The Mexican state: 1915-1973. An historical interpretation." Latin American Perspectives 2 (Summer): 48-63.
Lichtman, Richard
  1975   "Marx's theory of ideology." Socialist Revolution 5 (No. 1): 45-76.
Mannheim, Karl
  1936   Ideology and Utopia. New York: Harcourt Brace Jovanovich.
Noble, David W.
  1971   The Progressive Mind, 1890-1970. Santa Monica, CA: Rand Corporation.
Portantierro, Juan
  1974   "Dominant class and political crisis." Latin American Perspectives 1 (Fall): 95-120.

Sallach, David L.
    1974   "Class domination and ideological hegemony." Sociological Quarterly 15 (Winter):
            38-47.
Weinstein, James
    1968   The Corporate Ideal in the Liberal State. Boston: Beacon.
    1975   Ambiguous Legacy: The Left in American Politics. New York: New Viewpoints.
Wiebe, Robert
    1967   The Search for Order: 1880-1920. New York: Hill & Wang.

Chapter 7

Carchedi, G.
    1976   "The economic identification of state employees." Social Praxis 3, 1-2: 93-120.
Cockcroft, James D.
    forthcoming "Immiseration, not marginalization." Latin American Perspectives.
Ehrenreich, Barbara and Deirdre English
    1973   Witches, Midwives, and Nurses: A History of Women Healers. Old Wesbury, NY:
            Feminist Press.
Ehrenreich, John (Ed.)
    1978   The Cultural Crisis of Modern Medicine. New York: Monthly Review Press.
Friedland, Roger
    1980   "Class, power, and social control: the war on poverty," in M. Zeitlin (ed.) Classes,
            Class Conflict and the State. Cambridge, MA: Winthrop.
Gilbert, Neil and Harry Specht (Eds.)
    1981   The Emergence of Social Welfare and Social Work. Itasca, IL: F. E. Peacock.
Gough, Ivan
    1978   The Political Economy of the Welfare State. New York: Macmillan.
Johnson, Dale L.
    1972   "On oppressed classes," in J. D. Cockcroft, et al., Dependence and Underdevelop-
            ment. Garden City, NY: Doubleday.
Johnson, Dale L. and Christine O'Donnell
    1981   "The accumulation crisis and service professionals," in Economics Education Pro-
            ject (ed.) Crisis in the Public Sector. New York: Monthly Review Press.
Melman, Seymour
    1951   "The rise of administrative overhead in the manufacturing industries of the U.S.:
            1899-1947." Oxford Economic Papers January.
Patry, Bill
    1978   "Taylorism comes to the social services." Monthly Review 30 (October): 30-37.
Piven, Frances Fox and Richard Cloward
    1971   Regulating the Poor. New York: Vintage.
Reiff, R.
    1971   "The danger of the techni-pro: democratizing the human services professions."
            Social Policy 2 (May-June): 62-64.
Robinson, J. Gregg
    1982   "A class analysis of state workers," in Economics Education Project (ed.) Crisis in
            the Public Sector. New York: Monthly Review Press.

Chapter 8

Anonymous
    n.d.   An Historical Sketch of the State Normal College at Albany, New York and a
            History of Its Graduates for Fifty Years: 1844-1894. Albany: Brandow Printing
            Company.

Baxendall, Rosalyn, Linda Gordon, and Susan Reverby (eds.)
    1976   America's Working Women: A Documentary History—1600 to the Present. New
            York: Vintage Books.
Bernería, Lourdes
    1978   "Reproduction, production, and the sexual division of labor. International Labour
            Organization, WEP Working Paper.
Bernheimer, Charles Seligman (Ed.)
    1905   The Russian Jew in America. Philadelphia: J. C. Wilson Company.
Bobbitt, Franklin
    1913   The Supervision of City Schools: Some General Principles of Management Applied
            to the Problems of City-School Systems. Twelfth Yearbook of the National Society
            for the Study of Education, Part I.
Bronner, H. R. (Ed.)
    1920   "Statistics of state school systems." United States Bureau of Education Bulletin 11.
Buchanan, John T.
    1902   "How to assimilate the foreign element in our population." Forum 32.
Burritt, Bailey B.
    1912   "Professional distribution of college and university graduates." United States
            Bureau of Education Bulletin 19.
Butler, Nicholas Murray
    1889   "The training of the teacher." Century Magazine 16: 916-917.
    1899   "The beginnings of Teachers College." Columbia University. Quarterly I.
Calcott, Mary Stevenson
    1931   Child Labor Legislation in New York. New York: Macmillan.
Callahan, Raymond E.
    1962   Education and the Cult of Efficiency. Chicago: University of Chicago Press.
Carlson, Robert
    1970   "Americanization as an early twentieth century adult education movement."
            History of Education Quarterly 10: 440-464.
Coffman, Lotus Delta
    1911   The Social Composition of the Teacher Population. New York: Teachers College
            Press.
Cohen, David and Marvin Lazarson
    1972   "Education and the corporate order." Socialist Revolution.
College of the City of New York
    1925-26 City College Register.
Covello, Leonard
    1970   The Teacher in the Urban Community: A Half Century in City Schools: The Heart
            is the Teacher. Totowa, NJ: Littlefield Adams.
Cremin, Lawrence A.
    1961   The Transformation of the School: Progressivism in American Education, 1876-
            1957. New York: Random House.
Cubberly, Ellwood
    1934   Public Education in the United States. Boston: Houghton Mifflin.
Curoe, Phillip R.V.
    1926   Educational Attitudes and Policies of Organized Labor in the United States. New
            York: Teachers College Press.
Davies, Margery
    1979   "Women's place is at the typewriter: the feminization of the clerical labor force," in
            Z. R. Eisenstein (ed.) Capitalist Patriarchy and the Case for Socialist Feminism.
            New York: Monthly Review Press.
Ensign, Forest C.
    1921   Compulsory School Attendance and Child Labor. Iowa City: Athens Press.

Finn, Dan, Neil Grant, and Richard Johnson
    1977   "Social democracy, education and the crisis." Working Papers in Cultural Studies
            10.
Foner, Philip S.
    1972   History of the Labor Movement in the United States, Vol. I. New York: Interna-
            tional Publishers (original publication 1947).
Gersman, Elinor Mondale
    1970   "Progress reform of the St. Louis school board, 1897." History of Education Quar-
            terly 10: 3-21.
Greer, Colin
    1972   The Great School Legend. New York: Basic Books.
Gross, Magnus
    1904   "The College of the City of New York: some of its real functions." City College
            Alumni Quarterly 1 (No. 1): 1-4.
Gutman, Herbert
    1973   "Work, culture and society in industrializing America, 1815-1919." American
            Historical Review 78 (No. 3): 531-588.
Hammack, David
    1969   "The centralization of New York City's public school system, 1896: a social analysis
            of a decision." Master's essay, Columbia University.
Harris, Hannah Margaret
    1920   "Lessons in civics for the elementary grades of city schools." Bulletin 18 Bureau of
            Education. Washington, DC: Government Printing Office.
Historical Statistics of the United States from Colonial Times to the Present
    1976   Washington, DC: Government Printing Office.
Hogan, David
    1978   "Education and the making of the Chicago working class, 1880-1930." History of
            Education Quarterly 18 (No. 3): 227-270.
Jessup, Walter A.
    1911   The Social Factors Affecting Special Supervision in the Public Schools of the
            United States. New York: Teachers College Press.
    1916   The Teaching Staff. Cleveland: Survey Committee of the Cleveland Foundation.
Karier, Clarence
    1967   "Elite views in American education," in W. Laqueur and G. L. Mosse (eds.) Educa-
            tion and Social Structure in the Twentieth Century. New York: Harper & Row.
Katz, Michael B.
    1968   The Irony of Early School Reform. Boston: Beacon.
Lortie, Dan
    1975   Schoolteacher: A Sociological Study. Chicago: University of Chicago Press.
Mahoney, John J.
    1920   "Training teachers for Americanization." U.S. Bureau of Education Bulletin XII: 9.
Marx, Karl
    1973   Grundrisse (M. Nicolaus, trans.). Middlesex, England: Penguin.
McGurk, Josephine H.
    1934   "History of the Department and School of Education of the College of the City of
            New York." Master's thesis, CCNY School of Education.
Nagi, Mustafa H. and Meredith D. Pugh
    1976   "Status inconsistency and professional militancy in the teaching profession," in R.
            M. Pavalko (ed.) Sociology of Education. Itasca, IL: F. E. Peacock.
New York City Board of Education
    1910   Journal of the Board of Education of the City of New York.
    1927   Directory of the Board of Education of the City of New York.

Palmer, A. Emerson
    1905   The New York Public School. New York: Macmillan.
Perkinson, Henry J.
    1968   The Imperfect Panacea: American Faith in Education, 1865-1965. New York:
           Random House.
Poulantzas, Nicos
    1973   "On social classes." New Left Review 78: 27-54.
Ravitch, Diane
    1974   The Great School Wars: New York City, 1805-1973. New York: Basic Books.
Rudy, S. Willis
    1949   The College of the City of New York: A History. New York: City College Press.
Schwarzweller, Harry and Thomas A. Lyson
    1978   "Some plan to become teachers: determinants of career specification among rural
           youth in Norway, Germany and the U.S." Sociology of Education 51 (No. 1):
           29-43.
Scott, Donald
    1970   "The social history of education: three alternatives." History of Education Quarterly
           10: 242-254.
Thompson, E. P.
    1963   The Making of the English Working Class. New York: Vintage.
Van Denburg, Joseph
    1911   Causes of the Elimination of Students from the Secondary Schools of New York
           City, 1906-1910. New York: Teachers College Press.
The Wall Street Journal
    1979   "Education is basic at one-room school in rural Illinois." January 2, p. 1.
Weinstein, James
    1968   The Corporate Ideal in the Liberal State, 1900-1918. Boston: Beacon.
Whittemore, Richard F. W.
    1962   "Nicholas Murray Butler and public education, 1862-1911." Ph.D. dissertation,
           Teachers College.
Wright, Erik Olin
    1978   "Intellectuals and the working class." Insurgent Sociologist 3 (No. 1): 5-17.

Chapter 9

Benaría, Lourdes and Bruce Steinberg
    1979   "The dynamics of labor market segmentation." Unpublished paper, Department of
           Economics, Rutgers University.
Blauner, Robert
    1964   Alienation and Freedom. Chicago: University of Chicago Press.
Cashman, Michael
    1977   "DP salary survey." Datamaton 23 (November): 114-119.
Crompton, Rosemary
    1976   "Approaches to the study of white-collar unionism." Sociology 10 (September):
           407-424.
Devey, Barbara Tomaskovic and Donald T. Devey
    1979   "Rationalization in the computer field, with special emphasis on the role of women
           in the field." Unpublished manuscript, Boston University.
Dollars and Sense
    1979   "Computerizing your job." December.
Finerman, Benjamin
    1975   "Professionalism in the computer field." Communications of the ACM 18
           (January): 4-9.

Gallie, Duncan
    1978   In Search of the New Working Class: Automation and Social Integration Within
            Capitalist Enterprise. New York: Cambridge University Press.
Gilchrist, B. and R. E. Weber
    1975   "Discrimination in the employment of women in the computer industry." Com-
            munications of the ACM 18 (No. 7): 416-418.
Glenn, Evelyn Nakano and Roslyn L. Feldberg
    1977   "Degraded and deskilled: the proletarianization of clerical work." Social Problems
            25 (October): 52-64.
Greenbaum, Joan
    1976   "Division of labor in the computer field." Monthly Review (July-August): 40-55.
Hammond, Thomas H. and Jock H. Knott
    1980   A Zero-Based Look at Zero-Base Budgeting. New Brunswick, NJ: Transaction
            Books.
Lacatena, Marcoantonio
    1980   "Responding to DHE's management system." Voice of Higher Education. Union,
            NJ: Council of New Jersey State College Locals (AFT, AFL-CIO).
Neagius, Alan
    1978   "Proletarianization and class orientation among the new middle class: theoretical
            perspectives and empirical test." Unpublished paper, California State University,
            Northridge.
Pettigrew, Andrew W.
    1973   "Occupational specialization as an emergent process." Sociological Review 21
            (May): 255-278.
Singelmann, Joachim and Erik Olin Wright
    n.d.   "Proletarianization in advanced capitalist societies." Institute for Research on
            Poverty, University of Wisconsin, Madison.
Stoneham, P.
    1975   "The effects of computers on the demand for labor in the United Kingdom."
            Economic Journal 85 (September): 590-606.
Tuckman, Howard P., Jamie Caldwell, and William Vogler
    1978   "Part-timers and the academic labor market of the eighties." American Sociologist
            13 (No. 4): 184-195.
Van Arsdale, George
    1978   "Deprofessionalizing a part-time teaching faculty: how many, feeling small, seem-
            ing few, getting less, dream of more." American Sociologist 13 (No. 4): 195-201.
Vuskovic, Pedro
    1980   "Latin America and the changing world economy." NACLA Report on the
            Americas 14 (January-February): 2-15.

Chapter 10

Birenbaum, Arnold
    n.d.   "Pharmacy as a Social Movement." Unpublished manuscript.
Derber, Charles
    1982   Professionals as Workers: Mental Labor in Advanced Capitalism. New York:
            Oxford University Press.
Ehrenreich, Barbara and Deirdre English
    1978   For Her Own Good: 150 Years of the Expert's Advice to Women. New York:
            Anchor Press.
Ginzberg, Eli
    1979   "The professionalization of the U.S. labor force." Scientific American 240 (No. 3):
            48-53.

Kornhauser, William
    1963   Scientists in Industry. Berkeley: University of California Press.
Lasch, Christopher
    1977   "The siege of the family." New York Review. November 24.
Pample, Fred C., Kenneth C. Land, and Marcus Felson
    1977   "A social indicator model of change in the occupational structure of the United
            States: 1947-1974." American Sociological Review. 42 (December): 951-964.
Sennett, Richard and Jonathan Cobb
    1972   The Hidden Injuries of Class. New York: Vintage.

Chapter 11

Blumberg, Paul
    1980a   "White-collar status panic." American Teacher (April): 9-10.
    1980b   Inequality in an Age of Decline. New York: Oxford University Press.
Business Week
    1977   "The silent crisis in R and D." March 8.
Hirschorn, Larry
    1979   "The political economy of social service rationalization," in R. Quinney (ed.)
            Capitalist Society: Readings for a Critical Sociology. Homewood, IL: Dorsey
            Press.
Johnson, Dale L.
    1981   "Ideologues and executioners." Society (September-October).
New York Times
    1980   "High technology: a vibrant U.S. sector." August 20, P.A1.
Sobel, Richard
    1981   "White collar structure and class: educated labor reevaluated." Ph.D. dissertation,
            Department of Education, University of Massachusetts.
Sweezy, Paul
    1981   "Economic crisis in the United States." Monthly Review 33 (December): 1-10.
U.S. Department of Labor
    1979   National Survey of Professional, Administrative, Technical, and Clerical Pay.
            Washington, DC: Bureau of Labor Statistics, Bulletin 2045, March.
Wolfe, Alan
    1981   "Sociology, liberalism and the radical right." New Left Review 128 (July-August):
            3-28.

About the Authors

Each contribution to this volume represents original work undertaken by persons who are concerned with developing a more historical and dialectical social science than is current in the field. We have selected intermediate classes and the historical process of development as the theme of the volume and historical dialectics as the method. Though a very large share of responsibility for errors and misinterpretations are Johnson's, the book is an intellectual product of the collective activity of the following contributors:

David Eisenhower received his Ph.D. in sociology from Rutgers in 1977 with a theoretical dissertation on "Unproductive Labor and Crisis." He is currently Assistant Professor of Sociology at Manhattanville College, Purchase, New York, and teaches at the Labor College, New York.

Sherry Gorelick is a sociologist affiliated with Livingston College, Rutgers. Her book, a historical study of working-class Jews and Jewish mobility, was published by Rutgers University Press in 1981.

Michael Heffren is currently working on his doctoral dissertation in the Department of Sociology, Rutgers University, on a theme related to his contributions to this volume.

Dale Johnson is Coordinator of the Ph.D. Specialization in Political Sociology and Development, Rutgers University. He has published three books on Latin America and is editor of Sage Publications series "Class, State, and Development."

Christine O'Donnell, Assistant Professor of Sociology at Manhattanville College, Purchase, New York, completed her dissertation in the Rutgers Department of Sociology on women and drug addiction in 1979.

Martin Oppenheimer is a Livingston College, Rutgers, sociologist. He has published books and articles in the areas of political sociology and labor studies and is currently working on a book entitled *White Collar World.*